AF817627

Delhi Human Development Report 2013

The Delhi Human Development Report (DHDR) 2013 was prepared by the Institute for Human Development, New Delhi for the Government of National Capital Territory of Delhi. Contribution was received as part of the Planning Commission and UNDP partnership "Human Development: Towards Bridging Inequalities."

सत्यमेव जयते

Government of
National Capital Territory
of Delhi

DELHI HUMAN DEVELOPMENT REPORT 2013

Improving Lives, Promoting Inclusion

ACADEMIC FOUNDATION
NEW DELHI
www.academicfoundation.com

INSTITUTE FOR
HUMAN DEVELOPMENT
NEW DELHI
www.ihdindia.org

First published in 2013
by

ACADEMIC FOUNDATION
4772-73 / 23 Bharat Ram Road, (23 Ansari Road),
Darya Ganj, New Delhi - 110 002 (India).
Phones : 23245001 / 02 / 03 / 04.
Fax : +91-11-23245005.
E-mail : books@academicfoundation.com
www.academicfoundation.com

and

INSTITUTE FOR HUMAN DEVELOPMENT
NIDM Building, IIPA Campus
Indraprastha Estate, New Delhi -110002
Phone: + 91 11 2335 8166/2332 1610
Fax: +91 11 2376 5410
E-mail : mail@ihdindia.org
www.ihdindia.org

Cover photo credit: top-left: Paul Prescott | Dreamstime;
top-right: Indiapicture; bottom-left, centre and bottom-right: Haran.

Cover design: The Bookmint, New Delhi;
design copyright ©: Academic Foundation

Cataloging in Publication Data--DK
Courtesy: D.K. Agencies (P) Ltd. <docinfo@dkagencies.com>

Delhi human development report, 2013 : improving lives,
promoting inclusion.
p. cm.
Includes bibliographical references (p.).
ISBN 9789332700864

1. Economic indicators--India--Delhi. 2. Social indicators--India--Delhi. 3. Quality of life--India--Delhi. I. Institute for Human Development (New Delhi, India)

DDC 330.95456 23

Typeset by Italics India, New Delhi.

Printed and bound by The Book Mint, New Delhi.
www.thebookmint.in

Contents

IHD Team for the Preparation of DHDR 2013

Team Leader and Editor

Alakh N. Sharma

Associate Editors

Tanuka Endow
Nandita Gupta
Usha Jayachandran

Coordinators

Abhay Kumar
Preet Rustagi

Core Perceptions Survey Team

Nandita Gupta
Abhay Kumar
Rajesh Shukla (Principal Advisor)

Copy Editor

Anupma Mehta

Background Paper Writers

Sudhanshu Bhushan
Debabani Chakravarty
Amrita Datta
Tanuka Endow
Nandita Gupta
Usha Jayachandran
Abhay Kumar
Papiya Mazumdar
Sumit Mazumdar
Balwant S. Mehta
Shreya Sarawgi
Sandip Sarkar
Shivani Satija

Other Contributors

Sant Lal Arora
Vikas Dubey
Abhishek Kumar
Gaurav Mehta
Srabashi Ray
Samidha Sapra
D. G. Shreeram
Ramashray Singh
Rashmi Sinha

Steering Committee

Chief Secretary, GNCTD	Chairperson
Professor A.K. Shiva Kumar, Member, National Advisory Council	Member
Professor Niraja Gopal Jayal, JNU	Member
Dr. K. Seeta Prabhu, HDR Centre, UNDP	Member
Professor T.S. Papola, National Fellow, ICSSR	Member
Professor Ravi S. Srivastava, JNU	Member
Professor Alakh N. Sharma, Director, IHD	Member
Principal Secretary (Planning), GNCTD	Member
Principal Secretary (Health), GNCTD	Member
Secretary (UD), GNCTD	Member
Secretary (Education), GNCTD	Member
Secretary (Social Welfare & WCD), GNCTD	Member
Director (Planning), GNCTD	Member-Secretary

SHEILA DIKSHIT
CHIEF MINISTER

सत्यमेव जयते

GOVT. OF NATIONAL CAPITAL TERRITORY OF DELHI
DELHI SECRETARIAT, I.P. ESTATE, NEW DELHI-110113
PHONE: 23392020, 23392030 FAX: 23392111

FOREWORD

I am delighted to note that the second Delhi Human Development Report has been finalised. Delhi has changed significantly during the last seven years, since the first Report was published in 2006. We felt that it was time for a review as to how Delhi has fared since then and also to assess the progress achieved in the goals that we had set for ourselves.

I compliment the Institute for Human Development (IHD) for undertaking this work. I am happy that apart from secondary sources of data and information, the Report is also based on a survey of about 8000 households conducted by IHD to know what our citizens think and perceive of their lives and about city of Delhi.

We have made significant achievements in the last one decade or so. We have overhauled our transport system, we have seen great improvements in electricity and water supply, the quality of infrastructure in Delhi has improved substantially and so have indicators of health, education and environment. The per capita income in Delhi is highest in the country and its rates of growth have been robust despite the general economic slowdown witnessed across the globe.

I am happy to see that a very large proportion of Delhi citizens have said that they are satisfied with their quality of life, and even more have said that they are satisfied with their health, neighbourhoods and interpersonal relationships. These are positive signs. I am further driven to bolster these trends, and to delve into factors which are contributing to lesser satisfaction among people and sections.

It is heartening to know that people have appreciated our efforts to modernise the city transport systems. We are aware of the concerns particularly with regard to public safety, but we are committed to work towards a safer city with the help of citizens of Delhi. I congratulate the various departments of Government of Delhi and other organisations such as DMRC for their hard work. Nevertheless, we take the review in this Report with all seriousness and will sincerely work towards modernizing other departments and bringing about institutional improvements.

The Report also makes us aware of the vulnerability and needs of the elderly, women, children, the poor and some other social groups. We will continue to focus on their needs, so that all the citizens of Delhi participate in Delhi's development.

I once again congratulate the Institute for Human Development for preparing this Report. The Government of NCT of Delhi will seriously act on the suggestions and recommendations of the Report. The contents of this Report will be instrumental in guiding us to take further initiatives to ensure inclusive and all round development.

Sheila Dikshit

(SHEILA DIKSHIT)

सत्यमेव जयते

Empowered lives.
Resilient nations.

MESSAGE

We congratulate the Government of the National Capital Territory (NCT) of Delhi for preparing the second Human Development Report 2013 for Delhi.

Delhi occupies an important place in the country's development history and over the years has become the hub of education, industry, trade and commerce. As a result, the diaspora in Delhi is truly reflective of the diverse social, linguistic, and cultural traditions of the country.

This Report, while covering aspects central to the concept of human development such as health, education and standard of living, also places focus on the delivery of essential public services such as housing, water and sanitation, electricity and transport in an urban agglomeration. The Report strives to illuminate achievements, challenges and opportunities in human development, along with forward looking recommendations. Perhaps the most laudatory effort undertaken as part of this Report is the Public Perception Survey that has examined people's views and concerns on development in the city and recorded their aspirations.

We are indeed pleased to note the efforts that have been made to follow a participatory approach in the preparation of this Report. The foundation for all future initiatives must be imbued with the voice of the people, and this Report is a step towards promoting responsive governance. We are confident that the findings emerging from this detailed study and the recommendations suggested will resonate with planners and policy makers, and contribute towards giving shape to innovative development strategies.

We applaud the Government of the NCT of Delhi on the publication of the 2013 State Human Development Report and wish the Government of the NCT of Delhi success in its endeavors to promote human development.

Tuhin K. Pandey
Joint Secretary (State Plans),
Planning Commission, Government of India

Lise Grande
United Nations Resident Coordinator
UNDP Resident Representative

Preface

The discourse on human development has come a long way since the publication of the first global Human Development Report was published in 1990. Ever since then, people have become central to development issues, with the main concerns being that all sections of the society should benefit from economic prosperity, enjoy long, healthy and productive lives, and optimise their potential in all spheres.

Proceeding with a similar sensibility, the first Human Development Report for Delhi was published in 2006, and was structured around the central theme of 'Partnerships for Progress'. The Report highlighted the need for increased people's participation in order to achieve progress in human development on the basis of the partnerships forged between the community and the Government.

The theme of the Delhi Human Development Report, 2013, the successor to the first Human Development Report of 2006, is "Improving Lives, Promoting Inclusion". This theme is particularly relevant for Delhi in the context of the multi-layered society of this great megapolis, wherein the wealthy and the poor live side by side, where opulent mansions and crowded slums jostle for space with each other, and where people speak in myriad tongues and follow a multitude of cultures.

The economy of Delhi has witnessed a high growth rate during the last decade. Poverty has been reduced considerably. There has been an expansion in employment opportunities as well as in access to housing and many basic services. Public health facilities and educational opportunities have undergone tremendous expansion. This has been reflected in a very high level of satisfaction expressed by people across the board regarding the various aspects of life in Delhi. Notwithstanding the overall impressive gains accruing to various groups, however, disparities still persist amongst these groups. There are some particularly vulnerable groups of people such as the homeless, child workers, the differently-abled and the elderly, whose relative exclusion based on human development considerations, warrants focused attention from policy-makers. Public safety has recently emerged as a major area of concern bringing forth an important aspect of human development.

This Report has been prepared by a group of dedicated researchers at the Institute for Human Development (IHD), who have prepared background papers based on their subject matter specialization and has been synthesised and edited by an experienced team. The preparation of the Report has benefited from the involvement of a high level Steering Committee chaired by the Chief Secretary, GNCTD. The Report has been enriched by the views of the people of Delhi through a perceptions survey of about 8000 households, conducted by IHD, and also through focus group discussions (FGDs). The Report has benefited greatly from the organisation of various thematic consultations and a comprehensive stakeholder workshop inaugurated by the Chief Minister of Delhi, which entailed brainstorming sessions among national and international academicians and researchers, and discussions and feedback from Government officials/departments. These interactions helped garner a lot of enriching and useful inputs for incorporation into the Report. Our sincere endeavour in preparing this Report comes with the hope that it would become a tool for evidence-based policy formulations, thereby facilitating a better understanding of the various attributes that underlie the human development paradigm, especially in the context of Delhi.

It has been a great privilege for the Institute for Human Development to be associated with the preparation of the Delhi Human Development Report 2013. The Institute is grateful to the Government of Delhi for providing it this opportunity. The conduction of a Perceptions Survey, encompassing various issues directly related to human development, helps in bringing the voice of the residents of Delhi to the fore and highlighting people's feelings about the quality of their lives as residents of this city. Various interlinkages exist between the availability of human development-related services such as education, healthcare, basic services, and safety, and the perceptions of the people who avail of these services, especially the vulnerable and the marginalised. These links at the locality/neighbourhood, household and individual levels need to be understood closely in order to efficiently address the pervasiveness of various disparities as well as to assure better access and utilisation of essential services thereby promoting inclusion. The DHDR 2013 is a small but steady step in this direction.

Alakh N. Sharma
Director
Institute for Human Development
New Delhi

Acknowledgements

The second DHDR is an outcome of the strong commitment of the Government of National Capital Territory of Delhi (GNCTD) to enhance the human development scenario of the State. Following the path of the first report, this report is also a product of extensive engagements with government officials, academicians, civil society organisations, and last but not the least, more than 8000 people of Delhi from all the districts and from all sections of society who participated in the Public Perceptions Survey.

The genesis of this report would not have been possible without the dynamic initiative and support of the GNCTD. The necessary financial support was provided by Government of Delhi and Planning Commission – UNDP partnership 'Human Development: Bridging Inequalities' (HDBI). The project was executed at the Institute for Human Development (IHD), New Delhi, which accomplished this task by engaging various stakeholders and researchers.

Our foremost acknowledgement for this report is to the Chief Minister of GNCTD, Smt. Sheila Dikshit whose commitment to see it in the published form has throughout motivated the team to achieve this challenging goal within a very short span of time. Her keen interest, valuable suggestions, participation in the stakeholder's consultation meeting and overall her motive to periodically assess the human development situation in the State has brought out this publication.

We are also grateful to the Minister of Health and Family Welfare, GNCTD, Dr. A.K. Walia, who personally attended the consultation meeting on health and gave valuable suggestions.

We would like to acknowledge the valuable role played by all the members of the Steering Committee, which was especially constituted for accomplishing this task under the Chairmanship of the Chief Secretary, GNCTD, Mr. D.M. Spolia. We also offer special thanks to Dr. A.K. Shiva Kumar, Member, National Advisory Committee, Government of India, and a Member of the Steering Committee for his valuable advice. This Report would not have been possible without the relentless support provided by Dr. B.K. Sharma, Member Secretary, Steering Committee for the DHDR, 2013, who was present at every stage from its conception to its publication.

The Principal Secretary, Finance and Power, Mr. Shakti Sinha, Principal Secretary, Planning, Mr. A.J. Kurien, and Joint Director deserve our special acknowledgement as they led the work from the GNCTD. They facilitated in providing all the necessary inputs from the GNCTD, attended all the consultation meetings and gave their valuable feedback. They also ensured the smooth administrative support required for the publication of this Report.

We would like to acknowledge the contribution made by experts from different universities and institutions; officials from GNCTD, GOI and the National Capital Region Planning Board (NCRPB); and representatives from the various voluntary organisations that went through the draft chapter, attended the consultation meetings and gave important suggestions and critical comments which helped in enriching the report.

In the Livelihoods and Employment section, Prof. T.S. Papola, National Fellow, ICSSR; Prof. Prof. S.R. Hashim, Former Member, Planning Commission; Prof. Ajit Ghosh, Prof. J. Krishnamurthy, Prof. Sheila Bhalla, Prof. Harishwar Dayal, IHD; Dr. Sonalde Desai, Maryland University; Mr. A.K. Verma and Dr. D.P.S. Verma, GNCTD; Ms. Rashmi Singh, National Mission for Empowerment of Women (NMEW), GOI; Dr. Ritu Mathur, Dr. Swayamprabha Das, and Ms. Kavya Bopanna, UNDP; Ms. Naini Jayaseelan, Mr. M.L. Chotani and Mr. J.N. Barman (NCRPB); Dr. Milindo Chakravorty, Sharda University; Mr. Arbind Singh, NASVI; Dr. Nagendra P Singh, ASEED; Mr. Virender Gaur, CITU; Ms. Shaguna Kanwar, Aman Bharti; and Mr. B. S. Rawat have contributed immensely by going through the draft and attending the consultation meeting. We would like to thank them for providing significant inputs for the section.

In the Education section, we particularly wish to thank Prof. R. Govinda, Dr. Geetha Rani, Dr. Aarti Srivastava, National University of Educational Planning and Administration (NUEPA); Prof. Zoya Hasan and Dr. Saumen Chattopadhyay, JNU; Dr. Manisha Priyam, University of Delhi; Dr. Farida Khan, Jamia Milia Islamia University; Prof. N.K. Choudhary, Patna University; Mr. Diwan Chand, Mr. Rajendra Kumar, Dr. B.K. Sharma and Ms. Manju Sahoo, GNCTD; Prof. Dev Nathan and Prof. Atul Sarma, IHD, for providing critical inputs.

In the Health section, we particularly wish to thank Dr. Ritupriya Mehrotra, JNU; Mr. Patrick Mullen, The World Bank; Dr. N.V. Kamat, Prof. Richa Diwan and Dr. D.K. Diwan, GNCTD; Mr. K.D. Maiti, UNICEF; Ms.

Swayamprabha Das, UNDP; Dr. Nandita Saikia and Dr. William Joe, Institute of Economic Growth; Mr. Jagdeep S. Gambhir, Population Foundation of India; and Dr. Mira Shiva, AIDAN, for their contribution.

The section on Basic Services was enriched by the erudite comments of Mr. K. Dharmarajan, Expert Committees on Property Tax and MCD Act; Prof. Neelima Risbud and Dr. Vinita Yadav, School of Planning and Architecture (SPA); Prof. Dinesh Mohan, IIT Delhi; Mr. Jagan Shah, National Institute of Urban Affairs (NIUA); Dr. Renu Khosla, CURE; Mr. A.J. Kurien, Mr. R.K. Srivastava, Mr. V.V.V.J. Rajashekhar, Ms. Debashree Mukherjee, and Mr. Puneet Goel, GNCTD; Ms. Paramjeet Kaur and Mr. Sanjay Kumar, Ashray Adhikar Abhiyan; Ms. Ritu Sharma and Ms. Deepti Ann Joseph, Hazards Centre; Mr. Md. Noor Alam and Mr. Md. Muqueet Khan, MARG.

For the section on Public Safety, the comments received from Dr. Kalpana Viswanath, Jagori, Prof. Renu Adlakha, CWDS; Prof. Amitabh Kundu, JNU; Mr. S.K. Das, Chairman, S.K. Das Associated Architects, Mr. R. K. Singh, Former Home Secretary, GOI; Dr. T.N. Mishra, Former Director, National Police Academy; Dr. Suneeta Dhar, Jagori; Mr. Amod K. Kanth, PRAYAS; Ms. Vrinda Grover, Former Executive Director, MARG; Dr. Shubhra Sanyal, Mr. Kamlendra Prasad and Mr. B.N. Chattoraj, LNJN National Institute of Criminology and Forensic Science (NICFS); Ms. Nandita Bhatla and Ms. Sancheeta Ghosh, ICRW; Mr. Uday Sahay, SAUV Communications; Mr. K.K. Taneja, CPWD; Ms. Nayantara Singh, Centre for Women's Development Studies (CWDS); Dr. Abhinav Alakshendra, University of Florida; Dr. Pradeep Kumar Panda, Micro Insurance Academy; and Mr. Abhishek Rai, Advocate were very useful.

The section on People's Perceptions was enriched by the critical comments received from Prof. Ashwani Saith, International Institute of Social Studies (ISS); Prof. Savita Singh, IGNOU; Dr. Suraj Kumar, UN Women; Mr. Amitabh Behar, National Foundation for India (NFI); Prof. Amitabh Kundu, Prof. Ravi Srivastava, Prof. P.M. Kulkarni, Prof. Sachhidanand Sinha, Prof. B.S. Butola, Prof. Milap Punia, Dr. Anuradha Banerjee, Dr. Deependra Nath Das, JNU; Prof. Rajiv Malhotra, O.P. Jindal Global University; and Dr. Chetan Vaidya, SPA.

We would also like to thank the following staff members at IHD who have helped in the preparation of this report: Mr. Sudhir Malhotra, Ms. Jyoti Girish, Ms. Priyanka Tyagi, Ms. Kasturi Majumdar, Mr. S.P. Sharma, Mr. Shravan Kumar, Ms. Rekha Aswal, Mr. P.K Mishra, Mr. Sanjay Kumar Sharma, Mr. Phalguni Singh and Mr. Rajiv Ranjan.

We acknowledge the support of over 50 field investigators, who conducted the high quality fieldwork of People's Perceptions Survey for this report, as well as the following field supervisors: Mr. Rajoo Kumar, Mr. Jaswant Rao, Ms. Anita, Mr. Manish Kadam, Mr. Sanjay Kumar Mishra, Mr. Md. Ozair, Mr. Surveshwar Rao, Ms. Seema Madan, Mr. Shailesh Kumar and Mr. Dhan Bahadur. We also thank Ms. Shreiya Saxena, Ms.Vatsala Bhusry, Mr. Sujit Mridha, Mr. Jay Prakash Sharma and Mr. Deedar Singh for their contribution.

Last but not the least, our enormous gratitude goes out to the publishers, Academic Foundation, particularly, Mr. Sanu Kapila and Mr. Rituraj Kapila, for their cooperation in bringing out this Report in time, against all odds!

Abbreviations

AHTU	Anti-Human Trafficking Unit
ANCs	Antenatal Care
ANM	Auxiliary Nurse Midwife
ASER	Annual Status of Education Report
ASHA	Accredited Social Health Activist
AT&C	Aggregate Technical & Commercial
ATM	Access to Medicines
AVL	Automatic Vehicle Location system
BFA	Barrier Free Access
BOD	Biochemical Oxygen Demand
BPL	Below the Poverty Line
BRT	Bus Rapid Transport
BSUP	Basic Services for the Urban Poor
BTC	Basic Training
CAGR	Compound Annual Growth Rate
CBPACS	Ch. Brahm Prakash Ayurvedic Charak Sansthan
CBSE	Central Board of Secondary Education
CCE	Continuous and Comprehensive Evaluation
CDR	Crude Death Rate
CES	Consumption Expenditure Survey
CGHS	Central Government Health Scheme
CNBC	Chacha Nehru Bal Chikitsalaya
COD	Chemical Oxygen Demand
CPHEEO	Central Public Health and Environmental Engineering Organisation
CrPC	Criminal Procedure Code
CRS	Civil Registration System
CSB	Citizen's Services Bureau
CSE	Centre for Science and Environment
CSI	Commercial Secretariat Institute
CTC	Community Toilet Complex
CVDs	Cardio-vascular Diseases
CWSN	Children With Special Needs
DAK	Delhi Arogya Kosh
DAN	Delhi Arogya Nidhi
DCB	Delhi Cantonment Board
DCPCR	Delhi Commission of the Protection of Child's Rights
DDA	Delhi Development Authority
DERC	Delhi Electricity Regulatory Commission
DES	Department of Economics and Statistics
DGEHS	Delhi Government Employees Health Scheme
DHDR	Delhi Human Development Report
DJB	Delhi Jal Board
DLHS-RCH	District Level Household Survey – Reproductive and Child Health
DMPU	District Missing Persons Unit
DMRC	Delhi Metro Rail Corporation
DO	Dissolved Oxygen
DSCI	Delhi State Cancer Institute
DTC	Delhi Transport Corporation
DTU	Delhi Technological University
DU	University of Delhi
DUSIB	Delhi Urban Shelter Improvement Board
DVB	Delhi Vidyut Board
EDL	Essential Drugs List
EHV	Extra High Voltage
EML	Essential Medicine List
ENN	Early Neonatal
ESIC	Employees State Insurance Corporation
e-SLA	Electronic Service Legal Agreement
ETP	Effluent Treatment Plants
EVS	Everyday Science
EWS	Economically Weaker Sections
FGDs	Focus Group Discussions
FYP	Five Year Plan

GER	Gross Enrolment Ratio
GGSIP	Guru Gobind Singh Indraprastha
GIS	Geographical Information Systems
GNCTD	Government of National Capital Territory of Delhi
GPCD	Gallon Per Capita Per Day
GPS	Global Positioning System
GRCs	Gender Resource Centres
GSDP	Gross State Domestic Product
HCBS	High Capacity Bus System
HDI	Human Development Index
HDR	Human Development Report
HLEG	High Level Expert Group
HRH	Human Resources for Health
ICDS	Integrated Child Development Services
ICMR	Indian Council of Medical Research
ICTs	Information and Communication Technologies
IHBAS	Institute of Human Behaviour and Allied Sciences
IHD	Institute for Human Development
ILBS	Institute of Liver & Billiary Sciences
IMNCF	Integrated Maternal and Neonatal Care Facilities
IMR	Infant Mortality Rate
IPC	Indian Penal Code
IPD	In Patient Department
IRMA	Institute of Rural Management Anand
ISMH	Indian Systems of Medicine and Homeopathy
IT	Information Technology
ITCs	Industrial Training Centres
ITE	Institute of Technical Education
ITI	Industrial Training Institute
JBIC	Japan Bank for International Cooperation
JJ	Jhuggi Jhopdi
JJCs	Jhuggi Jhopdi Colonies
JJRC	Jhuggi Jhopdi Resettlment Colonies
JNNURM	Jawaharlal Nehru National Urban Renewal Mission
JSSK	Janani Shishu Kalyan Karyakram
JSY	Janani Suraksha Yojana
KV	Kilovolt
KVS	Kendriya Vidyalaya Samiti
LFPR	Labour Force Participation Rate
LIG	Low Income Group
LPG	Liquified Petroleum Gas
LRT	Light Railway Transit
MAIDS	Maulana Azad Institute of Dental Sciences
MCCD	Medical Certification of Cause of Death
MCD	Municipal Corporation of Delhi
MCH	Maternal and Child Health
MDGs	Millennium Development Goals
MGD	Million Gallons Daily
MHRD	Ministry of Human Resource Development
MIS	Management Information System
MMR	Maternal Mortality Rate/Ratio
MNCW	Maternal and Child Welfare Centres
MoHFW	Ministry of Health and Family Welfare
MoHUPA	Ministry of Housing and Urban Poverty Alleviation
MPCE	Monthly Per Capita Consumption Expenditure
MPD	Master Plan of Delhi
MRTS	Mass Rapid Transport System
MTP	Medical Termination of Pregnancy
MUZ	Multi-Utility Zones
MW	Megawatt
MWEs	Main Wage Earners
NCD	Non-Communicable Diseases
NCERT	National Council of Educational Research and Training
NCPCR	National Commission for Protection of Child Rights

NCR	National Capital Region
NCRB	National Crime Records Bureau
NCT	National Capital Territory
NCW	National Commission for Women
NDMC	New Delhi Municipal Corporation
NDPL	North Delhi Power Limited
NFHS	National Family Health Survey
NGOs	Non-Governmental Organisations
NHA	National Health Accounts
NHB	National Housing Bank
NIMS	National Institute of Medical Statistics
NN	Neonatal
NRHM	National Rural Health Mission
NSS	National Sample Survey
NSSO	National Sample Survey Organisation
NUEPA	National University of Educational Planning and Administration
OBC	Other Backward Classes
OOPE	Out of Pocket Expenses
OPD	Out Patient Department
PAN	Permanent Account Number
PG	Post Graduation
PHC	Primary Health Centre
PHTO	Public Health Technical Officers
PNG	Piped Natural Gas
PNN	Post Neonatal
PPP	Public Private Partnerships
PRUD	Promotion of Rational Use of Drugs
PSC	Private Stage Carriage
PUHC	Primary Urban Health Centre
PWD	Public Works Department
QOL	Quality of Life
RAY	Rajiv Awas Yojana
RBD	Registration of Births and Deaths Act
RCH	Reproductive and Child Health
RGI	Registrar General of India
RSBY	Rashtriya Swasthya Bima Yojana
RTE	Right to Education
RWA	Resident Welfare Association
SC	Scheduled Caste
SLL	Special and Local Laws
SMCs	School Management Committees
SNCU	Sick Neonatal Care Units
SRS	Sample Registration System
SSA	Sarva Shiksha Abhiyan
SSS	Samajik Suvidha Sangam
ST	Scheduled Tribes
T&D	Transmission and Distribution
TSS	Total Suspended Solids
TV	Television
UEE	Universal Elementary Education
UGC	University Grants Commission
UHC	Universal Health Coverage
UID	Unique Identification
ULBs	Urban Local Bodies
UNDP	United Nations Development Programme
UNESCO	United Nations Educational, Scientific and Cultural Organisation
UN-HABITAT	United Nations Human Settlement Programme
UNHCR	United Nations High Commissioner for Refugees
UNICEF	United Nations Children's Fund
UPSS	Usual Principal and Subsidiary Status
UTs	Union Territories
UTTIPEC	Unified Traffic and Transportation Infrastructure Planning and Engineering Centre
VAT	Value Added Tax
WHO	World Health Organisation
WPR	Workforce Participation Rate
YAP	Yamuna Action Plan
ZIPNET	Zonal Integrated Police Net

List of Tables, Figures, Boxes and Annexures

Tables

Figures

Boxes

Annexure Tables

Overview

The Delhi Human Development Report, 2013, has been structured around the theme '*Improving Lives, Promoting Inclusion*'. This theme encompasses all the fundamental concerns of human development, that is, improving people's capabilities; augmenting the choices available to them; assuring the progress of all segments of society in terms of income, education and healthcare; ensuring widespread access to basic civic amenities; and fostering a safe and enabling environment for the various population groups in the city. While examining all these issues through the lens of the disempowered and the marginalised, the *Report* keeps in focus the disparities that exist across various groups, and assesses the progress that has been made in bridging these.

The Report analyses issues regarding the status of human development in Delhi from two perspectives: first, the objective facts on the ground; and second, people's perceptions regarding these. The latter is based on the findings of a Perceptions Survey, conducted with a large and representative sample of around 8000 households, which probes how people rate various developmental issues as well as what their own aspirations are as the citizens of Delhi.

The main message that emerges from the Report is that the lives of the citizens of Delhi have indeed improved since the last assessment made in the Delhi Human Development Report, 2006, on the basis of most of the considerations mentioned above. Some of the pressing concerns of the 2006 Report have been addressed to a great extent. Delhi now has near-universal electrification. Poverty levels as measured officially, even though widely considered to be inadequate in capturing vulnerabilities, have been reduced substantially in recent years. Further, high economic growth has been sustained in the face of a nation-wide slump and the employment situation has improved. Access to most of the basic services and means of transport has also considerably improved. Schooling and higher educational opportunities have expanded considerably while people have been found to show an overwhelming preference for the public provisioning of health facilities.

Despite the above achievements, however, equity continues to be a concern with access to some of the services remaining riddled with disparities. The disparities are visible when various income groups and types of settlements are taken into account. There are gender gaps in work participation and literacy. There also appears to be an issue with regard to public safety for the citizens in the state. In addition, the increasing informalisation of employment in the city does not augur well for the overwhelmingly large proportion of workers who do not fall within the network of social protection.

The Report shows how even in the face of a declining housing shortage, the presence of homeless on the streets of Delhi and the sizeable population living in slums and other poor settlements reflects not just inequality, but also the loss of human dignity. Other vulnerable groups include child workers, children living on the street, the differently-abled and senior citizens, who are yet to fully partake of the human development process in the city. A levelling of living standards across different segments of the population depends critically on improved access to basic amenities, especially sanitation services. Although the access to public health facilities has improved, it still falls short of acceptable standards, particularly due to overcrowding, an inadequate health workforce and skewed facility locations, all of which have a bearing on the quality of services and responsiveness of the health system at large. Education opportunities, too, have widened but all socio-economic groups do not have similar access or class completion rates.

Public safety in peoples' perceptions is an area that the Report found to be of significant concern. Paradoxically, going by official statistics, Delhi has a lower rate of crime than many cities in the country. At the same time, women, and more so, children in the city were found to constitute very vulnerable groups, and in this regard, the Government needs to cover a lot of ground to restore people's faith in the police and the legal proceedings. Yet, overall the people surveyed gave a positive assessment to living in Delhi, expressing their satisfaction with most of the aspects of their life in the city, encompassing jobs, basic services, education, schooling, and healthcare.

In conclusion, the Report highlights the need: first, to focus on and reduce inequalities in human development indicators across gender, income groups and types of settlements; second, to ensure universal coverage for aspects such as basic healthcare and basic infrastructural services; third, and most importantly, to guarantee a safe environment for vulnerable groups, including children, the elderly and women. A strong case has been made for promoting the inclusion of all segments of society within the human development agenda, a process that can be expected to enrich lives across the board.

Delhi is a city with a great historical legacy and has survived the passage of time to become a bustling metropolis with nearly 17 million inhabitants. Presently, one of the most important hubs of trade, commerce and hospitality, and a centre for the Government in India, this capital city-state draws a large number of people from all over the country, seeking to improve their lives.

A unique city with a blend of the ancient and the modern, Delhi carries with it a slice of history, dotted as it is, with magnificent historical monuments. At the same time, it is a modern and sophisticated city with state-of-the-art airport, rail and road infrastructural facilities, stadia, museums and cultural centres. Delhi is also a city of aspirations and acts as a magnet for people from all over India, who throng the city to better their prospects, be it in employment or for education. In the political arena, the city acts as the centre for the Union as well as the Delhi Governments. In sports, Delhi has hosted the Asian Games in 1951 and 1982, and recently, the Commonwealth Games in 2010. At present, with an urban population over 16 million, it is the second largest urban agglomeration of the country.

Delhi's per capita income is amongst the highest in the country. The high growth rate of per capita income in Delhi has defied the downward trend at the all-India level. The estimated poverty rates have also seen a significant decline in recent times.

The average per capita income for Delhi, at more than Rs. 0.2 million per year in 2012-13 is nearly three times the estimate for the all-India average. During the seven-year period 2005-06 to 2012-13, the city's per capita income grew at the rate of about 7 per cent per annum, enabling it to become the richest state in the country. During 2012-13, the growth in per capita income was around 7 per cent vis-à-vis around 3 per cent for India. The sustained growth in per capita income has been associated with a reduction in poverty to single-digit figures (9.9 per cent) in 2011-12, from approximately 13 per cent in 2004-05. Notwithstanding the wide concern over the present official poverty line, which is indeed an under-estimate of the state of vulnerability, there has certainly been a decline in absolute poverty levels in Delhi.

Employment opportunities have expanded and the earnings of casual as well as regular workers have shown an increase. The female workforce participation has somewhat risen from its low base level.

The tightening of the labour market has possibly contributed to the lowering of poverty in Delhi. During the period 1999-2000 to 2011-12, an additional 1.3 million people were added to the workforce, reaching to 5.56 million. The female workforce participation rate, which was less than 9 per cent in 1999-2000, increased to over 11 per cent by 2011-12 and female unemployment also declined during this period. Considering the seven-year period of 2004-05 to 2012-13, the earnings of regular workers have shown an increase of 5 per cent annually; with the increase for female workers being higher than that for males. The increase in the earnings of casual workers was even greater, being roughly double than the corresponding all-India rate. Although the rate of migration seems to have stabilised in Delhi during the last one decade, at the absolute level, still around 75,000 people in a year migrate to the city in search of livelihoods and employment opportunities. The Report finds that the city has absorbed its migrant population rather well, with the migrants rating themselves better than the non-migrants in terms of several indicators of well-being. The positive trends in the labour market find an echo in the Perceptions Survey, 2013, wherein around one-third of the respondents perceived that work opportunities in Delhi had improved over the last three years, with a similar proportion reporting that the work opportunities continued to be average. What is of more importance is that two-thirds of households considered their household incomes to be stable.

On the basis of most educational indicators, Delhi is ahead of the rest of India. The city also provides huge opportunities for higher education as evidenced by the in-flow of a large number of students from other states. However, access to educational opportunities, even for basic education, remains disparate for different segments of the population, impacting their future capabilities.

Delhi's literacy rate, at around 86 per cent, is much higher than the all-India level (74 per cent). On an average, Delhi has 7.5 years of schooling as compared to the corresponding all-India figure of 4.8 years. Close to one-fifth of the population has acquired higher educational qualifications. The share of people with higher educational qualifications such as graduation and post-graduation is as high as 17 per cent vis-à-vis the corresponding all-India share of just 7 per cent. The Gross Enrolment Ratios (GERs) at the primary and upper primary levels are 127 per cent and 108 per cent, respectively, as opposed to the corresponding all-India figures of 116 per cent and 85 per cent, respectively.

Educational leverage has, however, not been available to all sections of the population equally. There is a considerable gender gap in literacy. Not only do the Scheduled Castes (SCs) and Muslims have lower representation in higher education, but the GER levels for SCs are low and are seen to decline gradually from the primary to the successively higher levels of schooling. This clearly reflects the difficulty in making the transition from one level of schooling to another for the SC children. The Perceptions Survey, 2013, reports that nearly 70 per cent of the illiterate population in the sample was concentrated in four types of settlements, viz. *Jhuggi Jhopri* (JJ) clusters, unauthorised colonies, JJ resettlement colonies and urban villages, thereby highlighting the need to enhance educational opportunities and generate awareness for better attainment.

There has been a consistent improvement in life expectancy over the last three decades along with improvements in public health facilities. A clear preference has been seen for public facilities for hospitalisation care, a trend reverse of that experienced in the other metros, and people are increasingly turning to public healthcare vis-à-vis private provisioning even for non-hospitalised services.

The reach of primary healthcare facilities in Delhi has expanded tremendously, propelled by dispensaries, mobile clinics, school health clinics and Primary Urban Health Centres (PUHCs), and the people have also shown a clear preference and growing reliance for publicly-provided healthcare facilities. The Perceptions Survey, 2013, corroborates these findings, as it shows that around three-fourths of the state's population indicated its 'habitual preference' for public health facilities; in low-income groups, such an indicated preference is almost universal. Significant efforts have also been made in facilitating equitable access to essential medicines distributed through primary and secondary facilities. This has been a result of a strong commitment on the part of the Government to a holistic, public health approach to the health system, marked by 'Mission Convergence', which gives due priority to the social determinants of health in policy formulations.

The provisioning of basic services in Delhi has greatly improved during the last ten years. However, barring electricity supply, disparities in the access to some of these services continues to prevail. The differential in terms of access varies with income categories as well as across different types of settlements.

Shelter: Despite the burgeoning population and the added pressure from in-migration, Delhi has witnessed an overall improvement in housing between 2001 and 2011, with the housing shortage declining from approximately 250,000 to 150,000 over the period under study. The quality of houses has also improved, and ownership of homes is high. During the course of the survey, people living in rented houses were found to be largely satisfied with their housing and a fair proportion of them were upbeat about the future outlook in terms of buying houses. The Government's initiatives to make Delhi a slum-free city through the implementation of plan programmes such as the Jawaharlal Nehru National Urban Renewal Mission (JNNURM), the Rajiv Awaas Yojana, schemes for constructing houses for the economically weaker sections (EWS) and building night shelters for the homeless, have, in all likelihood, contributed to a more positive outlook on the state of housing and shelter in the city.

In spite of the improvements seen in the housing sector, however, the fact that an estimated 50,000 homeless people continue to live on the streets of Delhi cannot be ignored. Ironically, the phenomenon of overcrowding in one-room living arrangements in poor habitations exists alongside a large number of houses in the city lying vacant. Slums, in particular, have poor living conditions, and lack many basic facilities such as water and toilet facilities within their premises. The plight of the homeless is much worse, with even their basic existence being threatened daily by a number of exploitative factors. There is thus an urgent need for effecting an expansion in affordable housing facilities in order to ensure that all the citizens of Delhi are to be able to access housing and other basic services equitably, and to live with dignity.

Water: With over 80 per cent of the households receiving water within their premises, Delhi has performed well vis-à-vis other metros in providing this vital facility to its citizens. Although the poor receive free water, their supply is plagued with shortages, especially in the summer months, and they also suffer from quality issues, thereby endangering health and hygiene. There is surface water deficit in the city and the groundwater is rapidly getting depleted in most of the districts, leading to a grave situation where water supply is concerned. The Perceptions Survey, 2013, shows that settlement-wise disparities exist in terms of rating the availability of water, posh localities, approved colonies and JJ resettlement colonies giving it a positive rating, but 70 per cent of the respondents in the unauthorised colonies and 40 per cent in the of JJ clusters respondents rate this service as below average.

Sanitation: The Census, 2011, pegs the availability of toilet facilities within the household premises in Delhi, at nearly 90 per cent with the remaining households using public facilities or open spaces. However, among the nearly 0.4 million households living in the slums, just 50 per cent have access to latrine facilities within premises. Around 56 per cent of the children in the slums defecate in the open with serious consequences for hygiene, security and environment. Perceptions regarding the cleanliness of public toilet facilities are very poor, with more than half the respondents according a below average rating to the same. Many settlements including slums also lack sewerage facilities. The open disposal of garbage and existence of open drains leads to the choking of these drains and flooding during the monsoons, especially in the poorer settlements.

Electricity: Electricity has nearly universal coverage (99 per cent of the households) in Delhi. The findings of the Perceptions Survey, 2013, reveal that almost 80 per cent of the respondents rated power supply in the city as above average. Reforms in the power sector seem to have yielded results with the supply of power greatly improving post-2002. However, residents from some poorer settlements cite erratic power supply, inflated bills and rise in power tariff as the common problem areas. The Perceptions Survey showed that 64 per cent of the respondent households rated the service of power supply personnel as above average, while those from the urban villages and JJ clusters were more dissatisfied on this front.

Transport: The citizens have benefited from the large strides made in the transport infrastructure in the city, which include the advent of the Metro, low-floor buses, construction of several flyovers, and erection of street lights, among other things. The Perceptions Survey, 2013, quite accurately finds that the transport scenario in Delhi is dominated by public modes of transport such as buses and the Metro while some people even walk to their destinations. However, the distribution of road space is lopsided with personalised vehicles accounting for the main share of vehicular traffic, indicating a need for increased attention to public transport. A need has also been articulated for turning more policy attention towards the users of non-motorised means of transport such as bicycles as well as towards pedestrians. People opt for buses because of their affordability, coverage, and safety aspects, but overcrowding and the non-availability of direct bus services to all destinations remain problem areas. While the male respondents reported that travelling in buses was time-consuming, for female respondents, on the other hand, it was the indecent behaviour of the bus staff/co-passengers that caused discomfort, thereby pointing towards the need for sensitising bus staff, staff and passengers on gender issues. The Metro was widely hailed as a welcome addition to the Delhi transport landscape, with the cleanliness and comfort for travel that it offered being cited as two of its main popular features. Men also approved of the fact that it is a safe mode of travel, while women claimed that the separate women's compartment in the Metro was a welcome feature. Again, overcrowding and the non-availability of direct Metro lines to all destinations and lack of availability of toilets at all stations were some of its cited handicaps.

Roads and Street Lighting: Only around one-third of the respondents of the Perceptions Survey, 2013, rated road conditions in their locality to be good. Respondents from the New Delhi district accorded higher approval ratings to road conditions while those from the North-west and North-east districts rated the same poorly. The locality-wise ratings indicated that the conditions of roads was the poorest in JJ clusters and unauthorised colonies. Improvements were, however, cited in the area of street lighting in Delhi, which had received attention during the Commonwealth Games, with more than 58 per cent of the respondents finding the condition of the same to be good. The Focus Group Discussions (FGDs), on the other hand, revealed that inner roads were not paved and street lights were often not functional in the poorer settlements, calling for attention to this area. It can be noted that many of the transport-related facilities are interlinked with safety, in general, and safety for women, in particular, and any policy efforts towards improving the same need to keep this underlying connect as a main focus.

If seen through the lens of human development, it is obvious that there has been considerable progress on many fronts in Delhi though there is still a need to make access to most services more equitable across population groups. The next section outlines some other pressing concerns and challenges for expanding the scope of human development attainment in Delhi in order to bring all sections of the population on board.

The prevalence of a high degree of informalisation of employment has increased the vulnerability of a majority of workers.

The high level of informalisation in the Delhi employment scenario is evident from the fact that 85 per cent of all workers are informal (taking into account those working in both the formal and informal sectors). This usually implies lower average earning levels as well as inferior work conditions vis-à-vis the formal workers. Nearly three-fourths of all workers and 97 per cent of the informal sector workers lack the cover of social protection. Further, a large proportion of regular workers have no written contracts and no access to social security. Some occupations are more vulnerable, such as sales (particularly retail) and service workers, domestic servants, transport workers, vendors and hawkers, security guards and construction workers. The manufacturing sector workers, whose numbers, contrary to expectation, have shown an increase, are also quite vulnerable, as is evident from their declining labour productivity. A large number of them are engaged in subsistence activities in poor work environments. The Perceptions Survey, 2013, finds that the proportion of households with their main wage earners engaging in unskilled low-paying jobs and reporting their incomes to be stable is low.

In the area of early childhood mortality, Delhi is a long way away from achieving the MDG targets. The per capita availability of public health facilities as well as health workforce also remains low in the city.

As regards the area of containing early childhood mortality, Delhi does not compare favourably with the other metros, accounting, as it does, for 28 infant deaths per 1000 live births, thus necessitating closer attention to arresting neo-natal deaths and ensuring universal institutional deliveries. Quantitatively, while both primary level clinics/dispensaries and secondary level hospitals have significantly increased their capacities, the per capita availability of public health facilities in Delhi continues to be low, with less than 2 clinics per a population of 10,000. The shortage of healthcare personnel remains a major handicap. As of 2012, less than 4 government physicians—including even specialists—were available for a population of 10,000. The policy flags that emerge from this include an urgent increase in the availability of clinics and health personnel, especially in view of the considerable in-migration and commuting experienced by Delhi and the resultant pressures on the health infrastructure.

The issue of safety for all, especially the vulnerable groups, from violence and discrimination, has become increasingly important in the human development discourse. With this perspective, an assessment of public safety issues in the city shows that while official statistics do not peg Delhi high in terms of the crime rate, its citizens, especially women, perceive public spaces to be unsafe. However, the statistics do reveal a disturbing trend of increasing vulnerability of children from a safety perspective.

The lack of services such as functional street lights and safe public toilets, especially in the poorer settlements, brought out by the Perceptions Survey, 2013, and the FGDs, reflects the inadequate attention being paid to gender-sensitive urban planning. This contributes to the fear of violence in public spaces, and is likely to adversely affect vulnerable groups like the economically weaker sections, women, the elderly and children. However, this perception has not always found an echo in the official statistics.

The Perceptions Survey, 2013, revealed that less than one-third of the respondents rated personal safety in Delhi as 'good' or 'very good' and the feeling that crime had gone up over the years was very high (cited by more than 90 per cent of the respondents). The Survey was conducted immediately after the tragic incident of December 2012, wherein a 23-year old girl was gang-raped, which must have contributed to this enhanced feeling of insecurity. Despite such an overall perception, however, a majority of the respondents (55 per cent) felt secure or very secure in the areas wherein they stayed, that is, in their immediate localities or neighbourhoods. While most women did not feel safe in public spaces, the workplace and public transport emerged overall as spaces perceived to be the least safe for women. Women, children and senior citizens were found to be more vulnerable. The Perceptions Survey, 2013, also found many respondents to be dissatisfied with the police in terms of the lack of both approachability and promptness of response displayed by police personnel.

The state of basic services available to the 0.4 million households living in slums is particularly poor. They lag behind the average levels for Delhi in terms of access to all basic amenities, except for electricity.

The Census, 2011, estimates show that a glaring gap exists in term of the access to basic services for slum households. While the gap between slum households and the Delhi average in household in terms of access to bathroom and latrine facilities within their premises is 38-40 percentage points, the gap in the availability of water within the premises is 27 percentage points. It is only with regard to power supply that slum-dwellers are found to be at par with the rest of Delhi, because of the achievement of 97 per cent electrification in the city. The contrasting situation of slum-dwellers *vis-à-vis* that of Delhi as a whole becomes apparent when it is seen that as compared to an average of 76 per cent households in Delhi accessing the three basic services of water within their premises, electricity and sanitation facilities, the corresponding share for slum households is just 44 per cent. As regards housing facilities, though the share of good and liveable houses and the slums is quite close for Delhi (at 97 per cent and 90 per cent, respectively), the caveat remains that the space/living conditions in slum houses and the houses found in many other settlements such as approved colonies, are vastly different and comparisons are not justified.

Many environmental concerns arise due to the lack of private toilets, open drains in some areas, especially in slums, open garbage disposal as well as the contamination of the surface water in Delhi.

The river Yamuna, Delhi's lifeline for water availability upto Wazirabad barrage, gets highly contaminated by uncontrolled flows of untreated waste from human settlements, as well as from industrial effluents. Open defecation leads to the incidence of faecal matter flowing into the river via open drains, as well as contaminating the immediate environment in the neighbourhood. The groundwater in many parts of Delhi suffers from high salinity and nitrate content. The Government thus needs to set into motion initiatives for addressing the pollution in the Yamuna, through implementation of the Yamuna Action Plan (which is being done in two phases, with the third phase on the anvil). Simultaneously, however, there is also a need to further raise public awareness against contaminating the river water.

Despite the challenges and problems of insufficient inclusion of different population groups on the human development front, it is heartening to note that according to the findings of the Perceptions Survey, 2013, the citizens of Delhi are satisfied with the quality of life they lead, as assessed on the basis of critical indicators like employment, education, and healthcare as well as other personal attributes. Even among the lowest income group, 64 per cent of the households reported being satisfied with the quality of life.

Satisfaction levels vary across age, gender, social groups, types of settlements, and whether the respondents were migrants or not, but the variation is not large. The largest variation was observed for different income classes, with 85 per cent of the highest income group expressing satisfaction with the quality of their lives and this share declining to 64 per cent for the lowest income group.

A common aspiration across communities was to secure a government job, mainly as a teacher or in the police department. While 30 per cent of the respondents felt that the number and quality of work opportunities in Delhi were average, a similar proportion felt that work opportunities had improved over time. What is more important is that household income was considered to be stable by more than 60 per cent of households. This share decreased in the case of households wherein the main wage earners were engaged in unskilled low-paying jobs.

Satisfaction with one's own health status was found to decline with age, with the decline being sharper among women. A huge proportion (90 per cent) of the respondents were found to be satisfied with their children's education and the satisfaction increased with rising levels of income. Educational opportunities for technical/professional courses were also rated highly, with 80 per cent of the respondents finding these to be 'above average'. Amongst the student respondents, government school students were more dissatisfied with their education vis-à-vis private school students.

A very interesting finding of the Perceptions Survey, 2013, pertained to people's rating of interaction with personnel from different government departments, with highest rating coming for the Delhi Metro Rail Corporation (DMRC), followed by electricity departments, the Delhi Transport Corporation (DTC), Delhi Jal Board (DJB), Delhi Traffic Police, Municipal Corporation of Delhi (MCD), and lastly, the Delhi Police. The most popular activities for spending leisure time were found to be watching television (63 per cent), followed by going for an outing or meeting friends (53 per cent). Reading as a leisure activity was found to be popular among the youngest age groups, but tapered off during the older years, re-emerging as a popular choice for people aged 60 years or more.

In conclusion, the Report reveals that Delhi has seen enhanced incomes, expansion in economic opportunities, and improved access to basic services, and other capability-enhancing measures during the last few years. However many challenges still confront the city in its quest to become a global, inclusive city.

There is a need to focus on reducing inequalities through greater formalisation, the universalisation of social security, economic enhancement of women, and improvement in the quality of services for achieving greater progress on the human development front. Enhancing the earnings of the low productive manufacturing sector and some subsistence services sub-sectors in the informal sector as well as better enforcement of laws for the promotion and protection of livelihoods, especially for those working in vulnerable occupations should constitute an important policy focus. Equitable distribution and access to resources in all aspects of life—such as housing, water, and toilets, among others—need further improvement. The education and health sectors need to see improvements in infrastructure, manpower, and the quality of service. An important step in this regard would be the periodic monitoring and assessment of public service delivery, and the setting up of accountability enhancing initiatives.

Two other important steps that are needed are: ensuring public safety for all citizens, and promoting environmental safety. Both are relevant for all sections of society, including women, children and the elderly. Building an equitable world-class city requires innovative measures which are supported by people's participation, the efficient functioning of public institutions, as well as good governance.

Indeed, the above-mentioned challenges are not unique for Delhi—similar disparities have emerged in most parts of India and the world too, in the wake of the march towards prosperity. However, these disparities at low levels of livings of a large section of the population become quite stark in the case of Delhi where huge improvements in infrastructure have taken place and enormous wealth has been generated. Given the potential of Delhi, in terms of both human and other resources, it is possible to address these concerns with the participation of all sections of citizens and various stakeholders, with the Government of Delhi taking the lead. If the aspirations of Delhi to become a world-class city have to be fulfilled, the challenge of making the benefits of prosperity available to the less privileged and to make it more inclusive must be met.

Map 1

National Capital Territory of Delhi with Districts

Map 2

District Level Population Density in National Capital Territory of Delhi

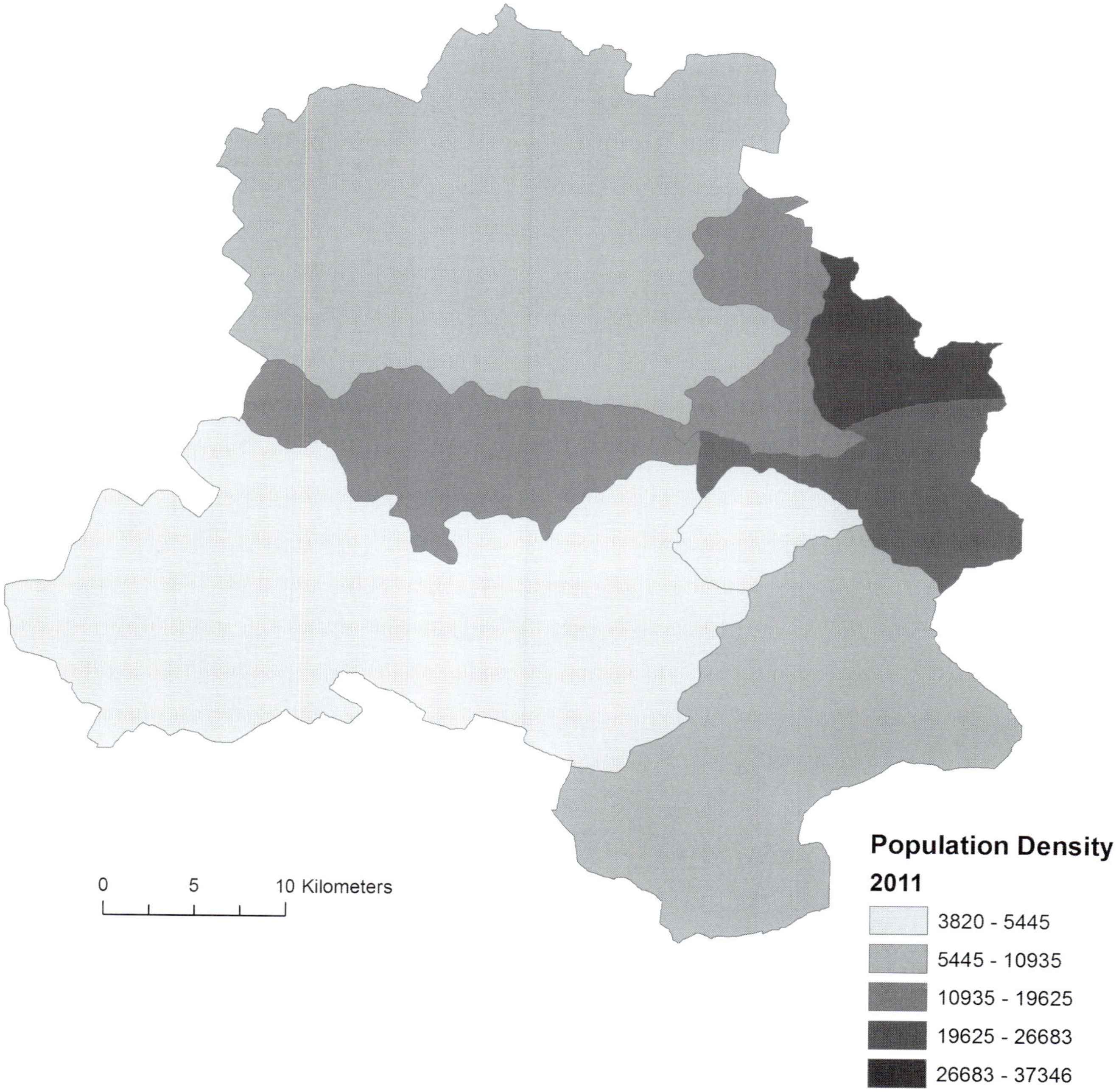

1

Introduction

1.1 Background

> "Human development, as an approach, is concerned with what I take to be the basic development idea: namely, advancing the richness of human life, rather than the richness of the economy in which human beings live, which is only a part of it."
>
> —Amartya Sen[1]

The human development approach has brought people to the centre-stage of discourses on development and policy-making, marking a shift away from approaches which focus on economic prosperity. Recognising that people are indeed the real wealth of a nation, the first global Human Development Report, published in 1990, pioneered a trend that has continued till today, at the global, national, regional and sub-regional levels. The second Delhi Human Development Report (DHDR), 2013, is presented here, a successor to the first Delhi Human Development Report, which was published in 2006.

The theme of the first Delhi Human Development Report, 2006, was citizen–government partnerships. Taking stock of the many achievements and shortcomings of life in Delhi, this Report concluded that Delhi's unparalleled economic expansion needed to go hand-in-hand with concerted efforts to improve the security and quality of life for its less fortunate residents. The Report spelt out a set of Delhi Development Goals,[2] which could only be achieved by fostering more partnerships between the Government, civil society organisations and the residents of Delhi. The targeted goals were to be attained by 2015. Since the target year of 2015 is yet to be reached, any evaluation of the achievements of those goals and targets would be a premature exercise. Nonetheless, as far as data permits, the second DHDR will attempt to locate Delhi's position vis-à-vis the goals and targets set by the DHDR, 2006.

The focus of the Delhi Human Development Report, 2013, is on *Improving Lives and Promoting Inclusion*. The Report delves into the perceptions and aspirations of the people of Delhi in terms of various human development-related issues. The quality of life enjoyed by an average citizen depends, to a great extent, on employment and livelihood opportunities, educational opportunities and attainments, the state of health and health services available, access to basic civic services and infrastructure, and last, but not the least, a safe and secure environment.

1. *http://hdr.undp.org/en/humandev/origins/*, Accessed on 13 March 2013.
2. Delhi Development Goals, Targets and Indicators have been adapted from the Millennium Development Goals (MDGs). There are 9 goals, 17 targets and 31 indicators.

The DHDR, 2013, analyses all the relevant human development issues in this context on the basis of various secondary sources of data as well as information about people's perceptions, gathered from a Public Perceptions Survey conducted by the Institute for Human Development (IHD) in 2013 (hereafter referred to as the Perceptions Survey, 2013).

The extensive Perceptions Survey, 2013, covering about 8000 respondents aged 15 years and above, was carried out on the basis of multi-stage probability sampling, by using Census 2011, ward level data and Census enumeration block maps. The survey was conducted during the period December 2012 to February 2013. Besides capturing people's perceptions and aspirations on development-related issues, the survey collected detailed information on the basic components of human development—income, health and education. It also collected information on living conditions and access to basic amenities such as water, sanitation, electricity, roads and transportation. Throughout the present Report, the analysis of the prevailing situation for various human development indicators from secondary sources of data has been complemented with findings from the Perceptions Survey, 2013 (see Appendix 1.1).

1.2 Delhi: A Unique City

Delhi is a unique city with a blend of the ancient and the modern. The imprints of its historical heritage on the cultural landscape of the city are as vivid as those from its modern-day infrastructural development. The city carries with it a slice of history, dotted as it is with magnificent structures such as the Qutub Minar, Red Fort, Purana Qila and Humayun's Tomb. The Qutub Minar, Red Fort and Humayun's Tomb are UNESCO World Heritage sites. At the same time, with its sprawling, modern airport, highly developed road and rail infrastructure, flyovers and bridges, Delhi has all the advantages of modern-day connectivity, which makes it a popular destination globally.

Delhi is a city of aspirations. This cosmopolitan city is a veritable melting pot of different cultures, religions and languages, and acts as a magnet for people from all over India. Living in a city that successfully hosted the Asian Games in 1951 and 1982, and recently, the Commonwealth Games, 2010, the citizens of Delhi have much to be proud of. Apart from being a modern, fast-developing metropolis, with state-of-the-art transport facilities, stadia, museums, multiplexes, wide tree-lined avenues and vibrant parks, Delhi also acts as the centre for Governments at both the Union and state levels.

Box 1.1

Delhi—A City with a Rich Heritage

Delhi has seen the rise and fall of many empires, which have left behind a plethora of monuments with the grandeur and glory of bygone ages. This is a city which traces its history to the *Mahabharata*, the great epic tale of wars fought between estranged cousins, the Kauravas and the Pandavas, for the city of Indraprastha.

The Mughals ruled Delhi in succession, starting from Qutab-ub-din to the Khiljis and the Tughlaqs. The city of Delhi passed into the hands of the British in 1803 A.D. In 1911, the capital of the British Empire was shifted from Calcutta to Delhi. After Independence, a kind of autonomy was conferred on the capital, but it largely remained a Chief Commissioner's regime. In 1956, Delhi was converted into a Union Territory (UT), and gradually the Chief Commissioner was replaced by a Lieutenant-Governor. In 1991, the National Capital Territory Act was passed by the Parliament and a system of diarchy was introduced under which the elected Government was given wide powers; except in the sphere of law and order, which remained with the Central Government. The actual enforcement of the legislation came into effect in 1993.

New Delhi, the capital of India, sprawled over the west bank of the river Yamuna, is one of the fastest growing cities in India. It is surrounded on three sides by the state of Haryana and to the East, across the river Yamuna, by the state of Uttar Pradesh (UP). Historically, the city has always been politically important with successive dynasties choosing it as their seat of power, between the thirteenth and the seventeenth centuries. The glorious legacy of those days is survived by important monuments in different parts of the city.

The myriad faces of the city are simply fascinating. In some places, it remains a garden city, tree-lined and with beautiful parks, but in others, it is congested and crowded with heavy traffic. Turbaned Sikhs, colourfully dressed Rajasthani and Gujarati women, Muslim shopkeepers along the lanes of Chandni Chowk in Old Delhi, Tibetans and Ladakhis manning the street stalls along Janpath, and Kashmiris selling wares in the handicraft emporia around Connaught Place, all these varied communities add to the cosmopolitan feel of the city. Soaring skyscrapers, posh residential colonies and bustling commercial complexes can be seen here rubbing shoulders with ancient historical monuments. Its boutiques and shopping arcades offer access to a wealth of traditional and contemporary crafts, from all over the country. The Old Delhi area, which looks entirely different from the New Delhi area, is located about 6 kms north of the city centre.

Source: *http://delhi.gov.in/wps/wcm/connect/DoIT/delhi+govt/travel/delhi+history,* Accessed on 14 May 2013.

For all its modern trappings and ancient charm, Delhi is, in another way, a city with two visages. Just as it is home to the affluent and the middle class, it is also inhabited by a large number of poor slum-dwellers, street children, homeless and differently-abled people. Are all these people, rich and poor, men and women, children and the elderly, the able and the disabled alike, able to access an acceptable quality of life, in terms of livelihoods, health and education facilities, as well as other basic services such as water and electricity? Equally important, are they living in a safe and secure environment? In an attempt to address these questions, the human development approach takes people of all hues on board. However, it is primarily through the perspective of the disempowered, marginalised humanity of this city, that this Report has approached the issues related to human development, recognising that if the fruits of development reach these people, then the entire society of Delhi would benefit.

1.3 Recent Changes in the Economy of Delhi

Delhi's evolution has deep and wide historical roots, which have left a profound impact on the cultural landscape of modern-day Delhi. Modern growth and development efforts, post-Independence, in general, and at the dawn of the new millennium, in particular, have contributed towards making Delhi a global capital city state. Plan documents suggest that the Tenth Five Year Plan (FYP) (2002-07) of Delhi constituted the golden era in its history of development. The major thrust of the Tenth FYP of the Government of NCT of Delhi (GNCTD) was on augmenting and strengthening civic amenities and infrastructure for transport, energy, water supply and sanitation, urban development, education, medical and public health sectors. In this Plan, special efforts were made to extend all essential civic amenities to the under-served areas of the capital city.

This was carried over even in the Eleventh FYP (2007-12), in which the GNCTD achieved major milestones

Box 1.2

Major Achievements of the Government of Delhi under the Eleventh Five Year Plan

Infrastructure: (i) With the completion of Metro's second phase more than two million commuters have benefited, (ii) As many as 3700 new low-floor buses and 300 new semi low-floor buses were added to the city's fleet,

(iii) A total of 50 flyovers/Rail Under Bridges (RUBs)/grade separators have been built.

(iv) More than 60 foot-over bridges/subways have been built.

Water supply: The capacity was enhanced to 855 MGD by the end of the Eleventh Plan.

Power: Reforms in this sector have reduced Aggregate Technical and Commercial (AT&C) losses from 54 per cent in 2002 to 15 per cent in 2011-12.

Health: (i) With the addition of more hospital beds, the availability of beds presently stands at 2.55 beds per 1000 population.

(ii) Three new super-specialty hospitals for liver, cancer and paediatrics were made functional.

Education: Six state universities/deemed universities and the Delhi Knowledge Development Fund have been set up.

Housing: (i) The Delhi Government has started building houses for the Economically Weaker Sections (EWS) under the Jawaharlal Nehru National Urban Renewal Scheme (JNNURM).

(ii) The Delhi Urban Shelter Improvement Board (DUSIB) has been set up for rehabilitating *Jhuggi Jhopdi* (JJ) clusters to achieve the goal of making Delhi a slum-free City.

Empowerment/Welfare of Women and Children: Various measures have been undertaken for the empowerment of women including the setting up of 54 new ICDS projects, sanction of additional honorarium for *anganwadi* workers, implementation of the *Ladli Yojana* and *Kishori Yojana*, offering of assistance by the Delhi Women Commission, and setting up of Gender Resource Centres. About 0.4 million senior citizens have benefited from the monthly pension scheme.

Sports: A major achievement of the city in this sphere was the successful hosting of the Commonwealth Games in 2010.

Source: Approach Paper to the Twelfth Five Year Plan of Delhi (2012-2017), Available at: *http://www.delhi.gov.in/wps/wcm/connect/DoIT_Planning/planning/important+links/an+approach+to+12th+five+year+plan+%282012-17%29*, Accessed on 12 April 2013.

in terms of infrastructural developments in the fields of water supply, power, transport, healthcare, education, and housing, among other human development indicators. In fact, human development goals were prominent in the Eleventh FYP, as the slogan for this Plan was 'Development with a Human Face and Making Delhi a Global City'. Thus, this Plan encompassed the twin goals of inclusive development and creating world-class infrastructure. Some of the achievements of the GNCTD under the Eleventh FYP are presented in Box 1.2.

The administrative and demographic contours of Delhi, along with its employment situation, are outlined next to identify the recent patterns of change. Some major changes that have come about in Delhi's economy in recent years are also presented and discussed here.

1.3.1 Administrative Set-up and Governance

Being the only city-state in the country, Delhi holds a unique position. Ever since Delhi was declared the Capital of India (on 12 December 1911), it has witnessed numerous intermittent amendments in its administrative status, with the only fact remaining constant being the multiplicity of authorities exercising administrative power. The Government of Delhi faces a challenging task in governing the city-state in view of the city's burgeoning population and the consequent pressures on infrastructure and civic services, with the task made more difficult because of the constant need for co-ordination

Box 1.3

Initiatives for Improving Governance

- *Bhagidari*: This initiative is about participatory governance and is based on the collaboration of multi-stakeholders such as citizens' groups, NGOs, and the Government. The process encourages citizen volunteerism and sharing of responsibilities between the Government and people. It facilitates public scrutiny of government functions and encourages people's active participation in the betterment of civil society (DHDR, 2006).
- *Mission Convergence (Samajik Suvidha Sangam)*: Mission Convergence was constituted to ensure the efficient and effective delivery of basic services and entitlements for the poor and marginalised. The mandate of the Mission was to bring together the plethora of schemes in order to eliminate duplication, strengthen implementation mechanisms by the use of Information Technology (IT), rationalise administration, and forge partnerships with civil society organisations for more effective delivery.
- *Citizen's Services Bureau (CSB)*: The CSB constitutes a unique IT initiative of the MCD to deliver its services electronically to the citizens of Delhi. The purpose of establishing the CSB was to provide all municipal services under one roof on payment of a small fee. The services that are provided here include registration of births and deaths, issuing of certificates, acceptance of applications for the issuing of all kinds of licences, renewal of licences, booking of community centres for holding private functions and receiving different types of payments.
- *Jeevan Centres*: Launched in February 2009, the project 'Jeevan'/ 'Sarkar Aapke Dwar' focuses on enhancing the quality of services available and on enabling the citizens to interact with the Government on a regular basis with speed, convenience, transparency, certainty and accountability at their doorsteps. All services are intended to be provided through a 'One-Stop-Shop' concept with an 'Anytime-Anywhere' facility.
- *Delhi (Right to Citizen to Time-bound Delivery of Services) Act, 2011*: Delhi is a frontrunner in initiating and implementing this Act for the time-bound delivery of services to its citizens. It also involves penal provisions for Government servants, in case of any default.
- *e-SLA*: The e-SLA is an electronic service level agreement that was devised to ensure the timely delivery of basic services to the citizens by fixing accountability. This is an information system which keeps a record of electronic submissions of service applications and their disposal. It also provides a tracking system to monitor the number of disposed and pending cases. Further, it helps the Government in tracking the performing and non-performing departments and personnel, and in taking timely corrective measures. In addition, it helps citizens track the status of their applications.
- *Green Bill*: This initiative is on the anvil and is expected to usher in considerable simplification in bill payment for the average citizens of Delhi. The Green Bill aims to integrate bills for various services such as water, electricity, phones (both fixed lines and cellular), cooking gas, etc., for which the consumer would have to pay just one bill for all the services. This bill has been conceptualised in order to synchronise the billing cycle of all the services offered on the same day.

Source: Compiled from *http://delhi.gov.in/wps/wcm/connect/DoIT/delhi+govt/delhi+home*, Accessed on 12 May 2013.

amongst multiple governing authorities. There is a dual jurisdiction in Delhi (of the Union Government and the state government), with the key functions of Delhi's administration being looked after by the Central Government, thereby posing challenges to the State Government in terms of making effective interventions and impacting its performance. The four major institutions governing Delhi are: the elected government of Delhi, office of the Lieutenant Governor, Municipal Corporation of Delhi (MCD) and the Delhi Development Authority (DDA). The latter three are accountable to the Central Government and hence, the elected government finds itself constrained while trying to effectively address the citizens' concerns.

With the existing complex administrative structure encompassing a vast area with a large population, the Delhi Government has had to turn towards many innovations in the area of governance. Most recently in 2012, two important amendments have taken place in the area of administration. The erstwhile single municipal body, which was serving 95 per cent of the area and 98 per cent of the total population in Delhi, was trifurcated. The trifurcation was done for bringing the Corporation closer to the people and for providing better delivery of services. The trifurcation of the MCD resulted in the formation of three different entities: the North Delhi Municipal Corporation (NDMC) with 104 municipal wards, the South Delhi Municipal Corporation with 104 municipal wards, and the East Delhi Municipal Corporation with 64 municipal wards. The second change involved the creation of two new districts by altering the boundaries of the nine existing districts. In a notification on 11 September 2012, the Department of Revenue, Government of NCT of Delhi created 11 districts and 33 sub-divisions/*tehsils* from the earlier 9 districts and 27 sub-divisions/*tehsils*. The two new districts are the South-east district with Defence Colony, Kalkaji and Sarita Vihar as its sub-divisions/'and Shahdara district with Shahdara, Seemapuri and Vivek Vihar as its sub-divisions. With the exception of North-west district, which has not witnessed any change in its existing sub-divisions and boundaries, all other districts have been altered and modified.[3]

The Delhi Government has envisaged and also launched a number of initiatives to improve governance in the city, and these have been done while keeping the citizens' interests at the forefront of policy-making (Box 1.3). Although a number of innovative steps have been taken by the Delhi Government, there is a need for greater generation of awareness among the people to take advantage of all these facilities. All these services also require supporting and efficient infrastructural developments on a large scale.

1.3.2 Population Dynamics

Delhi, akin to the other mega cities such as Mumbai and Kolkata, has recorded a significant decline in the population growth rate during the period 2001-2011. The fertility rates have been on the decline and as a result, the natural growth rate of the population has slowed down. However, one other important reason for the decline in the population growth rate of Delhi could be the development of satellite towns in the NCR region such as Gurgaon, Noida, Faridabad, Ghaziabad, Sonipat, and Meerut. The Census data shows that during the decade 2001-2011, the population growth rates in the urban areas of the constituent regions of the National Capital Region (NCR) other than Delhi such as Haryana (61 per cent), Uttar Pradesh (52.3 per cent) and Rajasthan (50.5 per cent), were very high. On the other hand, urban areas of Delhi registered a relatively low growth of 26.8 per cent during the same period. Despite recording the lowest population growth rate during the period 2001-2011 (20.96 per cent), Delhi still added nearly 2.9 million to its population during that decade.[4] With a birth rate of 17.5 per thousand and a death rate of 4.3 per thousand in Delhi, the contribution of the natural growth rate to the population of Delhi is 13.2 per thousand population (SRS, 2012). With its 16.3 million urban population, it is the second largest urban agglomeration in India. Mumbai is at the top with an 18.4 million population, while Kolkata ranks third with a 14.1 million population (Census, 2011).[5] However, Delhi's urban population growth is the fastest at 26.8 per cent, with Mumbai and Kolkata being way behind, at 12 per cent and 6.9 per cent, respectively. As a result, urban Delhi has added a population of nearly 3.4 million to its population during the last decade whereas Mumbai and Kolkata have added populations of only 0.2 million and 0.9 million to their urban areas, respectively. It is evident that Delhi is on the path of becoming the largest urban agglomeration of India. Delhi's rural population and area have been shrinking rapidly. In 1991, 53.8 per cent of the total area of Delhi (1483 sq km) was rural, which declined to 24.9 per cent in 2011. Similarly, the rural population in Delhi in 1991 was 10.07 per cent (0.95 million), which declined to 2.5 per cent (0.42 million) in 2011. More and more villages of Delhi are being declared as Census towns in each successive Census, resulting in a decrease in both the rural population and area (Economic Survey of Delhi, 2012-13). As per the Census, 2011, Delhi has 112 villages, 135 urban villages and 110 Census towns.

Economic growth and the accompanying livelihood and educational opportunities in Delhi have attracted people from all over India, who come to the city with dreams of building their future. Migrants not only from the neighbouring states such as Uttar Pradesh, Haryana and Rajasthan, but also from distant states like Bihar, West Bengal, Madhya Pradesh and many others throng the city. Although they form the backbone of Delhi's economy in many ways by providing invaluable labour and services, they also exert pressures on the civic services and other infrastructure of the city that are already strained.

1.3.3 Socio-religious Composition

The Scheduled Caste (SC) population comprises the largest proportion of poor and vulnerable in India

3. Department of Revenue, Government of NCT of Delhi, Notification dated 11 September 2012.

4. Except for the decade 1911-21 when it recorded a growth rate of 18.03 per cent.

5. As per the Census, 2011, Mumbai, Delhi and Kolkata are the three largest urban agglomerations in India, accounting for a population of more than ten million. All the three mega cities of India have recorded significant declines in their growth rate during the last decade.

(NCEUS, 2008). The proportion of SCs in the total population in Delhi has shown a declining trend over the last two decades. As per the Census 2011, the SC population of NCT Delhi was 2.8 million (comprising 16.7 per cent of the total population). In 1991 and 2001, this share was 19.1 per cent and 16.9 per cent, respectively. During the decade 2001-2011, however, the decline in the share of the SC population was relatively moderate.[6] The drop in the SC population in Delhi has taken place due to the larger share of non-SC communities in the migrant population. The proportion of the SC population is relatively higher in rural areas (19.6 per cent) as compared to urban areas (16.7 per cent).

Delhi does not have its own notified ST population. However, tribal people migrating to Delhi from other states comprise a small part of the population. Hindus form the largest religious category, with an 82 per cent share in the population (Census, 2001). Muslims and Sikhs are other important religious groups, comprising shares of 11.7 per cent and 4 per cent, respectively, in the total population. The population share of Jains and Christians in the city are 1.1 per cent and 0.9 per cent, respectively.

1.3.4 The Employment Scenario

Delhi's economy provides an opportunity to earn livelihoods and get better employment to both its original populace as well as the migrants who come here with a lot of aspirations. In terms of absolute numbers, there has been an increase in the labour force and workforce in Delhi during the period 2004-05 to 2011-12. However in percentage terms, the labour force participation rate (LFPR) and workforce participation rate (WPR) have almost remained stable. In 2011-12, the LFPR and WPR for Delhi were 35 per cent and 33.7 per cent, respectively. The gender gap in the WPR was also very high. In recent years, though, there have been welcome trends of continuous increases in the female WPR and decline in the proportion of unemployed females, indicating the successful creation of jobs for females.

Delhi's employment structure is dominated by three sectors—trade, other services and manufacturing. Two-thirds of female employment in the city is concentrated in other services, including financial, business services, public administration, education and healthcare, among others. However, there is cause for concern, given that employment in the organised sector has declined over the years as has occurred elsewhere in the country. Most of the employment generation in Delhi is currently taking place in the unorganised sector. The poor, who end

Box 1.4

Some Recent Milestones

Delhi Metro: A part of the Mass Rapid Transport System (MRTS), the Metro was introduced in 2002, and was expected to provide Delhi-ites with a safe, non-polluting and expeditious mode of travel within the city. It began its journey on the Red Line between the Shahdara and Tees Hazari stations. Subsequently, the Metro underwent major expansion in various phases and now it has other dedicated routes, viz., the Yellow, Blue, Green, Violet and Airport lines, which cater to the travel needs of the entire NCR region. With a current running length of about 190 kms,[7] work on the first two phases of the Delhi Metro has been completed. Besides the ongoing work on Phase III, during Phase IV, there are plans to increase the Metro line to around 245 km by 2021 (Twelfth Five Year Plan, 2012-17, and Annual Plan, 2012-13, Delhi). Within a span of ten years, the number of commuters using the Metro has gone up by 40 times, reflecting a clear preference of the citizens of Delhi for this fast and comfortable mode of travel.

Replacement of Blue Line Buses by the Corporate Sector Operator System: In order to improve the quality of the bus transport system with the addition of new low floor buses in the DTC fleet, the GoNCTD decided to replace the individual operator's blue line buses by the Corporate Sector system so as to maintain time schedule, quality of buses and road discipline on Delhi roads. At present, more than 500 Corporate Sector buses are serving commuters. Their number is going to cross 1000 by the end of this year.

Commonwealth Games (2010): The hosting of the Commonwealth Games in the city resulted in the overhauling of its physical infrastructure, including several modern flyovers, underpasses, foot overbridges, stadiums, multi-storeyed parking facilities, refurbished roads, and road signage. These modern-day infrastructures have changed the cultural landscape of Delhi.

6. At the national level, there has been an increase in the proportion of the SC population from 16.2 per cent in 2001 to 16.6 per cent in 2011.

7. *http://www.delhimetrorail.com/project_updates.aspx*, Accessed on 24 June 2013.

up getting jobs in the unorganised sector, often find themselves vulnerable due to the lack of both job security as well as social security, often working in conditions detrimental to their health. They largely end up finding their livelihoods in sectors such as construction, retail trade, transport, and solid waste management.

1.4 Human Development Issues

The human development approach goes much beyond income and focuses on reaching healthcare, nutrition, education, housing facilities and other basic services such as drinking water and electricity to the common people, so that they can enjoy an enriched life in a safe environment. It also examines the situation closely for all vulnerable groups such as the elderly, the differently-abled, children, etc., and in a rapidly changing urban milieu, for women, who constitute a particularly vulnerable group in terms of access to a secure environment.

In the recently published India Human Development Report, 2011, Delhi ranked second after Kerala in terms of the Human Development Index (HDI) (IAMR, 2011).[8] It ranked first according to the income index whereas for the education and health indices, it ranked second after Kerala. An encouraging aspect about Delhi's performance on the human development front is that it is not only better than other states, on an average, but that it is also better for all the socio-religious categories (ibid.). For instance, the performance of the SCs, Other Backward Castes (OBCs) and minorities in Delhi has also been relatively better vis-à-vis other states on several parameters. Thus, from an equity perspective, Delhi has fared better than most states. However, Delhi still has considerable scope to improve its HDI. In fact, it should aim at competing globally and set examples for the other states of India.

The Delhi Government had made inclusive development its focus, as reflected in the adopted theme 'Development with a Human Face' for the Eleventh FYP (2007-12). Future goals as envisioned in different policy documents including the Master Plan–2021 and the first Delhi Human Development Report (HDR), 2006, also indicate that the main thrust area is to ensure for all the citizens of Delhi a decent quality of life and to achieve environmentally sustainable development for the city. Some of these relevant issues are discussed in the subsequent sections in this chapter.

8. The HDIs were based on the 2007-08 data set.

1.4.1 Income and Poverty

Delhi had the highest average per capita income in the country during 2011-12 (Economic Survey of India, 2012-13). The advance estimates of per capita income for Delhi during 2012-13 peg it to be more than Rs. 0.2 million (ibid.) This is nearly three times the estimate for the all-India figure of Rs. 68,000. Similarly, the rate of growth of per capita income at constant prices was also higher at 7.1 per cent against an all-India average of 2.9 per cent during 2012-13. The growth of GSDP at constant prices (with 2004-05 as the base year) was 9 per cent in 2012-13.

Delhi's poverty level has remained lower than the all-India level. The recently released poverty estimates from the Planning Commission for 2011-12, using the Tendulkar Committee methodology,[9] suggest that the proportion of the Below the Poverty Line (BPL) population in Delhi is 9.9, which is less than half of the national average of 21.9 per cent. Using the same method, the proportion of the poor during 2004-05 was found to be 13 per cent for Delhi against an all-India estimate of 37.2 per cent. In absolute terms, the number of poor in Delhi was 1.7 million in 2011-12, which declined from 1.9 million during 2004-05. Bringing down the level of poverty is, therefore, still part of an unfinished agenda before the Government and needs to be tackled on a priority basis.

1.4.2 Education

Delhi has a variety of good quality schools, colleges and universities, as well as centres for research and higher education, and is a mecca of sorts for students from all over India and abroad. Its literacy rate at 86.3 per cent is substantially higher than the all-India average of 74.0 per cent. Although there is a gender gap in literacy, it has declined moderately over the years from 13.5 per cent in 2001 to 11.2 per cent in 2011. The literacy rate in Delhi is, however, still lower than that in the other mega cities such as Mumbai (90.8 per cent), Chennai (90.2 per cent), and Kolkata (88.3 per cent), and also in some other states such as Kerala, Mizoram, Goa and Tripura.

A sound elementary education provides the foundation on which the educational achievements of people can be based. Achievement of Universal Elementary Education (UEE) is a declared objective of the Government, and is also expected to strengthen the social fabric of democracy through the

9. As per the Tendulkar Methodology, the poverty line has been expressed in terms of the Monthly Per Capita Expenditure (MPCE) based on a Mixed Reference Period.

provisioning of equal opportunities to all. The Right to Education (RTE) Act (2009), mandates the provision of education as a fundamental justiciable right for 6-14 year-old children and has further strengthened the Government's resolve to attain this goal. The enrolment of students at all levels of schooling has continually gone up in Delhi during the period 2005-06 and 2010-11 (Economic Survey of Delhi, 2012-13). During 2005-06, the total enrolment of students in schools (primary to senior secondary level) was 3.4 million, which increased to 3.9 million during 2010-11. The gross enrolment ratio (GER) in classes I-V was 93.1 per cent (NSS, 2007-08). For classes VI-VIII, the GER was 115.1 per cent. Overall, the GER for classes I-VIII is 101.8 per cent. The increase in enrolment has been higher for secondary and senior secondary schools than at the primary and middle level school. The net attendance ratio (NER) during the year 2007-08 for classes I-VIII was 86 per cent (NSS, 2007-08), indicating gaps that still need to be bridged in school attendance. Therefore, it is imperative for the state to devise strategies to tackle the issues of attendance and retention for achieving better human development outcomes.

In order to attain the status of a fully literate state as well as the goals of universal enrolment, provisioning of quality education and educational infrastructure, the state needs to garner more resources in the education sector. Expenditure on education as a percentage of the Gross State Domestic Product (GSDP) was 1.60 per cent during the years 2010-11 and 2011-12.

1.4.3 Health

Over the years, Delhi has created a wide network of primary to tertiary healthcare systems, which not only cater to its huge population but also attract large numbers of patients from the neighbouring states. Apart from good healthcare facilities, health outcomes also depend on the availability of safe drinking water, sanitation facilities, better drainage facilities, and safe environmental conditions. There has been a tremendous increase and improvement in the capacity of healthcare facilities in Delhi. Spending on healthcare in absolute terms under its Plan expenditure increased from Rs. 14.8 billion to Rs. 28.2 billion during the period 2006-07 to 2012-13, which signifies an increase of more than 47 per cent. Despite such a trend, the pressures of its own population as well as of the neighbouring states bring the per capita availability of public health facilities in Delhi to less than 2 clinics per a 10,000 population (DHS, 2011). The inadequate availability of physicians and supporting technical manpower of para-medics is another major handicap. This puts the public health system under tremendous pressure with high case-loads and patients flocking the hospitals.

Delhi enjoys a relatively high life expectancy of 72 years, which is four years more than the national average of 68.[10] Also, there is little gender difference in this in the state. Since the 1990s, life expectancy levels in Delhi, among both males and females, have been higher than the national average. As a result, there is a growing elderly population that has special healthcare needs. The birth rate represented in terms of the total fertility rate (TFR) in Delhi is 1.8, which is among the lowest in India, and indicates the achievement of the replacement rate.[11] Similarly, the crude death rate in Delhi is also among the lowest in the country.

On the other hand, improving maternal health and reductions in child mortality remain a challenge. In 2007-08, the proportion of women who received adequate antenatal care (ANC) that is, coverage of at least three ANC check-ups was 72.7 per cent, and the proportion of institutional deliveries was 81.35 per cent (Annual Report on Birth and Death, DES, 2013). Although recent data of the Government of NCT of Delhi suggests that these proportions have improved, thereby making more births safer, nevertheless Delhi is still far from attaining the goals of universal ANC and institutional deliveries. Similarly, the infant mortality rate (IMR) at 28 per thousand live births (SRS, 2012) has shown a sluggish decline since 2006, making the Delhi Development Goals of 10 by 2015 unreachable. Delhi is also yet to attain universal immunisation coverage of children aged 12-23 months.

1.4.4 Gender Equality

Delhi, despite being one of the frontrunners in economic development, has experienced wide gender inequality in its development process. Indicators such as the sex ratio, literacy, WPR and similar indicators, reflect gender inequality in Delhi vis-à-vis other metropolises such as Mumbai, Kolkata and Chennai, as also other states. Although Mumbai (861) lags slightly behind Delhi (867) in its aggregate sex ratio,

10. Computed on the basis of SRS, 2010, data.
11. As per the State Civil Registration System, 2012, GNCTD, Delhi.

the child sex ratio, in particular, is alarmingly low in Delhi. The sex ratio has been a matter of concern for Delhi since long. It is among the lowest in the country, at 868 females per 1000 males (Census, 2011). Nevertheless, the Census, 2011, data shows that the gains in the sex ratio have been the highest for Delhi over the decade 2001-2011. This gain can be largely attributed to the gain in the sex ratio of the population aged 7-plus years. The gain in the child sex ratio is, however, still negligible and remains an area of concern.

The gender gap in literacy is also the highest in Delhi in comparison to the other four metros. Similarly, even in terms of the LFPR and the WPR, there still exists a wide gender gap. The labour force constitutes a little more than one-third of the total population in Delhi. However, only 11.1 per cent of the females have been recorded as participating in the labour force against 54.8 per cent for males (NSS, 2011-12). Even in terms of the WPRs, female workers are way behind their male counterparts. Despite a modest increase in the WPR for females and a decline for males during the decade 2001-2011, the gender gap between the male (52.7 per cent) and female (10.7 per cent) WPRs remains high.[12] There is thus a need to bridge such gender gaps in order to enhance the status of human development in Delhi.

1.4.5 Access to Basic Services

The major thrust of the last two Five Year Plans of extending the access of the population to basic services, especially to the under-served population, has resulted in wider proportions of the population gaining access to basic services such as electricity, water and sanitation. The Census, 2011, data reveals that the coverage of access to electricity in the state is nearly universal. More than four-fifths of the population in the city received piped water supply while three-fourths of the households had access to drinking water within their premises. The rate of access to sanitation facilities too has shown improvement, with nearly 90 per cent of the households having access to latrines within their premises. At the same time, the Census estimates for the slums reveal the existing disparities, with nearly 50 per cent of the slum households having no latrine facilities within their premises. Hence, apart from electricity wherein near-universalisation has been reached, the need to make access to water and sanitation universal continues to remain a challenge for the state. There are also gaps in the access and quality of water and sanitation for the poor settlements, which needs urgent attention.

1.4.6 The Environment

Rapid development processes and ever-increasing population pressures have posed enormous challenges in preserving environmental sustainability in Delhi. Several steps have been taken in the recent past to ameliorate the environmental situation. These steps include a massive focus on afforestation, the universal use of compressed natural gas (CNG) in commercial vehicles, a ban on plastics, better management of solid waste, treatment of waste water and many more, which have, in turn, yielded remarkable results, but nevertheless, many challenges still remain.

The available data suggest that in 1997, the percentage of the area under forest and tree cover was a meagre 1.75 per cent of the total area, which rose to nearly 20 per cent by the year 2011 (Economic Survey of Delhi, 2012-13). In 1997, the forest and tree cover was just 26 sq km, which rose to 299.6 sq km by 2009. Delhi has, therefore, added 91 per cent of its total forest and tree cover in the last decade. This is an incredible achievement. However, during the period 2009-2011, Delhi witnessed a decline in the forest and tree cover by 3.38 sq kms. This decline needs to be checked immediately and the focus on increasing the forest and tree cover in the state should continuously gain prominence so as to reach the harmonious level of one-third of its total area.

Controlling the levels of pollution—air, water, and noise—is also a challenge for the state as part of its endeavour to provide a healthy environment to its people. In 2011, there was a decline in the ambient air quality in the state, as the levels of all the air pollutants such as sulphur dioxide, nitrogen dioxide, carbon monoxide and suspended particulate matter were recorded to be high (Economic Survey of Delhi, 2012-13). Similarly, the quality of water in the Yamuna River has throughout withstood major challenges due to the discharge of untreated sewerage and inadequately treated industrial effluents. The enormous increase in the number of vehicles on the roads has also affected the prescribed decibel level of noise. The steps taken by the Delhi Government to improve the quality of the environment thus requires

12. The LFPR and WPR estimates are sourced from NSS 68th Round, 2011-12.

a major boost. It also necessitates the forging of effective partnerships between the government and citizens.

1.5 Vulnerable Groups

Any deficit in human development achievements impacts two special groups at two ends of the age spectrum: children and the elderly. The first group comprises young persons who are just starting their lives, but are already burdened with the cares of adults and much more, while negotiating a life on the streets and/or in a workplace, and facing security issues in the process. The other group comprises members who have mostly completed their prime years and look forward to enjoying the fruits of labour, but often feel alone, insecure and neglected by society. Another very important group that needs special attention is that of the differently-abled population.

1.5.1 Street Children and Child Labourers

These two groups of children—street children and child labourers—are not mutually exclusive, that is, there are street children who are child workers, but not all street children work. On the other hand, there are many child workers who do not live on the streets.

A recent survey by IHD and 'Save the Children' (2011) reported that there are around 51,000 street children (aged less than 18 years) in Delhi (IHD–Save the Children Report, 2011).[13] Such children include not only those who lack homes, but even those who live with their families but spend most of their time on the streets. Poverty, hunger, and the search for employment are the major factors that bring children on to the streets. Mostly male and largely illiterate, these street children were found to be engaged in rag-picking (20 per cent), street vending (15 per cent), begging (15 per cent) and working at roadside stalls and repair shops (12 per cent). Interestingly, the Survey found that 87 per cent of the street children paid for accessing toilet facilities in Delhi (with the figure being higher for girls at 90 per cent). There was also little awareness about the existing programmes among the children, and their access to support under these programmes was impeded by the lack of identity proof for these children.

A Report by the Ministry of Statistics and Programme Implementation (2012) provides estimates for child labour in Delhi, reporting that 11.8 per cent of the 5-14 year old children are working. Out of these, 2.2 per cent were engaged in paid work and 2.9 per cent were engaged in unpaid work (for someone other than members of the household in both cases). Notwithstanding debates regarding the definition of child labour, specially in the context of the Right to Education Act (2009), the NCPCR has called for an inclusive definition of child labour, incorporating all types of work, in agriculture and industry, at home, in hazardous or non-hazardous occupations, and including all children up to 18 years of age into the definition.[14] In order to address the issue of child labour more effectively, the Delhi Government has drawn up a detailed action plan based on the profiles of child labour in Delhi, which includes out-of-school children living with their parents, and children who have come from other states without their families.

1.5.2 The Elderly

With the changing fabric of society, wherein joint families are fast giving way to nuclear families, the elderly people have started feeling increasingly isolated and vulnerable. For those among the elderly aiming to lead an independent, active life, completing the daily round of chores or getting around the city can also pose considerable problems since enough public facilities are not in place. Thus, the elderly need special attention from the state.

The share of senior citizens (aged 60 years or more) in Delhi's population has risen over the last few decades. As per the 2001 Census,[15] the elderly constituted 5.2 per cent of the population in Delhi, which translates into 0.72 million people (0.37 million men and 0.35 million women). Higher estimates for the elderly have been provided by an independent survey at over 1.2 million for Delhi.[16]

13. UNICEF has defined street children as street-living children who ran away from their families and who live alone on the streets; street-working children who spend most of their time on the street fending for themselves, but who return home on a regular basis; and children from street families who live on the street with their families.

14. *http://ncpcr.gov.in*, Accessed on 4 April 2013.

15. This is the latest available official source of nation-wide data for this segment of population.

16. Agewell Foundation conducted a survey in 2012 on the elderly (60 years and above) in the Delhi NCR on a representative sample of 15,000 elderly people.

Although senior citizens face health-related problems, the perceptions regarding health issues are quite positive among them. According to the NSS estimates (60th Round, 2004), out of 12 per cent aged males reporting their illnesses, 66 per cent felt that the current state of healthcare in Delhi was good. Age-specific death rates are also better in Delhi than those at the all-India levels for most age groups.

Women are usually economically and educationally more vulnerable than men, and have much more care-giving responsibilities. Their financial dependence continues, and sometimes gets deepened, following widowhood. According to the Census, 2001, 46.6 per cent of the elderly women in Delhi were widows and formed an important proportion of the vulnerable in the city. The Delhi Government has launched a number of schemes to assist the elderly to enable them to conduct their daily lives in a safe and trouble-free manner. These range from the provisioning of monthly pension, old age homes, special health clinics, recreation centres, and concessional bus passes to comprehensive registration and supervision of senior citizens by the Delhi Police.

1.5.3 The Differently-Abled

Nearly 1.7 per cent of the population in Delhi or 0.23 million people, are differently-abled (Census, 2011). This includes those suffering from disabilities ranging from impairment in sight, speech, hearing, and mobility to psychological and mental handicaps. However, the largest proportion of the differently-abled comprised the visually impaired (50 per cent) and locomotive-disabled (27 per cent) population, which accounted for nearly three-fourths of the entire differently-abled population. These special groups require special treatment and infrastructure for mainstreaming. Over the years, Delhi has created some infrastructure to cater to the needs of this population in the form of schools, training-cum-product centres, sheltered workshops, and hostels for the college-going population. It also has a Plan scheme of monthly financial assistance worth ₹ 1500 for those with 40 per cent disabilities. Special camps have also been organised to extend the requisite services to this population group (Economic Survey of Delhi, 2012-13).

1.6 Sources of Data

This Report has used the latest statistics and information available on Delhi from secondary sources. These include the decennial censuses, including the Census, 2011; various rounds of NSSO data (particularly on employment) including the 68th Round (2011-12), other reports of the Government such as the Economic Survey of Delhi (2012-13), Economic Survey of India (2012-13), and Reports of various departments of the Government of NCT of Delhi. The report has also benefited from the latest data shared by the GNCTD. In addition, the report has used the findings of two large sample surveys conducted in Delhi by the Institute for Human Development (IHD) during 2010 and 2011. The first survey was carried out by IHD and the Institute of Rural Management (IRMA), Anand (referred to as the IHD–IRMA Survey) in 2010, which had a large sample of 2000 households drawn on similar lines as that of NSSO, and is representative of Delhi. The other survey was carried out in 2011 by IHD with support from Sir Dorabji Tata Trust (SDTT) (referred to as the IHD–SDTT Survey), which had a sample size of 3,000 poor households.

The People's Perceptions Survey (IHD—2013)

It is a well-known fact that Human Development Reports highlight the quality of the lives of people residing in various regions/countries/states, etc. For adding to the existing attributes that are considered to be a part and parcel of the human development paradigm, it becomes important to elicit people's own views, their established perceptions and suggestions, and to study them carefully to derive useful indications about the quality of their lives and their perceptions of public services. In tandem with the first Delhi Human Development Report, 2006, which presented empirical findings from a survey carried out to assess people's perceptions, a similar empirical exercise was carried out for the purposes of the Delhi Human Development Report, 2013, to identify the perceptions and aspirations of the residents of Delhi and add further value to the discussion on inclusive human development in the state.

Keeping the main objective as a representative state level survey to bring forth the public's perceptions on the quality of life and living standards in Delhi (including the living environment, basic amenities, healthcare, education and other facilities), the Perceptions Survey administered questionnaires to assess people's ratings of their access and contentment with the existing state of basic services. It was expected that the findings from this Survey would help in the formulation of future strategies and policy interventions. The target population for the study was the population aged 15 years and above, with the geographical target being the entire state and a sample size of 8029 households.[17]

The findings from the IHD Perceptions Survey throw very useful and relevant light on the state of various public services in Delhi and incorporate various elements of human development viz., livelihoods and employment, education, healthcare, basic services, and safety and security. They also study the perceptions of a cross-section of economic and social groups, districts and settlement types. Evidence-based findings from this survey, which are delineated in the various chapters of this Report, would go a long way towards facilitating the planning and execution of policy interventions for the state.

1.7 Structure of the Report

The second Delhi Human Development Report, 2013, presents a periodic review of the progress made as well as milestones to be reached in the sphere of human development, with a focus on inclusion, perceptions and equity. The suggested policy interventions and future strategies are evidence-based, with the aim of guiding future planning and programme implementation in the state. To start with, the state of employment and livelihoods in Delhi is presented in Chapter 2, wherein a detailed discussion of the levels and patterns of income and employment is presented. The chapter also presents recent trends in migration, drawing upon the findings from the Perceptions Survey, 2013, to highlight some interesting features of migration patterns in Delhi. This chapter also focuses on the challenges that the state faces in the sphere of employment and livelihoods, and identifies possible future strategies for addressing this issue. The human resource scenario is presented in Chapter 3, which details its composition in terms of the levels of education, the extent of inclusion, access and quality as well as the possible interventions needed to enable Delhi to attain universal literacy and ten average years of schooling by the year 2020. Keeping the universal coverage central to its theme, Chapter 4 reviews the health and healthcare scenario in Delhi. In this chapter, the successes achieved, the challenges that persist, the financial risk protection scenario, and the policy and programmatic responses put into place by the Government have been studied in depth and reviewed. This chapter also attempts to lay down a possible roadmap for achieving universal healthcare coverage in the state.

Taking the discussion on the various elements of human development beyond the parameters of income, education and health, Chapter 5 expresses the need to factor in the availability of and access to basic services such as housing, water, sanitation, electricity and transport, in the context of perceptions and inclusion. It explores the state of public provisioning in the area of housing and basic facilities as well as the access to basic services in slums and other types of deprived settlements, which throw light on the extent of inclusion/exclusion in the same. The chapter also draws on the findings of the Perceptions Survey, 2013, to highlight people's perceptions with regard to the access and functioning aspects of various public services. Safety and security are two essential aspects of human development, and the right to feel safe is an essential pre-requisite for leading a good quality of life. Chapter 6 presents the scenario on safety and security in an urban context with a focus on the vulnerable sections of the population such as women, children, and the elderly. It also draws conclusions on the basis of the findings of the Perceptions Survey, 2013.

Going beyond the traditional definition of human development, in this Delhi Human Development Report, 2013, an attempt has been made to broaden the scope of study to include various qualitative aspects of life such as leisure, contentment, feeling of safety and security, and people's perceptions on the quality of their lives. The Perceptions Survey thus helps focus on people's understanding of the quality of their lives, and feelings of safety and well-being. The findings from this survey are presented in Chapter 7, wherein the various aspects of well-being, as reported by the people of Delhi, are presented. Such an exercise adds another unique dimension to a better understanding of the human development paradigm, while facilitating a more holistic understanding of the latter. It needs to be stated that the findings from the Perceptions Survey, 2013, cut across the various indicators of human development presented in the chapters of this Report and are therefore presented accordingly in the

17. For details on the Survey, sampling procedures, etc., please see Annexure 1.1

relevant contexts at the appropriate places as well. The report concludes with Chapter 8, which outlines the milestones achieved by the citizens of Delhi from the human development perspective. It also indicates the challenges that remain in terms of achieving inclusion for all segments of the population, and suggests strategies for tackling the disparities that still persist.

Annexure 1.1

Perceptions Survey Methodology

1. Background

Human Development Reports provide a snapshot of the quality of life and quality of living experienced by the citizens of a region. While engaging in such an exercise, it is prudent to elicit people's own views, and determine their established perceptions and suggestions, amongst other indices and data. Noting the need for a people's review, the first Delhi Human Development Report (DHDR), which was released in 2006, included findings from a broad-based survey of households in Delhi. It was decided by the Steering Committee constituted for DHDR (2013) to conduct a similar empirical survey for eliciting information on perceptions, as also for some aspirations of the citizens of Delhi. While following this approach of taking people's viewpoints into account for assessing the various indicators of human development, the second DHDR employed both quantitative and qualitative research methods.

2. Objective

The main objective of this exercise was to undertake a representative state level survey to provide a glimpse into people's perceptions on the quality of life and quality of living in Delhi (including living environments, basic amenities, healthcare, education and other facilities). In this, it aims to examine the coverage and rating of the quality of services and people's access to those services. The findings from this survey were envisaged to feed into the formulation of effective policies and future strategies. The broad issues covered in the survey include the demographic profiles of the respondents and households, as also power supply, water supply and sanitation; transportation, roads and street lighting; access to medical and healthcare; access to basic education; housing; ownership of assets and future priorities; public and personal safety; quality of the environment; the economic environment; other perceptions,[1] and details of the main wage earner in the family.

3. Survey Approach and Design

3.1 Coverage and Design

The target population for the study included those aged 15 years and above, for whom representative estimates were sought. The geographical coverage of the survey included the entire state of NCT Delhi, covering all districts.

A three-stage stratified sample design had been adopted for the survey to generate representative samples. The Census urban wards, Census Enumeration Blocks (CEBs), and individuals aged 15 years and above formed the first, second, and third stage sample units, respectively. Sampling was done independently within each district and aimed to generate reliable district level estimates. Thus, the selection of the sample sizes and their distribution among the various stages were done on the basis of the derived level of precision for key estimates from the survey and the available resources.

While the first two stages of stratification in the survey used pre-existing sampling frames from the Census, 2011, the survey developed a sampling frame of households (individuals over 15 years age) during the third and last stage. The desired number of urban wards were selected independently from each sample district by deploying a probability proportion to population size (PPS) and constituted the first stage unit for the sample. A total of 40 urban wards were thus selected from 289 urban wards of Delhi.[2] The number of wards thus selected from each district varied between 3 and 7, depending upon the population of the district and the total number of such wards (Annex Table 1.1 and Map 3).

During the *second stage*, five CEBs from each sample ward were selected by adopting systematic random sampling. A total of 200 EBs were thus selected from the 40 sample wards. Census Enumeration Block maps of the 200 sample CEBs were used to identify the exact location for collecting the desired primary information for the survey.

During the *third stage*, all eligible individuals (aged 15 years and above), covering about 100 households, were listed in each sample CEB. Since public perception varies with age, gender and education, all the listed individuals were then stratified into 20 strata by using sex, age and education parameters (Table 1.2). Two individuals from each effective stratum were selected randomly. Thus, a total of 40 individuals were selected per sample EB, for collecting detailed information. While selecting the individuals for the Perceptions Survey, it was ensured that only one individual got selected from one household. Therefore, the selection procedure ensured the coverage of 'between households variability' by covering about a similar number of households in each sample EB.

A total of 50,593 individuals were listed from 20,301 households and 8029 respondents were finally surveyed for the public perceptions.

3.2 Data Collection Procedures

In this study, a listing proforma and a detailed public perception schedule were used to collect primary information. The schedule was pre-tested with a small number of respondents and accordingly desired changes

1. Other perceptions included problems of the locality in which the respondents live, day-to-day dealing with the personnel from the public departments of power, water, the Delhi Transport Corporation, the police, the Municipal Corporation, the Metro; satisfaction with life, preferred leisure activities, likes and dislikes in Delhi, etc.

2. This included all wards of the Municipal Corporation of Delhi (MCD), New Delhi Municipal Corporation (NDMC) and Delhi Cantonment Board.

Annex Table 1.1

Size and Distribution of the Sample

S. No.	District	Sample Wards	Sample Enumeration Blocks	Sampling Frame		Sample Households/ Individuals
				Listing of Households	Listing of Individuals (15+ years)	
1	North-west	7	35	3,322	8,610	1,407
2	North	3	15	1,677	3,738	602
3	North-east	5	25	2,619	6,696	1,005
4	East	4	20	2,006	5,004	799
5	New Delhi	3	15	1,526	3,995	600
6	Central	3	15	1,533	3,846	605
7	West	5	25	2,533	6,118	1,007
8	South-west	5	25	3,040	7,437	1,003
9	South	5	25	2,045	5,149	1,001
	Total	40	200	20,301	50,593	8,029

Annex Table 1.2

Stratification Criteria and Sample Size

Stratum No.	Stratification			Listing of Individuals (15+ years)	Sample Households/Individuals
	Gender	Age (In years)	Level of Education		
1	Male	15-30	Up to the Primary Level (5th)	2142	273
2	Male	31-45	Up to the Primary Level (5th)	2626	351
3	Male	46-60	Up to the Primary Level (5th)	1586	373
4	Male	15-30	Secondary Level (12th)	6646	629
5	Male	31-45	Secondary Level (12th)	5593	578
6	Male	46-60	Secondary Level (12th)	2305	460
7	Male	15-30	Graduate and above	2511	359
8	Male	31-45	Graduate and above	2200	366
9	Male	46-60	Graduate and above	1438	283
10	Male	More than 60	All Levels of Education	2152	370
11	Female	15-30	Up to the Primary Level (5th)	2351	367
12	Female	31-45	Up to the Primary Level (5th)	3956	497
13	Female	46-60	Up to the Primary Level (5th)	2125	546
14	Female	15-30	Secondary Level (12th)	4253	628
15	Female	31-45	Secondary Level (12th)	3101	528
16	Female	46-60	Secondary Level (12th)	1061	310
17	Female	15-30	Graduate and above	1393	304
18	Female	31-45	Graduate and above	1383	298
19	Female	46-60	Graduate and above	776	167
20	Female	More than 60	All Levels of Education	1495	342
		Total Sample Size		50,593	8029

were made in the content, wording as well as ordering of questions. Locally recruited graduate interviewers were engaged for the collection of primary data through the conduction of face-to-face interviews of the respondents.

Rigorous training of the field investigators selected for canvassing the survey schedules was accorded top priority. The main objective of the training was to ensure that not only were the investigators thoroughly comfortable with the schedules and the underlying concepts but perhaps more importantly, they could also convey the same to the respondents, who, it was envisaged, did not have the requisite knowledge and were in many cases illiterate. The training consisted of two parts, namely: 1) training of the supervisors, and 2) another round of 'on-site' training in different parts of the state, of the actual investigators who would administer the survey schedules under supervision. The interviews were conducted during the period 19 December 2012 through 15 February 2013.

3.3 Weighting

The interviewed sample information collected through the listing proforma and individual questionnaires were weighted to match the state's demographic parameters (such as sex, age, location, etc.). These parameters came from the Census, 2011. Weights were trimmed to prevent individual interviews from exerting too much influence on the final results. The use of these weights in statistical analysis ensures that the demographic characteristics of the sample closely approximate the demographic characteristics of the state population.

3.4 Perception and Survey Schedule

The Perceptions Survey schedule covered the Locational Details; Details of the Respondent; Household Details; Power Supply, Water Supply and Sanitation; Transportation, Roads and Street Lighting; Access to Medical and Healthcare; Access to Basic Education; Housing; Ownership of Assets and Future Priorities; Public Personal Safety; Quality of the Environment; Economic Environment; Other Perceptions,[3] and Details of the Main Wage Earner.

4. Focus Group Discussions (FGDs)

Apart from the quantitative survey, in-depth focus group discussions (FGDs) were also conducted in the poor localities across Delhi, with the objective of gaining a nuanced understanding of the issues and problems faced by people, especially among the poor and deprived.

The FGDs focused on aspects such as basic services, safety and security, education, healthcare, transport, women's issues, and the aspirations of the people. The respondents were asked to describe their access to basic services, the problems they faced with these services (such as seasonal problems, or problems pertaining to billing, repair and maintenance, etc.); they were also asked to rank the services on various aspects. Similarly, issues related to employment, livelihoods, quality of education, people's aspirations, mid-day meal schemes, and other social protection schemes were probed. Different social groups comprising women, children, and the elderly, among others, were asked to describe and rank their everyday concerns.

The FGDs were conducted among both mixed groups and in 'only women's groups' across 23 poor settlements.

Apart from the FGDs, which were conducted to analyse the above-mentioned issues, specific FGDs were also conducted to understand the safety concerns of the people. These FGDs were carried out in six localities in the city, namely Mongolpuri (North-east) Harsh Vihar, Ashok Vihar (North-west), Satyavati Railway Colony, Sultanpuri (North-west), Patel Nagar (West), Pahar Ganj (Central), and Raghuvir Nagar (West), with both women and men. In particular, 'only women's FGDs' were conducted in various locations across the city to understand the different issues that concern women's safety. In addition, interactions with police personnel were also carried out in order to obtain their perspectives. It should be noted that the fieldwork was conducted soon after the incident of 16 December 2012, which might have influenced the responses of the public, particularly with regard to the issue of safety in Delhi.

5. Household Income Categories

A common problem faced by most of sample surveys is the under-statement of economic data (income, expenditure and savings) by the respondents. And invariably doubts are raised over the reliability of such data. Experience shows that there are difficulties in the collection of reliable income data in the field due to ambiguities in the choice of unit of sampling, sampling frame, reference period of data collection, and even items of information. However, in the current survey, an attempt has been made to collect details of 'perceived monetary income', which includes all income received by the household as a whole, and by each of its members, during the reference year, by asking a single income question, "What is your annual household income from all sources?" In order to arrive at a better interpretation, households have been categorised into five income groups (based on the reported annual income)—Lowest (Less than Rs. 60,000); Low (Rs. 60,000–Rs. 1,20,000); Lower Middle (Rs. 1,20,000–Rs. 2,40,000); Middle (Rs. 2,40,000–Rs. 6,00,000); and Highest (More than Rs. 6,00,000).

3. Other perceptions included problems encountered in the locality in which the respondents live, day-to-day dealing with the personnel from the public departments of Power and Water, the Delhi Transport Corporation (DTC), police, the Municipal Corporation of Delhi (MCD), the Metro; satisfaction with life, preferred leisure activities, likes and dislikes in Delhi, etc. *(AQ: The content of this footnote has been repeated in Ch. 1)*

Map 3

Sample Wards of Perceptions Survey, 2013

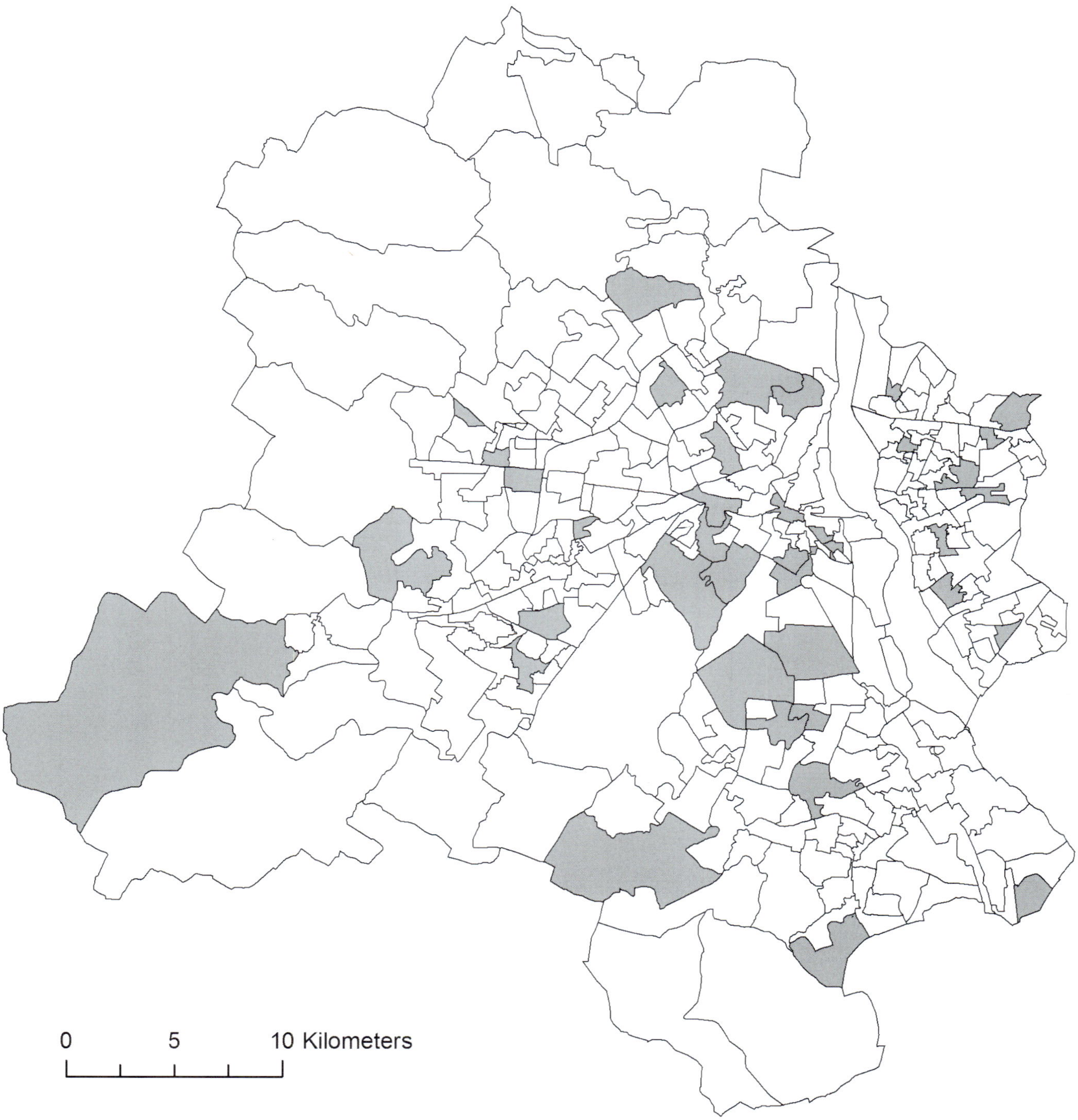

2

Livelihoods and Employment

2.1 Introduction

Delhi, the capital of India, is among the top 40 cities[1] in terms of wealth ranking in the world. It is the hub of trade, commerce and industrial activities in northern India and has a huge potential for success in today's creative economy. It is the most prosperous state with the highest per capita income of more than Rs. 0.2 million in 2012-13 among all the states of the country.

The growth of the state's population during the decade 2001-2011 was 21 per cent, which dramatically declined from 47 per cent during the previous decade of 1991-2001. As mentioned in the introductory chapter, this reduction may be attributable to a drop in the fertility rate and a substantial increase in population in other towns of the National Capital Region (NCR).[2] In addition, it seems that the rate of in-migration in Delhi has declined or at least stabilised, and a large number of migrants are now settling down in other expanding towns of the NCR (Economic Survey of Delhi, 2012-13).

A district-wise analysis of the population reveals a clearer picture, indicating that two of the districts, that is, the New Delhi and Central districts, registered negative growth during the previous decade. The removal of slum clusters from Yamuna Pushta and simultaneous large-scale commercialisation have led to a fall in population as a rather large number of people have been either displaced or shifted out. The conversion of residential areas into commercial areas is also visible in Central Delhi, with the people of these areas preferring to move out to more modernised housing in other parts of Delhi or the NCR (Figure 2.1). On the other hand, the growth of the population in the South-west district is attributed to the incidence of people flocking to the relatively new areas such as the sub-city of Dwarka and other new settlements. The next fastest growth has occurred in the North-west district of Delhi, which includes areas such as Narela, Alipur, Mongolpuri, Wazirpur and Rohini. It is home to several rehabilitation colonies now occupied by people displaced from elsewhere or from the industrial estates in the city. The growth of numerous unauthorised colonies in the West district of the city has also led to an increase in its population size, with a similar situation prevailing in the South district too. As for the North district, while these factors hold true there too, the advent of the Delhi Metro and many flyovers has led to large-scale demolition and a consequent decline in population in the Kashmere Gate area. Due to this process of displacement, a large number of people have left the city or have shifted to the peripheral regions of the national capital. Apart from a drop in the fertility rate and the fact that a significant portion of the population has not been counted in the Census due

Figure 2.1

District-wise Population of Delhi, 2001 and 2011

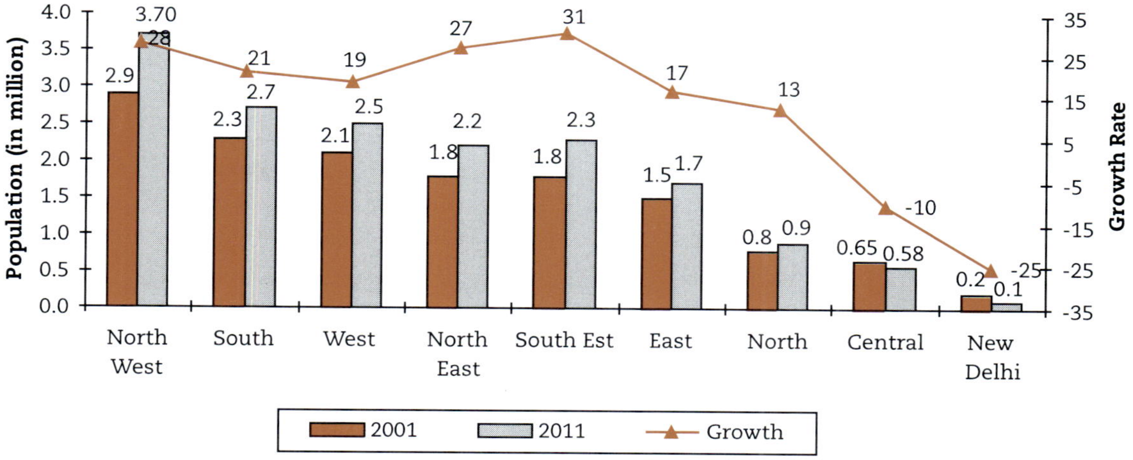

Sources: Census of India, 2001 and 2011.

1. Ranked 37th according to the World Wealth report, 2011.
2. As per information obtained from the Delhi Urban Shelter Improvement Board, only 32,000 displaced families, or around 1,50,000 people, have been officially relocated in rehabilitation colonies and the rest were displaced due to ineligibility for rehabilitation. They may have settled in slums elsewhere or in other parts of the NCR.

to their migration to the peripheral regions of the city may also be responsible for the sharp drop in the population growth rate in Delhi.

An important and positive demographic feature is the increase in the sex ratio of the state from 821 to 866 during the last decade 2001-2011. The literacy rate has also registered an upward trend, rising from 81.67 per cent in 2001 to 86.34 per cent in 2011, with the male and female literacy figures being 91.03 per cent and 80.93 per cent, respectively.

Although the rate of migration seems to have declined or at least stabilised, Delhi continues to be a favourite destination for a large number of people seeking livelihood and better employment opportunities. The city has been registering robust growth in infrastructure and economic growth for the last several years. All these have contributed to an increase in employment and other economic opportunities in the city. This chapter provides details of the income growth, patterns of employment creation, the issue of migration and vulnerability in the livelihood opportunities of the workers.

The sources of data for this chapter are the Employment and Unemployment Surveys of the National Sample Survey Organisation (NSSO); the People's Perceptions Survey, 2013, conducted by the Institute for Human Development (IHD); the Census of India, 2001 and 2011; and a large primary survey conducted by IHD and the Institute of Rural Management (IRMA), Anand on informal employment in 2010 (henceforth referred to as the IHD–IRMA survey). Apart from these sources, other secondary information from the Government of Delhi like Economic Surveys and other public documents have also been used for the chapter.

2.2 Economic Activity

2.2.1. Level and Patterns of Income Generation

State Income

The Gross State Domestic Product (GSDP) of the state increased three-and-a-half times from Rs. 10,030 billion in 2004-05 to Rs. 36,570 billon in 2012-13 at current prices. The per capita income (GSDP) of Delhi crossed Rs. 0.2 million per annum in 2012-13 at current prices, which is around three times higher than the national average, and the highest in the country. During the years 2005-06 and 2012-13, the growth rates of per capita income of Delhi throughout exceeded the corresponding rates at the all-India level (Figure 2.2). The GSDP at constant prices also recorded an increase of 6.1 per cent during the period 1999-2000 to 2004-05 and of 11.9 per cent during the period 2004-05 to 2011-12.

Figure 2.2

Growth of State Domestic Product, Delhi and India during 2005-06 to 2012-13

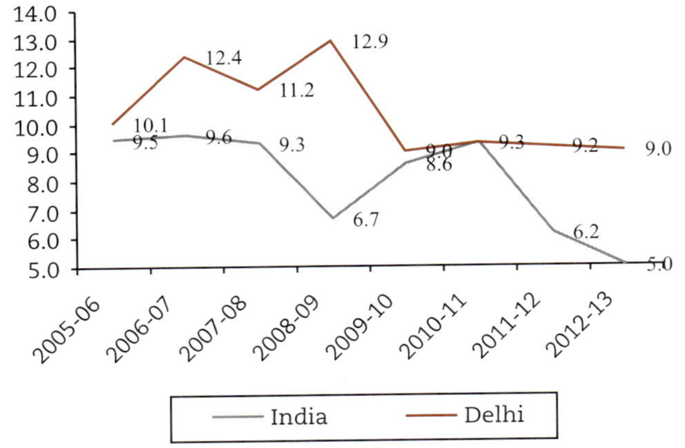

Source: Economic Survey of Delhi, 2012-13.

An assessment of the per capita real income of Delhi also indicates that it is consistently higher than the national average and increased almost two-fold at constant prices (2004-05) from 2004-05 to 2012-13 (Figure 2.3). The growth of per capita real state income has also been consistently higher than the growth of the national per capita real income. It recorded an increase of around 6.9 per cent in Delhi as compared to 2.9 per cent of the national per capita real income during 2012-13 (Figure 2.4).

Figure 2.3

Per Capita Real Income of Delhi and India (in Rs. hundred thousand and at constant 2004-05 prices)

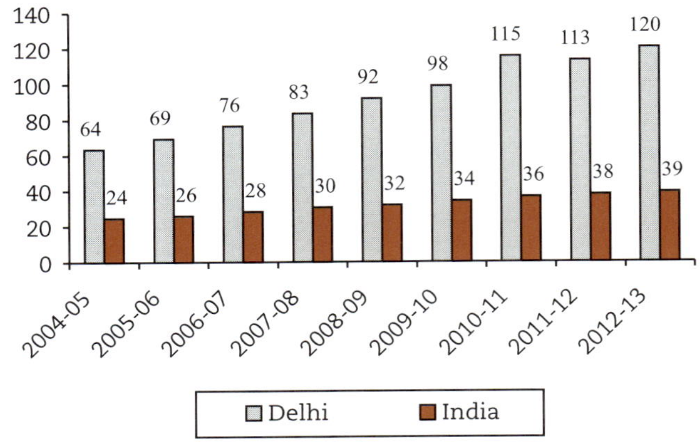

Source: Economic Survey of Delhi, 2012-13.

Figure 2.4

Growth Rate of Per Capita Real Income of Delhi and India from 2005-6 to 2012-13

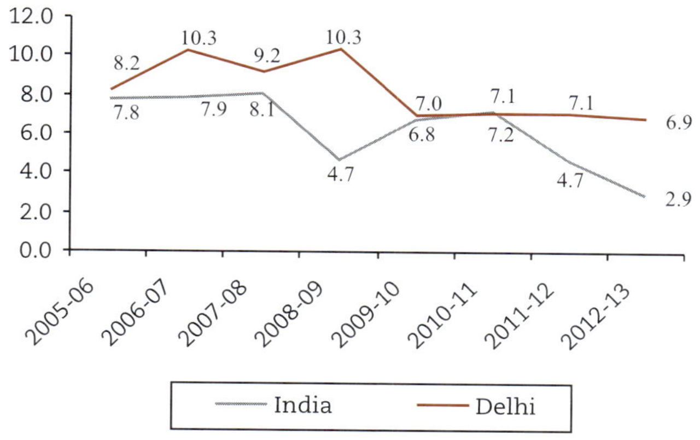

Source: Economic Survey of Delhi, 2012-13.

Sectoral Composition of the State Income

The tertiary sector is the key driver of Delhi's economy. Its contribution is consistently very high and has increased over the years from 80.5 per cent in 2004-05 to 85.8 per cent in 2012-13. This sector consists of trade, hotels and restaurants, transport, communications, financial and insurance services, real estate, public administration and other social and personnel services. In contrast, the contribution of the primary and secondary sectors has been shrinking over the years. The contribution of the primary sector is almost negligible at less than 1 per cent at present. The share of the secondary sector declined from 18.5 per cent in 2004-05 to 13.6 per cent in 2012-13.

The decline in the share of the primary sector is the outcome of the declining rural and cultivable area as a result of the rapid pace of urbanisation and alternative uses of the available agricultural and rural land which provide higher returns. The share of the secondary sector has declined due to the displacement of industrial units and the closure of polluting industrial units due to the strict enforcement of environmental pollution standards. The closure of industrial units in the unapproved industrial areas has also contributed to the decline of contribution by the manufacturing sector to the economy. On the other hand, improvements in civic infrastructure, and the transport, communication, trade, storage, health, education and other sectors have helped to considerably promote the tertiary sector (Economic Survey of Delhi, 2012-13).

Incidence of Poverty

The high level of growth has also contributed to a decline in poverty over the years. Currently, less than 10 per cent of the state's population is below the poverty line (BPL), as per the latest NSSO quinquennial survey round of 2011-12. Albeit, this poverty line is a gross under-estimation of the level of poverty, as a whole, and there is a need to consider wider aspects in measuring poverty in a metropolis like Delhi where the cost of living is high. Nevertheless, there has certainly been a decline in absolute poverty levels in Delhi as compared to other parts of the country. In view of the significantly high growth rate in Delhi, however, the extent of decline in poverty in the state was expected to be more than what has been witnessed.

2.3 Level and Patterns of Employment Generation

2.3.1. Participation in the Labour Market

The Labour Force Participation Rate (LFPR) in Delhi has increased marginally from 34 per cent in 1999-2000 to 35 per cent in 2004-05, but it remained almost constant during the period 2004-05 to 2011-12. Although the female participation rate of Delhi has been low in comparison to the corresponding all-India rate for all these years, yet there was a continuous increase in female participation during this period, from 8.8 per cent in 1999-2000 to 11.1 per cent in 2011-12, though the male participation rate remained the same during the period under consideration. However, there is a strong gender disadvantage in labour force participation, since it is much lower in the case of females as compared to males for all the years. During the year 2011-12, women's participation was just 11 per cent, which is around five times lower than that of males (54.8 per cent) (Table 2.1). The participation rate of women in Delhi is around 40 per cent lower than the urban female participation rate for India as a whole. An important aspect of female labour force participation is that while in the case of males, it does not vary substantially across educational levels, in the case of females, it is clearly U-shaped, with a much higher level on the right side. The female participation rate for graduates and above is almost double the second highest category of 'not literate females', who participate in the labour market in large numbers (Table 2.2). This is also reflected in the higher work participation of women at the top income level—the participation of women in the highest expenditure quintiles is the highest, but this trend has not been noticed in the case of males.

Table 2.1

Labour Force Participation Rate (LFPR) and Workforce Participation Rate (WPR) (UPSS) in Delhi

Gender	Years		
	1999-00	2004-05	2011-12
Labour Force Participation Rate (LFPR)			
Male	54.9	56.1	54.8
Female	8.8	9.4	11.1
Persons	33.9	35.2	35.0
Workforce Participation Rate (WPR)			
Male	53.1	53.5	52.7
Female	8.3	8.8	10.7
Persons	32.7	33.5	33.7

Note: The LFPR is the percentage of persons in the labour force to the total population, while the WPR is the percentage of persons in the workforce to the total population.

Source: 55th, 61st and 68th.Rounds, NSSO.

Table 2.2

Labour Force Participation Rate in Delhi by Educational Level (of Age 25 Years and Above), 2011-12

Education	2011-12		
	Male	Female	Persons
Not literate	70.9	8.6	25.1
Up to the Primary Level	73.8	2.8	44.3
Primary Level	91.9	7.4	58.6
Middle Level	96.9	1.2	57.5
Secondary Level	91.3	1.8	55.1
Higher secondary Level	94.6	4.3	55.1
Graduate + Level	83.1	15.9	56.9
Total	88.3	7.6	49.7

Source: National Sample Survey, 2011-12.

The total number of workers in Delhi increased from 4.4 million during the year 1999-2000 to 4.9 million during the year 2004-05, and further to 5.6 million during the year 2011-12. In the case of unemployed, there was an increase of about 87,000 during the period 1999-2000 to 2004-05, but it declined by 24,000 during the next seven years. Interestingly, the number of female workers almost doubled during the period 1999-2000 to 2011-12, while the number of female unemployed declined during this period from 33,000 to 32,000 (Table 2.3).

A comparison of the unemployment rates of Delhi with those of urban India as a whole indicates that the overall unemployment rate is slightly higher in Delhi (4 per cent) as compared to that of urban India (3.4 per cent) during the year 2011-12. However, it is comparatively less in the case of females (4.3 per cent) as compared to that of males (3.9 per cent) (Table 2.4).

Table 2.4

Unemployment Rate (UPSS) Delhi and Urban India

		1999-00	2004-05	2011-12
Delhi	Male	3.0	5.1	3.9
	Female	7.3	8.0	4.3
	Persons	3.6	5.4	4.0
Urban India	Male	4.6	3.8	3.0
	Female	5.7	6.9	5.2
	Persons	4.8	4.5	3.4

Source: 55th, 61st and 68th Rounds, NSSO.

2.3.2. Composition of Employment

A comparison of the primary, secondary and tertiary sectors shows a sharp decline in the primary sector from 3.0 per cent to 0.3 per cent during the period 1999-2000 to 2009-10. The tertiary sector share grew

Table 2.3

Labour Force, Work Force and Unemployed (in '000)

	1999-2000			2004-05			2011-12		
	Male	Female	Persons	Male	Female	Persons	Male	Female	Persons
Labour Force	3,986	526	4,512	4,521	635	5,156	4,980	877	5,857
Work Force	3,860	493	4,353	4,315	595	4,909	4,789	846	5,635
Unemployed	126	33	159	206	40	246	191	32	222

Source: National Sample Survey, 1999-2000, 2004-05 and 2011-12.

from 64.9 per cent to 67.6 per cent during this period but the share of the secondary sector declined only marginally from 32.5 per cent to 32.1 per cent during the corresponding period.

The employment scenario in Delhi is dominated by the following four sectors: (i) trade, hotels and restaurants, (ii) manufacturing; (iii) public administration, education, health and other services; and (iv) finance, real estate and business activities. Interestingly, more than 50 per cent of the female employment is concentrated in the public administration, education and health sectors. During the ten-year period from 1999-2000 to 2009-10, the highest increase in the share of employment was in the finance, real estate and business sectors (8.2 percentage points), followed by manufacturing (2.4 percentage points), transport, storage and communication (2.1 percentage points), and trade, hotels and restaurants (1.6 percentage points). During the year 2009-10, the trade, hotels and restaurants sector accounted for 30.5 per cent of all employment, followed closely by manufacturing, which accounted for 27.6 per cent. The finance, real estate and business sector accounted for 12.3 per cent of the total employment and 9.3 per cent was accounted for by transport, storage and communication (Table 2.5). On the other hand, the largest decline in employment share was observed in public administration, health and other services (9.3 percentage points) followed by the construction sector (2 percentage points). The manufacturing sector showed a contrasting picture, registering an increase in employment share but a decline in the GDP share, accounting for low labour productivity. This points to the creation of low productive jobs in this sector. Another interesting point is that public administration, health and other services show a decline in employment growth but an impressive rise in productivity. As a whole, the secondary sector exhibits much lower productivity (its share in state GDP is around 13 per cent but its share in employment is much higher at 32 per cent) as compared to the tertiary services sector, whose share in the state income is around 85 per cent but that in employment is only around 67 per cent.[3]

2.3.3. Recent Pattern of Employment Growth

The pattern of employment growth during the year 2005-10 has also been analysed at a more disaggregated level (4-digit level) by classifying the industries into the following three categories: (i) Industries having an employment share of more than 0.5 per cent and those having generated some additional employment during 2005-10, (ii) Industries having an employment share of more than 0.5 per cent, but having witnessed some decline in employment during the period 2005-10, and (iii) Emerging industries for which the growth of employment during this period was impressive (more than 25 per cent), irrespective of their share of employment. Some of the important industries in these three categories are discussed below (see Annex. Tables 2.1a, 2.1b, and 2.1c).

Table 2.5

Employment by Industry in Delhi, 1999-2000, 2004-05 and 2009-10

Industry	*Years*		
	1999-2000	2004-05	2009-10
Agriculture and Mining	3.0	0.6	0.2
Primary Sector	3.0	0.6	0.3
Manufacturing and Electricity	25.6	25.2	27.6
Construction	6.5	6.5	4.5
Secondary Sector	32.5	31.8	32.1
Trade, Hotels and Restaurants	28.8	27.4	30.5
Transport, Storage and Communication	7.2	8.2	9.3
Finance., Real Estate And Business	4.1	8.1	12.3
Public Administration, Education, Health and Others	24.8	24.0	15.5
Tertiary Sector	64.9	67.7	67.6
Total	100.0	100.0	100.0

Source: 55th, 61st and 68th Rounds, NSSO.

Six industries in the first category show a net increase in employment to the tune of more than 50,000 during the period 2005-10. In the case of the 'wholesale and retail trade' sector, these industries are: (i) Retail sale of food, beverages and tobacco in specialised stores (1,81,000), (ii) Wholesale of other intermediate products, waste and scrap (63,000), and (iii) Sale, maintenance and repair of motorcycles and related parts and accessories (54,000). Most of the employment generated in the 'wholesale and retail trade sector' is of the self-employment type. In the manufacturing sector, it mostly pertains to the manufacture of luggage, handbags, and the like (1,69,000). Out of 1,69,000, about two-thirds of the

3. The employment figures quoted are for the year 2009-10 while the state income figures pertain to the year 2012-13.

workers were regular workers while the remaining were self-employed. The other two industries are: (i) Software publishing (51,000), relating to the computer sector, and (ii) Investigation and security activities (50,000), relating to the other business sector. The employment generated in these industries was mostly of the regular type (see Annex Table 2.a).

The emerging industries having high growth rates of employment (of more than 50 per cent per annum) during this period are those dealing in the: (i) Manufacture of luggage, handbags, and the like (51 per cent), (ii) Manufacture of ferrous alloys (113 per cent), (iii) Manufacture of basic precious and non-ferrous metals, (iv) Wholesale of other intermediate products, waste and scrap (51 per cent), (v) Cargo handling (66 per cent), (vi) Computer hardware consultancy (55 per cent), (vii) Advertising (129 per cent), (viii) Investigation and security activities, and (ix) Dramatic arts, music and other arts activities. Out of these nine industries, in two industries (that is, investigation and security activities; and dramatic arts, music and other arts activities), the maximum employment generated was of the self-employment type, and in the remaining seven industries, it was mainly of the regular type. Some of these industries relate to modern services (that is, advertising, computer hardware consultancy, and investigation and security activities), the growth of which is good for the state but there are some industries (that is, wholesale of other intermediate products, waste and scrap), which might be causing pollution (see Annex Table 2.b).

The industries having a share of employment of more than 0.5 per cent and where the net decline in employment was more than 50,000 during the period 2005 to 2012 are: (i) Embroidery work, *zari* work and making of ornamental trimmings by hand (82,000), which is a traditional industry, (ii) Other retail sale in specialised stores (73,000), and (iii) Building of complete constructions or parts thereof; civil engineering (63,000) (see Annex Table 2.c). The above analysis at the disaggregated level shows that Delhi is witnessing a significant change in the pattern of employment growth. Several new industries, particularly in the service sector, have emerged in recent years. On the other hand, some traditional industries, in both manufacturing and services, have shown a decline. This pattern needs to be studied in depth through primary data.

2.3.4. Growth of Organised and Unorganised Employment

The employment in organised sector in Delhi during the period 2000-07 showed a marginal decline from 0.85 million in 2000 to 0.83 million in 2007, after which it increased to 0.86 million in 2011. During the same period, employment in the organised private sector showed an increasing trend but from a low base. It increased from 0.22 million in 2007 to 0.27 million in 2011, but this could not arrest the decline in organised sector employment because of the large decline in organised public sector employment.
Of the 0.86 million (8.6 lakhs) total employment in organised sector, close to 70 per cent of all organised employment in Delhi is in the public sector while the rest is in the private sector. The Central Government and quasi-Central bodies account for nearly 58 per cent of the employment, while the State Government and quasi-State bodies account for about 28 per cent and the rest (about 14 per cent) is accounted for by local bodies (DGET, 2013) (Figure 2.5).

Employment in the public sector, especially the Central Government, quasi-government and local bodies shows a declining trend while that in the Government of the National Capital Territory (NCT) of Delhi showed a positive growth from 1,13,000 in March 2000 to 1,27,000 in March 2009, which recorded a growth rate at 1.14 per cent per annum. The breakdown of public sector jobs shows that the public sector workers are largely employed in the Central Government followed by that in quasi-Central Government bodies. Two-fifths of the public sector workers are employed by the State Government, quasi-State and local bodies.

With the level of employment generation in the organised sector being low, most of the employment generation (around 85 per cent of the total, which includes the self-employed) in Delhi has taken place in the unorganised informal sector. The NSS survey of the 67th Round, 2010-11, pertaining to unincorporated non-agricultural enterprises for the year shows that retail trade (except for motor vehicles and motorcycles) dominates unorganised sector employment, accounting for a share of nearly 28.2 per cent. The other important sub-sectors of employment were: Manufacture of wearing apparel (8 per cent), wholesale trade, except motor vehicles and motorcycles (7.3 per cent), food and beverages, and service activities (6.4 per cent), other personal service activities (maids, hairdressers, pet care, etc.) (4.8 per cent), education (3.5 per cent), wholesale and retail

Figure 2.5

Growth of Organised Sector Employment in (in hundred thousand) 2000-20011

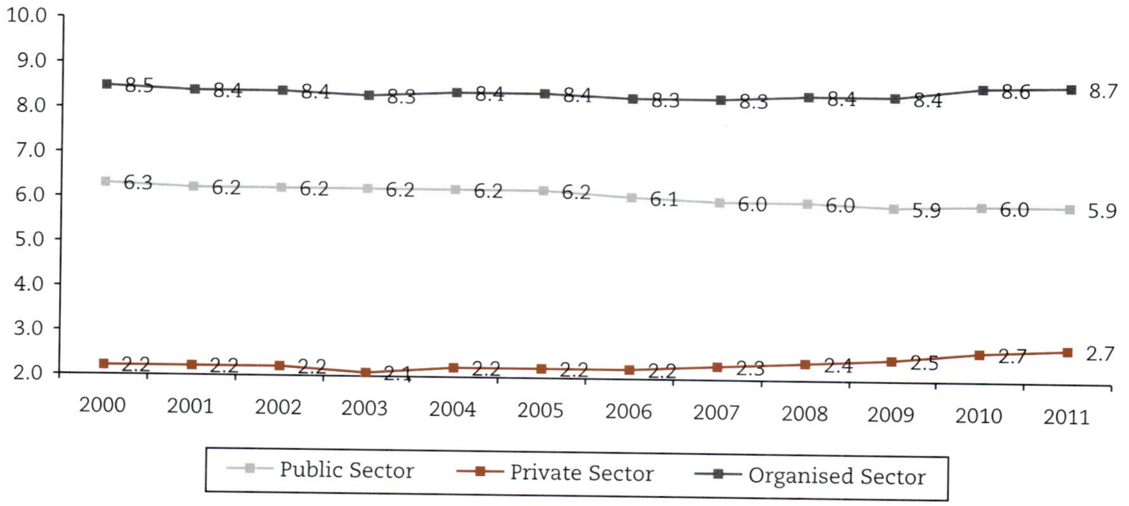

Source: DGET, Annual Employment Review, various years.

trade, and repair of motor vehicles and motorcycles (3.2 per cent), and human health activities (3 per cent). The above industries together accounted for about two-thirds of the employment in all the 65 sub-sectors of unorganised sector employment.

2.3.5 Employment Status and Earnings of Workers

Notwithstanding the growth in unorganised sector employment, Delhi has witnessed an increased trend in the growth of regular workers. The status of employment shows that about 63 per cent of the workers are regularly employed, and about one-third are self-employed, while casual labourers account for a low share of only 3.5 per cent. This is quite in contrast with the picture of urban India wherein the percentages of regular, self-employed and casual workers are 42, 43, and 15, respectively. Further, the share of regularly employment increased by about 10 percentage points during the period 1999-2000 to 2011-12. The share of self-employment increased by 6 percentage points, but most importantly, the share of casual workers declined by 4 percentage points during the corresponding period (Figure 2.6).

Figure 2.6

Status of Employment, 1999-2000, 2004-05 and 2011-12

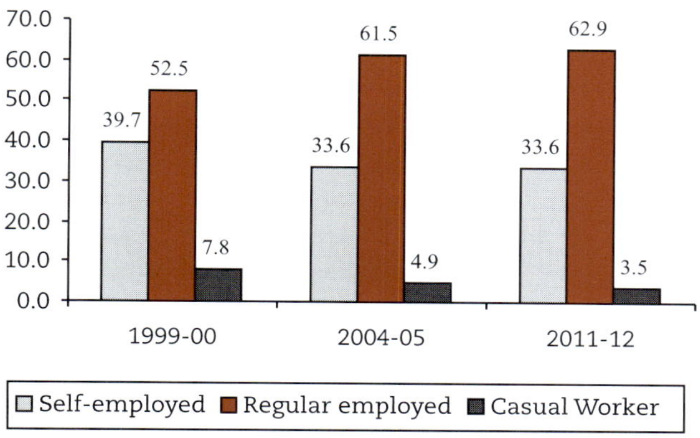

Source: NSS Surveys, Various Rounds.

Earnings of Workers

Along with an expansion in employment opportunities for wage and salary employment, there has also been increase in the earnings of workers. The average per day earning of regular workers increased during the period 2004-05 to 2011-12 (at constant 2004-05 prices) at 4.5 per cent per annum. The increase was higher for females (6.6 per cent) than for males (4.7 per cent). While this rate of increase for males in Delhi was similar to the corresponding all-India figures, in the case of females, it was somewhat higher than the all-India figures. Similarly, the average wage of casual workers increased substantially at a rate which was twice of the corresponding all-India rate during the same period, reflecting the working of two factors—tightening of the labour market for casual labourers, which largely includes manual work, with a possibly lower supply and regular increase in the statutory minimum wages (Table 2.6).

Table 2.6

Growth of Wage Rate, 2004-05 to 2011-12 (Age Group of 15-59 Years)

Delhi/All India	*Male*	*Female*	*Total*
Regular Workers			
Delhi	4.1	6.6	4.5
All-India	4.2	4.7	4.2
Casual Workers			
Delhi	10.3	-	10.9
All-India	4.9	5.5	5.2

Source: National Sample Survey, 2004-05, 2011-12.

2.4. Migration Level

As mentioned earlier, there are indications that the rate of migration in Delhi has somewhat declined or at least, it is stabilising, as a large number of migrants are settling in other parts of the NCR. However, even now, it is estimated that about 75,000 persons per year are still migrating to Delhi (Economic Survey of Delhi, 2012-13).

Some recent patterns in migration can be observed from the Perceptions Survey, 2013. The survey shows that around 16 per cent of the total population of Delhi comprises migrants, taking into account the 20 years duration of migration. If the duration of migration is limited to 10 years, as is generally done, the proportion of migrants falls to around 9 per cent. This estimate pertains to individual migrants, and if the migrant households (defined as those having at least one migrant) were to be considered, the proportion of migrant households in the total households would be much larger (IHD–IRMA, 2010).[4] The proportion of migrants is 4.6 per cent in the case of a duration ranging between 6 and 10 years, and 4.1 per cent in case of a duration of less than 5 years, implying that there has been a small decline in the incidence of migration during the last five years or so. An analysis of the reasons for migration reveals an interesting picture, with the proportion of migrants in search of employment and better employment opportunities showing a clearly declining trend. On the other hand, the proportion of those migrating for the purpose of education and training shows an increasing trend. The number of migrants coming to Delhi for pursuing education, and acquiring skills and training in various disciplines has increased more than twice during the last ten years, with the highest proportion being registered during the last one year alone. The proportion of people who migrate in search of employment and better employment opportunities has declined from around 60 per cent to 32 per cent, and form 28 per cent to 21 per cent, respectively, during the corresponding period. This indicates that migrants might be preferring other places for employment opportunities than Delhi as compared to ten years ago. There may be several reasons behind this decline in the migration to Delhi for employment reasons, including the high cost of living (food, housing, transport, etc.) in Delhi as compared to that in other towns and cities (Table 2.7).

Table 2.7

Reasons for Migration by the Years of Migration

Reasons for Migration/ Years of Migration	*Years of Migration*				
	Up to 1 Year	*2-5 Years*	*6-10 Years*	*> 10 Years*	*Total*
In Search of Employment	31.9	42.3	51.5	59.5	50.7
In Search of Better Employment/Higher Salary and Wages	21.3	16.0	24.2	27.8	23.0
To Take up Better Employment/Higher Salary and Wages	5.4	2.6	6.8	3.9	4.4
Education and Training	40.4	32.5	12.9	6.2	17.6
Others*	1.0	6.6	4.6	2.6	4.2
Total	100.0	100.0	100.0	100.0	100.0

Note: Others* include poverty, abuse, discrimination and natural disaster.
Source: Perceptions Survey, 2013.

4. The IHD–IRMA Survey had also found that around 8.5 per cent of the individuals (considering up to 10 years of migration) are migrants and that 16 per cent of the households are migrant households.

An assessment of the state-wise share of the population migrating to Delhi indicates that the incidence of migration is the highest from Uttar Pradesh (UP) (47 per cent), followed by Bihar (31 per cent). There has been a rapid increase in the share of migration from Bihar, of nearly 2.5 times from 13.6 per cent in 2001 to around 31 per cent in 2013. On the other hand, barring the states of UP and Bihar, the respective shares of migration of all other states have shown a decline, albeit at varying rates (Table 2.8).

Table 2.8

State-wise Share of Migration in Delhi, 2001 and 2013 (Percentage of the Total Migrants)

States	Years	
	2001	2013
Uttar Pradesh	43.13	46.50
Bihar	13.63	30.70
Haryana	10.43	4.10
Rajasthan	5.16	2.90
West Bengal	3.22	2.90
Others	24.43	12.90
Total	100.00	100.00

Sources: 1. For the year 2001: Census of India, 2001;
2. For the year 2013: Perceptions Survey, 2013.

As pointed out earlier, the occupations of the main earners of the migrant households in Delhi also show a changing picture. The proportion of migrating professionals has increased while that of service workers and skilled low-paid workers has declined over the years, except in the case of unskilled low-paid workers, whose share has marginally increased. Delhi has limited space and the character of the activities being undertaken here is also changing. The number of low-paid and service workers migrating to Delhi is thus gradually due to the high cost of living and possibly also because of the recent increase in the availability of more options in the peripheral areas of the NCR or in some other cities of the country (Table 2.9). More than half of the recent migrants are highly educated (at the level of graduates and above), and they constitute the largest proportion of the total migrants. The proportion of migrants with educational levels below graduation, on the other hand, has been continuously declining over the years (Table 2.9). This again shows that because of the changing activity patterns in the city, persons with a higher level of skills are now migrating to Delhi.

The remittance pattern shows that as a whole, around 44 per cent of the migrants send remittances to their native places. Three-fourths of the migrant households belonging to the highest income group

Table 2.9

Occupation of Main Migrant Earners and Highest Educational Level in the Migrant Family by Duration of Migration Years of Migration

Occupation	Up to 1 Year	2-5 Years	6-10 Years	> 10 Years	Total
Professional	12.1	11.0	6.3	5.2	7.6
Semi-professional	8.5	11.2	8.7	14.3	11.5
Service Workers	20.1	24.0	36.0	31.8	30.1
Skilled Low-paid Workers	12.2	15.2	21.3	28.6	21.7
Unskilled Low-paid Workers	18.3	8.2	18.1	19.1	15.6
Others (Students)	28.8	30.5	9.5	1.0	13.5
Total	100.0	100.0	100.0	100.0	100.0
Educational Level					
Illiterate	4.9	6.5	2.9	3.5	4.3
Primary Education	3.3	5.3	16.7	12.4	11.1
Secondary Education	17.7	18.6	30.0	40.2	29.8
Senior Secondary Education	8.5	11.3	16.4	16.9	14.7
Higher Education	65.6	58.3	34.0	27.0	40.1
Total	100.0	100.0	100.0	100.0	100.0

Source: Perceptions Survey, 2013.

remit money whereas only one-third of the migrant households belonging to the lowest income category of households remit money to their native places. This indicates that the lowest income households are not able to remit because of the higher level of minimum expenditure that they have to incur to survive in the metro city.

It is interesting to note the perceptions of migrants with regard to the availability of employment of opportunities as well as some indicators of satisfaction. As can be seen from Table 2.10, migrants have been able to avail of the numerous economic opportunities in the city. Around 60 per cent of the migrants interviewed during the Perceptions Survey, 2013, revealed that employment opportunities for working age men have improved in their households, whereas this percentage was only around 51 per cent for non-migrants. Only 8 per cent of the migrants reported that their incomes during the last three years had declined, whereas around 11 per cent of non-migrants reported such a decline (though the improvement in the case of non-migrants was higher than that of migrants) (Table 2.10). Not surprisingly, migrants, as a whole, have somewhat higher satisfaction levels as compared to those of non-migrants. As can be seen from the bottom section of Table 2.10, except the quality of life, in terms of the three other aspects—healthcare, neighbourhoods and overall achievements in life—the levels of satisfaction among the migrants are higher than those of non-migrants. However, it should be kept in mind that this does not necessarily indicate a higher level of well-being among migrants. Instead, most of the migrants may be comparing their present conditions with their initial conditions, which would have been generally inferior to the present conditions.

As a whole, there have been important changes in the pattern of migration in Delhi, and the city is becoming more selective in migration towards the more educated and skilled people. This conforms to the changing pattern of the growth structure and income generation in the city, which are dominated by the services sector, wherein higher levels of skills and education are required. The prevalence of advanced educational and training facilities in Delhi also attracts a large number of people. Further, the scarcity of space and rising costs of living compel the poor and less educated migrants to look for employment opportunities at other places around Delhi or elsewhere. Nevertheless, it has been observed that the city of Delhi has successfully absorbed migrants from all parts of the country, and this migrant population in Delhi largely feels satisfied with regard to the various aspects of the quality of life and livelihoods in the city.

Table 2.10

Availability of Employment Opportunities, Income Opportunities and Satisfaction Levels among Migrants and Non-Migrants

(a) Rate of Availability of employment opportunities for working age men in the households (% distribution)

	Migrants	*Non-migrants*
Good	59.8	51.1
Average	21.8	31.3
Poor	18.4	17.5
All	100.0	100.0

(b): Experience of Improvement/Deterioration in Income during the Last Three Years

Change in Income Levels	*Migrants*	*Non-migrants*
Improved	22.2	27.6
Remained Same	69.5	61.7
Deteriorated	8.3	10.7
All	100.0	100.0

(c) Satisfaction Level with Regard to Various Lifestyle Indicators

Lifestyle Indicators	*Migrants*	*Non-migrants*
Health	86.1	80.9
Quality of life	73.4	75.3
Neighbourhood	82.4	79.1
Overall Achievements in Life	64.0	61.3

Source: Perceptions Survey, 2013.

5. Informality, Vulnerability and Inequality

Although there has been a rather decent growth of employment in Delhi, most of the employment as elsewhere in the country is being generated in the unorganised sector, wherein the quality of employment is low and offers no social security. This can be seen by assessing the distribution of formal and informal workers. The informal (unorganised) sector comprises all unorganised enterprises, defined as all unincorporated private enterprises (owned by individuals or households) that employ less than ten workers. On the other hand, informal employment includes all those, whether employed in unorganised enterprises or in the organised sector, who have no access to social security benefits or security of tenure. There can, therefore, be informal workers in the organised sector and formal workers in the unorganised sector. The IHD–IRMA Survey, 2010 shows that the size of the formal sector (42 per cent) in Delhi was significantly higher than that in India as a while (16 per cent) in 2010. This is because the people in Delhi are mostly self-employed or regular workers, while a very small proportion of them are casual workers. However, an analysis of the workers' distribution across formal and informal employment indicates that around 86 per cent of all workers are informal workers (with the corresponding proportion for all- India being around 92 per cent). This reveals that though the size of the formal sector is very large in Delhi as compared to India as a whole, most employment created in Delhi is informal in nature. This can also be observed by looking at the matrix across sectors and workers. This clearly indicates that about two-thirds of the formal sector workers are informal workers, which implies increasing informalisation of the formal sector (Table 2.11).

Table 2.11

Formal and Informal Sector and Workers' Matrix, 2010

	Formal Sector			*Informal sector*		
	Male	*Female*	*Total*	*Male*	*Female*	*Total*
Formal Worker	31.1	54.9	33.9	*	*	*
Informal Worker	68.9	45.1	66.1	100.0	100.0	100.0

Note: * Negligible.
Source: IHD-IRMA Survey, 2010.

The workers face a high level of vulnerability. About half of them have no written contracts and 6 per cent of them work under written contracts of less than one year (Figure 2.7). As such, in a majority of the cases, employment in regular works provides some relief to them in terms of regular incomes but not in livelihood protection. This is also reflected in the low coverage of social protection available to them. Around four-fifths of the workers do not have any social protection (with the insecurity affecting around two-thirds of the workers in the formal sector and as many as 93 per cent in the informal sector).

Figure 2.7

Written Contracts of Regular Workers in 2010

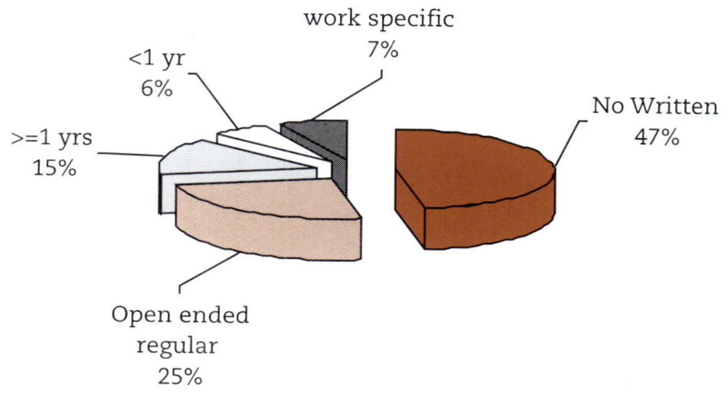

Source: IHD-IRMA Survey, 2010.

The inequality between formal and informal sector workers is also reflected in some other indicators. The average number of years of schooling in the case of informal workers is 7.1 years, whereas in the case of formal workers, it is 11.1 years. Less than one-tenth of the informal workers have higher education, whereas more than half of the formal workers have higher education. Similarly, while about 15 per cent of the formal workers have acquired technical or vocational education, the percentage is as low as 2 in the case of informal workers. All these have contributed to their earning differentials. The average monthly earning of male formal workers was nearly three times higher than that of their informal counterparts. In the case of informal female workers, the differences were even higher, with the earnings of female formal workers being about 4.5 times higher than those of the informal female workers (Table 2.12).

Table 2.12

Educational Achievements and Monthly Incomes of Informal and Formal Workers in Delhi in 2010

	Informal Workers	*Formal Workers*
Educational Qualifications		
Mean years of schooling	7.1	11.1
% of workers with higher education	9.6	53.4
% of workers with technical education	2.3	14.7
Average monthly income (Rs.)		
Male	6,175	18,082
Female	3,886	17,295

Source: IHD-IRMA Survey (2010).

Table 2.13

Top Ten Occupation Groups by Quintile Income Classes in terms of Share of Employment

Occupations	*Bottom three quintiles*	*Fourth quintile*	*Highest quintile*	*Share in employment*
Shop workers, assistants, peons, delivery boy, waiters	71.6	20.5	7.9	18.4
Construction workers, masons, plumbers, painters, welders	85.1	13.6	1.3	16.7
Managers, operators, officers, engineers	17.0	19.8	63.2	13.4
Small shop keepers, traders	35.2	26.1	38.7	12.7
Transport workers, drivers, conductors, rickshaw pullers	66.8	25.6	7.5	9.1
Street vendors, cobblers, other service providers on the streets	68.8	26.3	5.0	5.6
Domestic workers, cleaners, washermen, caretakers, gardeners	89.6	8.4	2.1	5.6
Clerks, defence workers, police personnel, constables	13.2	17.9	68.9	3.5
Electricians, mechanics, fitters, repairers	61.8	19.4	18.8	3.4
Home based workers, artisans, tailors, blacksmiths	64.4	23.8	11.9	3.4

Source: IHD-IRMA Survey (2010).

The detailed sectoral distribution of workers shows that the poor workers are concentrated in: (i) Private households with employed persons; (ii) Other community and personal activities; (iii) Agriculture, and (iv) Construction. On the other hand, members of middle- and high-income households are working in administrative jobs in the education, health and social work, financial intermediation, public administration and real estate sectors. The workers in manufacturing, hotels and transport, and wholesale and retail trade were equally distributed across all the income group households .

Ten broad groups of occupations constitute 92 per cent of the total employment in Delhi (Table 2.13). There is a clear distinction between workers across occupations and income groups of professionals and people involved in administration and trade belonging to higher income quintile. On the other hand, those engaged as shop workers and assistants, peons, construction workers, transport workers, street vendors, domestic workers, and household workers report very high levels of vulnerability in terms of income.

The distribution of occupational status as per the Perceptions Survey, 2013, reveals that the main earners belonging to the lowest household income are largely engaged in unskilled, service work and low-wage skilled jobs. On the other hand, the main earners belonging to highest income category are mostly engaged in professional and semi-professional jobs. A similar trend can be observed in the case of the spouse of the main earner of the highest income and lowest income categories, wherein the spouses of the main earners of the highest income categories are engaged in professional or semi-professional jobs while the spouses of the main earners of the lowest income categories are involved in unskilled low-wage and service work. As mentioned earlier, the female work participation rate of the highest income group is more than double of that of the lowest income group (13 per cent as against 4.8 per cent). It increases the earning differential of households of the lowest and highest income categories.

This differentiation in earning opportunities, which is primarily caused by the level of education of both the main earners and their spouses, is also reflected in the differential perception of economic opportunities. The household perception about the present economic environment reveals that households belonging to the highest income group are more confident and optimistic about the male and female employment opportunities and improvement in the family income. On the other hand, households belonging to the lowest income category are less confident about employment opportunities and improvement in their incomes. Although there are differences of opinion between the highest income group and the lowest income group households, yet a substantial proportion of workers in the lowest income group perceive that they are in the middle income category (46 per cent) and have stable household incomes (49 per cent) and access to good opportunities for male (41 per cent) and female (36 per cent) employment (Figure 2.8).

Figure 2.8

Household Perception about Economic Environment

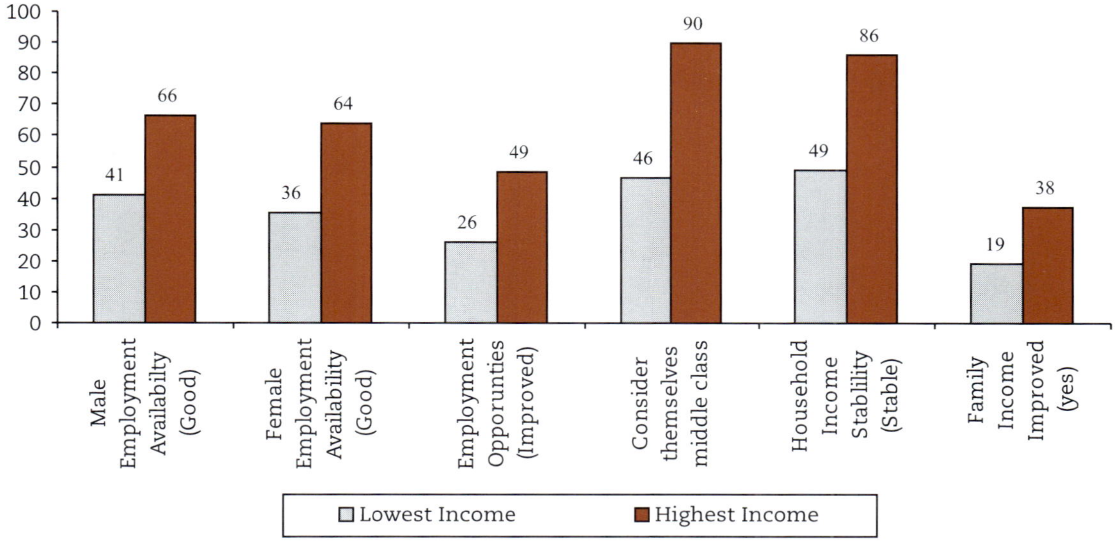

Source: Perceptions Survey, 2013.

Table 2.14

Access and Ownership to Consumer Assets

Monthly Income Group	*Scooter*	*Cycle/Rickshaw*	*Car*	*Cable TV*	*AC*	*Refrigerator*	*Laptop/Desktop*
Lowest	18.0	25.0	2.9	58.1	2.9	35.6	4.4
Low	35.1	25.9	7.1	77.6	7.1	59.0	7.1
Lower Middle	49.9	22.0	14.7	85.9	16.6	76.3	14.8
Middle	62.3	14.4	35.7	91.6	39.0	88.6	24.7
High	55.0	7.2	59.2	95.5	72.8	96.2	18.6
Total	40.7	21.9	15.7	78.9	17.3	65.3	12.0

Source: Perceptions Survey, 2013.

The ownership and access of consumer assets is an important indicator of well-being (Table 2.14). As expected, the proportion of households owning various consumer assets goes up monotonically in the higher income groups. Around three-fourths or a higher proportion of the lowest income households possess consumer assets like electric fans, cooking gas and television (not presented in the table). Around half of the households belonging to the lowest income class have cable connections and coolers in their homes. The difference is clearly visible in terms of ownership of luxury items (like refrigerators, air conditioners, car and laptop) between the lowest and highest income households though the ownership of some of the luxury items among the lowest income households needs to be noticed.

The size of dwellings reveals rather extreme inequality in Delhi. More than half of the lowest income households live in one-room dwellings. In contrast, 40 per cent of the households in the top income group live in houses with three and more rooms. Further, around 45 per cent of the people from the lowest income category were found to be paying monthly rents in the range of 20 per cent to 40 per cent. The people belonging to the second lowest income category also end up paying around 40 to 45 per cent of their monthly income as a rent. This also partially explains the declining trend of migration due to employment and population growth in Delhi in recent years.

Thus, though as a whole, the labour market in Delhi has tightened in the wake of high economic growth leading to expanding employment opportunities and enhanced earnings of the workers, this has been the consequence of increasing informalisation in the labour market. The labour market also exhibits vulnerability in terms of low coverage of social protection and a high level of inequality in the levels of living and earnings.

2.6 Conclusions and Policy Paradigms

The analysis undertaken in this chapter suggests that Delhi has witnessed expanding income and livelihood opportunities during the last 12 years or so. This has also led to a tightening of the labour market with increased employment opportunities and earnings. The proportion of regular workers has increased at the expense of the self-employed and casual workers. The labour force participation of females and their earnings have also increased. The most important part of this tightening of the labour market is reflected in the high growth of earnings of both regular and casual workers, particularly the latter.. There has also been a churning in the labour market, characterised by a significant growth of some modern industries and the decline of employment in some sub-sectors of both traditional industries as well as some modern industries. Delhi continues to attract a large number of migrants. However, it seems that the rate of migration (not the absolute levels) has declined or at least stabilised in recent years. This may be because of the incidence of a large proportion of migrants settling in other parts of the NCR and commuting into Delhi for work. The proportion of those migrating in search of employment shows a declining trend, while the number of those migrating for acquiring higher education and training shows an increase. Further, the proportion of professionals amongst migrants has increased, while that of service and low-paid workers has declined. Delhi has thus absorbed the high rate of migration rather well, with the migrants being largely satisfied in terms of various indicators of satisfaction levels, vis-à-vis the non-migrants in the city.

These positive trends have, however, been accompanied by some disquieting features. There has been a high degree of informalisation in the labour market, with around 86 per cent of the workers found to be informal workers. Around three-fourths of the workers have no social security benefits, which indicates a high level of vulnerability in livelihoods. There are also acute earning differentials between the formal and informal workers, along with huge disparities in the levels of livings. The labour productivity of the manufacturing sector is much lower as compared to that of the services sector. Of course, these trends are not confined to Delhi alone, and have been taking place in most parts of India, and indeed all over the world.

Emerging Policy Paradigms

Several programmes and policies are already being implemented for the promotion and protection of livelihoods in Delhi. Some of the important measures that are needed, as emerging from this analysis, include:

- Gradual formalisation of informal workers in terms of registration, contracts and provision of legal space for work.
- Enlarging and strengthening of social protection in terms of pension, healthcare and maternity benefits and specific needs of vulnerable sections.
- Policies for providing affordable housing for the poor.
- Shifting the low productive workers in the sub-sectors of manufacturing to higher value industries, either in manufacturing or services.
- Initiation of effective policies and programmes of credit, technology, skill upgradation and training for the low productive sectors, particularly the manufacturing sub-sectors.
- Better enforcement of laws for the promotion and protection of livelihoods, especially for those working in vulnerable occupations in terms of low earnings and higher uncertainty in livelihoods.
- Contextualisation of development planning in Delhi in terms of urban and livelihood planning of the NCR because of the existence of large inter linkages.

Annex. Table 2.1a

Important* Industries at the Four-digit Level Generating Additional Employment during 2005-2010

Broad Sector	*Sub-Sectors*	*Additional employment generated*	*Share in employment*	*Growth in employment during 2009-10*	*Employment Status*		
					Self-employed	*Regular*	*Casual*
Manufacturing	Manufacture of luggage, handbags, and the like, saddlery and harness	1,69,361	3.9	51	38	62	0
	Manufacture of corrugated paper and paperboard and of containers of paper and paperboard	26,109	1.4	9	57	39	4
	Printing [Includes printing of newspapers, magazines, periodicals, journals and other material for others on a fee or contract basis]	25,354	1.2	12	16	84	0
Wholesale and retail trade	Maintenance and repair of motor vehicles [including washing and polishing, etc.]	35,993	1.4	16	27	73	0
	Sale, maintenance and repair of motorcycles and related parts and accessories	54,202	1.3	47	60	40	0
	Wholesale of other intermediate products, waste and scrap	63,427	1.5	51	58	42	0
	Retail sale of food, beverages and tobacco in specialised stores	1,80,570	9.8	10	91	9	0
	Retail sale of textiles, clothing, footwear and leather goods	35,248	4.7	3	72	28	0
	Retail sale of household appliances, articles and equipment	28,900	2.3	6	81	19	0
Transport	Freight transport by road	36,523	2.5	7	43	57	0
Communication	Telecommunications	29,530	1.4	12	15	85	0
Real Estate	Real estate activities with own or leased property	28,166	0.7	33	78	22	0
Computer	Computer hardware consultancy	30,794	0.7	55	0	100	0
	Software publishing	50,700	1.3	32	14	86	0
Other Business	Advertising.	26,611	0.5	129	86	14	0
	Investigation and security activities	49,945	1.1	82	3	97	0

Note: *Industries having a share of employment of more than 0.5 per cent in 2010.

Source: National Sample Survey (NSS), 1999-2000, 2004-05 and 2009-10.

Annex. Table 2.1b

Important* Industries at the Four-digit Level with High Growth of Employment during 2005-10

Broad Sector	*Sub-Sectors*	*Additional employment generated*	*Share in Employment*	*Growth in employment during 2009-10*	*Employment Status*		
					Self-employed	*Regular*	*Casual*
Manufacturing	Manufacture of vegetable and animal oils and fats	10,842	0.27	39	0	100	0
	Manufacture of cordage, rope, twine and netting	7781	0.19	39	0	100	0
	Manufacture of luggage, handbags, and the like, saddlery and harness	1,69,361	3.88	51	38	62	0
	Printing [Includes printing of newspapers, magazines, periodicals, journals and other material for others on a fee or contract basis]	22,212	0.59	32	48	52	0
	Manufacture of soap and detergents, cleaning and polishing preparations, perfumes and toilet preparations	18,787	0.46	40	42	58	0
	Manufacture of ferro alloys	23,111	0.47	113	0	100	0
	Manufacture of basic precious and non-ferrous metals	20,953	0.47	58	100	0	0
	Manufacture of machinery for textile, apparel and leather production	7408	0.19	38	0	100	0
	Manufacture of parts and accessories for motor vehicles and their engines	21,229	0.59	29	20	80	0
Electricity, gas and water	Collection, purification and distribution of water	1267	0.04	27	26	74	0
Wholesale and retail trade	Sale, maintenance and repair of motorcycles and related parts and accessories	54,202	1.27	47	60	40	0
	Wholesale of other intermediate products, waste and scrap	63,427	1.45	51	58	42	0
Supporting transport activities	Cargo handling	21,010	0.46	66	0	100	0
Insurance	Life insurance	13,208	0.39	26	0	100	0
Real Estate	Real estate activities with own or leased property	28,166	0.75	33	78	22	0
Computer	Computer hardware consultancy	30,794	0.69	55	0	100	0
	Software publishing	50,700	1.35	32	14	86	0
Other Business	Advertising	26,611	0.54	129	86	14	0
	Investigation and security activities	49,945	1.05	82	3	97	0
Recreation, culture and other	Dramatic arts, music and other arts activities	4428	0.10	58	100	0	0

Note: *Industries having the employment growth of more than 25 per cent per annum during 2005-10.

Source: National Sample Survey (NSS), 1999-2000, 2004-05 and 2009-10.

Annex. Table 2.1c

Important* Non-farm Industries with Declining Employment during 2005-10

Broad sector	*Sub-sectors*	*Decline in employment*	*Share in employment*	*Rate of decline*
Manufacturing	Embroidery work, zari work and making of ornamental trimmings by hand	-82287	1.02	-17.5
	Manufacture of other fabricated metal products	-15022	0.76	-6.5
	Manufacture of furniture	-27201	0.90	-9.0
Construction	Building of complete constructions or parts thereof; civil engineering	-63294	3.62	-5.8
Trade	Other retail sale in specialised stores	-73065	1.24	-14.4
Communication	Courier activities other than national post activities	-9646	0.62	-5.3
Other business	Accounting, book-keeping and auditing activities; tax consultancy	-14721	0.76	-6.3
	Photographic activities	-36326	0.86	-11.5
Education	Primary and secondary education	-84777	2.15	-11.0
Health and social work	Hospital activities.[Includes the activities of general and specialised hospitals]	-18915	0.94	-6.5

Note: *Industries having their share of employment more than 0.5 per cent in 2010.

Source: National Sample Survey (NSS), 1999-2000, 2004-05 and 2009-10.

3

Education

3.1 Introduction

Delhi is a city of heterogeneous cultures wherein people of different socio-economic groups, religious faiths and nationalities live together. Education and the cultural environment, which nurture tolerance and support the higher ideals of life, bear a special importance to cosmopolitan Delhi. All forms of education and training have the potential to enhance capabilities, which can be further transformed into well-being and economic benefits. Education creates conducive social and cultural environments, enabling people to live in peace and harmony. However, harmony in society is possible only if access to education and the possibilities for upward mobility are made available to a majority of the people. In this context, the status of education in Delhi acquires added importance. In this chapter, we present the human resource scenario in Delhi along with its composition in terms of the levels of education and the various interventions that have been put into place in order to address the educational challenges faced by the state. The vision for the future in the sphere of education for Delhi would thus entail improvements in the quality of education, coupled with inclusive access aimed at reaching the goal of a fully literate state, with an average of ten years of schooling for its entire population by the year 2020.

3.2 Human Resource and Composition by Levels of Education

3.2.1 Findings from the Perceptions Survey

A large-scale survey for assessing people's perceptions (hereafter referred to as the 'Perception Survey, 2013') was conducted by the Institute for Human Development (IHD), which investigated the quality of human resources by levels of education. This survey covered a population above 15 years of age and reported that a large proportion of the population in Delhi was highly qualified, having acquired degrees from various higher education institutions. Close to one-fifth (17 per cent) of the population possessed graduate and postgraduate qualifications with 2 per cent having professional and higher research degrees. In absolute terms, out of the total fifteen years and above population estimates of 11.8 million for Delhi, 2.0 million were graduates and postgraduates, and 0.27 million possessed professional and higher research degrees, showcasing the presence of human resources of high quality in the state (Figure 3.1). This is in sharp contrast to the all-India scenario wherein approximately 7 per cent of the population above 15 years of age possessed higher education qualifications (NSS, 2009-10). Further, approximately one-third of the population possessed matriculate and higher secondary qualifications. What is of essence is that the primary and middle school graduates (who together comprise 39 per cent of the total population) are able to acquire higher education or appropriate skill sets, and the existing 18 per cent of the illiterates have been converted into literates by imparting necessary skills to them, thereby making their upward transition a reality.

Figure 3.1

Delhi: Human Resource by Levels of Education

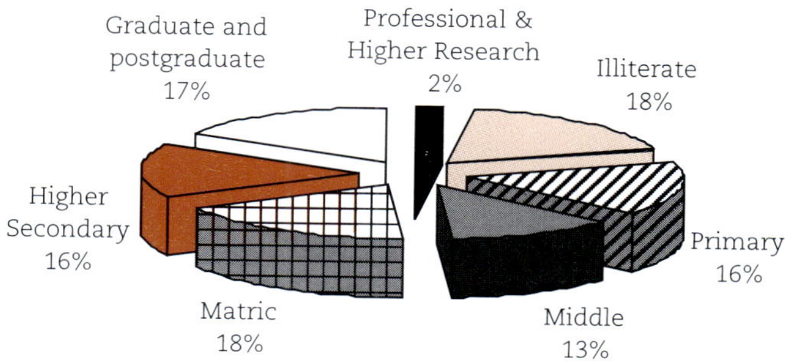

Note: Percentages presented as a proportion of population in the 15 years and above age group.

Source: Perceptions Survey, 2013.

It would be interesting to further probe the social, economic, religious and other characteristics of those possessing higher educational degrees in Delhi. In terms of the social composition, 75 per cent of those possessing higher educational degrees belonged to the general category. The reserved categories including the Scheduled Castes (SCs), Scheduled Tribes (STs) and Other Backward Castes (OBCs) constituted a small proportion of the higher education graduates at 12, 1 and 12 per cent, respectively.[1] Thus, higher educational qualifications were clearly not fairly represented amongst the population groups. This was particularly true of the SCs, who constituted 27 per cent of the total population, out of which only 12 per cent were higher educational graduates (Figure 3.2). The survey also found that while Muslims in Delhi constituted 12 per cent of the total population, only 4 per cent of this population comprised graduates. The SCs and Muslims were also found to show low representation amongst the population groups with higher educational qualifications. Thus, the SCs and Muslims emerge as the two important target groups in whose case the transition to higher education needs to be promoted for ensuring a prosperous and progressive

1. It may be noted that in the total population of 11.8 million, the percentages of persons belonging to the general, SC, ST and OBC categories are 51.8, 27, 2.1 and 19.1, respectively.

Delhi. Another significant finding of the Perceptions Survey is that a large proportion of the graduates earned monthly incomes ranging from Rs. 20,000 to Rs. 50,000 (while 39 per cent of these were graduates and postgraduates, 32 per cent were professionals or higher research degree holders). Further, close to two-thirds of the graduates lived comfortably in authorised colonies.

Figure 3.2

Per cent Distribution of Graduates with Higher Education Qualifications and Population

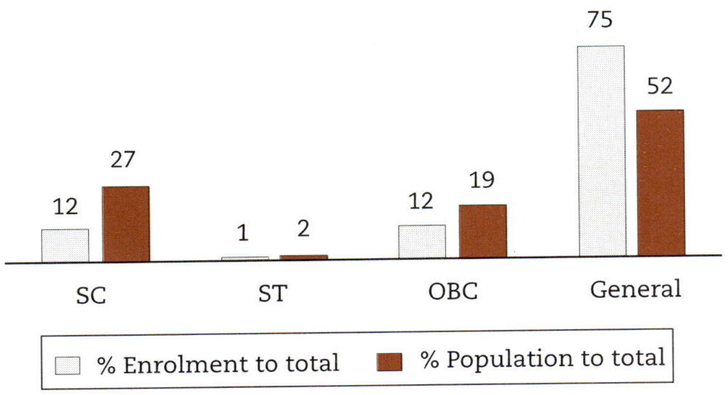

Source: Perceptions Survey, 2013.

An important target group in Delhi comprises people who live in unauthorised colonies, urban villages, *Jhuggi Jhopri (JJ)* or slum clusters and JJ resettlement colonies. They also constitute vulnerable groups, irrespective of their caste and religion, with many of them engaged as temporary, casual or self-employed workers. These groups cannot be ignored as they are the providers of important services and contribute significantly to economic activities in Delhi. The Perceptions Survey provides useful information regarding the levels of education for the population aged above 25 years, residing in these areas. Approximately 5.6 million people, constituting 48 per cent of the total population, live in these four types of settlements in Delhi. The Perceptions Survey finds that amongst all the illiterate respondents, 68 per cent live in these settlements, while 56 per cent of those who have education up to the primary and middle school levels also reside here. What, therefore, emerges as an important policy direction here is the need for strategic interventions to improve the education and skill status of persons living in these settlements. This, in turn, would necessitate the monitoring and supervision of targets under the literacy and universal elementary education programmes of the Sarva Shiksha Abhiyan (SSA), which, in turn, would contribute immensely towards making the education scenario more inclusive in Delhi, one of the basic tenets of the Twelfth Five Year Plan, thereby enhancing the capabilities of the vulnerable populace in the process. Another interesting feature observed during the survey is that as regards the occupational structure and levels of education of the respondents, almost 22 per cent of the population above 15 years of age comprises professionals and semi-professionals working in different capacities, a majority of whom possess higher educational qualifications. Service workers constitute 30 per cent of the population and play an important role in terms of their contributions. However, 85 per cent of these service workers are either illiterate or have differing levels of school education. The unskilled and skilled but low-paid population, with mostly low levels of education, constitute 20 per cent and 23 per cent of the population, respectively, and constitute the target age group of people who need to be imparted skills on a priority basis. Thus, three categories of workers in the city, viz., service workers, skilled but low-paid workers, and unskilled workers (constituting 74 per cent of the population) possess low levels of education. The introduction of policy interventions aimed at upgrading the skills of the working population and certifying the same is the need of the hour in order to augment the market value of these workers. In this context, a major policy prescription that clearly emerges from the survey is the need for initiating skill development programmes in partnership with various non-governmental organisations (NGOs) and industry associations for upgrading and promoting skill building among this target population.

3.2.2 *Average Number of Years of Schooling*

The average number of years of schooling is a good indicator of the quality of human resources in a particular sample group.[1] Using data from the National Sample Survey (NSS) 66th Round (2009-10), Figure 3.3 presents a comparative picture of the average number of years of schooling for Delhi

1. The average number of years of schooling is calculated by assigning weights equal to the percentage distribution at each level of schooling and by subsequently multiplying the weights with the number of years of schooling at each level of education (including illiterates, 0, primary level, 5, and so on) and then by summing them up and dividing by the total weights, that is, 100. Thus, if 40 per cent of the population is illiterate and 60 per cent of them are educated up to the primary level, then the weights would be 40 and 60, respectively, and the levels of education identified as the number of years, that is, 0 and 5, would be multiplied by 40 and 60, respectively, and then added. The numerator would then be 300 and the denominator, 100. The average number of years of schooling in this example would then turn out to be 3.

and all-India, disaggregated by social groups. On an average, the population in Delhi has 7.5 years of schooling as compared to the corresponding all-India figure of 4.8 years of schooling. For all social groups too, Delhi fares better with regard to the average number of years of schooling with the exception of the STs, who may be showing a downward bias in this area due to their small sample size.

Figure 3.3

Average Years of Schooling, 2009-10

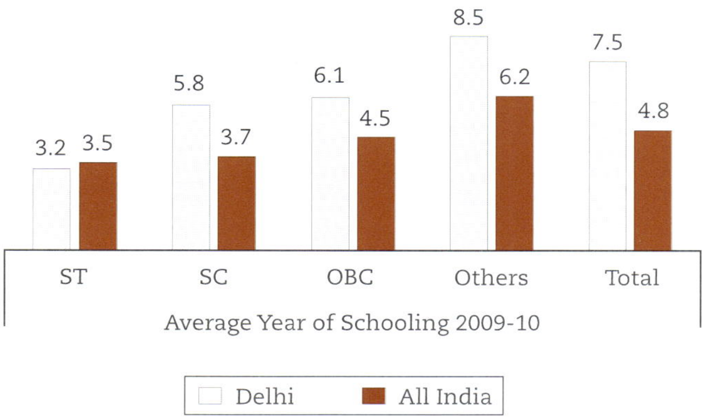

Source: NSS 66th Round (2009-10).

Figure 3.4

Average Years of Schooling for Delhi: 1993-94 to 2009-10

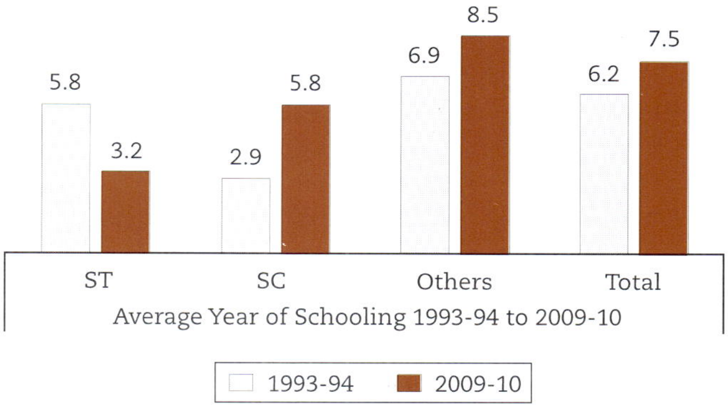

Source: NSS (1993-94 and 2009-10).

A comparison of the average number of years of schooling over two NSS time points, viz., 1993-94 and 2009-10 (Figure 3.4) reveals an improvement from 6.2 years to 7.5 years. The SC population shows a marked improvement in the average number of years of schooling from 2.9 years to 5.8 years during the period under consideration, which could be a reflection of the various interventions undertaken

Box 3.1

Pathways to Achieving Ten Years of Average Schooling in Delhi by 2020-21

A total number of ten years of schooling may be fixed as a norm to be achieved by 2020-21 to bring Delhi at par with many developed nations. This may be considered as representative of a very high quality of life, almost similar to that of the developed countries. Such a norm means that on an average, every person should have acquired education up to the secondary school level. A projection exercise was carried out in order to understand what needs to be done to achieve this norm for Delhi by 2021. The resultant projection was that no person in Delhi should be illiterate or have education below the primary level by 2020-21. In order to achieve this, what is needed is include improvements in the transition of students from primary to middle levels such that 15 and 25 per cent of the population have acquired education up to the primary and middle school levels, respectively, representing an increase from the present (NSS estimated level in 2009-10) proportion of 11.8 per cent to 25 per cent at the middle school level. Further, there is need for substantially enhancing the capacity to accommodate secondary and senior secondary level students to ensure that the proportion of those with secondary level education increases from 13.8 per cent in 2009-10 to 20 per cent in 2020-21, while the proportion of those with senior secondary level education increases from 13.7 per cent to 20 per cent during the corresponding period. Simultaneously, there is need for expanding the capacity of tertiary education institutions to ensure that the proportion of those with tertiary level of education increase from 17.1 per cent in 2009-10 to 20 per cent by 2020-21. There could be various pathways to achieve this targeted average number of ten years of schooling. A reasonable pathway could be to increase capacity at the primary and upper primary school levels by at least 100 per cent, at the secondary and senior secondary school levels by 50 per cent, and at the tertiary education levels by 20 per cent. Such an expansion is, however, based on the existing population numbers. Surely, by 2020-21 there would also be an absolute increase in the population as compared to the population in 2009-10. Any planning exercise geared to meet this expansion path must thus also take into account the absolute increase in the population. This means that the capacity expansion would be a multiple of what is envisaged above. The multiplier would depend on the proportion of increase in the population in 2020-21 over that in 2009-10.

Source: Details of calculations presented in Annexure 3.1.

by the state government under the SSA. Surprisingly, the average number of years of schooling for the STs shows a decline over the same period from 5.8 years to 3.2 years, which could be a result of the large-scale migration of the illiterate ST population from other states into Delhi, or due to the bias resulting from the small sample size. Hence, various strategies aimed at inclusion for enhancing the average number of years of schooling for the state need to keep these findings on SCs and STs as the focal points for implementing their intervention plans.

3.3 Status of Education

Delhi is the academic hub of India, and is responsible for nurturing human resources across the country by providing education and skills of the highest standards. A significant point to be noted is that many political discussions and socio-cultural discourses are profoundly supported by research institutions, universities and NGOs in Delhi, which also has one of the largest densities of institutions, scholars of repute, and varied groups of student communities in the country. The universities in the city attract students from all over the country as well as from abroad, making it the educational and cultural centre of the country. The city also witnesses the inflow of private capital at all levels of education. Since Delhi is a part of the National Capital Region (NCR), the growth of educational institutions in Delhi should be seen as part of the NCR planning process for human development.

3.3.1 The Literacy Rate

Literacy is an integral and indispensable element of educational development. It can pave the way for facilitating reductions in population growth, child mortality and poverty, and the attainment of both gender parity as well as sustainable and holistic growth. It also provides for the nurturance of democratic values such as freedom and peace among the people (Sen, 1999). Delhi, the second most populous metro of the country after Mumbai, with a population of 16.3 million, recorded a literacy rate of 86.21 per cent in 2011, showing an increase of around 4.54 percentage points over the corresponding figure for Census 2001 (see Table 3.1). In 2011, within Delhi, the literacy rates varied from 82.8 per cent to 89.3 per cent amongst its districts (with North-east Delhi reporting the lowest literacy rate and New Delhi the highest) (Figure 3.5).

One of the most significant developments in the city has been the narrowing of the gender gap in the literacy rate, representing a drop of 2.53 percentage points, which is also the highest fall recorded in this sphere so far. The gender gap in literacy now stands at approximately 11 percentage points (Census, 2011). While there has been a narrowing down in the gender gap in literacy, the overall literacy rate in Delhi is below the corresponding figures for the cities of Mumbai, Chennai, Bangalore and Kolkata, with Mumbai recording the highest percentage of 91 in 2011.

Table 3.1

Literacy Rates (percentage) in India and Delhi: 1981–2011

Census Year	*India*			*Delhi*		
	Total	*Male*	*Female*	*Total*	*Male*	*Female*
1981	43.57	56.38	29.76	61.54	68.4	53.07
1991	52.21	64.13	39.29	75.29	82.01	66.99
2001	64.80	75.30	53.70	81.67	87.33	74.71
2011	73.00	80.90	64.60	86.21	90.90	80.80

Note: The literacy rates for the years 1981 to 2011 relate to the population aged 7 years and above.

Source: Socio-Economic Profile 2011-12, Available at *www.delhiplanning.nic.in* accessed on 07 May 2013.

The gender gap in the literacy rate in 2001 was the highest in the South, North-east and North-west districts of Delhi, but this scenario showed a change in 2011, with the East, North and South districts showing the largest gender gap in literacy rates (Figure 3.6). Over the period 2001-11, the East and West districts reported a worsening in the gender gap in literacy while the North-east district reported the sharpest decline in the gender gap for this indicator. What is worth noting is that in 2011, even within the highly literate districts such as New Delhi and South-west Delhi, the gender gap in literacy was relatively high (Figure 3.6). Thus, there is need for a focused strategy for enhancing the female literacy rate in Delhi, within the framework of the 'Sakshar Bharat' programme of the Government of India.

3.3.2 The Gross Enrolment Ratio

The role of Universal Elementary Education (UEE) in strengthening the social fabric of democracy through the provisioning of equal opportunities to all is a declared objective of human development. The Gross Enrolment Ratios (GERs) in 2010-11 at the primary and upper primary levels in Delhi are 127 and

Figure 3.5

District-wise Literacy Rates (per cent) in Delhi 2011

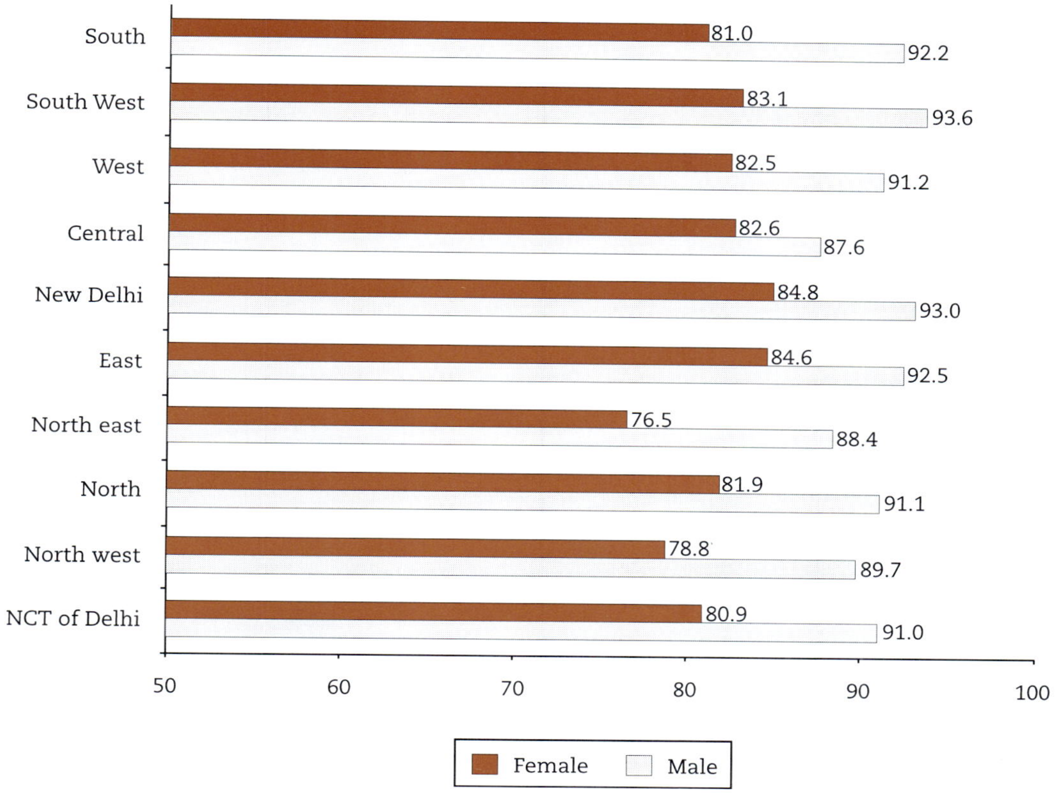

Source: Census of India, 2011.

Figure 3.6

Gender Gap in Literacy Rate (per cent) 2001 and 2011

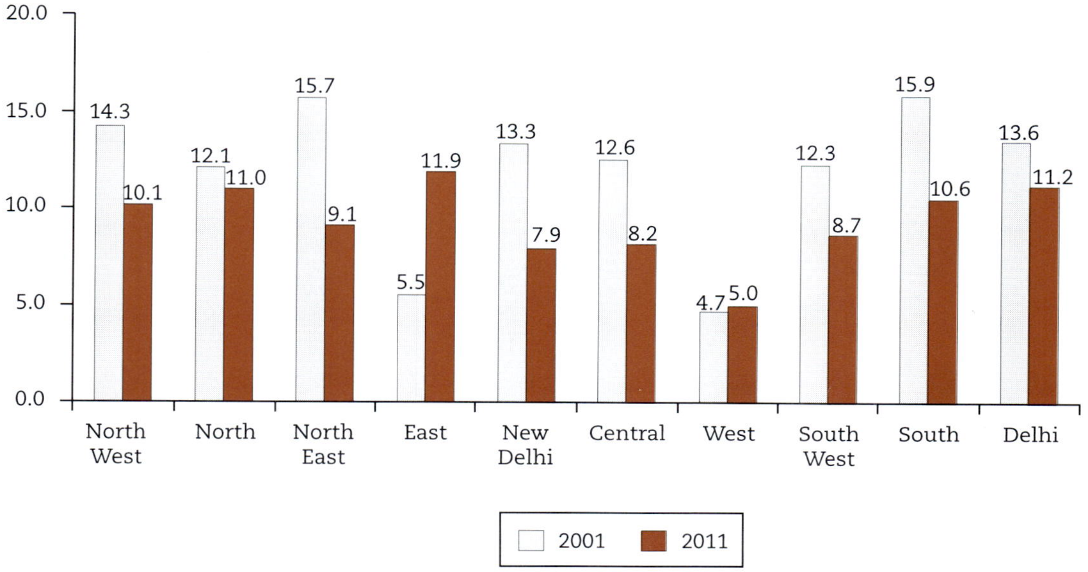

Source: Calculated from Census of India, 2001 and 2011.

108, respectively, as opposed to the corresponding all-India figures of 116 and 85, respectively.[1] The GERs for the SCs at 69.5 per cent and for the STs at 54.1 are rather low and highlight the need for specifically targeted interventions (Figure 3.7). The GER for SC children has fallen to 54.1 per cent at the upper primary level and witnessed a further drop to 64 and 38.6 per cent at the secondary and senior secondary levels, respectively (Figure 3.8), thereby clearly indicating the difficulties faced by students belonging to these communities in making the transition to higher levels of education. The low transition from the primary to upper primary levels and further to higher levels of school education needs to be probed in terms of the vulnerability of the weaker sections to move forward, and the lack of adequate number of institutions to enrol students or of the latter's promptness to join the labour market, among other factors. In a study conducted in the slum areas of Delhi, Chugh (2011) finds that the incidence of drop-outs at the secondary level of schooling is more prevalent in the slums which are inhabited by migrants from other states. Chugh reports that low achievers and students from the low socio-economic backgrounds are at a much higher risk of dropping out of school, which could be due to several reasons such as inadequate parenting, inability to afford educational expenditures, poor schooling infrastructure, de-motivated teachers, pressures to augment family incomes, parental perceptions that schooling has limited economic returns, peers with low aspirations, poor nutrition and health, and the existence of too few role models in the community. Yuko (2009) reports an attendance of 54.5 per cent among slum children in the areas she surveyed for her study, with 14.1 per cent drop-outs (ever attended school) and 31.5 per cent for those who never attended school. The study also highlights the fact that almost all slum children were enrolled in government schools, with the two main factors contributing to the high level of drop-outs among these children being financial reasons and the negative perception of education among their parents. being cited as two of the main factors contributing to their dropping out.

1. The GER is calculated as the ratio of the number of students in a given class or set of classes to the number of children in the appropriate age group. The Net Enrolment Ratio (NER) is a better means of capturing figures for age-appropriate enrolment, but it is difficult to obtain age-wise enrolment information/data.

Figure 3.7

Gross Enrolment Ratio, 2010-11

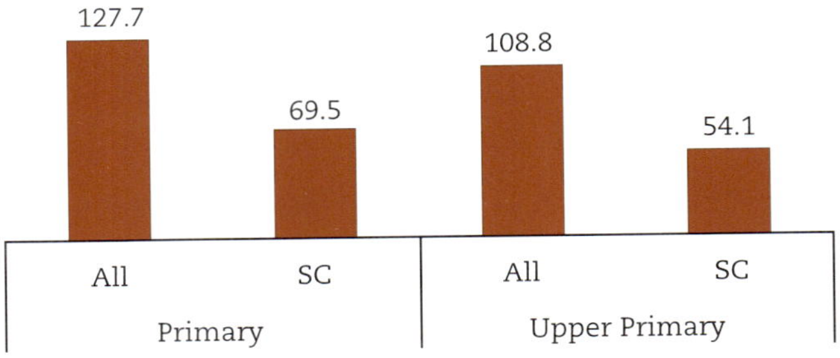

Source: Selected Educational Statistics, 2010-11, Ministry of Human Resource Development (MHRD), Government of India.

Figure 3.8

Gross Enrolment Ratio (2010-11)

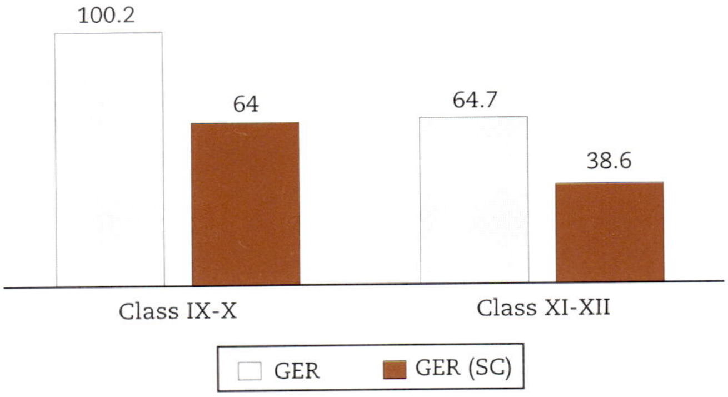

Source: Selected Educational Statistics, MHRD, Government of India, 2010-11.

3.3.3 Elementary Education: Salient Features

Some of the salient features of the elementary education scenario in Delhi can be encapsulated here. In Delhi, primary education is mainly the responsibility of local bodies—the Municipal Corporation of Delhi (MCD), the New Delhi Municipal Corporation (NDMC) and the Delhi Cantonment Board (DCB). However, the Directorate of Education has also introduced primary classes in 364 Sarvodaya Vidyalayas of the Government of NCT of Delhi. In 2010, there were 5043 schools in Delhi, including 2613 pre-primary and primary schools, 588 middle schools, and 1872 secondary/senior secondary schools providing enrolment to 3.9 million children and with a total teaching staff of 0.11 million (Table 3.2). Of the total 5043 schools, 2666 were government schools and 2377 private schools, indicating a significant role played by the private sector. In order to increase access, the Directorate of Education and the MCD have set up 83 new schools, upgraded 144 and bifurcated 25 existing schools during

Box 3.2

Special Features of Primary and Upper Primary Schools in Delhi, DISE 2010-11

- The density of primary and upper primary schools per 10 square kilometres in Delhi was 29 and 16, respectively, in 2010-11, which signifies one of the highest figures in India. Paradoxically, however, the number of schools per 1000 child population (aged 6-11 years) is only 3, which is one of the lowest in India. This aptly reflects the relative shortage of primary and upper primary schools in the city.
- A feature worth noting is that the average number of classrooms per school was 16 and that the average number of teachers per school was 15, which is reportedly the highest amongst all states. Therefore, though the number of schools in the city is in short supply, the size of the schools is quite large and partly compensates for the shortage of schools.
- As many as 98 per cent of the upper primary schools (including both government and aided schools) report having less than 220 working days in a year.
- In terms of the basic facilities, all schools had drinking water facilities and 80 per cent had girls' toilets.
- A significant proportion of 80 per cent of the schools also reported having functional computer facilities.

Source: DISE, 2010-11, NUEPA, Delhi.

Table 3.2

School, Enrolment and Teachers in Schools in 2010-11

	Higher Secondary Education (Universities and Colleges)	*Senior Level*	*Secondary Level*	*Middle Level*	*Primary Level*	*Pre-primary Level*	*Total*
Number	207	1392	480	588	2563	50	5073
Enrolment	2,81,987	4,23,950	6,33,842	9,82,949	17,31,123	1,48,601	39,20,465
SCs as a percentage to the total	13.3	11.6	12.7	9.8	10.5	7.6	10.7
STs as a percentage to the total		0.5	0.4	0.3	0.4	0.3	0.4
Teachers	4467	68,255	10,859	7482	28,688	188	1,15,472

Source: Statistical Hand Book, 2012 Education, Available at: *http://www.delhi.gov.in/wps/wcm/connect/doit_des/DES/Our+Services/Statistical+Hand+Book/*; accessed on 10th May 2013.

the Eleventh Five Year Plan. Because of the space constraint, a majority of these schools are run in double shifts.[2] The enrolment of students in primary and upper primary schools was approximately 1.73 and 09 million, respectively, in 2010-11, while at the secondary and senior secondary levels, it was 0.6 million and 0.4 million, respectively.[3] Also, at all levels of education, females comprised 46-47 per cent of the total enrolment, reflecting gender parity in this sphere.

An important feature of education in Delhi is the marked presence of private schools with 28.4 per cent of all school-going children at the primary and upper primary levels attending private schools (Economic Survey, 2012-13). This proportion increases to 42.71 per cent for the secondary and senior secondary levels, indicating the preference among students for private schooling at higher levels of education (Table 3.3).

2. Source: 'An Approach to the Twelfth Five Year Plan', Government of Delhi, Chapter 7, Available at: *http://www.delhi.gov.in/wps/wcm/connect/DoIT_Planning/planning/important+links/an+approach+to+12th+five+year+plan+%282012-17%29*; accessed on 15th May 2013.
3. Selected Educational Statistics, 2010-11, MHRD, Government of India.

Table 3.3

Share of Private Sector in Enrolment

Classes	*Private (in million)*	*Percentage in Private*
Primary and middle levels	0.38	28.4
Secondary and senior secondary levels	1.09	42.7
All	1.48	37.7

Source: Economic Survey, 2012-13, Government of Delhi.

Under Article 21A of the Constitution of India and its consequent legislation, the right of children to free and compulsory education (Right to Education [RTE] Act, 2009) became operative on 1 April 2010. The RTE Act stipulates necessary interventions by the government to realise the goal of universalisation of elementary education. To this end, the target to be achieved by the state government by putting into place various interventions includes: decreases in the pupil–teacher ratio from the existing 46 to 40 at the primary level and from 39 to 35 at the upper primary level. Training has been imparted to 2142 educational administrators in concurrence with the RTE Act provisions. All schools have adopted the Continuous and Comprehensive Evaluation (CCE) scheme. Although currently, School Management Committees (SMCs) do not exist, necessary steps are underway to make them a reality soon. According to the NCERT 3rd Round survey, the students in Delhi have excelled in three subjects—Mathematics, Hindi and Everyday Science (EVS)—and the performance of children is above the national average in class V. In order to enable the Government of NCT Delhi to fulfil all the clauses of the RTE Act, there is need for regular monitoring by a Committee of Experts and of apprising the Government of all the findings through monitoring of reports. In this regard, the role of the SSA in the implementation of the RTE is worth mentioning. Under the SSA, assistance is provided for recruitment and training of teachers, development of infrastructure, and procurement of textbooks, among other things. It also entails the creation of additional posts for teachers to maintain the prescribed norms of the teacher–pupil ratio in all Government schools, provide educational facilities to all children of school-going age by opening new schools and additional sections in all classes, and provision of free-ship quotas for the Economically Weaker Section of Students (EWS) in private schools, among other measures. The private schools that have not been allocated land at concessional rates are reimbursed the cost of the free-ships given to EWS category students admitted by such schools. The expenditure on the scheme is shared between the Central and state governments in the 65:35 ratio. Improved implementation of the RTE can be achieved by bringing schools run by different managements under one umbrella thus facilitating better co-ordination.

3.3.4 Education for Children with Special Needs (CWSN)

Every disabled child has his/her own strengths and weaknesses. It is the responsibility of the State and educated citizens to create enabling conditions for allowing them to lead a life of dignity. As per the Results Framework for SSA Goals, 2013-14,[1] there are 17,474 children with special needs (CWSNs) enrolled in schools or alternative systems including home-based education in Delhi. The educational requirements of children with special needs have seen a transition from special schools to integrated schools and eventually to inclusive schools. The RTE (2009) mandates the complete inclusion of all children in the schooling processes with a special emphasis on CWSNs. It calls for the placement of CWSNs into neighbourhood schools with necessary support services. Inclusion of all children, including CWSNs, would then facilitate the achievement of UEE. Within the SSA, there is a zero rejection policy for CWSNs with a special provisioning of Rs. 3,000 per annum for every CWSN per annum. It also provides guidelines for Barrier Free Access (BFA) for all children, which is not just limited to buildings and physical infrastructure, but also extends to the curriculum and teaching–learning processes in order to address the various learning needs of CWSNs.[2] It is important to note the efforts made in this direction by individuals and institutions in Delhi, which have contributed towards addressing the educational needs of CWSNs.[3] A report by Deshkal, UNICEF and Care Foundation (2010)[4] on inclusive classrooms very aptly points out, "For classrooms to be fully inclusive, it should be ensured that the curriculum is accessible to and relevant for all children in terms of what is

1. Available at: *http://ssa.nic.in/pabminutes-documents/Pab%20 Minutes%202013-14/Delhi/Annexure%20-%20IV%20Result%20 Frame%20Work%20Delhi.pdf*; accessed on 15th May 2013.
2. Ibid.
3. Examples of schools and children with special needs who have benefited from inclusive education provided by some schools in Delhi can be accessed at the following websites: *purti.org/our-work*, *www.marshaforest.com/centreproject/html* accessed on 17th May 2013.
4. "Inclusive Classroom, Social Inclusion/Exclusion and Diversity: Perspectives, Policies and Practices", Deshkal, UNICEF and Care Foundation (2010).

taught (content), how it is taught (method), how the children learn best (process), and how it relates to the life experiences of the children and the environment in which they live and learn. In order to be inclusive of children with different backgrounds and abilities, curriculum material needs to be sensitive to the diversity of children and their circumstances."

3.3.5 Educational Performance/Achievements

An analysis of the Class XII Central Board of Secondary Education (CBSE) results for the year 2012[5] shows that one-third (33.7 per cent) of the students from private schools, more than half (56 per cent) from government schools, 7.1 per cent from government-aided schools, 3.1 per cent from Kendriya Vidyalayas (KVS) and 0.3 per cent from the NDMC schools appeared in the CBSE Board examinations, and reported almost similar pass rates. This brings out the fact that though private schools do play an important role in the sphere of higher education in Delhi, government schools also have an equally pivotal role to play. While the success rate in private schools was 90 per cent, the corresponding rate for government schools was 87.72 per cent, reflecting that government schools in Delhi do not lag behind private schools in terms of the performance of students the Class XII Board examinations. Remarkably, girls' schools showed pass percentages of 91 per cent as opposed to 81 per cent for boys' schools. However, an issue of some concern is the fact that only 7 per cent of the students appeared in the examination from the Science stream and 6 per cent from the vocational stream as opposed to 68 per cent from the Arts and 20 per cent from the Commerce streams, pointing towards the need to promote the science and vocational streams. Another area of concern is the low pass percentage in Economics in government schools. Some of the schools, including Urdu schools, where the pass percentage is below 50 per cent also need attention.[6] Learning achievements at the primary level for slum students reveals that schools managed by the MCD reported the lowest mean scores—13 per cent learners reported achievement scores of less than 20 per cent (Agrawal and Chugh, 2003). Recent studies by ASER (2012) confirm the poor learning achievements of primary level students in the rural areas.

5. Directorate of Education, Government of Delhi.
6. *Source*: Directorate of Education, Analysis of CBSE Results, 2012, Available at: *http://www.edudel.nic.in/Result_Analysis/2012/ResultCBSE12th2012.pdf*; accessed on 13th May 2013.

3.4 The Higher Education Scenario

In the field of higher education, there are 160 colleges in the city, which includes 83 Delhi University (DU) colleges, 77 colleges affiliated with the Guru Gobind Indraprastha (GGSIP) University in 2012. An issue that needs to be addressed is the fact that DU, Jawaharlal Nehru University (JNU), and Jamia Milia Islamia University, though located in Delhi, are Central universities and thus do not have any quota or preference for Delhi students. The South Asia University is a welcome addition, making Delhi an education hub for neighbouring countries. The Delhi Technological University (DTU) has been a milestone in equipping Delhi with world class education, research and innovation capabilities. The Indira Gandhi National Open University (IGNOU) facilitates admission to all students seeking higher education, training and research in varied fields. In the field of professional and technical education, Delhi has 107 degree and postgraduate level professional and technical educational institutions affiliated to the GGSIP University, DU and other universities. The well-known All India Institute of Medical Sciences (AIIMS), Indian Institute of Technology (IIT), and Indian Statistical Institute (ISI) add special status to the state by promoting sheer excellence in education. There are 11 deemed universities specialising in different disciplines as well. There are 21 diploma level institutions, which includes 12 Government/aided polytechnic institutions and 9 private sector institutions. The number of certificate level institutions in the form of Industrial Training Institute (ITI) and Industrial Training Centres (ITC), Basic Training Centres (BTC) and Commercial Secretariat Institute (CSI) reached 75 in 2010, which includes 17 Government ITIs and 56 private sector ITIs. The total enrolment in diploma and certificate level courses is 22,185 and the total number of teachers is 1,434 teachers (Table 3.4). The setting up

Table 3.4

Number of Technical Education Institutions under the Directorate of Training and Technical Education, Government of NCT of Delhi

	ITIs	*ITCs*	*BTC*	*CSI*	*Polytechnics*	*Total*
Number of institutions	17	56	1	1	21	95
Students	7545	1762	512	155	12,211	22,185
Teachers	521	242	32	3	636	1434

Source: Statistical Hand Book, 2012 Education, Available on *http://www.delhi.gov.in/wps/wcm/connect/doit_des/DES/Our+Services/Statistical+Hand+Book/*; accessed on 10th May 2013.

Box 3.3

Three Flagship Universities in the State—A Much Needed Initiative

- For focused development in the field of higher education, the Government of NCT of Delhi established a separate Directorate of Higher Education in the year 1997. Delhi Government also established three State Universities namely, Guru Gobind Singh Inraprastha University, National Law University and Bharat Ratna Dr. B.R. Ambedkar University in the year 1998, 2008 and 2008, respectively.
- The Guru Gobind Singh Indraprastha (GGSIP) University was established in 1998 as an affiliating and teaching university with a focus on professional education. The University is functioning from its new campus at Dwarka. There is a proposal to establish another (East) campus of the University at Surajmal Vihar, for which the necessary clearances are in process. With an enrolment of 62,000, the University has 13 Schools of Studies in its campus. In addition, 77 self-financing institutes and 23 Government institutes are affiliated to the University. The Bharat Ratna Dr. B.R. Ambedkar University was established by the Government of NCT in the year 2008, and it comprises 10 Schools of Studies covering 9 programmes, with 629 students enrolled in 2011-12.
- The National Law University (NLU), established by the Government of NCT of Delhi, in 2008, is one of the premier law institutes in the country. It was established with the vision to create a global legal institution which would compete with the best outside India. In 2011-12, it had 6 academic programmes with 337 students enrolled in them.

Source: Government of NCT of Delhi, Directorate of Higher Education, Twelfth Five Year Plan.

of GGSIP University, Ambedkar University, National Law University (NLU), Indraprastha Institute of Information Technology, DTU, Delhi Pharmaceutical Science and Research University, Delhi Institute of Tool Engineering, Institute of Heritage Management and Research has also contributed, to a great extent, in making Delhi an educational hub (Box 3.3).

3.5 Issues and Interventions to Promote Education

The educational progress attained in Delhi so far has been the result of cumulative interventions over the years. While market forces have created spaces for the privileged classes and the poor have not benefited much from the expansion of private schools and colleges, planning processes have played a significant role in providing educational benefits to the poor. The recent planned interventions that have been undertaken by the state towards educational development include:

- Setting up of a new a Technical University for Women, two new Medical Colleges, a Para-medical Staff Training Institute, a world class Skill Development Centre in collaboration with ITE, Singapore, and a Regional Vocational Training Institute, among others, all of which would contribute towards facilitating improvements in higher and professional education in both quantitative and qualitative terms.
- The Master Plan of Delhi (MPD–2021) recommends that there should be one senior secondary school for every 10,000 population. As per the recommendation, 550 new senior secondary schools need to be set up during the Twelfth Five Year Plan period for a projected population of 19.0 million by 2017. This, in turn, requires massive investments in the form of school infrastructure as well as the recruitment of teachers and other support staff. The private sector could also be a partner in the investments required if the Delhi Development Authority (DDA) allots land to develop private schools at concessional rates with the condition that these schools allocate 25 per cent of their seats under the free-ship quota to the economically weaker students.
- Despite a high literacy rate, the prevalence of a gender gap in literacy is a matter of concern. There is thus need for coordinated and integrated efforts through planned schemes like Ladli, better scholarships, free transport facilities for girl students in the rural areas, and the programme for empowerment of women through Gender Resource Centres and ICDS projects for reducing this gender gap.
- The Government of Delhi has started a number of programmes to improve the

Box 3.4

Delhi: Initiatives in Higher Education during the Twelfth Plan

1. Financial assistance for students of economically weaker sections: The Government of NCT Delhi has framed the 'Yuva Nirman Scheme' under 'The Delhi Higher Education Aid Trust', whereby scholarships are to be provided to the socially and economically backward students of state universities and affiliated institutes on a merit-cum-means basis. There is also provisioning for scholarships/reimbursements of half the tuition fee for professional courses to students whose maximum family income from all sources is Rs. 0.2 million.
2. Award for college lecturers: In order to incentivise lecturers to impart quality education, a cash prize of Rs. 75,000 is slated to be given to the best lecturer in each of the 28 colleges funded by the Government of NCT of Delhi and affiliated to the University of Delhi.
3. Promotion of sports facilities in University Colleges: A proposed outlay of Rs. 25 million has been allocated under the Twelfth Plan to promote sports facilities in Delhi University Colleges.
4. Award for meritorious students in Government-funded colleges: A cash award of Rs. 10,000 is proposed to be given to the toppers of Arts, Science and Commerce streams in all Delhi University colleges.
5. Construction of hostels for college-going female students in Delhi: At present, five DU colleges namely, Miranda House, Lady Shri Ram (LSR) College, Indraprastha (IP) College, Lady Irwin College and Daulat Ram College have hostel facilities. In view of the acute scarcity of hostels for girls, the Twelfth Plan has made an allocation for constructing hostels in DU colleges.
6. Sufficient allocations have been made under capital expenditure for strengthening the Directorate of Higher Education, and for construction of the Ambedkar State University and East Campus of the GGSIP University, Law University and new buildings of DU colleges.

Source: Government of NCT of Delhi, Directorate of Higher Education, Twelfth Five Year Plan.

quality of education in government schools. The impact of these programmes is also visible in the results of the secondary and senior secondary CBSE examinations. However, there is still scope for further improvement. The difference in the performance of the Pratibha Vikas Vidyalayas above other government schools showcases the quality of education offered by them and the need to bring other government schools up to the same standards. However, in view of the lack of timely allotment of suitable sites to the Government of Delhi and the MCD for opening new schools, the classes in these schools are being held in tents and semi-pucca buildings. Thus, a proper land allotment policy needs to be implemented so that allotment of the new sites for schools can be done 5-6 years in advance to facilitate the timely construction of school buildings so that stop-gap measures do not have to be resorted to.

- The MPD–2021 recommends the holding of second shifts in schools in view of the problem of land and space. Private schools could be allowed to hold second shifts in their school complexes if they fulfil all the requirements prescribed by the Directorate of Education.
- While at the primary and middle levels, 28 per cent of all children attend private schools, this proportion is much higher at 42 per cent for the secondary level.[1] Such an imbalance needs to be addressed by instituting more government secondary schools to improve access especially for children belonging to the economically backward classes.
- The Directorate of Education has developed computerised modules for Management Information Systems (MIS) for the following areas:

  i) Transfer/posting of teaching and non-teaching staff;

1. Government of NCT of Delhi, Directorate of Higher Education, Twelfth Five Year Plan.

ii) Personal information system;

iii) Students' enrolment;

iv) Financial budget control;

v) School Infrastructure;

vi) Attendance of employees on the Internet; and

vii) On-line admission in Government schools under the Directorate of Education.

- The holding of second shifts for classes have become more acceptable in the state with the aggressive expansion of technical education institutions over the last 4-5 years. The phenomenon of female students being increasingly able to avail of hostel and food facilities has also resulted in higher enrolments.

3.6 Challenges and Strategic Thinking in Education

While the Government of Delhi has undertaken various planned interventions in the sphere of education, there are many challenges that still need to be addressed, some of which include: maintaining the teacher–pupil ratio as per the norms; provision of support to the economically weaker categories of students; ensuring autonomy in the management of institutions; setting up of an independent accreditation body for schools and independent evaluations of learning achievements. If all these measures were to be implemented, they would go a long way in promoting inclusion and quality in education.

Some of the other challenges in the sphere of education in Delhi that need to be addressed are as follows:

- Delhi is a state wherein shadow education is on the rise, and tuitions and coaching centres are mushrooming. The factors that give rise to this phenomenon may be a matter of academic debate; however, it is definitely both the cause as well as the effect of a class divide in education. This can be countered through interventions aimed at strengthening mainstream education and containing the proliferation of coaching and tuition centres.

- The Government of Delhi has taken necessary steps for the implementation of the Right to Education (RTE) Act. However, as noted above, the problem of co-ordination in implementing the RTE in schools under different managements still remains.

- The University of Delhi attracts a large number of students for admission into its different colleges every year. Even though students manage to secure college admission, finding proper accommodation remains a challenge as most colleges have limited hostel facilities. Nearly 30 per cent of the students (approximately 19,000 in number) enrolling across DU colleges come from outside Delhi and compete for just 1,000 seats in the campus hostels. The remaining almost 18,000 first-year students have to turn elsewhere for accommodation every year. Such students then have to seek accommodations at exorbitant rents and also have to face the concomitant problems of food and hygiene. Foreign students and women students, too, do not have separate hostels.[1] Hence, there is an urgent need to expand hostel infrastructure in the colleges of Delhi University.

- Municipal schools in the national capital face a severe shortage of teachers. According to official data, 5,568 posts for teachers are lying vacant in around 1,750 schools run by the three civic bodies.[2] The erstwhile MCD has since been trifurcated. Before the trifurcation, the MCD had filled 3,848 posts of teachers during the years 2009-10 and 2011-12. However, 5,568 posts still continue to remain vacant (The Tribune, 2 September 2012). Many DU colleges and departments are also functioning with ad hoc teachers due to a large number of vacancies that are yet to be filled since 2008. More than 40 per cent of the teaching positions in colleges are lying vacant and the situation could worsen with teachers recruited as far back as 1969 due to retire in the near future. While ad-hoc teachers have teaching duties similar to the permanent ones, they have to renew their contracts every four months, and are also not entitled to receive benefits like medical allowances or

1. *India Today*, 5 July 2012.
2. *The Tribune*, 2 September 2012.

basic reimbursements. This lack of benefits and the sustained insecurity among the adhoc teachers thus leads to a serious drop in the quality of their teaching as well as in the research environment. The problem of shortage of teachers in DU colleges, therefore, needs to be dealt with urgently (The Times of India, 16 January 2012).

- There are 12 fully sponsored colleges run by the Delhi Government. Another 16 colleges are funded to the extent of 5 per cent by the Delhi Government. The need of the hour is thus to support all the 28 colleges through Plan funding by strengthening sports, hostel and residential infrastructure.

Strategic thinking in education in the context of the capital state of Delhi is also required for facilitating the implementation of the following measures:

- Innovative thinking for a Meta University in Delhi is underway and the Jamia Milia Islamia, DU, JNU, and IIT, New Delhi are envisaged to play a role in the same. Meta Universities enable the sharing of learning resources from different universities by using the latest technologies for the benefit of students. They represent second generation universities, which are free from physical boundaries with the ability to operate in virtual space, taking advantage of the innovation and flexibility possible in such domains. Under the Cluster Innovation Centre of Delhi University, the 'Master of Mathematics Education' is a Joint Degree being offered jointly by DU and Jamia Milia Islamia University.

- The introduction of the four-year undergraduate progamme (FYUP) in DU has also been a radical move. The Delhi University's Academic Council gave its nod to convert the coveted three-year undergraduate programme into four years, with the entire structure of the traditional course coming in for a major overhaul from the 2013-14 session onwards. The course will now give the students the option to discontinue the programme after two years with an associate degree, after three years with a Bachelor's degree, and acquire an Honours degree after completion of all the four years. Sports and cultural activities would form part of the curriculum and the course would be multi-disciplinary, allowing students to choose subjects across streams. However, the launching of this programme in Delhi distorts the three-year undergraduate structure prevalent in the rest of the country, and experts feel that such a sudden change in the under-graduate structure demands wider consultations and careful implementation.

- Government school reform necessitates the devolution of greater autonomy in management to school authorities. The 73rd and 74th Constitutional Amendments require Panchayati Raj and local administrative bodies, the third-tier of administration in villages and urban areas, to manage local schools. However, much of the administrative controls over schools in Delhi still rest with the state and Central governments. The Right of Children to Free and Compulsory Education Bill, 2009, mandates the setting up of SMCs, with parental and community representation. Although this is a welcome move, the SMCs need to be empowered with the necessary controls over school management covering the areas of recruitment of qualified teachers and removal of irresponsible staff, thereby increasing accountability and enhancing community involvement.

- The introduction of performance pay incentives for teachers (both individual and group) constitute another reform measure that would encourage better teaching and learning outcomes and quality of education. As the names suggest, the first incentive has been provided to teachers whose class-group has shown improvements in learning outcomes and the latter incentive is provided to the entire group of teachers under whom students show overall improvements across the board.

- The quality of education received by students is paramount and over-rides all other concerns. Rather than allowing for the continued emphasis on enrolments, learning outcomes need to become the prime area of attention of public policy. Undertaking an independent assessment of learning achievements is the only way of ensuring this and it could serve as a starting point for future educational policies. For instance, independent studies of learning achievements by the NGO Pratham, published in the latter's Annual Status of Education Report (ASER), 2012, show that less than 50 per cent of Standard V children are able to read textbooks prescribed for Standard II.

- The setting up of an independent accreditation body for schools would help inform and empower parents to make the right choice of schooling for their children. An alternative could be the setting up of a State Institute for Learning Assessments, which would study and assess the school-wise academic performances of students (from, say, Standard III onwards) and would help in defining the standards of learning achievements for both government and government-aided schools, thereby making them more performance-oriented.

3.7 In Summary

The basic motivation for the discussion presented in this chapter has been to convey that Delhi, being the capital of India, is a state that occupies a place of unique importance. People of varied backgrounds, both national as well as international, cultures, religions and social groups, live together here in a state of peace and harmony, while engaging in various economic, political and administrative activities. This necessitates the promotion of a culture of humanism, tolerance and togetherness that can only be sustained through a high-quality, purposeful and inclusive education system. Delhi is the academic hub of India, and is responsible for nurturing human resources with education and skills of the highest standards. Further, since Delhi is a part of the NCR, the growth of educational institutions in the city should be seen as part of the NCR plans for human development.

In 2011, Delhi recorded a literacy rate of 86.3 per cent, which signified an increase of approximately 4.7 percentage points over 2001. There is also a variation in literacy rates across districts. The gender gap in literacy stands at close to 11 percentage points, despite there being a narrowing down in the same over the decade 2001-2011. The policy pointer that emerges from these findings is that given a relatively persistent and high gender gap in literacy, strategies for promoting female literacy need to be prioritised as short-term policy interventions. The prevalence of low GERs for the SCs and STs in 2010-11 (69.5 and 54.1, respectively) at the primary and upper primary levels, and even lower GERs for the same social groups at the secondary and senior secondary levels highlight the possible difficulties in transitioning faced by children hailing from these social groups, including vulnerability, lack of appropriate institutions for enrolment or their willingness to join the labour market. Hence, there is a need to provide incentives in policy design for ensuring success in the transitioning of these children to higher levels of education, especially the socially and economically weak students. The educational participation of slum children in Delhi is mainly in government schools, however these children subsequently drop out from school due to financial reasons or the negative perception of schooling by their parents.

While primary education is principally the responsibility of the state government in Delhi, the private sector does play a prominent role in providing the same. Space constraints for running schools compels a majority of the schools to run double shifts.

There does seem to be gender parity in school enrolment at the primary level, which is an encouraging phenomenon. The presence of the private sector in schooling is more marked at the secondary and senior secondary levels, covering close to 42.7 per cent of those who attend school (Economic Survey, 2013). Various interventions aimed at implementing the RTE Act (2009) have also been put into place to realise the goal of UEE. What is thus needed is regular monitoring and effective implementation of the various Clauses of the RTE Act by a committee of experts and the subsequent apprising of these measures to the Delhi Government. The RTE Act also needs to be implemented more effectively by bringing schools run by different types of management under a uniform structure of management, which would help address all issues pertaining to coordination. The same Expert Committee could also examine various aspects leading to dropouts and lacunae in the learning achievements, particularly of children from the unauthorised settlements. The role of the SSA in implementing the RTE would then be optimally utilised. For children with special needs, it is imperative to ensure adequate and requisite training for teachers, coupled with the institution of curricular and other support systems. The efforts and initiatives already being made by certain schools to address the issue of CWSNs are commendable. Data on educational achievements in Standard XII reveal that government schools are now at par with private schools in terms of students' performance, with girls' schools registering a higher pass percentage as compared to boys' schools.

The average number of years of schooling for Delhi calculated by using the NSS 66th Round data (2009-10) has been found to be 7.5 years at the aggregate level. When disaggregated by social groups, Delhi fares well except for the STs (which could be showing a downward bias as a population group because of small sample size). When the trend in the average number of years of schooling is studied over the period 1993-94 to 2009-10, SCs show an improvement from 2.9 years to 5.8 years, which could be attributed to the interventions under the SSA that are specially targeted for this social group. The STs, on the other hand, show a decline in this indicator over the same time period from 5.8 years to 3.2 years, which could be attributed to either the high in-migration of the illiterate ST population into Delhi or small sample size biases. Inclusive education strategies, therefore, need to focus on these two population groups in particular, when aiming to achieve advances in the average number of years of schooling. In order to reach a target of ten years of average schooling for Delhi's populace by the year 2020-21, it is estimated that capacities at the primary and upper primary levels need to be increased by at least 50 per cent, at the secondary and senior secondary levels by 60 per cent, and at the tertiary levels by 25 per cent.

The higher education scenario in Delhi is very promising, with 160 colleges operating in 2012, including 83 in DU, and 77 affiliated with the GGSIP University. Since DU, JNU and Jamia Milia Islamia University are Central universities, they offer no quota or preference for Delhi students. In the field of professional and technical education, Delhi has 107 degree and PG level professional and technical educational institutions that are affiliated to the GGSIP University, DU, and other universities. The well-known institutions—AIIMS, IIT, and ISI add special status to the state by promoting sheer excellence in education. There are 11 deemed universities specialising in different disciplines as well.

The area that needs to be addressed in the field of higher education in Delhi is an expansion of hostel infrastructure in the Delhi colleges, coupled with improvements in quality, and filling up of all teacher vacancies through government consultations with the University Grants Commission (UGC) and DU. There is also a need to strengthen mainstream educational structures in terms of quality and inclusiveness in order to bridge class and social divides. It is necessary to make private institutions partners in the development of education rather than allowing them to function as instruments of division in the social and economic structure of Delhi. Furthermore, education should create a climate of healthy debate on all matters that make India a prosperous and progressive nation.

The main findings from the Perceptions Survey (2013) highlight the need for first, facilitating the upward educational transition of those having acquired education up to the primary and middle school levels, who comprise over one-third of Delhi's population, thus enabling them to acquire higher education or skill sets. The conversion of illiterates into literates with adequate skill sets is also a priority area. Second, the SCs and Muslims constitute only a small proportion of those having acquired higher education, thereby emerging as the two critical target groups for whom the transition to higher education levels needs to be the focus for policy interventions. Third, low education and literacy levels among the population residing in unauthorised colonies, JJ clusters, urban villages and resettlement colonies call for strategic interventions coupled with monitoring and close supervision of targets under the SSA. Some policy imperatives are thus needed to help push the vulnerable population groups up on the literacy and education ladders, and to make the educational processes in Delhi more inclusive. Fourth, when studied by occupational structure, three categories of workers constituting almost three-fourths of the population, viz., those in the service industry, and skilled but low-paid and unskilled workers possess low levels of education. What is needed is an upgradation of the skills of this set of workers with appropriate certification in order to improve their market value and employability. This can be achieved by forging partnerships with NGOs and industry associations to upgrade and promote skill formation among this group of workers.

Some of the recent planned interventions to promote educational development in the state, especially for the poor and underprivileged sections, need to be highlighted. These are detailed here. First, the setting up of various higher educational institutions to improve the professional education scenario in the state during the Twelfth Plan period (including the setting up of a Technical University for Women, two new Medical Colleges, a Para-medical Staff Training Institute, and a world class Skill Development Centre in collaboration with ITE, Singapore). Second, in accordance with the MPD–2021, the setting up of 550 new senior secondary schools along with the requisite infrastructure and teaching staff is on the anvil. Third, initiatives such as Ladli, offering of scholarships and free transport facilities for female children in rural areas, setting up of Gender Resource Centres for female empowerment and ICDS projects have been instituted to effectively address the existing gender gap in literacy; Fourth, a number of programmes have been initiated to help improve the quality of education in government schools, the impact of which is seen in the results of the secondary and senior secondary CBSE examinations. Fifth, the advent of computerisation and introduction of MIS' for education-related information, including student enrolment, transfer/posting of teaching and non-teaching staff, Personal Information Systems, financial budget control, school infrastructure, and employee attendance have been significant achievements in the sphere of education in Delhi. Finally, with second shifts gaining acceptance, expansion of technical institutes, and increase in female enrolments in higher education, the accompanying availability of hostel and food facilities needs to be enhanced.

Along with the myriad planned interventions that are being put into place in the education sector, many challenges still exist that need to be effectively addressed for making the education system in the state more inclusive and egalitarian. Some of these possible interventions are:

1. Maintaining the teacher–pupil ratio as per norms;
2. Providing greater support to the economically weaker categories of students;
3. Introducing autonomy in the management of institutions;
4. Setting up an independent accreditation body for schools and for the conduction of independent evaluations of learning achievements;
5. Interventions aimed at strengthening mainstream education in order to control the phenomenon of shadow education and the proliferation of coaching and tuition centres;
6. Better coordination in implementing RTE in schools under different managements;
7. Enhancement of the hostel and residential infrastructure;
8. Tackling the shortage of teachers in municipal schools;
9. Filling up of teacher vacancies in DU colleges and various departments;
10. Innovative thinking for the setting up of a Meta University which would facilitate the sharing of learning resources from different universities by using the latest technologies;
11. Transitioning to the FYUP in DU, with regard to which many experts feel that sudden changes in the education structure demand wider consultations and careful implementation.
12. Introducing performance pay incentives as a reform measure to encourage better teaching and learning outcomes;
13. Undertaking independent assessments of learning achievements to examine the quality of education, which may serve as a starting point for the introduction of future educational policies. The setting up of an independent accreditation body for schools would also inform and empower parents to make the right choice for their child's schooling. An alternative could be the setting up of an independent body (such as a State Institute for Learning Assessment) that would study and assess the school-wise academic performances of students (from, say, Standard 3 upwards).

Annex 3.1

Annexure Table 3.1 gives the assumed distribution of population in 2020-21, as against the already existing distribution of population in 2009-10 by levels of education. The hypothetical distribution in 2020-21 assumes that the population is at least educated up to the primary level. It is clear that with a hypothetical distribution in 2020-21, the average number of years of schooling is 10.3 years. (For calculation, see Footnote 2 of the chapter). It has been noted in the text that the average number of ten years of schooling could be achieved through many pathways, assuming different distributions of population by levels of education. If the hypothetical distribution of the population assumed here is followed, then at the middle level, expansion has to take place by roughly 100 per cent, at the secondary and senior secondary levels by roughly 50 per cent, and at the tertiary level by roughly 20 per cent. It may be noted here that since in 2020-21, there would be an absolute increase in the population as well as that compared to the level of population in 2009-10, the capacity expansion would be a multiple of the capacity expansion envisaged above. The multiplier would depend on the extent of increase in the population in 2020-21 over the population in 2009-10. Thus, assuming that the population increases by 50 per cent, the capacity expansion then at the middle (including the primary level), secondary, and senior secondary and tertiary levels would have to be 150, 75 and 30 per cent, respectively. However, this method of arriving at capacity expansion represents a crude methodology. The exact capacity expansion necessitates a detailed planning exercise which would take into account the complete age cohort.

Annex Table 3.1

Assumed Distribution of Population in 2020-21, Against the Existing Distribution of Population in 2009-10 by Levels of Education

Educational Attainment	2009-10	2020-21	Capacity Expansion, Assuming the Existing (in per cent)	Capacity Expansion, Assuming a 50 per cent Population Increase in the Population (in per cent)
Illiterate	17.8	0		
Below the primary level	11.6	0		
Primary level	14.2	15		
Middle level	11.8	25	100	150
Secondary level	13.8	20	50	75
Senior secondary level	13.7	20	50	75
Tertiary level	17.1	20	20	30
Total	100.0	100		

4

Health and Healthcare

4.1. Introduction

It is widely acknowledged that health constitutes a core pillar of human development, and is a key indicator for assessing achievements in capability enhancements and well-being. The indicators of health serve as essential components of the Human Development Index (HDI) and the Multidimensional Poverty Index (MPI). Health outcomes are considered as useful measures of how development policies and interventions have reduced deprivations and bridged social disparities. Concerns on health thus stem from both implicit and instrumental premises. Good health is a cherished goal as it helps in realising human capabilities and thus contributes to well-being. Healthy people are more productive and their contribution augments economic development and fuels growing incomes. On the other hand, ill-health stifles the full realisation of psychological, social and economic capabilities, and has financial implications in terms of loss of income and productive time as well as the need to avail of medical care. Thus, the manner in which nations and regions influence the health outcomes of their populace through different policies and interventions often shapes their larger development prospects.

While policy-makers and the development community are well aware of the importance of good health, the real challenge lies in context-specific assessments of priorities and the utilisation of appropriate and efficient instruments in implementing required reforms. Often, preponderance with vertical programmes and target-driven approaches could fail to ensure an inclusive and equitable distribution of resources and sustainability of health programmes. Structural inequalities owing to disparities in income, education and living conditions lead to the inequitable use of public programmes and interventions, thereby making the health systems less responsive to the needs of vulnerable populations. Again, there always remains the tough balancing act for policy-makers between multiple challenges and fewer instruments (including fiscal prudence). Achieving inter-sectoral coordination and convergence, both within public agencies as well as across the diverse set of stakeholders, is always easier said than done, but has a significant bearing on the degree of responsiveness of health outcomes to policies and programmes.

The spate of reform measures during the last decade that have swept across health systems including in India, instil optimism that health policy-makers are increasingly becoming responsive towards evidence-based decision-making, keeping equity and efficiency central to their concerns. Recent such measures undertaken in India include: the National Rural Health Mission (NRHM) (launched in 2005), which has significantly revitalised rural health care delivery through a largely participatory, convergent approach of planning and decision-making; and recent initiatives in financial risk protection including the flagship Rashtriya Swasthya Bima Yojana (National Health Insurance Scheme), (started in 2008) of the Central Government, which provides cashless hospitalisation facilities to the poor and currently covers about 35 million families nationwide.[1]

The renewed recognition of the importance of the social determinants of health, and the emergence of universal coverage as the avowed milestone for health systems reflects adherence with the larger global thinking on health. A recent body of work needs mention as it has been instrumental in raising further awareness about health systems and policy. Marmot (2007) and Marmot *et al.* (2010) highlight the pathways in health systems 'from root causes to fair outcomes' to place equity in health and healthcare outcomes at the centre-stage of health system goals. They argue that a synergistic view is needed of how inequalities in basic living standards and opportunities constrain the attainment of good health, and equitable access to health services. They posit health outcomes in the larger context of socio-political and economic policy, and reaffirm the importance of health from the perspective of all-round human development.

The notion of universal coverage is conceptually identical. Its ultimate motivation is to eliminate inequity in all its manifestations from health systems by ensuring equitable service access, reducing avoidable and disproportionate risks of ill-health among the vulnerable populations, and extending adequate financial risk protection to ensure that health systems are fair, responsive, and effective. Universal coverage is considered to be the ideal pathway to progress and better outcomes for developing country health systems, and success stories from countries such as Thailand, Sri Lanka, Brazil and Mexico illustrate the same.[2] In India, the universal health coverage agenda has been significantly furthered by the constitution of a High-Level Expert Group (HLEG) by the

1. Data provided at the RSBY national web portal, Available at: *http://www.rsby.gov.in/*, Accessed on 17 July 2013.
2. For case studies on illustrations of the UHC concept, see HLEG (2011).

Planning Commission in 2011, to deliberate on the mechanisms for moving towards effective, equitable, and universal health coverage. In its Report (HLEG, 2011), the Group made a set of recommendations and prescriptions, some of which have been incorporated in the Twelfth Five Year Plan. This development raises hopes that health policy and programmes in India would increasingly take into consideration the conceptual moorings and initiate required reform measures to ensure good health for all at affordable costs.

This chapter draws its motivation primarily from the universal coverage paradigm, which has equity and quality central to its agenda. It reviews the health and healthcare scenario in Delhi, and presents a snapshot of the current trends in key population health indicators over the last decade. While assessing the financing aspect of healthcare, it focuses on the cost of illness and medical services, and evaluates the extent of financial risk protection. It discusses the challenges confronting the health system, and reviews the policy and programmatic responses introduced in recent years, trying, in effect, to identify the possible roadmap towards achieving effective and universal coverage of health services. It draws extensively from published official data and service statistics as well as household survey data, including those collected through a number of past studies conducted by the Institute for Human Development (IHD), including a recent People's Perceptions Survey (2013).

4.2. Health Scenario in Delhi – Status and Recent Trends

We commence with a quick look at the demographic scenario in Delhi, including the size, composition and characteristics of the population which constitute the main aspects of the health system. Delhi constitutes around 1.5 per cent of the national population of 1.22 billion (Census, 2011), with the state's share of the national population remaining almost constant over the last decade. It has a high population density of 11,297 persons per sq. km. (the highest in India), and a highly variable population base because of a nearly equal number of people commuting into Delhi every day for work and business as well as to seek medical care especially from the suburbs, predominantly from the new twin cities of Noida and Ghaziabad to the east and Gurgaon to the south in the neighbouring states of Haryana and Uttar Pradesh, respectively. All this makes it very difficult for planners and policy-makers to ascertain the actual demand for public health utilities.

Within the confines of the state's boundaries, however, the pace of demographic change has witnessed a clear deceleration. Over the last three Census periods (1991, 2001 and 2011), Delhi has registered a fall in the rate of growth of population. The decline in the decadal population growth by almost 27 percentage points (the highest decline registered across the country) indicates a slowing momentum of demographic changes. Fertility levels in Delhi have also been falling at a rapid rate with the total fertility rate at replacement levels of 1.7[3] (NFHS-3, 2005-06), clearly indicating that the state's population is heading towards stability.

4.2.1 Mortality

Overall, Delhi has shown significant improvements in its vital statistics pertaining to the population over the last three decades, demonstrated by the following developments:

- Persistent rise in the life expectancy, also across gender (Table 4.1): the expectancy of life at birth, a key component of the UNDP's HDI calculations, at 72 years, is better than the national average of 68, with females showing a higher level than males of almost 75 years. Since the 1990s, life expectancy levels in Delhi among both males and females have been better than the national average.

Table 4.1

Life Expectancy at Birth across Gender, Delhi and India 1990-2010

	Sex	*Life Expectancy at Birth*		
		1990	*2004*	*2010*
India	Male	59.3	63.6	65.4
	Female	60.6	66.5	68.4
Delhi	Male	65.7	68.3	71.7
	Female	68.9	71.9	74.2

Source: Calculated from life tables using age-specific death rates (ASDRs) from the Sample Registration System (SRS) Data Reports, relevant years.

- Gains in life years are reflected in the level of mortality in Delhi over the recent years, with reductions in the crude death rate (CDR)

3. The latest estimates on fertility in Delhi, according to the State Civil Registration System, 2012, is 1.8 (Communication from Directorate of Family Welfare, Department of Health and Family Welfare, GNCTD).

from 4.7/'000 in 2004 to 4.2/'000 in 2010 (SRS data reports, relevant years) being much better than the national averages for both the years considered (7.5/'000 and 7.2/'000, respectively). The overall mortality scenario in Delhi has also been much better than in the other three metro cities, with the city-state consistently recording the lowest death rate of approximately 4.5/'000 population throughout the last decade (SRS Statistical Report, 2009).

- Infant mortality in Delhi, at 28 (per '000 live births),[4] in 2011, remains one of the key indicators, which, however, falls short of being impressive.[5] This figure for the IMR and its pace of reduction pales in comparison to the corresponding figures in some larger states such as Maharashtra (25) and Tamil Nadu (22) (RGI, 2012), which also have substantial rural populations, higher levels of poverty and a less intensive network of public health infrastructure. In fact, the IMR in the city of Delhi (33 during 2004-09) was higher than in all the three other metros of Kolkata (25/'000), Mumbai (21/'000), and Chennai (19/'000) (RGI 2011).[6]

Delhi's commitment to reduce the IMR in a time-bound manner has been enshrined in the Delhi Development Goals (2006), or more recently by the Delhi State Health Mission, to 15 per 1000 live births by 2015 (DHDR, 2006). Calculations based on the present trend of IMR reductions from the SRS-based estimates clearly show that Delhi is still quite far from achieving the pegged goals (IMR of 15).[7] Over the period 2006-12, the IMR reduced annually at a rate of around 5.4 per cent. If such a pace can be termed as the 'business as usual' scenario, Delhi can only hope to reach the threshold of 15 in distant 2023 (Figure 4.1). In a 'deadline-set' scenario pegging the target year at 2015, the IMR would need to be reduced by almost 12 per cent annually. In a'doubling-up' scenario, reductions by about 10 per cent per annum would allow Delhi to reach the target IMR of 15 in 2018.[8] In this context, it would be helpful to understand a few details about the infant mortality scenario in Delhi, for example, where such deaths are clustered, and what steps need to be taken to achieve a faster pace of decline in the same. Demographers and health experts believe that reductions in the IMR require different interventions at different stages of its decline path. Reducing the IMR from very high levels (say around 80-100) would involve taking into account and addressing the incidence of deaths due to infectious diseases such as diarrhoea, pneumonia and other major killer diseases during infancy, and improving the coverage of institutional deliveries. However, the decline becomes more elastic at lower ranges, similar to the levels that Delhi is experiencing, (an IMR of 25-30). Accordingly, two areas of attention are imminent, viz., reducing deaths during the neo-natal period and universalisation of maternal and newborn care through formal, institutional systems.

Segregating infant deaths into early neo-natal deaths (within the first seven days of birth), late neo-natal deaths (between the first to the fourth week of life) and post-neo-natal deaths (age of 28 days to one year) can indicate the time periods in the life of an infant when mortality risks are clustered and are thus the highest. Unfortunately, such segregated data are not readily available from common sources such as the

4. Most recent (2011) SRS estimates (RGI, 2012).
5. Alternative estimates of IMR, from the Annual Report on Registration of Births and Deaths in Delhi, 2012, brought out by the Directorate of Economics and Statistics and the Office of the Registrar General, provides a figure of 23.9 infant deaths per 1000 live births for 2012. See the detailed report available at: *http://www.delhi.gov.in/wps/wcm/connect/73b95e00408f7b6db48cff1dfb6415f9/report+final.pdf?MOD=AJPERES&lmod=935641067&CACHEID=73b95e00408f7b6db48cff1dfb6415f9* (Accessed on 17 August 2013). Although, these two estimates (SRS and CRS) are not directly comparable due to the use of differing methodologies, and estimates based on Civil Registration System on which the DES estimates are based tend to be under-estimates of infant deaths (based on self-reported, or infant deaths in medical institutions only), the decline seems impressive. However, in recent years the CRS-based estimates have indicated an irregular decline, as a result of much could not unfortunately be made out of the DES estimates.
6. According to the latest SRS (October 2012) Report, the IMR of urban Delhi is 26/1000 live births, which is significantly higher than that of urban Maharashtra (17) and Tamil Nadu (19), and at an equal level with that of urban West Bengal and Karnataka.
7. The IMR reduction experience presents a better picture, if we consider the State CRS figures (22) for 2011; nevertheless, we retained SRS figures for a longer time-series and comparability with national patterns. Interestingly, if we consider the CRS level of 22 as the baseline value for the 'reduction–projections' shown in Figure 4.1, the IMR needs to be reduced by about 8 per cent annually, as compared to the present (SRS-based) rate of 5.4 per cent, and the required projected rate of 12 per cent annually to attain the goal of 15 by 2015.
8. Note that these projections are based on the IMR levels of 2011 for which the SRS figures are the latest available. If in the ensuing period, that is, 2011-13, the IMR has fallen by a faster rate, perhaps the trajectories would be slightly modified for each of these scenarios.

Figure 4.1

Projected Levels of Infant Mortality Rate and its Reduction for Delhi, Based on Observed Rate of Reduction* between 2006-12

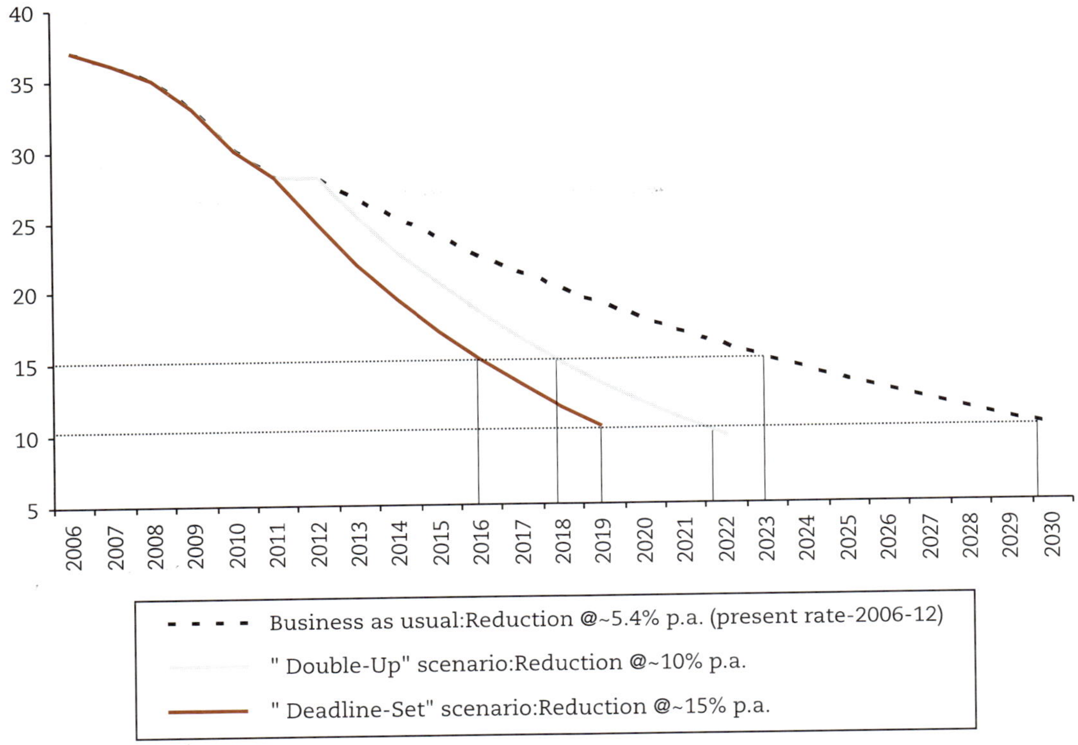

Note: *Based on SRS figures from 2006 to 2012.

Source: Calculated from the SRS-based IMR levels for Delhi, SRS Bulletins, relevant years.

Figure 4.2

Ratio of Neonatal/Postneotal Infant Deaths, Delhi 2001-2011

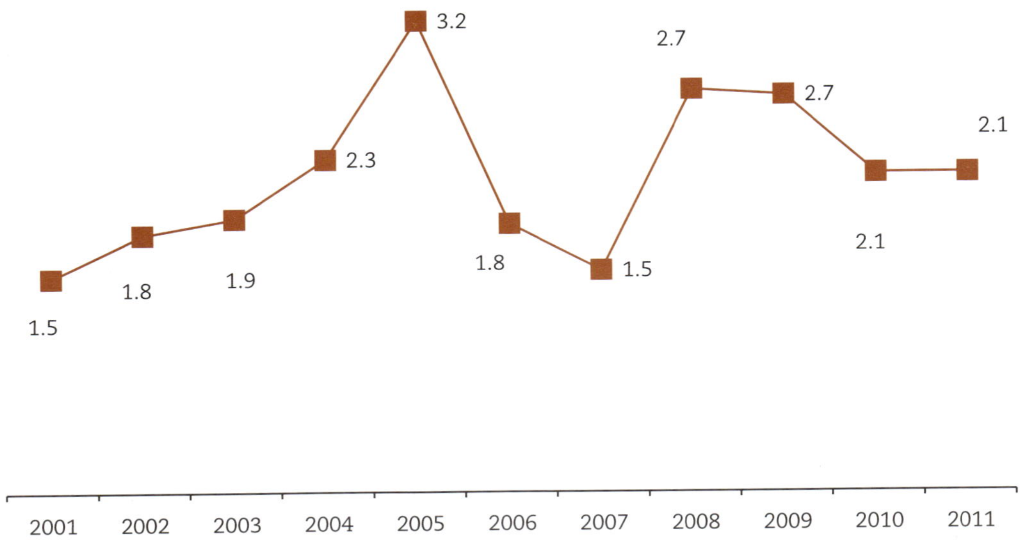

Source: Calculated from CRS data for Delhi, relevant years.

SRS.[9] A recent attempt[10] finds that in Delhi (Table 4.2), most neo-natal deaths take place during the first four weeks after birth (and are even more concentrated during weeks 2-4). The decline in infant deaths during the post-neo-natal period is much faster (62 per cent) as compared to the declines achieved during the neo-natal (35 per cent) and early neo-natal (26 per cent) periods.

Table 4.2

Components of Infant Mortality

Time Periods	*ENN*	*NN*	*PNN*	*Infant*
1981-86	24.3	36.9	30.4	66.2
1987-92	21.5	29.4	26.8	55.4
1993-98	24.3	29	17.6	46.1
1999-2005	17.9	24	11.5	35.2

Source: NIMS, ICMR and UNICEF (2012).

The predominance of neo-natal deaths is also evident from CRS data (DES, 2012a) on the reported number of infant deaths (Figure 4.2). For every single infant dying after completing the first month, there are almost two infants observed to be dying below the age of one month. The recent trends demonstrated by the incidence of neo-natal and post-neo-natal deaths in Delhi strongly indicate an urgent need for stressing on mortality risk reductions among infants aged less than a month. How fast and effectively would Delhi have to reduce its mortality risks among infants, in order to stay on track to reach its stated targets, crucially hinges on how the health system, in particular, and other stakeholders, in general, respond to the challenge of bringing down the levels of neo-natal mortality, along with the pace of such reductions.

Conventional proximate determinants of infant mortality include the household environment, maternal characteristics (mothers' education and age at childbirth), poverty and living conditions. One of the major challenges for arresting infant mortality pertains to deliveries conducted at home, which keep women out of the coverage of essential maternal health services. This aspect is elaborated in the next section yet it also needs to be stressed here that efforts aimed at reducing neo-natal mortality, and improving the survival prospects of infants need to ensure that all pregnancies are within the coverage of qualified, professional assistance, which is significantly instrumental in bringing down the risks of newborn deaths during the first few days and weeks after birth.[11] A few studies in India find a strong influence of socio-economic factors in explaining infant survival in urban settings (Goli *et al*., 2013). Despite evidence of weakening in recent years (Singh *et al*., 2011) the socio-economic disparities in childhood mortality, for example, are found to persist through indirect effect via factors such as mother's education. In another analysis, the Gini coefficient of child mortality (denoting socio-economic inequality) in Delhi was found to be quite high (seventh in an all-India ranking), although indicating a marginal decline during the early 1990s and mid 2000s (NIMS, ICMR and UNICEF, 2012).

Maternal mortality is another aspect of the vital statistics for population in Delhi that warrants attention. According to the state's Civil Registration System (CRS), which is the only regular information source for maternal deaths in the state, Delhi's performance in terms of reducing the maternal mortality rate (MMR) to below 100 deaths per 1,000,00 live births by 2015, and further to less than 50 by 2020, seems to be on track (DES, 2013). In 2012, the

9. Some estimates are available though within the reported hospitals, death data analysed by the Directorate of Family Welfare for the periods 2008-09 and 2009-10.

10. NIMS, ICMR and UNICEF, 2012.

11. In a stakeholder workshop organised at IHD in April 2013, as a part of the DHDR preparation exercise, to discuss the background paper (Mazumdar and Mazumdar 2013), which served as the basis for this chapter involving health policy-makers, medical professionals, academics and representatives of civil society groups and community-based organisations active in Delhi, a common concern raised by the health administrators and medical doctors was the issue of 'floating demand', that of sick infants and neonates born outside Delhi, mostly in the rural areas of the neighbouring states, coming to the state-run hospitals to seek treatment—which inflates the 'real' neo-natal mortality scenario in Delhi. In their opinion, such 'out-born' infants, are often from domiciliary deliveries, or other high-risk pregnancies, and often arrive at the hospitals at an advanced, futile state. Since such deaths get recorded in Delhi, the available figures constitute an over-estimation of the real infant and neo-natal mortality scenario. While such assertions may not be entirely invalid, anecdotal evidences also suggest that pockets of deprivation and low awareness levels, coupled with poor neo-natal care practices often lead to high risks for the newborn, more so for those residing in poor living conditions such as slums or the *Jhuggi Jhopdi* (*JJ*) clusters. In fact, while recognising such gaps in conventional service delivery systems and typical risk profiles, the Government has initiated a spate of measures targeting these vulnerable, high-risk groups. These include earmarking 200 beds in 14 selected hospitals catering mostly to infants, primarily those belonging to low-income neighborhoods, and assigning Accredited Social Health Activist [ASHA] workers to pre-identified families for delivering home-based newborn care, and proper capacity building of health workers (Directorate of Family Welfare, GNCTD, unpublished correspondence).

Figure 4.3

Decadal Trend of Estimated Maternal Mortality Ratio in Delhi (2001-2012)

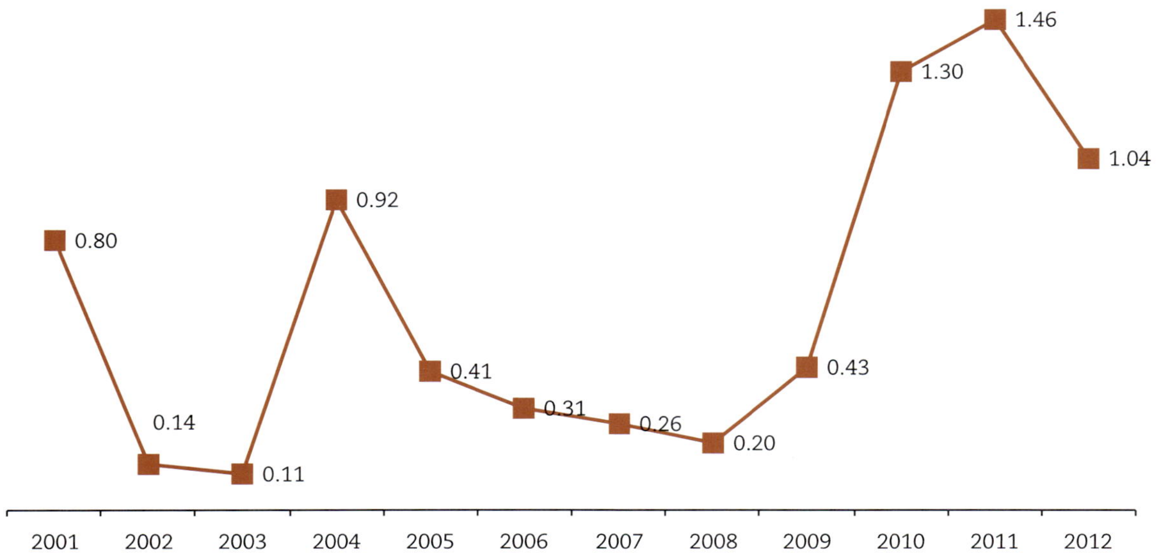

Source: Calculated on the basis of data given in Table (i), Vital Statistics by Sex, 2001-2012, DES, 2013.

CRS estimates put the MMR levels at 104, falling from about 130 in 2010 and 146 in 2011. The trends in MMR levels, based on the CRS data, are shown in Figure 4.3. It is not directly possible to account for the fall in MMR during the year 2011-12, in the absence of detailed data, while the spikes in 2010 and 2011 could be largely because of better reporting of maternal deaths due to conducting a higher proportion of deliveries in health facilities. Although the MMR estimates from CRS are not suitable for trend analysis and can be influenced by irregular fluctuations, one can expect these rates to even rise a little in the coming years with better reporting and ultimately levelling off as a result of higher coverage. Detailed studies based on verbal autopsy would allow for better analysis of the levels and risk factors associated with maternal deaths. In the absence of such detailed data, reductions in the MMR levels could at best be achieved and consolidated through proper screening of high-risk pregnancies, and ensuring that deliveries are monitored and conducted in health facilities. Additionally, basic and emergency obstetric care facilities need to be strengthened in health institutions, particularly those catering to the poor and economically weaker sections.

4.2.2 Causes of Death

As compared to other metros and even some other states, Delhi has a strong system of annual registration of total and institutional deaths. With the medical certification of causes of death made compulsory in 2003, by bringing in all government and private hospitals under the purview of the provision of 10(3) of Registration of Births and Death Act, 1969, the process of Medical Certification of Cause of Death (MCCD) in Delhi has shown remarkable improvements. The 'cause of death' data is a very useful source of information for understanding the levels and trends of different diseases responsible for deaths, which, in turn, also facilitates the current assessments of the burden of diseases. The latest Report on Medical Certification of Causes of Death (MCCD) in Delhi (DES, 2013), reports the major (identified) causes of death among infants to include septicaemia, slow foetal growth and foetal under-nutrition, birth asphyxia and other prenatal causes (DES, 2013). Pneumonia in infancy, which is generally considered to be a major killer disease among infants, contributes to a meagre share of institutional infant deaths. An unpublished analysis of infant death records from government hospitals reveals that in the case of nearly 24 per cent of the infant deaths, the proximate cause was septicaemia, 25 per cent were premature deliveries, 14 per cent were due to birth asphyxia, and 16 per cent were attributable to respiratory infections.[12] While most of these causes could be prevented through timely

12. Unpublished correspondence from the Directorate of Family Welfare, Department of Health and Family Welfare, GNCTD.

medical interventions and better newborn care, this segregation of the proximate causal factors for infant deaths indicates the gaps in reaching out to the mother during the pre-natal, natal and perinatal periods, with the required services.

The profiling of the major causes of death, as available from the 'Cause of Death' statistics from the 2011 Report on MCCD (DES, 2012b) points towards non-communicable diseases (that is, neoplasm, circulatory, injury or other external causes) as the reasons for a considerable proportion of total institutional deaths (36 per cent) in recent years, with an almost equal share across gender (36.9 per cent for males and 37.2 per cent for females). Nevertheless, infectious and parasitic diseases still account for about 15 per cent of the total recent institutional deaths, indicating an incomplete epidemiologic transition as far as the cause of deaths is concerned. Interestingly, respiratory illnesses, which are widely considered to be influenced significantly by exposure to and the quality of outdoor ambient air and indoor pollution, are responsible for only about 6 per cent of the reported deaths. Overall, nearly one-fourth of the deaths occur due to unspecified causes. Although it has not been discussed in detail here, it may be noted that disaggregating the MCCD data (DES, 2012b) by age for major 'killer' diseases, throws up a few interesting facets of the disease epidemiology in Delhi. First, among the major infectious diseases responsible for deaths, tuberculosis (TB) is the cause of the largest number of adult deaths in Delhi and pneumonia for children. Secondly, all the three major non-communicable diseases, that is, cancer, heart diseases and diabetes, showcase casualties in the prime productive ages of 45-64 years. A rising burden of such diseases having differential fatality rates across age groups (with a higher impact in the productive ages), could adversely affect life expectancy levels and have a considerable economic impact. However, being entirely sourced from published 'cause of death' statistics, disaggregating these data further to observe the socio-economic gradient in both mortality levels and its major causes is not possible.

4.2.3 Morbidity Levels and Patterns in Delhi

Information on health status and illnesses in India continues to remain rare in the absence of regular health surveys. The latest NSS 60th Round Survey on morbidity (2004-05), which is almost a decade old, reports the morbidity prevalence rate in Delhi at 16, and an incidence rate of 7, both of which are much lower than the national average. For more recent estimates on the health scenario and the pattern of the disease burden in the state, the hospital-based disease surveillance system in Delhi is a rich, but unexploited information source.[13] On the basis of the most recent year (2010) for which such hospital-based data on disease conditions is available, it has been found that more than two-thirds (67 per cent) of the reported cases sought treatment for infectious and communicable ailments, while the remaining were affected by chronic, non-communicable conditions (DHS, 2011). This clearly reflects the 'double burden' of both communicable and chronic diseases, indicating an incomplete epidemiological transition, which could be explained by the heterogeneity in the demographic and socio-economic composition of the population.

The burden of disease statistics further reveals that for communicable diseases (Figure 4.4), a major share is attributable to acute respiratory infections (43 per cent), followed by acute diarrhoeal diseases (23 per cent). For non-communicable diseases, on the other hand, cardiovascular problems including cerebrovascular diseases (16 per cent), hypertension (19 per cent), and ischemic heart disease (6 per cent) were the major ailments for which patients sought treatment. Another 20 per cent of the reported cases were accounted for by cancers and diabetes (combined for Type I and Type 2). Diseases related to the respiratory system such as asthma and bronchitis, also formed considerable proportions of the reported cases (8 per cent and 5 per cent, respectively). Notably, indicating a growing burden of injuries, nearly one-fifth of the reported cases were related to accidents and other traumas.

Non-communicable diseases also have significant human development consequences. Evidence suggests that contrary to common perceptions, most of the chronic, so-called 'lifestyle diseases' not only afflict the rich, but rather the poor also face disproportionate risks of exposure to such diseases and their risk factors with more severe welfare consequences (Kar *et al.*, 2010; Jeemon and Reddy, 2010; Reddy *et al.*, 2007; Misra *et al.*, 2001; Rastogi *et al.*, 2004). It is thus likely that a large contributor to

13. Given the fact that more than 95% of illness-episodes in Delhi get treated, a strong hospital information system, or disease surveillance system can be a cost-effective alternative to gain valuable insights into the burden of diseases, and their possible risk-factors. At present the Annual Report of the Directorate of Health Services, compiled by the State Bureau of Health Intelligence, is the only source of tabulated disease, and site-specific information. See DHS (2011) for the latest published Report.

Figure 4.4

Burden of Diseases in Delhi, 2011

Percentage Distribution of Communicable Diseases from Hospital Statistics, Delhi 2010

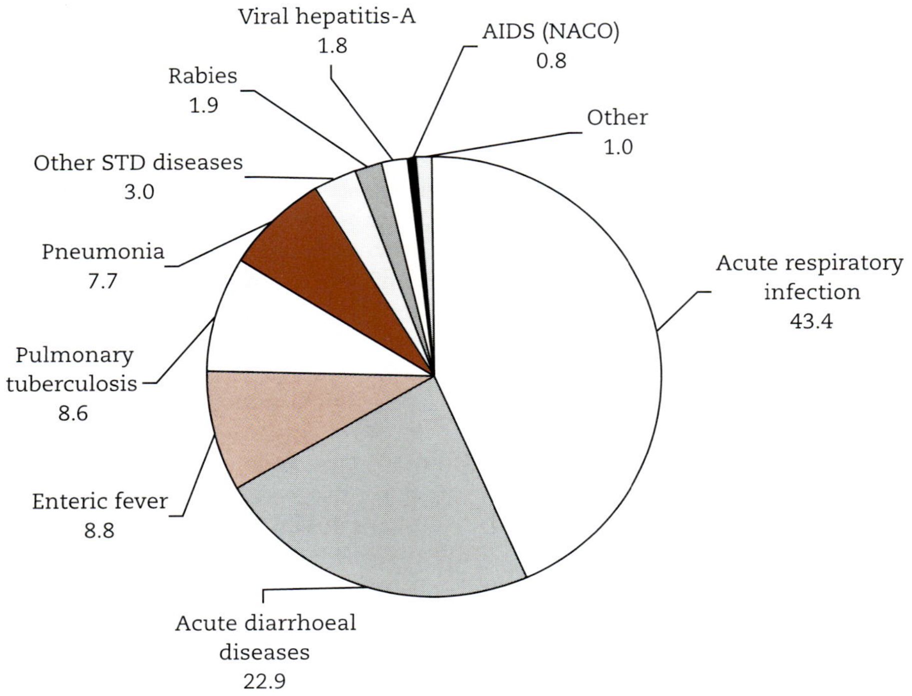

Percentage Distribution of Non-communicable Diseases, Accidents and Injuries from Hospital Statistics, Delhi 2010

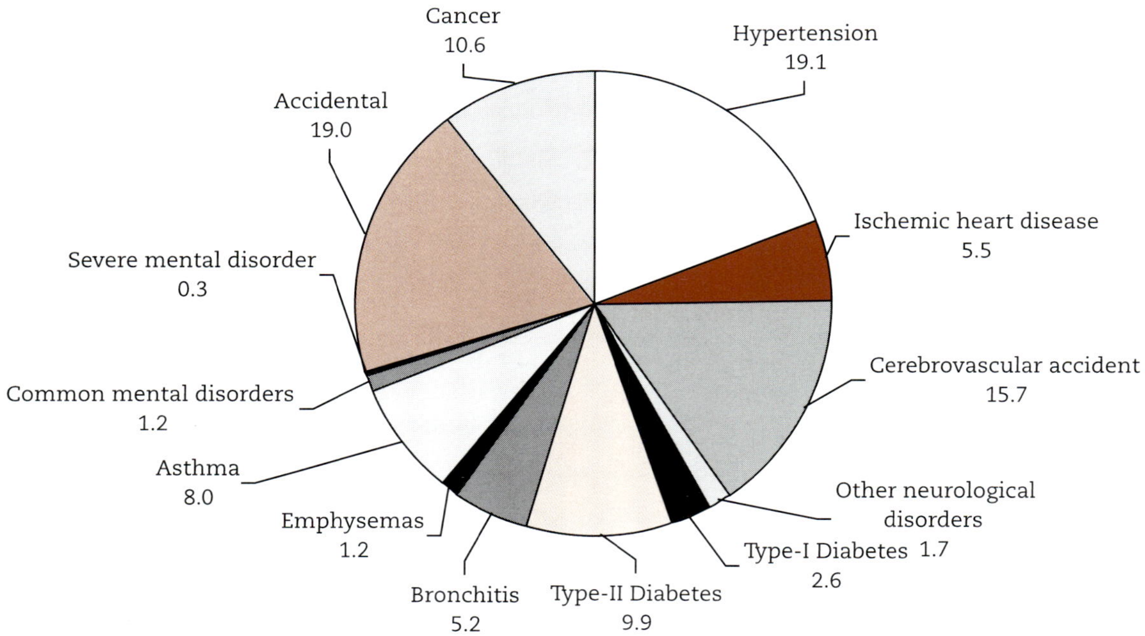

Source: DHS (2011).

the growing burden of chronic diseases in Delhi is the poor, less-educated population residing in slums and other low-income localities, with limited means to afford the economic impacts of chronic ailments, especially for the productive age groups. Thus, the need of the hour is to design appropriate policies and interventions for effectively managing non-communicable diseases, with a greater emphasis on the poor and socio-economically vulnerable population.

Recognising the rise in chronic diseases (lifestyle diseases), the State Government has adopted a holistic approach, focusing more on the preventive and promotive aspects, rather than the costlier option of curative care. The latest budget speech of the Chief Minister (2013) sums up the Government's focus on these key aspects through efforts to "... spread awareness of the insidious nature of lifestyle diseases.....people are encouraged to adopt healthy lifestyles".[14] A few recent initiatives by the State Government such as the setting up Tobacco Cessation Clinics, declaring 2013 as the 'Year of Awareness for Prevention and Early Detection of Diabetes and Hypertension', and observing the last day of every month as 'Dry Day' for not selling tobacco-related products, can be seen as steps in the right direction.[15] With a majority of the Indian Systems of Medicine and Homeopathy (ISMH) dispensaries now functioning along with the allopathic dispensaries, patients now have a larger choice of healthcare providers in a single facility. Although alternative therapies are being preferred (*ayurvedic*, *unani* and homeopathy), broad-based service packages are also being provided. What needs to be accorded due priority includes scaling up of efforts involving routine population-based screening, ensuring the availability of necessary drugs for chronic conditions under the essential drug lists, better monitoring mechanisms through surveillance systems, and emergency facilities for the management of critical conditions.

A related aspect in the context of the burden of diseases and the population health status is the growing share of the aged population, with unique geriatric health needs. Given Delhi's increasing life expectancy levels, and changing demographic structure following rapid decline in the fertility rates, addressing the health needs of the elderly is a key aspect towards improving the quality of life and well-being of the aged. The Twelfth Plan approach document specifies that a large proportion of the 60+ years population can be expected to suffer from a myriad chronic health conditions and that people in this category are in need of timely interventions. A number of studies (Mazumdar and Mazumdar, 2013) indicate a significant prevalence of functional limitations and psychiatric disorders amongst the elderly, apart from the common chronic and degenerative ailments reported by them. There is an emerging need for comprehensive geriatric care within the primary healthcare framework, to enable the elderly to access their health care needs. Although the response of the health system towards this emerging challenge has been lukewarm, it appears to be headed in the right direction. Some of the interventions that are already in place include facilities for screening aged persons for undiagnosed diseases and disabilities at dispensaries, introducing Senior Citizen Health Cards for keeping a record of such screenings, organisation of 'Sunday Clinics' exclusively for senior citizens in all government hospitals, and the promotion of greater social linkages through senior citizens' clubs.[16]

As this section illustrates, the health system in Delhi is beset with multiple challenges. Risks of infant, and particularly neo-natal deaths persist and necessitate the targeting of pockets wherein these death risks continue to be clustered. The burden of disease too indicates a mixed epidemiological scenario, similar to that observed in other fast-developing states and regions in the country. Acknowledging the socio-economic differentials that are likely to accompany such a transitional health scenario and the steady inflow of patients from across the country to seek care from the impressive health infrastructure network in the city-state, it is imperative for the provisioning and delivery of services to accommodate such need factors.

4.3. Coverage of Health Services and Equity in Access

4.3.1 Universal Health Coverage (UHC)

Universal Health Coverage (UHC) aims at ensuring the availability and accessibility of health services at affordable costs, which, in turn, lead to health

14. Page 20 (English version) of the Budget Speech of the Chief Minister of Delhi, Mrs. Sheila Dikshit, delivered during the presentation of the Annual Budget, 2013-14. The full text of the speech is available at: *http://delhi.gov.in/wps/wcm/connect/lib_finance/Finance/Home/Budget/Budget+2013-14/Budget+Speech++2013-14+English* (accessed online on 20th August, 2013)
15. Official communication from the Directorate of Health Services, GNCTD.
16. *Op. cit.*

Box 4.1

Twelfth Plan Recommendations on Universal Health Coverage (UHC)

Universal coverage is one of the cornerstones of the National Health Mission (NHM), following up on the footsteps of the NRHM. The Draft Twelfth Plan document acknowledges Universal Health Coverage (UHC) as a core component of social security. It reaffirms the key recommendations of the High-Level Expert Group (HLEG) on UHC which include:

1. Increase in public expenditure on health to 2.5 per cent of the GDP by the end of the Twelfth Plan and allocating 70 per cent of the expenses on primary healthcare.
2. Ensuring equitable access to medicines, vaccines and healthcare technologies, accompanied by an expanded Essential Drug List and rational drug use.
3. Strengthening of Human Resources for Health (HRH) through increased availability and dedicated training systems for frontline workers.
4. Offering of a National Health Package as an entitlement for all citizens to essential health services, with due considerations for equitable access in urban areas and focusing on the health needs of the urban poor.
5. Development of specialised Health Systems Management Cadres across the states, and the all-India and state level public health service cadres to strengthen the UHC system.
6. Encouraging the setting up of participatory Health Councils and improving access to health services for women, girls and other vulnerable groups.

Source: Adapted from Planning Commission, 2013 (p. 12, Box 20.1).

outcomes that are equitable across income groups, social status, occupations/livelihoods, religions, and ethnicity, or across any other disaggregation. The guiding principles are universalisation, equity, non-exclusion, non-discrimination, and comprehensive good quality healthcare. The underlying objective is to improve health outcomes across population groups, reduce financial risks associated with ill-health, and ensure equity in access. The World Health Assembly, 2005, led by the UHC movement, reiterated the need for all governments to strengthen their health systems, to ensure that people had access to health services and that they did not suffer financial hardships while paying for the same. Currently, about 30 middle-income countries across the world have already implemented programmes aimed at transitioning to the UHC, while many other low-income countries are in the process of doing so (Giedion *et al.*, 2013).

In India too, there is increasing affirmation of the principles and mechanics of universalising healthcare. This stems from a realisation that if implemented in a planned, synchronised and cost-effective manner, UHC holds the key to equitable and effective health coverage for all sections of the populace. The Planning Commission, in its reaffirmation of the recommendations of the High Level Expert Group on UHC (HLEG, 2011), has laid out the core strategies that would form the basis of health strategies in the Twelfth Five Year Plan (Box 4.1). The UHC vision in India proposes that every citizen be entitled to essential primary, secondary and tertiary healthcare services, guaranteed by the State (HLEG, 2011). As defined by the HLEG, it includes different dimensions of universal health assurance with appropriate quality including promotive, preventive, curative and rehabilitative health services at different levels. Besides being inclusive, all these services are slated to be delivered at affordable costs, so that people do not suffer financial hardships in the pursuit of good health (HLEG, 2011). The Government is mandated to act as not only the provider of health and related services, but also the guarantor and enabler. The vision is to ensure the coverage of health services for all citizens, through the financial protection of services at the primary, secondary and tertiary care levels, with a choice to access care from public sources or from contracted-in private providers. The reforms in the health sector needed to achieve this vision include health financing and financial protection; health service norms; human resources for health; community participation and citizens' engagement; access to medicines, vaccines and technology; and management and institutional reforms.

4.3.2 Health Service Coverage—The Building Blocks

The preparedness for UHC needs a well-built network of public health centres providing quality health services. In the NCT of Delhi, a number of agencies (both public and private) provide healthcare infrastructure and services. In the public sector, the major service providers include the Department of Health and Family Welfare, Government of NCT of Delhi (Directorate of Health Services and Directorate of Family Welfare), and three local government bodies, viz., Delhi Municipal Corporations (DMC), the New Delhi Municipal Council (NDMC) and the Delhi Cantonment Board (DCB). In addition, there are health facilities and institutions operated by the Central Government and different government departments and agencies. Several non-government organisations (NGOs) and a vibrant private sector also provide healthcare services, which are coordinated by the Directorate of Health Services through a set of regulations and guidelines. The private entities in healthcare vary widely, ranging from NGOs and charitable institutions targeted towards the poor to private sector super-specialty hospitals equipped with state-of-the-art international standard facilities. An amorphous, parallel market for healthcare, manned by a motley mix of unqualified, informal medical practitioners or *quacks*, traditional healers and therapists also serves a section of the population, in the lanes of the urban villages (*gaons*) or the JJ colonies and slums, which represent diverse cultures and are home to a steady stream of migrants from other states.

Adequacy of Service Coverage

The public sector health facilities in Delhi are organised in a typical hierarchical manner, with service norms that are specific to a largely urban population. Primary Health Centres or urban PHCs provide basic healthcare services while following a proper referral system.[17] With the State Government and other agencies realising the importance of universal coverage as far back as 2006, the coverage of the unserved areas became a priority intervention under the Delhi State Health Mission, supported by the Government of India (GOI) under the National Rural Health Mission (NRHM). Through this activity, 56 new centres have been opened, covering around three million of the hitherto unserved/underserved population for the provision of basic primary healthcare. These are known as 'Seed Primary Urban Health Centres' (PUHCs) and are subsequently expected to be subsumed into more comprehensive structures. All these PHCs are equipped with basic laboratory facilities, and offer a variety of services including reproductive healthcare, immunisation, family planning, general OPDs, and referral services. The seed PUHCs and certain dispensaries have also started their outreach activities in vulnerable locations, with the help of Auxiliary Nurse Midwives (ANMs) and Accredited Social Health Activists (ASHAs). The aim of these activities is to ensure outreach services in all areas having vulnerable populations. The MCD operates Maternal and Child Welfare (MNCW) centres, with a large pool of ANMs[18] and ASHAs[19] engaged in outreach services that are specifically concerned with maternal and child health. For the smaller unserved clusters requiring outreach activities in primary health services, an efficient network of mobile health clinics was operationalised in 1989, and a present, there are 90 such clinics, of which 77 cover JJ clusters while 13 cover construction sites. A total of 430 locations are currently being covered, with half of the clinics being run through PPP initiatives launched in collaboration with several NGOs. Over the last five years, more than two million patients have been attended to every year at these clinics, making these mobile health facilities significant additions to the conventional PHCs. Mobile dispensaries also offer various services including basic healthcare, family welfare, child immunisation, and health education, while providing medical assistance to certain vulnerable groups, and during large religious gatherings and certain occasions such as *melas*, sports events, and sudden disease outbreaks. In recent initiatives, mobile clinics have reached out to the under-served but high-risk groups by providing services in night shelters, and among the homeless population at certain marked sites. In addition, the MCD runs 29 mobile clinics with the same objective. Similarly, in order to cover important yet traditionally under-served segments of the population, such as school-going children and adolescents, the School Health Scheme (under the rubric of the *Chacha Nehru Sehat Yojana*) of the

17. These are often referred to interchangeably as dispensaries, government health centres, or Delhi Government dispensaries.

18. ANMs are employed as unique outreach workers in Delhi. The efficient functioning of ANMs can help in ensuring better accountability and monitoring, and help prevent duplication or overlapping due to the presence of a number of different supervising agencies/authorities.

19. Delhi is the first state in India to have an urban ASHA initiative. This also offers ASHAs incentives for increasing their motivation, retention and participation in the RCH programme.

Box 4.2

Chacha Nehru Sehat Yojana **(School Health Schemes)**

The School Health Scheme in Delhi was launched in the year 1979, initially in six schools targeted to improve the health and nutrition status of children and to provide them with useful education on hygiene. It has grown to its present proportion of 104 School Health Clinics operating across the districts in Delhi. The specific services offered through these clinics relate to the promotion of positive health, prevention of diseases, early detection, diagnosis, treatment of disease, and referral services to higher health centres for the individuals who require further treatment and management. The school health clinics are set up in school premises for easy accessibility specially meant for children studying in government and government-aided secondary schools (DHS, 2013). Each clinic serves a cluster of 8-10 schools located within a radius of 8-10 km., and targets about 10,000 children. Each of the districts has one special referral centre for services related to the eye, ear, nose, throat and dental treatment of the children who are referred from their respective school clinics. School-going children, who are not covered by any regular school health clinic, are covered under specific mobile clinics set up for them. Under this scheme, approximately one million students were screened for diseases, deficiencies and disabilities, 20,000 students were provided free spectacles, more than 50,000 students have been referred for various treatments, 2.7 million children were dewormed in a single day and 27,046 were given the TT vaccine while and health talks given to 25265 students.

Source: Different official publications and periodic reports of DHS, GNCTD.

Government offers an example of a successful experiment in the area of healthcare (see Box 4.2).

The dispensaries run by the DHS and other government bodies act as frontline health outlets, providing treatment for common ailments, essential medicines, and a number of preventive and health-promoting activities. These dispensaries are envisioned to play a key role in the bottom-up planning and development approach for the health sector. According to the latest available statistics on primary health facilities in Delhi (see Annexure table 4.1), 671dispensaries are directly run by the state and the three local governments.[20] With a population base of 16.7 million, a simple back-of-the envelop calculation yields an estimate of about 1.85 dispensaries for a population of 10,000, or roughly about one primary level facility for a population of 25,000 or 5000 families. The inclusion of the 746 additional primary health facilities, which however exclusively serve certain specific categories of the population such as government and public sector employees, and defence personnel, pushes up the ratio to about 4 health facilities for a population of 10,000. However, these ratios mask the actual availability across habitations/areas, given that primary health facilities are not uniformly spread across all areas/localities.[21] Being the first point of care, primary level clinics in Delhi need to respond effectively and efficiently to the growing demand for healthcare in the city.[22] These facilities need to be strengthened through systematic planning – for setting up new facilities and augmenting the functioning of the existing ones – by focusing on locality specific services and required capacities.

At the secondary and tertiary levels, Delhi can boast of a large pool of hospitals run by different government bodies. Apart from handling the usual patients, these hospitals provide emergency services and surgical care, and work as higher level referral facilities for the primary level dispensaries

20. The 671 dispensaries are organised as follows: 317 allopathic dispensaries/health posts (256 run directly by the State Government, including 57 seed PUHCs, and 61 run by the three local urban local bodies [ULBs]) and 354 AYUSH dispensaries (among these, the State Government directly operates 35 *ayurvedic*, 97 homeopathic and 17 *unani* dispensaries) (*Source*: Official Communication dated 3rd July from Health and Family Welfare Department, GNCTD).

21. In a pioneering attempt, the DHS has mapped all the government health facilities for each district and produced a set of GIS-based maps which are available online at *http://www.delhi.gov.in/wps/wcm/connect/DoIT_Health/health/our+services/map+info+delhi+govt.+hospitals*. The maps clearly indicate that primary level health facilities are highly localised in most districts. A drawback of the maps, however, is that they are not overlaid with other demographic and spatial details such as ward level population concentrations, types of localities, etc., which would allow the proper assessment of spatial distribution adjusted for the need factors.

22. Since 1998, 122 new allopathic government dispensaries and PUHCs have been opened till date; another 18 are currently at various stages of planning and implementation. An estimated 1.20 crore (12 million) patients are treated annually in the government dispensaries at present. (Source: Communication received from the State Health Intelligence Bureau, Directorate of Health Services, DHFW, GNCTD).

Box 4.3

The Delhi 'Model' of Rational Drug Use

Realising the crisis situation in terms of access to drugs faced by the patients visiting government health outlets and their dissatisfaction with the quality of free drugs offered by dispensaries and hospitals, the Government of Delhi adopted a comprehensive Drug Policy in 1994. Delhi was and still is one of the few states to have a policy that targets the availability and accessibility of free drugs for those in need. The onus of this lies with an NGO, the Delhi Society for the Promotion of Rational Use of Drugs (DSPRUD), which works in close collaboration with the Delhi Government and other important stakeholders. The DSPRUD's first recommendation of an Essential Drugs List (EDL) came into existence in 1997; this helped in setting up a centralised, pooled, procurement system of drugs and influenced their rational use. The EDL is mandated for revision every two years. The financial sustainability of drug purchase is ensured by adopting a rigorous selection of suppliers, having a minimum annual threshold turnover and by introducing Good Manufacturing Practice inspections to protect the quality of supply. The bulk purchase of prudently selected EDL drugs is estimated to save almost 30 per cent of the annual drug bill of the Government of Delhi. This further facilitates the procurement of more drugs and has improved availability in more than 80 per cent of the health facilities. Today, with a significant quantum of funds incurred for procuring medicines from the EDL, the Government of Delhi has become one of the largest purchasers of medicines in India. Its drug stock is well distributed among patients, with 80 per cent of the prescriptions complying with the EDL, and 70-95 per cent of the patients reporting receiving the prescribed drugs. The 'Delhi Model' is certainly a success story of free and quality drug access and distribution, which has been achieved with minimal additional expenditure, but by implementing major changes in the managerial system.

Source: Chaudhury *et al.*, 2005.

functioning across the districts.[23] In an important move to promote equity in access for private hospitals including the super-speciality segments, 44 private hospitals (built on land made available to these agencies at concessional rates by the State Government) are required to provide free treatment to patients from the economically weaker sections (EWS). These hospitals are mandated by legislation to reserve at least 25 per cent of their out-patient consultations and 10 per cent of their in-patient admissions for the EWS category, as also approximately 650 free beds and 100 critical care beds. Furthermore, in a recent directive, all health institutions in the state, irrespective of their being under the purview of the public or private sector, are bound by law to attend to all medical emergency cases brought to them (especially victims of crimes and or road accidents).[24] This is indeed a welcome directive and consistent with the provisions of universal coverage for medical emergencies.

The latest data provided for this Report by the Directorate of Health Services indicates that government hospitals offer 24,181 functional beds (out of a total number of 25,982 sanctioned as in July 2013). Additionally, a total number of 19,838 functional beds are available at private or voluntary organisations, nursing homes/hospitals (DHS, 2013). At present, 111 hospitals run directly by the state and the three local bodies are available for everyone in need of these services, irrespective of any qualifying criteria, thereby putting the average population served per hospital bed in Delhi at 395. Including only the beds in the public sector, the average population served works out to be 720, and is the seventh highest in the country as of 2012 (ibid.). Notably, as also in the case of primary health clinics, a few public sector hospitals are either restricted to only a limited group of residents (such as Central/State Government employees, public sector unit (PSU) employees, etc.), or those working in formal enterprises (such as the ESIC hospitals). The very notion of universal coverage implies unrestricted access to services, which, under the present service organisation norms, are only

23. As in 2012, the Government of Delhi had 37 hospitals functioning under the administrative control of the Department of Health and Family Welfare. Apart from this, the MCD runs 61 hospitals, offering a wide range of services across different medical streams. Details of the hospitals run by the other agencies are as follows: NDMC, 4, DGHS, 7, CGHS, 3, Department of AYUSH, 3, the Railway Ministry, 2, the Defence Ministry, 3, ESI Corporation, 4, and autonomous bodies under the Ministry of Health and Family Welfare, 2. In addition, there are 124 public hospitals in Delhi, and approximately 856 hospitals run by the private sector (as in 2012). (Source: Official Communication dated 3rd July from Health and Famly Welfare Department, GNCTD)

24. Ref. GO, numbered F.24/20/2003/NH/DHS/HQ/15341-018, 16047-219, 16227-238 , dated 21 February 2013.

available to a minority. A rethinking of the viability of these 'exclusive' criteria, given the prevailing shortfall in the available health facilities and the targeted goal of the Government of NCT of Delhi to provide three hospital beds per 1000 people, is thus imperative. As per the Twelfth Plan Approach Paper, the State Government plans to add 14,302 new hospital beds across both the public and private sector hospitals, during the period 2012-17 to reach a bed–population ratio of 3 per thousand by 2017 (at a projected population of 19 million of the NCT of Delhi). While such expansion plans are needed to meet the growing need and demand for health services, they also require supportive policies and efforts by other agencies,[25] which are directly or indirectly involved in the healthcare sector.

The availability of hospital beds in Delhi has almost doubled during the last 15 years, from 24,025 beds in 1997 to 44,019 beds in 2013, with 13 new hospitals added over the last 10 years. In spite of pressing problems such as the availability of land, the Government is moving ahead with 19 new hospitals, which are at various stages of planning and implementation (DHS, 2013). At present, the state government runs 39 hospitals, of which 6 hospitals[26] have been recognised as Centres for Excellence for the high quality of services they provide, and for serving as the benchmarks for secondary and specialty care. While such expansion has undoubtedly added substantially to the scale of service provision, certain undesirable consequences of a heavier secondary and tertiary level have also emerged. Often, referral mechanisms are broken with a bye-passing of primary clinics by patients seeking services in the bigger hospitals, with a significant proportion of them arriving from neighbouring states. Apart from leading to overcrowding and efficiency losses, this also adversely affects the quality of services.

25. A major challenge with regard to expansion stems from the non-availability of appropriate land in Delhi. As mentioned by the Directorate of Health Service, many similar projects are awaiting clearance from the Delhi Development Authority (DDA).This involves the availability of adequate and suitable sites for the construction of new hospitals, which the DDA would have to allocate, and the requirement for higher FAR to enhance hospital buildings and facilities.

26. These include the: Institute of Liver and Biliary Sciences (ILBS), Delhi State Cancer Institute (DSCI), Maulana Azad Institute of Dental Sciences (MAIDS), Institute of Human Behaviour and Allied Sciences (IHBAS), Ch. Brahm Prakash Ayurvedic Charak Sansthan (CBPACS), and Chacha Nehru Bal Chikitsalaya (CNBC).

Availability of Healthcare Providers[27]

In terms of the adequacy of health professionals and the larger health workforce, the scenario in Delhi is quite grim.[28] If the population figures for 2011 are considered for the NCT of Delhi, a paltry 2 healthcare providers were available for a population of 10,000. The scenario remains much the same across all the districts. The manpower planning for the healthcare sector in Delhi thus needs to be at an entirely different scale if the state aims to achieve universal coverage.

In 2012, there were 6533 doctors in government hospitals across different streams and types (DHS, 2012), converting into 3.89 doctors per 10,000 population (ibid.).[29] This is a rough estimate of doctor availability in secondary and tertiary healthcare and needs more refined data with appropriate disaggregation (streams of medicines and types of hospitals), in order to assess the actual availability of doctors in general practice in the government sector. These also include specialists and other categories which, in reality, are not available as part of the general practice, thereby further lowering the ratio. Officials and policy-makers in the State Government health department too admit the challenge of ensuring an adequate number and distribution of the health workforce in the state, which, however, remains crippled with a weak supply chain and shortage of manpower. There is an even greater need

27. All calculations in this section are based on the figures provided by the Directorate of Health Services in the recent official publication, HMIS reports, Annual Reports (such as DHS, 2012) and personal communications from officials of the Department of Health and Family Welfare, GNCTD, unless otherwise stated.

28. In the absence of any internationally acceptable gold standard for assessing the sufficiency of the health workforce available, WHO maintains that about 23 healthcare professionals (counting only physicians, nurses and midwives) are required and consistent with achieving adequate coverage rates for 'key primary healthcare interventions prioritised by the Millennium Development Goals' (WHO Health Statistics, 2009, Table 6, Health Workforce, Infrastructure and Essential Medicines, WHO 2009). Available online at: *http://www.who.int/whosis/whostat/EN_WHS09_Table6.pdf*, The Human Resources Background Paper I of the Universal Health Coverage India Group maintains a slightly different ratio of 24:5. See Rao, K.D. (undated), "Situational Analysis of the Health Workforce in India", Available at: *http://uhc-india.org/uploads/RaoKD_SituationAnalysisoftheHealthWorkforceinIndia.pdf* . Last accessed on 30th April, 2013

29. The conventional indicator of the doctor–population ratio, however, only provides a gross idea about the availability of physicians, while the 'actual' availability needs to be calculated by taking into account the type of specialised services provided by doctors of different categories, as they often do not attend to the health needs falling beyond their specialty.

for these services at the primary care level, where only two medical officers, on an average, attend to as many as 400 patients per day. The cumulative number of OPD/emergency patients visiting the Delhi Government hospitals/dispensaries was over 33 million in 2011-12, and over five lakh patients were admitted in Delhi Government hospitals.[30] In terms of sheer numbers, the above figures are almost twice the population of Delhi.

Some measures have been initiated to tackle the dearth of available health workforce such as outsourcing of non-clinical services (for example, sanitation and security of hospitals and dispensaries) and partial contracting-in of paramedics (such as nursing staff, laboratory technicians, OPD registration services, oxygen and other equipment suppliers and maintenance persons). However, even these measures have largely failed to compensate for the short supply of key personnel such as resident technicians (radiologists, anaesthetists, etc.).Close to 40 per cent of the sanctioned posts for medical officers, and 20 per cent for other support staff in health facilities that are directly run by the State Government remain vacant.[31] The scarcity of the health workforce is likely to adversely impact the quality of service provision. More efficient solutions, involving both short and long-term strategies, are needed to meet the growing demand and service expansion, and for ensuring the quality of services being delivered. This Report notes a few possible options in this direction including allowing teaching facilities in some of the larger hospitals, hiring retired physicians, and rotating shifts/operating hours for providing health facilities.

Access to Medicines—The 'Free Medicines for All' Mechanism

In India, the high prices and poor availability of medicines, and low affordability amongst the patients are some of the key barriers to access to treatment (Cameron, *et al.*, 2011). Further, high out-of-pocket expenses (OOPE) on medicines are often responsible for increasing health expenditures and consequently even impoverishment among the consumers of healthcare services. Thus, poor availability and unreliable quality of drugs and public health facilities force people to seek treatment and purchase medicines from the unregulated private sector, often at inflated costs (Selvaraj and Karan, 2009; Also see Garg and Karan, 2009.) Recent policy statements have identified inefficient and iniquitous financing mechanisms, high drug prices, faulty procurement and distributional policies, irrational medicine use and the lack of adequate regulations as the major barriers affecting Access to Medicines (ATM). They recommend the implementation of the 'free essential medicines for all' programme throughout the country,[32] which is being proposed as a way of ensuring regular, equitable and affordable access to quality medicines for all under the universal health coverage (UHC) agenda.

In Delhi, the efforts of the Government to ensure universal coverage and equitable access of drugs by providing both generic and branded drugs free of cost through the network of health facilities to all patients, irrespective of any criteria, is a strong step towards universal coverage and ensuring equitable access to medicines. It also facilitates lower treatment costs, and financial risk protection, especially for the economically weaker sections. Aided by a strong civil society movement (Box 4.3), the so-called 'Delhi Model' remains a pioneering example of rational drug use based on a responsive, realistic essential drug list, efficient procurement and distribution policies, and stringent quality monitoring systems. In fact, Delhi is one of the first states to have a Drug Policy dating back to 1994. Government facilities at the primary, secondary and tertiary levels are also mandated to provide essential medicines free of cost to all patients. These medicines are procured on the basis of the Essential Medicine Lists (EML) suggested by the expert committee and a strong system of review,[33] distinct for both dispensaries

30. Communication received from DoHFW, GNCTD.

31. Recently, governmental action for augmenting the recruitment process through the state cadre formalised through UPSC and contractual engagements through the Delhi State Health Mission (under the NRHM) has narrowed this gap significantly (Source: Official Communication dated 13th August from Health and Famly Welfare Department, GNCTD).

32. See Chapter 2, "Access to Medicines, Vaccines and Technology, in High-Level Expert Group Report on Universal Health Coverage for India", Available at: *http://planningcommission.nic.in/reports/genrep/rep_uhc0812.pdf.* Also see, for the Recommendations on 'Access to Medicines' by Working Group-4 (WG-4) of the Planning Commission. *http://164.100.47.5/newcommittee/reports/EnglishCommittees/Committee%20on%20Health%20and%20Family%20Welfare/45th%20report.pdf;* For the detailed report of the Parliament Standing Committee on Health, and *http://planningcommission.nic.in/aboutus/committee/wrkgrp12/health/WG_4drugs.pdf* for the report of the Planning Commission Working Group (WG-4) on drugs.

33. They are selected with due regard to public health relevance, evidence of efficacy and safety, and comparative cost-effectiveness. This list is a dynamic list and is revised every two years. The procedures for updating the list are in line with the WHO-recommended process for developing clinical practice guidelines. Its key components comprise a systematic approach to collecting and reviewing evidence

Box 4.4

Recent Measures and Strategies towards Inclusive Service Delivery and Effective Coverage in Delhi

- Encouraging holistic healthcare through lifestyle modifications and an integrated effort to reduce tobacco consumption. Dry days for tobacco-related products being observed on the last day of every month.
- Sunday Clinics offering for specialised geriatric care in designated hospitals; introduction of the Senior Citizen Health Cards as a part of the health screening of the elderly at dispensaries.
- Allowing a wider basket of choices—the cafeteria approach—of health service types; most of the ISMH dispensaries now function at buildings of allopathic dispensaries.
- Address public health emergencies such as risks of dengue through a multi-disciplinary, public health approach involving system-wide actors (such as the Dengue Task Force) and the use of government hospitals as sentinel surveillance centres. Strengthening of disease surveillance systems in hospitals and across communities.
- Introduction of a number of measures to control and treat tuberculosis (TB) such as free diagnosis and treatment for MDR-TB, TB control services in night shelters for the homeless, and empowering widows of TB patients to serve as community DOTS providers.
- Stress on behaviour change communication to contain the spread of non-communicable diseases (NCDs); setting up of a dedicated diabetes care unit at the Guru Tegh Bahadur Hospital and augmentation of dialysis facilities through the public–private–partnership (PPP) mode.
- Provision of quality 'home to hospital care' in an equitable way whereby the Centralised Accident Trauma Services (CATS) already run 151 ambulances across Delhi free of cost, and 100 more ambulances are slated to be added during the current financial year.

Source: Communications and awareness/publicity documents of the Department of Health and Family Welfare, Government of NCT of Delhi.

and hospitals. However, the inferences that can be drawn from the existing policy documents (such as the Directorate of Health Services Annual Reports), and the available official statistics do not allow assessments about the scale of coverage, or a disaggregated view of the benefits accruing across socio-economic groups. One of the major limitations in this sphere is the paucity of empirical studies for assessing the impact of equitable service access resulting from these policy measures. Clearly, it is imperative to conduct further research on these issues.

Thus, in Delhi, the movement towards universal coverage continues to be a formidable challenge, primarily due to supply side imbalances (the scale of physical infrastructure and health manpower), and the burgeoning demand. Nevertheless, the State Government has launched a number of sector-specific, issue-based programmes and interventions to address the specific needs of certain population groups or to cater to unique disease or service delivery requirements. Some of the recent measures among these are summarised in Box 4.4. The impact of the recent measures in terms of improving service delivery, increasing the quantum of health facilities for addressing shortages in service availability, compensating for the deficit of human resources through alternative means, is discussed in the following sections. These measures have helped improve reliance on public health facilities and benefited vulnerable groups through increased utilisation levels. The consolidation of these gains, and the continued commitment to achieve universal coverage necessitate a significant scaling-up of the existing services, backed by key policy measures such as the easy availability of drugs and diagnostic services for ensuring risk protection.

---

and a transparent development process with several rounds of review (see "The Concept of Essential Medicines", Government of Delhi, Available at: *http://delhi.gov.in/wps/wcm/connect/bde05d8041c46b66ab43fb08d0e5d97a/THE+CONCEPT+OF+ESSENTIAL+MEDICIN ES.pdf?MOD=AJPERES&CACHEID=bde05d8041c46b66ab43fb08d0e5d97a*, Accessed on 8 April 2013). At present, the EML in Delhi is based on 2010 recommendations put forward by the expert committee, which involves a selected range of medicines to be procured by the Central Drug Procurement Agency, for consumption at both the levels of government dispensaries and hospitals.

4.3.3 Service Utilisation Patterns and Barriers to Access

The usage patterns of healthcare services constitute a core aspect of any health system. An assessment of the different barriers to service access is necessary for identifying the optimal pathways needed for extending universal coverage. The health service utilisation for in-patient and out-patient care in Delhi has been studied here by using data from the NSS 60th Round on morbidity (2004-05) and three household surveys conducted by the Institute of Human Development (IHD), in Delhi over the period 2011-2013. In 2004-05, the morbidity prevalence in Delhi was about 1727 per 1 lakh persons (1.6 per cent ailing within a 15-day reference period), with an estimated 2.53 lakh hospitalised cases. As compared to national averages, it reflected a relatively better health profile for the residents of Delhi (DES, 2006). The NSS 60th Round data (2004-05) brings forth another important observation with regard to the public/private service mix in the state. The hospitalised care sought by patients from public institutions in both rural and urban Delhi—46 per cent and 59 per cent, respectively—was higher than the corresponding national figures of 42 per cent and 38 per cent, respectively. However, the service utilisation for non-hospitalised ailments reverses the above pattern, with only 23 per cent of the residents in urban Delhi reportedly seeking treatment from public facilities, which is marginally better than the corresponding figure of 19 per cent for India overall (NSSO, 2006).

However, recent household surveys conducted by IHD indicate a growing reliance by a majority of Delhi's population on the public sector for their healthcare needs. This has also been brought out in the findings of the IHD-SDTT Survey (2011) and the recent Perceptions Survey (2013).[34] Some of the main findings of these surveys conducted by IHD are as follows:

First, independent of the type of services (inpatient or outpatient) used, there is a growing reliance on government health facilities, as the '*most preferred option*' or '*habitual choice*', which is a probable testimony to the State Government's efforts to facilitate better access to and utilisation of public health facilities, especially during the last decade. Nearly 60 per cent of the respondents reported seeking treatment from government institutions during their most recent use (Table 4.3). In order to elicit household preferences on the utilisation of health facilities, during the second survey, respondents were also asked about their usual or habitual preference for health services, irrespective of actual usage. Two-thirds of the respondents indicated their preference for public health facilities (hospitals, clinics and dispensaries), while only 58 per cent preferred private physicians and clinics.[35]

Second, the scenario is more positive in terms of the socio-economic gradient in service utilisation patterns. The IHD-SDTT survey, focusing primarily on the low-income population groups with vulnerable livelihoods, reports a strong reliance of the poor households on public hospitals, and to some extent, on informal providers. Amongst the households reporting illness (of any members during the year preceding the survey), 51 per cent sought treatment (both ambulatory and hospitalisation services) from public health facilities, while only 27 per cent sought the services of qualified private providers (Kumar *et al.*, 2012). The Perceptions Survey also clearly brings forth the socio-economic gradient in the treatment-seeking behaviour of households in Delhi (Table 4.3). The poor and vulnerable households identified using multiple yardsticks (that is, household income categories, household asset ownership, low-paid occupations, education of the household head, locality and an aggregate vulnerability index),[36] which demonstrate a much higher utilisation of public health services (based on their last experience of health services usage). In contrast, a majority of the households having lower scores as per the aggregate

34. The IHD-PPS survey refers to a Public Perceptions Survey conducted by IHD in 2013 specifically for preparing the Second Delhi Human Development Report (DHDR). The survey, details of which are provided in Chapter 1 has also collected information on a few parameters pertaining to health service access, use, quality and financing.
The IHD-SDTT survey conducted during 2011 by the Institute for Human Development (IHD) with support from Sir Dorabji Tata Trust (SDTT) had collected data from about 3000 households, which were mostly poor.

35. Note that both of the 'preference' questions elicited multiple provider preference. Taking account of the multiple responses, the 'relative' preference pattern indicates that 47 per cent of the respondent-households usually rely on public health facilities, 38 per cent on private physicians, clinics, or private hospitals, 7 per cent on unqualified medical practitioners or quacks, 3 per cent on different facilities provided by charitable organisations, and another 5 per cent generally use employer-provided, or otherwise mandatory health facilities (such as the CGHS or ESIC facilities).

36. The aggregate vulnerability index is based on a simple, equally-weighted additive combination of 5 variables: income classes, asset ownership terciles-groups, educational level of the respondent, major occupation of the household, and type of locality. The aggregate score thus derived was divided into three equal size classes—low, medium and high, wherein a low score denoted higher 'aggregate' vulnerability, and vice versa.

vulnerability index, and denoting the economically well-off households, sought health treatment from private sources.

Taken together with the continued expansion of public healthcare facilities in Delhi, the findings from the Perceptions Survey indicate the positive impact of such changes in terms of the equitable usage of government health facilities among the weaker economic sections, and their growing reliance on the public health system. While such trends bode well for universal coverage, the health system still continues to face the major challenges of consolidating the equity gains through supply side interventions and ensuring the responsiveness of service delivery.

Utilisation of Maternal and Child Health Services

A crucial determinant for improving the survival prospects of both pregnant women and newborn infants is the coverage offered by maternal and child healthcare services, including ante-natal care, risk reduction during pregnancies, institutional deliveries and full immunisation coverage. These issues are discussed here with a particular emphasis on socio-economic differentials for the purpose of understanding equity in coverage and service delivery.

According to the NFHS-III (2005-06) and DLHS-RCH III (2007-08) Rounds, Delhi shows satisfactory coverage in terms of mothers receiving institutional care during the last pregnancy, especially in comparison to the national level scenario. Data accessed from the Office of the Directorate of Family Welfare for 2011 shows that about 84 per cent of the deliveries in Delhi were conducted in health facilities, of which about two-thirds took place in government hospitals. In addition, around 66 per cent of the domiciliary births were also found to be assisted by doctors, and trained nurses/midwives, which made those births safe.

Research on the subject of maternal healthcare has highlighted notable socio-economic differentials in ante-natal care coverage with regard to women residing in the non-slum areas. It has been found that those with secondary level education are more likely to receive ANC services from health professionals (Gupta, *et al.* 2009, cited in Mazumdar and Mazumdar, 2013). Disaggregated data from the DLHS-RCH III (2007-08) also reveals socio-economic differentials in delivery care and continued inequalities in the use of maternal health services in Delhi (Mazumdar and Mazumdar, 2013). The inequities in institutional care during delivery partly arise due to the inadequate coverage of the basic preventive services. These include ante-natal screening facilities, particularly for those belonging to the weaker sections, who also constitute the potentially high-risk pregnancies. This

Table 4.3

Socio-economic Differentials in the Type of Health Services Utilisation: Delhi, 2012-13

Attributes	*Government*	*Private*
Income Groups		
Low income	75.4	20.5
Lower-middle income	63.7	32.0
Upper-middle income	54.9	39.6
High-income	44.9	53.5
Household Asset Index		
Low	71.9	23.6
Medium	62.8	32.4
High	41.2	55.3
Education Levels		
Primary	68	26.2
Higher secondary	62.2	33.6
Graduation and above	44.9	52.8
Type of Occupation		
Lower paid-occupations	66.0	28.8
Service workers	62.3	34.1
Semi-professionals	50.6	43.8
Professionals	44.6	53.2
Locality		
JJ cluster/colony	72.6	21.9
Unauthorised colony	63.2	32.7
Urban village	73.7	23.9
Approved colony	51.8	43.1
Walled City	66.9	29.7
Posh locality	44.7	55.3
Aggregated Vulnerability Index		
High	71.0	24.8
Medium	59.9	34.2
Low	43.1	53.8
Aggregate Split	61.5	34.8
Total (N)	4,941	2,792

Source: Perceptions Survey, 2013.

necessitates according high priority to ante-natal care through interventions such as early screening and home-based counselling and monitoring of pregnant women. The Government of Delhi has taken several initiatives in this sphere, including the Delhi Initiative for Safeguarding Health of Adolescents (DISHA),[37] which is being conducted through the JSY, the JSSK and the *Mamta* schemes, and provision of free transport to the pregnant women from the home to the hospital and back home in order to promote institutional deliveries. The state has also planned stricter implementation of the Janani Shishu Suraksha Karyakram in all its 32 hospitals and 31 maternity homes by launching mass awareness generation programmes. A fleet of 120 new ambulances has been added to be used for facilitating the free transportation of pregnant women, merely by dialling the toll-free number 102.[38] Under the JSSK, further efforts are being planned to tie up with the Jan Ahaar scheme to provide nutritious food for pregnant women. Reductions in maternal mortality are also planned through multi-faceted operations including the linking of primary healthcare facilities to secondary hospitals and first referral units (FRUs), strengthening blood bank services that are equipped to provide essential blood to patients/referral units for handling ante-partum and post-partum haemorrhage cases, making contraceptive services accessible to everyone, and making the MTP service provisioning easily available.

In Delhi, approximately two-thirds (63 per cent) of the children aged 12-23 months received complete immunisation coverage against six major killer diseases, as compared to the corresponding average figure of 44 per cent for India as a whole (NFHS III, 2005-06). Meanwhile, the corresponding DLHS-RCH III (2007-08) figure is 67 per cent. The district-wise vaccination coverage was found to range around the 50 per cent mark for children residing in the northern (in both the North-east and North-west districts) parts of the state, pointing towards a clear spatial zone in urgent need of a massive scaling-up of immunisation coverage. Recent estimates from the UNICEF's Coverage Evaluation Survey (2009) indicate the level of immunisation coverage in Delhi to be 72 per cent. However, despite these improvements, inequities continue to persist. According to the DLHS-RCH III state report for Delhi (IIPS and MoHFW, 2010, cited in Mazumdar and Mazumdar, 2013), child immunisation levels are found to vary with the mother's education levels. While close to half of children of illiterate mothers received full immunisation, more than three-fourths of those with mothers who had completed matriculate level of education were found to be fully immunised.

Recent policy measures appear to be aimed towards ensuring universal immunisation coverage, and in fact expanding the vaccination schedules by consistently incorporating new vaccines such as MMR (1999), hepatitis B (2001), typhoid (2004) and the pentavalent *Haemophilus influenzae* type B (HiB) vaccine (2013).[39] The Pulse Polio Programme in Delhi is considered as a model, as it provides a template for convergent intervention strategies aimed at ensuring universal coverage by reaching out to children from the under-served, vulnerable communities and families.

In a nutshell, while both maternal and child health coverage indicators are likely to have improved in recent years in Delhi,[40] issues of inequity in access to these basic but crucial preventive services persist and need to be addressed. A few recent initiatives indicate that the State Government has been taking positive steps to address issues related to equitable and quality MCH service coverage.[41]

37. The State has created 162 adolescents' reproductive and sexual health clinics named as DISHA, which provide comprehensive services for the adolescents for preventive, promotive, curative and referral services on growth and development, sexual and reproductive health, nutrition, contraception and behavioural issues. Provision of nutritional counselling and iron and folic acid tablets to the adolescent are targeted for this age group, to alleviate anaemia and its intergenerational effects.

38. Briefing notes from the Department of Health and Family Welfare, Government of NCT of Delhi.

39. Communication from the Directorate of Family Welfare (DFW), Government of NCT of Delhi.

40. A recent survey conducted by the Government of India and WHO in the North-east district has confirmed that the state has achieved a Maternal Neonatal Tetanus Elimination status in early 2013, which is an indirect substantiation of improved coverage, which now needs to be consolidated further by the state. Source: DFW, Government of NCT of Delhi.

41. In order to increase the coverage and reach to the hitherto unreached women and children, the areas have been mapped for the ANMs, with each ANM being accountable for all the pregnant women and children residing in her earmarked area. In addition to this, around 3800 ASHAs cover a population of around seven million, and have been selected and trained to mobilise the beneficiaries from the community to avail of the available health services, provide information and advice on basic health issues, and offer basic health aid like distribution of ORS/Paracetamol tablets before referring the patient to the health centre. She is also being trained for counselling the mothers on care during the post-partam period and basic home based new born.
The Mother and Child Tracking System (MCTS), which is being implemented in Delhi, constitutes another

4.3.4 *Quality of Care for Services Offered at Healthcare Facilities in Delhi—Insights from the People's Perceptions Survey*

The fundamental aims of UHC are to reduce barriers to access to services and promote equitable use by ensuring that the services offered are in synchronisation with the users' needs and expectations, and incorporate attributes of both technical and interpersonal dimensions of quality of care in delivering services. However, since studies on users' perspectives demand data and necessitate specific study designs, they are usually rare. In Delhi, a few studies, such as those undertaken by Jishnu Das and Jefferey Hammer (Das and Hammer, 2007; 2005; 2004) provide some interesting facts about how the quality of healthcare varies according to localities, providers' motivations, and between the public and the private sector. For example, they find that the poor tend to visit providers who are less knowledgeable, with both the public and private providers in poor neighbourhoods having lower competence. More importantly, the studies highlight that motivations and incentives often influence the quality of medical advice and services: public providers are apparently less reluctant to perform in keeping with their competence, while those in private practice tend to over-exert themselves through additional diagnostics, over-medication, etc. The studies indicate that private physicians, even those with lower competence levels, provide 'better care on an average' than their better-qualified counterparts from public hospitals.

As part of the Perceptions Survey, 2013, the respondents were asked about the three aspects of health services accessed by them during their recent visits which they have liked best. The responses included cost of treatment (58 per cent), effectiveness of the treatment and medicines prescribed (57 per cent), and the skill and competency of the physician/staff (50 per cent). These three attributes also conform with the three aspects of publicly-provided services, viz., lower costs or affordability, technical competence, and the effectiveness of medication. These findings indicate that public health services score reasonably well in Delhi in terms of the technical aspects of service quality. However, as regards the two interpersonal dimensions of the quality of care: friendliness and courtesy of the physicians/staff, and the ease with which they administered the treatment and the medicines, the responses obtained during the Perceptions Survey, 2013, showed that a much lesser proportion of the respondents (32 per cent and 23 per cent, respectively) rated them as satisfactory. Only a small proportion of the respondents (17 per cent) found the overall cleanliness of the public health facilities conforming to their liking.

On the other hand, two-thirds of the respondents rated 'overall cleanliness' as the most popular aspect of private health facilities. The interpersonal quality of care, that is, the friendliness and clarity of communication of the health personnel in private facilities was also rated highly (48 per cent) as compared to public facilities. With regard to the two technical aspects, that is the competence of the service provider and efficacy of treatment, private health facilities were rated as marginally better than the public facilities (by 61 per cent and 55 per cent of the respondents, respectively). However, it must be noted that, as illustrated in Table 4.3, the users of private and public health facilities are distinctly different in terms of their background characteristics—income, education, occupation and overall vulnerability. Hence, these differentials are not directly comparable but are at best indicators of the aspects of the service quality found to be satisfactory by their respective users.

The Perceptions Survey, 2013, also tried to identify what the respondents disliked most about the public/private health services accessed by them. A significant proportion of users of public health facilities cited long waiting times (89 per cent) and lack of privacy during consultations/or overcrowding (49 per cent) as the factors most disliked by them. About a quarter (24 per cent) reported that cleanliness levels and the environment at the health facility were below their expectations. Lastly, 41 per cent of the respondents cited the long distances they had to travel to reach public health facilities as a factor they disliked, which indicates that geographical accessibility of the health facilities continues to be a significant issue at least for part of the population. On the other hand, a very small proportion (13 per cent) considered treatment costs in public facilities to be higher than expected. The responses of the users of private facilities for the same clearly brought out an indicative divide. While about 6 respondents in 10 considered waiting time to be a hindrance in private facilities as well, more than 56 per cent considered the costs of

important initiative for tracking all pregnant women and children to ensure the delivery of appropriate care. As on 14 August 2013, around 4 lakh women and 3.9 lakh children have been registered on the MCTS portal over the last two years. Efforts are being made to universalise the utilisation of MCTS system by all MCH care providers. Source: DFW, Government of NCT of Delhi.

treatment to be high, something they disliked the most. Approximately one-third (37 per cent) of the respondents also felt that private facilities were not available close by and rated distance as one of the factors they disliked.

The Perceptions Survey, 2013, brings to the fore a few interesting dimensions of the quality of healthcare services in Delhi. While people rate both the public and private health sectors on a near-equal footing with respect to the technical aspects of care, the users of public facilities appear to be attracted more by the lower costs of treatment, which is understandable because a larger proportion of the respondents belong to households from the lower socio-economic strata. This alone is indicative of the fact that the public health facilities have achieved effective outreach towards the priority sections of the population. Also, the fact that the users of public facilities rate the effectiveness of treatment and the perceived competence of the providers quite high, speaks well of the overall quality of these services. The users' responses also highlight the various areas of concern, including cleanliness, the environment at the facilities, overcrowding and lack of privacy, and long waiting times. The private sector, on the other hand, fares well in terms of the aspects of cleanliness and bedside manners of the physicians towards their patients, but it is still considered a costly option by a major share of the respondents. While the users of the private sector mostly belong to the economically better-off households with lower socio-economic vulnerability, their cost concerns make a strong case for better coverage and greater efficiency of public sector health services to ensure that low-cost, effective, and patient-sensitive options are available for the masses in Delhi.

4.4. Financial Risk Protection

Along with equitable access to quality healthcare services, the other core tenets of universal coverage are a reduction in barriers to financial accessibility and extension of adequate, effective risk-protection against the financial impact arising out of illness. The Indian scenario is characterised by private, out-of-pocket expenditures incurred on treatment and related expenses, with the impacts often being catastrophic and leading to impoverishment, particularly among those with limited means and vulnerable livelihoods (Shiva Kumar, *et al.*, 2011). In this section, the existent patterns of healthcare financing in Delhi are assessed. An attempt has also been made to identify the major issues plaguing the health system with regard to adequate financial risk protection.

4.4.1 Public Spending on Health and Healthcare Services

Public spending on health and related services in Delhi accrues from three major sources—directly from the State Government, as support from the Central Government for Centrally-sponsored schemes or national programmes, and from the local bodies, viz., the New Delhi Municipal Corporation (NDMC), Municipal Corporation of Delhi (MCD) and the Delhi Cantonment Board. Multiple public financing sources make any study of flow of finances, in both absolute and sectoral terms, difficult. Also, the amounts collated from different sources do not always match, primarily due to different definitions and accounting principles. However, the broad picture emerging from most of the available sources suggests that public spending on health services in Delhi has been consistently on the rise. According to the budgetary analysis reports of the State Government, spending in absolute terms has increased, more than doubling from about Rs. 11 billion in 2006-07 to about Rs. 28 billion in 2012-13.[42] Although subject to certain qualifications (see Footnote 42), the increase in public spending seems impressive. It is, however, lesser so, when the growth in outlays is observed in proportion to the total budgetary outlays—it has increased from about 8.1 per cent in 2006-07 to about 9.9 per cent in 2012-13. A publication of the Reserve Bank of India—*State Finances: A Study of Budgets of 2010-1*—reveals the positive aspect of public health spending in Delhi, including family welfare and other allied expenditures (Reserve Bank of India, 2011). The statement (Statement 42, p.186) puts the expenditure on health services as a ratio of aggregate expenditure in Delhi at about 8 per cent in 2010-11, the highest in the country and almost double of the national average (4.3 per cent). The 2012-13 edition of the report is even more promising—it revises the estimate to 9.3 per cent, and pegs the figures for the two subsequent financial years at a phenomenal 9.9 per cent. Thus, Delhi is probably the first state in the country to spend almost 10 per cent of its budget on health. The recently published *Economic Survey*

42. The figures are taken from different years of the publication, *Analysis of the Budgetary Transactions of State Government*, published annually by the Directorate of Economics and Statistics, Government of Delhi. The reported values are for the expenditure under the head, "Medical and Public Health". The figure for 2006-07 also includes expenditures of the local bodies, but that for 2012-13 is only for the state government's budgeted estimates. The figures given here can be considered as a partial estimate of the total public spending on health and allied services in the state, as it excludes contributions from the Central Government, and does not includes expenditure incurred on family welfare services, contributions to ESIC and Delhi Arogya Nidhi, and medical education and training.

of Delhi, 2012-13, highlights the share of health in development plans—an additional indicator of the 'fiscal priority' accorded to this sector. It shows that the proportion of Plan expenditure on health in Delhi has hovered around 12 per cent since 2004, but was worth almost Rs. 16 billion, that is, 12.2 per cent in 2011-12. As in the earlier instance, this figure too suggests a better public financing pattern in Delhi as compared to the other larger Indian states.

Generally, in India, the dearth of a regular system of national health accounts plagues any assessments of trends in public spending on healthcare across states, on the one hand, and more importantly comparisons of the relative role of public financing vis-à-vis private, mostly out-of-pocket spending on health and healthcare services, on the other. The most recent National Health Accounts (NHA), published in 2009, pertains to data till 2004-05, when the last National Health Survey (containing private health expenditure data) was conducted by the NSSO (60th Round). According to the NHA 2004-05 (MOHFW 2009), Delhi with a per capita public health spending of Rs 560 is ranked 6th nationally (with the average at Rs 242). A crucial gap in the available NHA estimates is the lack of comparative estimates for the post 2008-09 period, which, as the budgetary estimates for Delhi (and also for a few other states) indicate, public spending on healthcare and health services received a fillip, and have started to climb up remarkably with significant support from the Central Government under the National Rural Health Mission (NRHM). Such a positive turnaround in the levels of public spending was mooted in the report of the National Commission on Macroeconomics of Health report (MOHFW, 2005), though it fell short of the avowed goal of raising national levels of public spending to 2-3 per cent of the GDP.[43] More recently, the Ministry of Health and Family Welfare, Government of India, had provided some estimates of the per capita 'health expenditure', following which in 2008-09, the same for Delhi stands at Rs. 840; by this estimate—wherein the national average is put at Rs. 503 – Delhi is ranked ninth among all the states and UTs in India.[44]

43. Interestingly, in the recently published High-level Expert Group Report on UHC (HLEG, 2011), a 'normative expenditure' threshold of ₹ 2000 per capita was conceived to be required for UHC goals in the 'special-category' states (as defined by the NRHM), which includes Delhi. Assuming the current levels of public outlays on health (as a proportion of the state GDPs), the report estimates Delhi's public spending in 2019-20 to rise to Rs. 2855, thereby significantly exceeding the 'normative threshold' and in fact, making it the only state (with a population of 10 million or above) to do so (HLEG, 2011, pp. 108-09).

44. See Response to the Lok Sabha Question—MoH&FW, 18 December 2009. 'State-wise per capita Expenditure on Health', Available at: *http://pib.nic.in/newsite/erelease.aspx?relid=56240*, Accessed on 18 December 2009.

4.4.2 Private Spending on Health and Healthcare Services

It is now well-acknowledged that in India, a large part of the health expenditure is private and largely borne out-of-the-pocket. From the perspectives of universal coverage and economic welfare, it is important to understand the gaps in health financing mechanisms. The patterns and composition of private spending help in ascertaining the economic impact of health shocks on the vulnerable sections, who have little access to formal risk-protection mechanisms. The NHA (2010) estimates for India reveal that a whopping 71 per cent of the private health expenditures are borne by households, of which a major proportion is out-of-pocket, with little coverage from formal risk-pooling mechanisms. In Delhi too, private expenditure accounts for more than two-thirds (77 per cent) of the total health expenditure, which is relatively better as compared to most other states with the exception of Himachal Pradesh (58 per cent), Karnataka (72 per cent) and Rajasthan (76 per cent), which report lower proportions of the total health expenditure accounted for by private sources.

An analysis of the recent consumption expenditure surveys of the NSSO, for example, the 55th (1999-2000), 60th (2004-05) and 66th (2009-10) Rounds for Delhi indicate that households spend about 3 per cent of their total non-food expenditures and around 2 per cent of their total consumption expenditures on medical care, with the levels remaining virtually unchanged over the five years covered by the NSSO rounds (Mazumdar and Mazumdar, 2013). A comparison of household outlays on medical care in Delhi with that of the rest of urban India reveals that households in Delhi spend significantly lesser proportions of their consumption expenditures on medical care. The NSS 66th Round (2009-10)[45] data shows that medical care expenditures as a proportion of the non-food and total consumption expenditures work out to be 5 per cent and 8.5 per cent, on an average. There could be three possible reasons for explaining such an expenditure pattern in Delhi: *first*, lower morbidity (and hospitalisation) experienced by the population vis-à-vis their counterparts from other urban centres across India; *second*, lower average cost of treatment/medical expenses borne by the households, probably due to higher coverage and utilisation of government health services; and *third*, a markedly different consumption pattern in

45. Table 6A, NSSO 66th Round Report on Consumption Expenditure

Delhi that is biased more towards the non-medical care components of non-food expenditures (such as education and entertainment).

At the aggregate level, the proportion of medical care expenses in the household's aggregate consumption expenditure masks socio-economic differentials and inequalities in financing medical care. The IHD–SDTT survey allows for some useful disaggregated analyses. The survey results suggest that households with higher education levels spend significantly more on healthcare. The average expenses on medical care were found to be highest amongst high-income households and the least for families in the lowest income bracket. Notably, while households relying on formal, qualified private physicians spent the most, treatment from public sources was also found to be costly enough. However, it was actually the informal providers, which about one-fifth of the households subscribed to, who were reported to be the least expensive, which clearly explains why they were found to constitute the most attractive healthcare option by the lowest income category households (Kumar *et al.*, 2012).

Another study which provides useful information on the dimensions of health financing in Delhi was conducted by IHD-IRMA (2010-11),[46] and covered a larger sample with better representation of the population of Delhi. The findings from this survey also indicate that the economically better-off pay more for medical care (by a multiple of about 9), and that treatment in government hospitals is no less costlier than seeking treatment from private physicians or hospitals (Mazumdar and Mazumdar, 2013), which is a cause for concern. If the results of both the above mentioned surveys are taken together, it appears that the poor and the vulnerable households appear to be cushioned somewhat, most likely due to the fact that they settle for less costly options (such as local government clinics, rather than government hospitals or unqualified/semi-qualified private physicians rather than bigger hospitals or more qualified physicians).

A related concept, and one which is employed extensively in the health financing literature, is that of catastrophic expenditure on healthcare, and the consequent impoverishment it causes. Any household spending on healthcare is considered to be catastrophic when it is required to reduce its basic expenditure in order to cope with healthcare costs (Xu *et al.*, 2003), though there is little consensus on the threshold to be used. However, the convention is to either use a higher threshold, for example, 40 per cent of the household's capacity to pay (that is, non-food consumption expenditure) (op. cit.), or a combination of thresholds, such as 10 per cent, 20 per cent, 30 per cent and 40 per cent. An analysis of the IHD-IRMA data shows that a significant proportion of the households in urban Delhi did experience financial catastrophe situations when paying for the treatment of their ailing family members. The proportion of households experiencing catastrophic situations following the heavy expenditure incurred ranged from about 9 per cent to about 3 per cent, on an average. In absolute numbers, out of an estimated number of 23,06,903 (23 lakh plus) households in urban Delhi, 2.16 lakh households spent 10 per cent or more of their *capacity to pay* (non-food consumption expenditure) on medical care; At subsequent higher thresholds of 20 per cent, 30 per cent and 40 per cent, it amounted to about 1,27,000, 88,000, and 65,000 households, respectively.[47] The evidence, however, is not clear that catastrophic expenses are more likely to be experienced by the poor, in terms of household consumption expenditure classes. Nevertheless, households relying more on informal means of occupation/employment show more than three times the incidence of experiencing financial catastrophe (at the lowest threshold), which then tapers off to twice the incidence at the highest threshold of the households' capacity to pay for health services, indicating some amount of socio-economic gradient in the risks of financial catastrophe due to healthcare-related costs.[48]

The results from the household surveys studied in this section indicate a diverse picture of private healthcare financing in Delhi. Although the poor and socio-economically vulnerable families spend less on health services as a proportion of their incomes, they are at higher risks of experiencing catastrophic

46. The study (2010-11) conducted by Institute for Human Development (IHD) and Institute for Rural Management - Anand (IRMA) was primarily related to informal employment, migration and social protection in urban India, and involved a detailed household survey in two Indian cities, Delhi and Ranchi. The urban Delhi sample of about 2000 households were drawn with a sampling design similar to that of NSSO and is representative of urban Delhi.

47. The population level estimates were worked out by applying the multipliers calculated through a detailed technique closely resembling that followed by the NSSO CES surveys.

48. Detailed discussions and results are available from the background paper to this chapter. See Mazumdar and Mazumdar (2013) for a detailed analysis on health financing aspects reported in this section by using the IHD household surveys.

expenses leading to further impoverishment. The poor, in the absence of formal risk-pooling safety nets, insure their costs of illness by accessing the services of low-cost informal practitioners, or government clinics. This highlights the issue of financial risk protection as a key corrective action against the inequity-encouraging private out-of-pocket health expenditures.

4.4.3 Financing Healthcare—Role of Risk Protection and Equitable Coverage

The analysis presented in the previous sections clearly points towards a predominance of private, out-of-pocket spending on medical services by households, and socio-economic differentials in household budgetary outlays on medical care. These findings for Delhi are comparable to those for the rest of the country too. However, what makes the case of Delhi different is that it exhibits one of the highest (higher than the national average too) levels of public expenditures on healthcare and medical services. Nevertheless, the fact that a considerable proportion of the households spend a significant part of their incomes on availing of treatment for their ailing family members, raises important issues with regard to financial risk protection, universalisation of coverage and insuring against unanticipated health shocks.

Irrespective of the source of data used, and indicating a near-constant pattern over much of the past decade, the financing pattern of healthcare-related expenses by the households indicates a common thread—the unanimous predominance of out-of-pocket spending, drawn out of current income or past savings, with very little support extended by formal insurance mechanisms. Disaggregated data for total healthcare-related expenses by different financing sources from the NSSO 60th Round data (2005-06) shows that 92 per cent of the expenses incurred by households in Delhi on non-hospitalised ailments, and 89 per cent of the expenses incurred for hospitalised ailments were financed out of the incomes of households and/or their past savings. About 7 per cent of the hospitalisation expenditures and about 4 per cent of the expenses on other ailments were supported through borrowings, while friends and relatives helped contribute about 2 per cent of the hospitalisation expenses. About 2 per cent of the total medical expenses for non-hospitalised ailments were also financed out of the sale of assets and mortgages (NSSO, 2006). The IHD-SDTT Survey (referred to earlier) finds that nearly one-fifth of the households faced risks of indebtedness likely to arise from the loans they raised to finance health treatment costs. Data obtained from the more recent Perceptions Survey, 2013, also shows that only a small proportion of the households were able to support their medical expenses via alternative insurance and risk protection mechanisms (such as employer-supported healthcare). In the case of major illnesses, requiring hospitalisation or surgeries, the proportion of households tapping into their savings (69 per cent) was the highest, followed by those using their current income (59 per cent) and social network-based informal risk-sharing through financial help received from friends and neighbours (47 per cent).

The financing pattern for medical expenses in Delhi also shows a distinct socio-economic gradient, reflecting inequities in the same. Households belonging to low-income classes and high vulnerability groups were found to fall back more on informal sources of risk-sharing via borrowings from relatives/neighbours to finance their medical expenses. On the other hand, most of the households reportedly benefiting from formal sources of risk-sharing (mainly employer-provided or subsidised government health schemes) belonged to the economically better-off sections. Such formal means of social safety nets against health shocks, mostly available to those holding organised, formal sector jobs, eludes the poor and vulnerable, who tend to be concentrated in informal, unorganised sector jobs. Clearly, there is a pressing need for targeted social health insurance alternatives.

Pronounced gaps in financial risk protection amongst priority groups have also been found from other household surveys. The IHD-IRMA survey found that households/persons predominantly relying on work in the informal sector were spending more than twice (4.3 per cent) of their capacity to pay[49] on healthcare. In comparison, those engaged in formal sector jobs (1.6 per cent), and thus having better incomes and lower vulnerability, were spending much lesser proportions of their household non-food expenditures on healthcare. Such inequities in risk protection were also evident from the Perceptions Survey, 2013, which reports that low-income, vulnerable households prefering to use public hospitals and health facilities could manage to cover only about 6 per cent of their medical expenses through any form of risk protection (formal or informal). On the other hand, those with higher incomes and lower vulnerability disproportionately

49. Defined as per capita household non-food consumption expenditure.

enjoyed coverage of about 20 per cent of their medical expenses from formal sources (mostly extended by their employers). In the case of major illnesses, the disparity in financial risk coverage becomes quite stark. While the better-off households manage to get almost a quarter of their medical expenses covered through formal sources, for the highly vulnerable households, the formal safety nets account for less than 2 per cent of their expenses. Besides intra-community or intra-family informal credit support (accounting for about 27 per cent of the expenses), these households have no option but to rely on their own finances or resort to other sources of credit to finance their healthcare needs. With such a skewed pattern of formal safety nets and risk protection mechanisms in play, it is implicit that the poor and vulnerable households, with informal means of livelihoods and incomes, continue to face high financial risks in the face of health shocks, which has wider implications for human development and welfare outcomes.

4.4.4 Assessing Institutional Mechanisms Towards Financial Risk Protection

Delhi, being the national capital and a thriving metro city, has one of the best networks of healthcare facilities and service providers in the country. As the statistics reported in the previous sections on the spread and growth of government health infrastructure indicate, the state has also been largely responsive in catering to the needs of the vulnerable populations and poor communities and localities by providing a wide array of urban health centres, dispensaries, secondary and tertiary care hospitals, and mobile health clinics, among other facilities. While this augurs well in terms of the desirable steps towards ensuring equitable access and universalising healthcare coverage, the scenario of healthcare financing viewed in terms of the coverage of formal risk protection instruments does not seem to echo these positive developments. In fact, as the subsequent discussion in this section indicates, such coverage remains very low with the risks of perpetuating inequities in financing, which goes against the basic foundations of universal coverage.

The strategies adopted by the State Government to ensure equity in healthcare financing, and extension of financial safety nets to the vulnerable families is largely indirect and follows from the Government's initiatives and interventions to ensure equity in access to healthcare and to reduce the different barriers towards 'effective coverage'. As illustrated by the seminal work by Tanahashi (1978), ensuring effective coverage through supply side interventions facilitating better accessibility and network of health facilities; making drugs, equipments and health workforce available at easily accessible locations; and having specific interventions such as the Mobile Health Scheme for hard-to-reach populations is consistent with the concepts of universal coverage. However, care must be taken to ensure that the utilisation patterns justify a positive benefit incidence of the government's expenditure. If the poor enjoy a greater share of the public health services, which appears to be the fact as evident from the Perceptions Survey, 2013 (Table 4.3)—suggesting benefit incidence to be progressive in nature, equity in access to healthcare facilities and services can encourage equity in financing as well, and help extend financial risk protection through such intervening pathways. In the absence of detailed, disaggregated household survey data linking utilisation and financing behaviour, it is difficult to comment conclusively on such linkages and the success of the health system to ensure overall equity and on-track towards universal coverage. However, relying solely on a positive benefit incidence of the 'in-situ' strengthening of the healthcare infrastructure and service delivery mechanisms may not be adequate as those households, particularly from the low-income, vulnerable segments, who continue to remain outside the coverage of publicly-provided healthcare services can be disproportionately exposed to risks of further impoverishment, resulting from high out-of-pocket expenditure incurred in receiving treatment from sources other than the free, public services.

Nevertheless, the State Government has also been proactively pursuing the agenda of financial risk protection through a number of equity-sensitive programmes and interventions. These include the twin schemes—*Delhi Arogya Nidhi* (DAN, the State Illness Assistance Fund) and the *Delhi Arogya Kosh* (DAK), apart from schemes such as the Delhi Government Employees Health Scheme (DGEHS), and other national health insurance programmes such as the Employee's State Health Insurance Scheme (ESIC) and the *Rashtriya Swasthya Bima Yojana* (RSBY). The DAN and DAK schemes are designed to provide cash assistance to patients from the economically weaker sections (and having the relevant entitlement cards) for treatments involving high financial costs. The DAK is specifically aimed at supporting dialysis-related expenses, in government and empanelled private hospitals. Both the DGEHS, which caters to government employees and the ESIC, which caters to other organised sector employees, cover the relevant population segments and offer the risk-pooling support only to a miniscule proportion of the population, which indicates that they are against the basic principles of equity by supporting the better-off instead of those with lower economic capacities. Adding to these, a number of measures such as the facility of free beds in the 44 designated private hospitals mentioned earlier, or offering free treatment for low-income families in specialty hospitals are appropriate steps towards attaining equity in financing patterns and safeguard vulnerable families against health expenses-induced shocks.

The only other scheme, prioritised towards targeting the poor is the RSBY. A nationwide scheme, and billed as the world's largest targeted national health insurance programme, the RSBY generated a lot of promise when it was launched. Under this scheme, cashless hospitalisation facilities are provided in designated hospitals (with about 70 per cent in the private sector) for a maximum amount of Rs. 30,000 per year for five members in the eligible poor households identified from a roster of below the poverty line (BPL) families. Using strong technology support via smart cards and stringent norms of identifying health facilities, insurance providers and administrators, the RSBY allows the tracking of each enrolled beneficiary household, thus keeping a tab on the functioning of the scheme. By providing adequate financial cover to poor households against severe illnesses and facilitating a broader choice of quality healthcare providers, the RSBY aims to ensure equity in financing and delivery of healthcare. However, since the RSBY is still in its early years, it may be a little premature to comment on its effectiveness in terms of financial risk protection and as a key vehicle to achieve universal and inclusive service coverage. The scheme's performance varies considerably across the country and mixed results have been obtained. However, inequities persist even in terms of enrolling the 'eligible' beneficiaries, and consequently in disbursing the benefits. A few studies have identified structural barriers that permeate information gaps in terms of the awareness of the schemes, which, in turn. keeps enrolment rates down. More often, families outside the 'enrolment coverage' are those that are in most need of insurance support (for a review, see Palacios, *et al.*, 2011). Such information asymmetries can be equally responsible for the low awareness relating to other equity-sensitive interventions and initiatives of the Government, such as free beds in private hospitals or the illness assistance funds, and may not always guarantee coverage to the most needy, particularly with a clear demand-based orientation.

Estimates suggest considerable gains by enhancing the coverage of schemes such as RSBY (Mazumdar and Mazumdar, 2013), as a collateral initiative to reap increasing returns and leverage efficiently from the already pro-public sector tilt in the service mix and utilisation patterns evident in Delhi. In fact, we argue for universalising a RSBY-type of health *entitlement* system, covering all types of healthcare services—hospitalisation as well as outpatient, clinic-based consultation services with cashless service usage options through suitable platforms, independent of whether the poor opt to use the services of the public sector (which are already cashless at the point of care) or designated private sector 'outlets'. Delhi could probably take a leaf out of recent pilots under the RSBY to engage community-based groups and other non-government entities to provide cashless outpatient services to the beneficiaries, and to introduce such schemes in the coming days.

However, in view of the fact that at present, the bulk of the state's budgetary outlay on health services, as discussed above, is committed towards strengthening service delivery and further bolstering the health infrastructure—physical and health workforce—introducing a large-scale financial protection mechanism or a 'scaled-up' version of the RSBY might not sound feasible, form the viewpoint of both operational as well as fiscal prudence. Nevertheless, and as this chapter had identified, the policy-makers need to take into cognizance the fact that notwithstanding the impressive network of health facilities and growing public reliance, more so among the poor, relying solely on a purely supply-side driven system to ensure universal coverage with equitable outcomes may not be the best idea. Demand side barriers arising out of low awareness and other information asymmetries, coupled with imperfections in service delivery mechanisms, can crowd out the poor and vulnerable people from the service nets, and skew the benefit incidence. Further research evidence could greatly aid the policy-makers in drawing up suitable roadmaps for such integrated strategies that draw the best from present arrangements, and simultaneously repair the lacunae in effective coverage through appropriate social safety nets.

It is evident that the health system in Delhi presents a mixed bag of performances, and has some commendable achievements to its credit. At the same time, however, it faces strong challenges arising out of its commitments to its citizens in terms of ensuring that they enjoy long, healthy, productive lives and that they have easy access to reliable, effective medical care. Glimpses of the spirit of universal coverage can be seen in the health service delivery system and in prioritisation of interventions for the vulnerable populations. In view of the challenges that Delhi faces on the healthcare front, and building on its recent achievements, the next section puts forth a set of measures aimed at informing future strategies for health system reforms in order to achieve universal, effective coverage.

4.5. The Way Forward

This chapter reviews the current status and future prospects of the health system in Delhi, from the perspective of universal coverage and its significance in ensuring human development outcomes. It is quite apparent that the health system in Delhi is faced with multiple challenges, some unique to the city-state. These include steady streams of 'floating' populations from the neighbouring states who come to the capital to seek treatment for emergencies and for general healthcare needs; vulnerable groups such as the homeless, or those engaged in high-risk livelihoods; and a growing share of the aged populace requiring assistance amidst fragmenting social support systems. The new and emerging concerns in healthcare, which Delhi shares with most of the urban health systems in the transitional economies across the developing world, include balancing environmental concerns with development pursuits, addressing wider health and well-being concerns of the swelling ranks of adolescents, and ensuring preparedness for medical emergencies such as sudden epidemics or acts of violence. All these require careful consideration and synergistic action involving a wider array of stakeholders. Some of the major findings highlighted in this chapter are as follows:

- There is need to meet the persistent challenge of improving the survival prospects of newborns while ensuring that all births take place under institutional care, and are followed by proper care of the newborn.

- The burden of disease scenario only reaffirms the emergence of the 'double burden' of persisting communicable diseases and the growing predominance of chronic diseases. More often, it is the poor and socio-economically vulnerable population groups that are unequally exposed to both disease and premature mortality risks. Clearly, the interventions and policies need to be more pro-active and inclusive and should aim to extend effective coverage to the under-served as a development priority.

- The high reliance of the poor on public health facilities points towards the need for expansion of health infrastructure and the provisioning of free medicines to encourage desirable service usage patterns. On the other hand it is imperative to address the various drawbacks in the system pertaining to the quality of services, and a highly stretched out health workforce, which prevents optimal utilisation of potential and equitable service coverage.

- Financial protection remains inadequate—it seems that weak convergence and the lack of an integrated approach prevent the State from ensuring the optimal implementation of the various programmes available (including national schemes such as the RSBY and the state's own illness assistance funds). Several barriers exist, hampering adequate financial risk protection for those most in need of such safety nets. Low awareness amongst the poor, weak efforts by the government to reduce information gaps, stringent eligibility criteria and long-drawn out processes for availing of the benefits often leave the poor with inadequate and ineffective financial coverage. What is needed instead is increased broadbasing of social insurance measures such as the RSBY by extending their coverage to outpatient services as well, with the State providing the additional budgetary support. The government needs to recognise that universal coverage calls not for multiple, overlapping schemes, but for a single, integrated and effective financial risk protection measure that can be availed of by the poor, without any barriers.

In an attempt to put Delhi's health system in perspective, five major achievements of the state's growing health system and five major challenges, termed as the '5*5 *dashboard*' (Box 4.4) have been delineated here. However, this is neither an exclusive nor an exhaustive list, and necessitates debate and consultative processes involving the major stakeholders in the healthcare domain of Delhi.

Box 4.5

Key Challenges and Achievements of the Health System in Delhi: THE 5*5 DASHBOARD

The Five Challenges

1. A slower-than required decline in infant mortality rate, with higher deaths concentrated in the neonatal period. Inequities in providing preventive maternal and child health services, including lower levels of institutional deliveries.
2. Growing burden of noncommunicable diseases, with mortality risks disproportionately concentrated in economically active ages. Continued threat of infectious conditions especially respiratory ailments possibly linked to ambient air quality.
3. Severe shortages of manpower well below recommended levels, including both physicians and paramedics.
4. Persistent concerns about interpersonal aspects of quality including communication, privacy and long waiting times in public health facilities even as lower costs, effectiveness of treatment and provider competence continues to attract patients to public facilities.
5. Inadequate financial risk-protection, particularly amongst those with informal livelihoods with a considerable number of households still facing risks of very high medical expenses.

The Five Achievements

1. Impressive network of primary health care facilities, propelled with dispensaries, mobile clinics, school health clinics and PUHCs and a strategic approach to reduce IMR and MMR through integrated approaches.
2. Phenomenal increase in reliance on public health facilities, with desired coverage among lower socioeconomic and vulnerable groups and localities, and marked decline in the use of unqualified medical practitioners.
3. Commendable efforts in facilitating equitable access to essential medicines distributed through primary and secondary facilities. Likely contribution in reducing average medical expenses, and improving equity in financing.
4. Significant developments in health information systems, particularly related to Medical Causes of Institutional Deaths, aided by a fast-improving Civil registration system
5. Strong commitment to a holistic, public health approach to the health system, marked by 'Mission Convergence' according due policy-importance to the wider, social determinants of health

In order to ensure universal coverage with equity and quality, six major policy recommendations may be made for prioritising policy interventions to ensure maximum benefits for all sections of the state's citizens, irrespective of their social, economic, locational, and cultural affiliations.

- *Ensure universalisation of in-health facility childbirths along with integrated maternal and neo-natal care facilities (IMNCF)*. For potentially high-risk pockets, such as slums and localities with predominantly vulnerable populations, a set of 24*7 maternity centres should be provided with the recommended basic and emergency obstetric care facilities, and provisions for Sick Neo-natal Care Units (SNCU).

- *Institute an integrated, population-based screening mechanism involving ASHAs/ANMs and voluntary organisations for early screening of high-risk pregnancies, likely cases for domiciliary deliveries, non-adherent cases for communicable diseases therapies and NCDs.* For the latter, innovations in screening could involve sensitisation of lifestyle education and Sunday camps involving the RWAs. These platforms can also be used to screen and counsel the growing elderly population of Delhi for emerging health risks such as mental health conditions and degenerative disorders.

- *Invest in human resources for health to match the growing demand for qualified manpower to deliver a scaled-up primary health service sector*. As an option, the state can consider developing a cadre of Public Health Technical Officers (PHTOs) with an intensive six-semester training programme on basic epidemiology, public health, social and preventive medicine, pharmacology and health management. The PHTO cadre will be health facility managers, incentivised to build individual PUHCs as Centres for Service Excellence.

- *Address the growing demand for public primary health facilities through a streamlined system of matching efficiency indicators with the available manpower planning. Explore additional options of service delivery including an accountable system of contracting-in private practitioners on standardised incentive structures and starting evening clinics in popular service locations.* A maximum threshold of patients, preferably 200 per 6-hour working-shift, can be set to assess and identify centres with regular patient overloads. For these 'priority popular' centres, local private practitioners may be contracted in for certain days on a standard incentive schedule. Another option is to consider starting 'Evening Clinics' in these locations, with options for specialist consultations on certain days of the week. In popular locations, special day-long weekend clinics could be run, with a compensatory week-day off for the manpower involved.

- *Ensure the universal coverage of financial risk protection schemes and avoid duplication of coverage. Scale-up enrolment and coverage of the RSBY through sustained information campaigns, while building on innovative measures such as using the Gender Resource Centres (GRCs) or dedicated drives focusing on vulnerable livelihood sectors. Consider extending RSBY coverage to out-patient consultations for rationalising out-patient loads in clinics.*

- *Develop a strong facility-based disease surveillance system with an integrated electronic backbone.* The system would be instrumental in capturing surveillance data from community level screening, dispensaries, mobile health/ school health clinics and hospitals based on a real-time software platform enabled by user-friendly data entry devices. There is need to develop brief, standardised data entry protocols suitable for different platforms (mobiles, smartphones, tablets, PCs, etc.) and data flow that can be coordinated through the DPMUs. A committed data user community could be identified, involving interested sections of the health administration, academia and civil society for aiding evidence-based decision-making.

Annex Table 4.1

Organization of Health Service Delivery in Delhi

District	Type of Facility									
	Dispensaries/ health posts (Allopathic) run by DHS	Dispensaries/ health posts (Allopathic) run by NDMC/ MCD/Delhi	Dispensaries (AYUSH)	Primary Urban Health Centres (Under (NRHM)	School Health Clinics	Maternal and Child Welfare Centres (MCD)	Hospitals		Super-Speciality hospitals	Teaching Hospitals
							Pub.	Pvt.		
1	2	3	4	5	6	7	8	9	10	11
Central	15	18	40	57	6	23	19	50	3	10
East	27	2	45	66	15	13	10	95	0	1
West	34	12	58	35	18	28	11	195	1	2
North	18	7	31	27	4	13	8	41	1	3
South West	39	5	30	19	10	6	10	82	2	4
North East	36	2	32	85	12	16	12	56	3	3
North West	54	11	77	77	17	29	23	173	0	0
South	33	4	41	64	22	30	18	165	3	4
Total	256	61	354	430	104	158	111	857	13	26

Note: 1. Figures in col 3 include 57 seed PUHCs.
2. Col 7: these are the locations served by mobile clinics, at present 90 vans are deployed.

Source: Communication from DoH&FW, GNCTD, dated: July 3, 2013.

5

Shelter and Basic Services

5.1 Background

Health, education and living standards, the three main components of the Human Development Index (HDI), are usually captured by life expectancy at birth, the mean years of schooling/expected years of schooling and the gross national income per capita.[1] Progress in these three dimensions has various underlying implications. For instance, improvements in health indicators could reflect progress on a host of inter-related fronts such as access to food, shelter, drinking water and sanitation facilities. Similarly, improvements in living standards reflect better access to the aforesaid services as well as to some other basic services such as electricity and transport, especially in the urban context. The Twelfth Five Year Plan in India, with its focus on inclusive growth, recognises the importance of improving access to basic amenities for all people.[2] Inclusive growth must not only translate into lower poverty levels, improved health outcomes, improved access to education, and better opportunities for wage employment and livelihoods, but "it should also be reflected in improvement in provision of basic amenities like water, electricity, roads, sanitation and housing" (p. 2, Approach Paper to the Twelfth Five Year Plan). The Delhi Human Development Report (2006) highlighted the deprivation faced by many of Delhi's citizens in these very basic areas and discussed the related inequities that exist. Some of the pressing issues that were highlighted and discussed in the 2006 report included the deficient quantity and poor quality of water, and housing shortages.

Given the important role that basic services play in facilitating and enhancing various human development outcomes, it is imperative to focus on the access to and quality of basic amenities which impact the average citizen's daily life in Delhi. In this chapter, an attempt has been made to explore the state of government provisioning in the crucial areas of housing and basic facilities such as water, sanitation, electricity, and transport, among other things, and analyse the successes and challenges in these areas. The scenario in the slums of Delhi and a few other types of settlements in the context of specific deprivations has also been examined. The underlying motive of this exercise is to understand the extent of inclusion in the access to various basic facilities for slum-dwellers, which has important implications for policy interventions aimed at achieving inclusive growth and human development.

1. *http://hdr.undp.org/en/statistics/hdi/*, Accessed on 3 April 2013.
2. Approach Paper to the Twelfth Five Year Plan, Available at: *http://planningcommission.nic.in/plans/planrel/12appdrft/appraoch_12plan.pdf*, *Accessed on 3 April 2013.*

5.2 Shelter

'*Shelter is important because it protects us from the elements, provides us with a basic sense of security, and a place for our families to interact. But it is also linked to other aspects of what we consider "normal life": privacy, independence, dignity, safety. Shelter is fundamental to the enjoyment of many human rights*' (Quick Facts, Shelter and Human Rights: UNHCR, Canada, 2010).[3] Housing does not simply signify a roof above one's head, or a space enclosed within four walls. It is the place that people head towards at the end of a hard day's work, or where families, including small children as well as the elderly, spend a large number of hours in a day, and where the family members have access to decent accommodation with enough space for all of them. However, the world over, the pressures of increased population, urbanisation, land scarcity and migration to urban centres have either pushed a large number of people into living in sub-standard housing or rendered them homeless. The latter group comprises persons who use any temporary shelter they can find or often sleep in the open, braving the weather and lacking any security. In the context of a metropolis like Delhi too, the living conditions and basic facilities in slums and some other types of settlements do not come anywhere close to the concept of 'decent' housing. A sizeable proportion of the homeless population living here does not have access to even basic shelter, leave alone any other support service. The congestion in the Delhi (NCT) region has led to the pressures on residential spaces and basic services, coupled with an escalation in land prices. The price index for housing for industrial workers (base year 2004-05) showed an increase of 11.3 per cent over 2010-11, which was slightly lower than the all-India figure of 11.8 per cent, but much higher compared to the figures prevalent in the other metros such as Chennai (6.6 per cent) and Kolkata (4 per cent) (Economic Survey of Delhi, 2012-13).

Among all the states and Union Territories (UTs), Delhi had the highest population density in 2011, at 11,297 people per sq. km. The population in Delhi has touched 16.75 million, as per the Census, 2011 estimates (Economic Survey of Delhi, 2012-13), despite a decline in the decadal population growth rate from 47 per cent during the period 1991-

3. *http://www.humanitarianforum.org/data/files/resources/802/en/shelter_human_rights.pdf*, Accessed on 4 April 2013.

Figure 5.1

Households by Owership Status (2011)

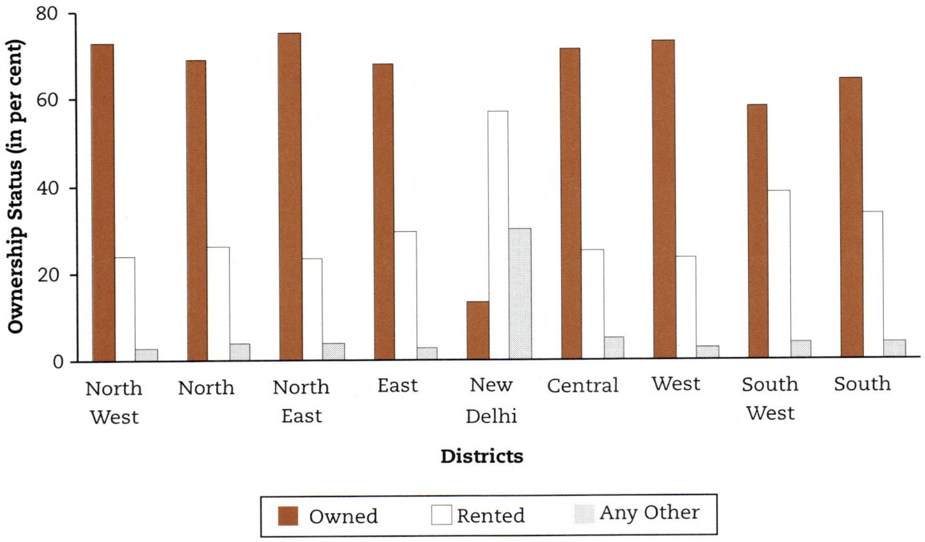

Source: Census, 2011.

2001 to 21 per cent during 2001-2011. The city is overwhelmingly urban, with 75 per cent of its total area (1483 sq. km.) falling in an urban jurisdiction. In the urban areas, the population density is as high as 17,664 persons per sq. km (Economic Survey of Delhi, 2012-13). In contrast, the rural population now stands at only 4.19 lakhs.[4] The Delhi Government's approach towards housing keeps the common citizen central to its ideology and aims at providing affordable housing for all, especially the economically weaker sections of society, in accordance with the National Urban Housing and Habitat Policy, 2007.[5]

The demand for shelter in Delhi is relentless, as more and more people continue to throng the metropolis, due to population growth as well as migration. In-migration during the decade 1991-2001 was 2.22 million, as compared to 1.64 million during the preceding decade of 1981-91 (Census figures cited in the Delhi Human Development Report, 2006, p. 41). Although, the annual population growth rate has declined during 2001 to 2012 and the migration rates also seems to have stabilised, as mentioned in Chapter 2, an estimated 78,000 migrants come to Delhi annually.

5.2.1 Availability and Ownership of Housing

Despite the challenges of population growth, migration and land availability, housing stock in Delhi has increased over the years, while the gap in housing shortage remains. According to the Census 2011 estimates, there were 3.341 million households, residing in 3.176 million houses, which clearly indicate a shortage in housing. Houses in Delhi are not only used for residential purposes, but also have commercial use. Out of 4.61 million houses in 2011, only 4.09 million were occupied, and of the occupied houses, 77.6 per cent were being used for residential purposes. As regards the other uses, 9.2 per cent of these housing units were being used for shops/offices, 3.4 per cent for residential- cum-other purposes, and 5.8 per cent for entirely non-residential purposes. The quality of housing in Delhi has improved over the last decade, with the share of 'good' houses having increased from 58 per cent in 2001 to 66 per cent in 2011.[6] Nearly one-third of the

4. Statement 2.15 in the Economic Survey of Delhi, 2012-13, Available at: *http://delhi.gov.in/DoIT/DoIT_Planning/ES2012-13/EN/ES_Chapter percent202.pdf*), Accessed on 14 April 2013.

5. The National Urban Housing and Habitat Policy, 2007, focuses on providing "Affordable Housing to All", with special emphasis on the Economically Weaker Sections (EWS) and the Lower Income Groups (LIG). Available at: *http://mhupa.gov.in/policies/duepa/HousingPolicy2007.pdf*, Accessed on 14 April 2013.

6. The Census classifies houses as 'good', 'liveable' and 'dilapidated', in accordance with whether these are in good condition and need no repair, need minor repairs, or need major repairs, respectively.

houses need minor repairs and only 3 per cent are in a dilapidated condition and require major repairs (Census, 2011).

The ownership of houses in Delhi is also high, with 68 per cent of the households owning houses and 28 per cent living in rented premises (Census, 2011). The district-wise data reveals housing ownership to be higher in the northern than in the southern districts (Figure 5.1), with New Delhi being the only district having a higher share of rented than owner-occupied housing (many residents also avail of government accommodation in New Delhi).

The high share of housing ownership in Delhi is a positive reflection of the housing situation and the official estimates too show that housing shortage has declined over time, from 2,53,679 in 1991 to 1,53,597 in 2011. This shortage also includes the homeless population and those living in *kuchcha* houses. The decline in housing shortage in the state has, however, primarily taken place between 1991 and 2001, with little improvement being seen in the situation during the last decade, and is reflected in the reduction of housing shortage by just 1.7 per cent. Other sources indicate that housing shortage may not be as low (Annexure 5.1). For instance, as per the estimates for the housing shortage provided in a Report released by the Ministry of Housing and Urban Poverty Alleviation (MHUPA) in 2012, estimates for housing shortage in Delhi are much higher at 0.49 million,[7] showing a decline from approximately 1.1 million in 2007 (MHUPA).[8]

Even if the housing stock and the number of households grow at matching rates, shortages may persist because the houses that are being built may not be affordable by the homeless and other poorer sections of the population. In fact, the Delhi city index (RESIDEX) for tracking prices of residential properties used by the National Housing Bank (NHB) shows a steep upward rise from 100 in 2007 to 202 during the first quarter (January-March) of 2013.[9]

7. *http://mhupa.gov.in/W_new/urban-housing-shortage.pdf*, Accessed on 10 April 2013. Estimates provided by the Technical Group on Urban Housing Shortage (TG-12) (2012-17) constituted by the NBO, Ministry of Housing and Urban Poverty Alleviation. The estimate is based on Census and NSS 65th Round results on 'Housing Conditions and Urban Slums', July 2008-June 2009.

8. *http://mhupa.gov.in/ministry/housing/HOUSINGSHORTAGE-REPT.pdf*, Accessed on 11 July 2013.

9. *http://www.nhb.org.in/Residex/delhires.php*, Accessed on 10 July 2013.

5.2.2 Crowding and Housing Density

Housing ownership encompasses a wide range of housing types. Unbundling housing ownership based on the Slum Census, 2011, reveals that in the Delhi slums, 0.27 million households (out of a total of 0.384 million households) had their own houses, that is, the ownership was as high as 70 per cent.[10] However, 0.146 million households (accounting for 54 per cent of the households that owned houses) lived in single-room accommodations. The phenomenon of one-room cramped accommodation/shanties in slums in the name of a 'house' is well-known, with many house-owners also lacking tenure security. This is true even for new resettlement colonies wherein the beneficiaries are entitled to short period leases. Clubbing such dwellings with houses wherein the middle classes and rich people reside could be misleading.[11]

Figure 5.2

Distribution of HH by Household Size (Per cent) 2001-2011

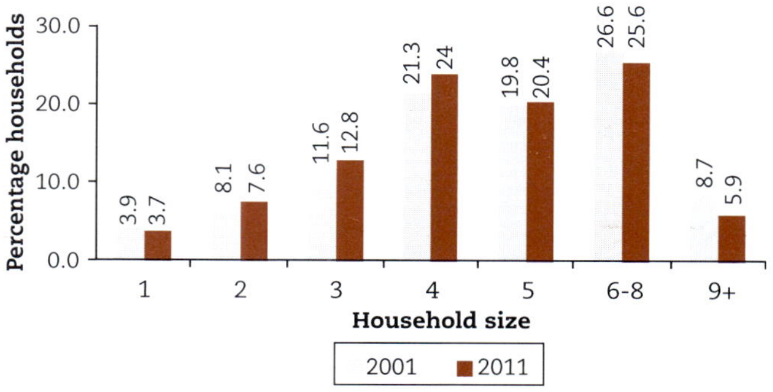

Source: Census of India, 2001 and 2011.

The relatively higher ownership among poorer households is reflected in large families staying in one/two room accommodations. The distribution of households by size (Figure 5.2) shows that in Delhi, in 2011, around a quarter of the households had 6-8 family members while 44 per cent of the households had family size of 4-5. Also, 32 per cent of Delhi's households lived in one-room accommodations. Despite their large household sizes, families are clustered in one and two room accommodations (Figure 5.3), reflecting housing congestion. The Perceptions Survey data, 2013 reveals that on an average, about 2.5 persons live in one-roomed accommodations, and this figure is the highest

10. *http://www.censusindia.gov.in/2011census/hlo/Slum_table/hl-slum/SHH1604-crc.pdf*, Accessed on 11 July 2013.

11. A detailed discussion on housing and basic services in slums/JJ clusters follows later on in this chapter.

for *Jhuggi Jhopdi* (JJ) clusters at 3.5. Paradoxically, a number of vacant houses (11 per cent) in Delhi have been found to be coexisting with the crowding and congestion. Considerable variation is seen in the district-wise share of vacant houses with the North-west and South-west districts reporting 14 per cent vacant houses and the Central district having the lowest corresponding share of 6.74 per cent. It is interesting to note that despite the housing congestion, Delhi is better placed in terms of housing as compared to the other metropolises. The percentage of households living in a single room is 63 per cent in Mumbai, 42 per cent in Kolkata, and 39 per cent in Chennai (as per Census, 2011, estimates).

Figure 5.3

Housing Occupancy Status in Delhi

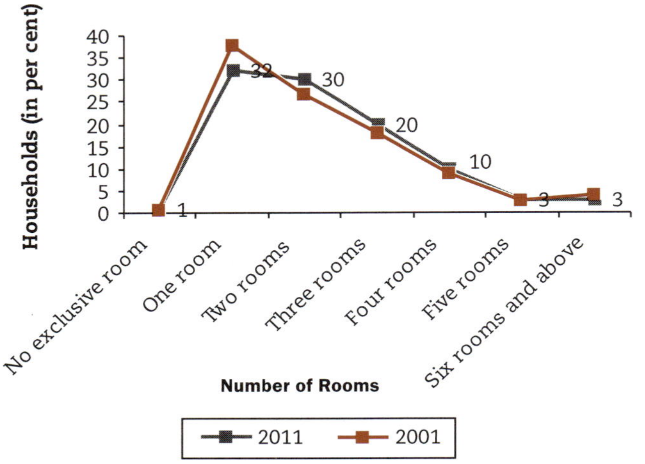

Source: Census of India, 2001 and 2011.

5.2.3 Rented Households, Rent Paid and Their Satisfaction Levels

The Census, 2011, shows that in Delhi, approximately 28 per cent of the households live in rented accommodation. As pointed out in chapter 2 on employment and livelihoods, lower income groups in Delhi spend very large proportions of their income on rent. In the lowest income category, around 45 per cent of the households were spending 20-40 per cent of their incomes on rent.

In order to ascertain the satisfaction levels in terms of housing quality and the amount of rent paid, the Perceptions Survey, 2013, divided people's satisfaction levels into three categories, viz. fully satisfied, somewhat satisfied, and not satisfied. The Survey found: *First*, on an average, 59 per cent of the tenants were somewhat satisfied, while 22 per cent were fully satisfied with their housing quality and the amount of rent they were paying. This pattern was similar across social and religious groups. Almost 54 per cent of the households belonging to higher income categories responded as being fully satisfied, and considering that there were more tenants in the higher income groups, it may be surmised that those who were paying high rent were also availing of good quality housing. *Second*, people residing in rented houses largely showed a positive outlook with approximately one-fifths of them reporting that they intended to buy a house within the next three years. Of these households, 42 per cent reported that they actually expected to be able to buy a house within

Figure 5.4

Proportion of Tenant Respondents (per cent) who think they can buy house in the next 3 years

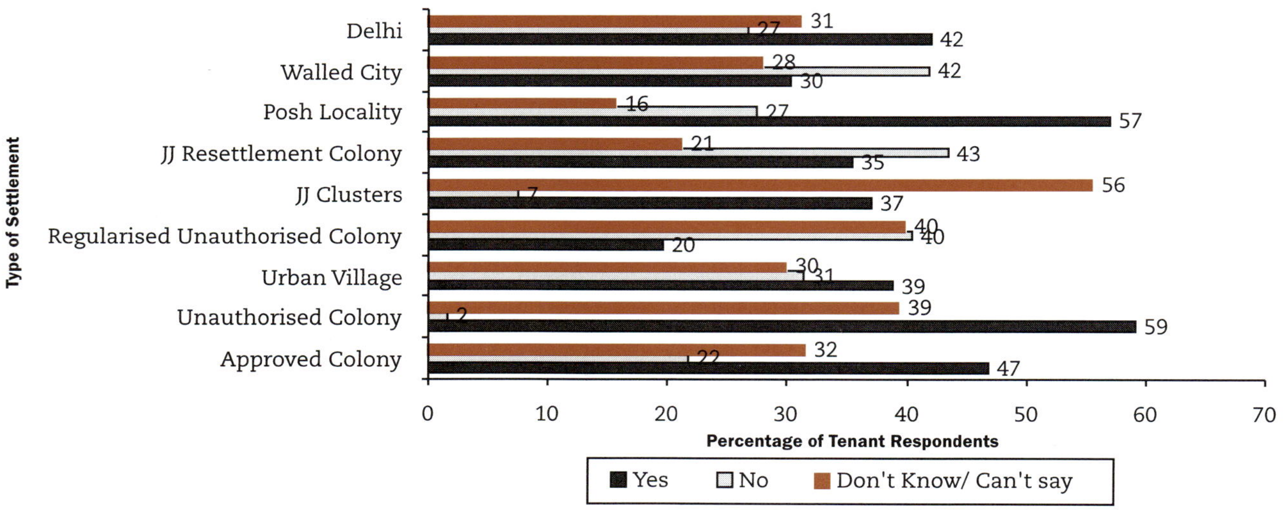

Source: Perceptions Survey, 2013.

the next three years (Figure 5.4). *Third*, almost 60 per cent of the respondents living in unauthorised colonies and 57 per cent residing in posh localities expected to be able to buy a house within the next three years. Except for the regularised unauthorised colonies, other settlements revealed 30-47 per cent of the respondents as being confident about being home owners. However, those who felt that they would not be able to buy a house within the next three years accounted for a high share (40 per cent or above) in the JJ resettlement colonies, the Walled City and regularised unauthorised colonies. A large share of the respondents in the JJ clusters did not reply in either 'yes' or 'no'.

5.2.4 The Homeless

Homelessness is a global phenomenon and millions of people all over the world are found to be spending their lives on pavements, on roadsides, railway platforms, in subways, under bridges, at their workplaces, in temple premises and so on—these are the people who lack a permanent place to call 'home'. Many factors contribute to this disturbing phenomenon, including rapid urbanisation, population pressures, and rural–urban migration, among others. In the Indian context, it has been found that extreme poverty in rural India causes many people to leave their homes and migrate to big cities. Unable to cope with the migratory shift, they end up becoming homeless. Natural disasters also act as a trigger for migration to urban centres as a survival strategy (Government of NCT of Delhi, Homeless Survey, 2010).

With an estimated 13 million homeless across the country, homelessness is not a phenomenon peculiar to Delhi, though the latter had an estimated homeless population of 56,000 in 2010 (ibid.).[12] The plight of the homeless in Delhi was recognised by the Supreme Court, which in January 2010 directed the Government of Delhi, the MCD, the NDMC and the Delhi Cantonment Board to set up a minimum given number of temporary and permanent shelters and community kitchens for them and to issue AAY ration cards to them.[13] It also directed the State Governments and Union Territories (UTs) to undertake a detailed survey on the homeless at the earliest and submit the detailed reports through their affidavits. Following this, in June-December 2010, a survey of the homeless population in Delhi was conducted at the behest of the Delhi Government, as an instrument for ensuring the rights of homeless citizens.[14] The homeless in Delhi also stand to benefit from another important order in February 2010, whereby the Supreme Court mandated the following for all state governments and ULBs for cities covered under the JNNURM and having a population of more than 5 lakhs.[15]

- One 24-hour, 365-days-a-year, homeless shelter with a capacity of 100 persons for every population size of one lakh.
- Basic amenities including mattresses, bed rolls, blankets, portable drinking water, functional latrines, first aid and primary health facilities, and de-addiction and recreation facilities, among others.
- Thirty per cent of the shelters to be special shelters for women, the old and infirm, and to function as recovery shelters).

5.2.5 Government Initiatives

With the aim of making Delhi a slum-free city, the Delhi Government has, in its approach to the Twelfth Five Year Plan, outlined mission objectives that embrace human development goals, irrespective of class and status, including: environmentally

12. A study undertaken by the Institute for Human Development in 2007 pegged the number of shelter-less persons in Delhi at 46,788 in 2007 (IHD, 2007).

13. The details of the directive are: to set up at least 100 temporary shelters for people living in the streets within one week, to build at least 140 permanent shelters for people living in the streets by December 2010, to set up at least 500 community kitchens across the city and provide nutritious and cheap cooked food, to issue AAY ration cards to all homeless people in Delhi with a validity of at least two years, which could be renewed, should they remain homeless in the city by 31 March 2010, and to file an affidavit to the Supreme Court on the steps undertaken to protect the food and shelter rights of homeless people in the city by 15 February 2010, Available at: *http://www.righttofoodindia.org/data/homelessness_data/July_2011_report_urban_homeless_national_advisor_on_homeless_to_the_comiissioners_of_supreme_court.pdf*, Accessed on 12 July 2013.

14 The survey was supported by GNCTD and UNDP. Mission Convergence, the flagship programme of the Delhi Government, selected St. Stephen's Hospital as the Mother NGO for the survey.

15. *http://www.righttofoodindia.org/orders/interimorders.html*, Accessed on 10 February 2013.

Box 5.1

Homeless in Delhi: A Snapshot

There are very few studies on headcount of the homeless population Delhi. A survey conducted by the IHD-GNCTD (2007) revealed a shelter-less population of 46,788 in Delhi. According to another study by the GNCTD-UNDP (2010), the shelter-less population in the city numbers 56,000. The main observations from the GNCTD-UNDP Survey (2010) for the homeless in Delhi were as follows:

- A majority of the homeless were men (85 per cent) and young adults.
- A majority of the homeless people were working and were productive citizens of the city.
- The motivation to migrate was a result of the poor state of the rural economy.
- Most of the homeless slept on the pavements and at workplaces, cooked their own food and consumed water from unsafe sources.
- A large number of the homeless were children, and more than 20 per cent of them were less than 18 years old.
- The ratio of homeless girls falls sharply as they enter puberty and adulthood.
- Harassment from the police is a major problem faced by the homeless besides other difficulties.

The homeless in Delhi were concentrated in three districts, accounting for 61 per cent of the total: 25 per cent in the Central district, 19.3 per cent in the North-west district, and 16.8 per cent in the South district. They were usually rag-pickers, rickshaw-pullers, construction workers, and porters, among others. Their contribution was invaluable in running the city's business and easing the daily life of its people.

The Survey Report outlined the need for the following in its recommendations:

- More appropriate and affordable shelters;
- Special shelters for women, children, families, the disabled and the destitute;
- Access to subsidised food rations for the homeless;
- Locations with a high density of homeless to be provided with additional public taps, drinking water facilities and public toilets;
- Sensitisation of the police about the needs of the homeless; and
- Issuance of Identity cards for the homeless.

Sources: IHD-GNCTD,/Shelter-less Persons in Delhi', 2007; and GNCTD-UNDP Study on Homeless in Delhi, 2010.

sustainable urbanisation; provisioning of basic amenities in all habitats irrespective of their status; urbanisation for more inclusive growth with provisioning for social services; skill development and policy initiatives for productive employment for EWS workers; and convergence of all programmes to make Delhi a slum-free city, urbanisation with preservation and conservation of its built heritage to make Delhi a Heritage City of global standards.[16]

The Delhi Government is only one of the many players in the housing sector because land, land development and public housing are under the jurisdiction of the Delhi Development Authority (DDA). However, with the introduction of the Jawaharlal Nehru National Urban Renewal Mission (JNNURM)[17] scheme, the Delhi Government is now

16. An Approach to the Twelfth Five Year Plan (2012-17), Available at: *www.delhi.gov.in*, Accessed on 12 May 2013.

17. The Mission Statement of the JNNURM includes attention to reforms and fast-track planned development of the identified cities. The focus is on ensuring efficiency in urban infrastructure and service delivery mechanisms, community participation, and accountability of ULBs/ Para-statal agencies towards citizens. There are two sub-missions under the JNNURM: (i) for urban infrastructure and governance, and (ii) for basic services to the urban poor. Source: *http://jnnurm.nic.in/wp-content/uploads/2011/01/PMSpeechOverviewE.pdf*, Accessed on 12 May 2013.

Box 5.2

Some Policy Landmarks of the Delhi Government in the Area of Shelter and Housing

Night Shelters including Mobile Shelters by DUSIB (Delhi Urban Shelter Improvement Board)

The scheme aims to provide night shelters and mobile shelters to the shelter-less population. The DUSIB has setup 150 night shelters in all parts of the city. Of these, 66 night shelters are functioning in permanent structures and 84 in temporary structures. These night shelters have also been provided with the basic facility of Sulabh Shauchalayas. The upgradation of 52 community halls into night shelters is in progress.

The Jawaharlal Nehru National Urban Renewal Mission (JNNURM)

Under this Central Government scheme, infrastructure building, improving quality of services and spatial development of the city have been brought into focus to facilitate qualitative improvements in urban areas. It also includes the provisioning of low-cost houses and upgradation of slums by providing basic services to the urban poor.

Under the Basic Services for the Urban Poor (BSUP) scheme under the JNNURM, the Government of India has approved 17 EWS housing projects for construction. These projects together would provide 67,784 dwelling units for the poor in Delhi. Of these 14,844 units have already been constructed, while issues in beneficiary selection etc remain, and about 1,505 households have been allotted flats or have been issued letters of allotment.

In another initiative, the Government of the National Capital Territory of Delhi (GoNCTD) has conferred ownership/ freehold rights to about 45 JJ resettlement colonies, which were held on lease/license basis till June 2006. This conferment promises tenure security to almost 1.25 million persons (2,50,000 plot-holders/ households) on payment of a conversion charge. This conferment is also being considered for other such settlements.

Rajiv Awas Yojana (RAY)

RAY is a significant policy guideline under the JNNURM for enabling slum redevelopment, rehabilitation and promotion of affordable mass housing. It envisages a 'slum-free city' in which every citizen has access to basic civic and social services and decent shelter. It aims to achieve this vision by encouraging states/UTs to tackle the problem of slums in a definitive manner, by using a multi-pronged approach. It focuses on bringing all the existing slums, notified or non-notified, within the formal system and enabling them to avail of the same level of basic amenities as the rest of the town. It aims to provide support to states for redeveloping all the existing slums in a holistic and integrated way, and to create new affordable housing stock. About 250 cities are expected to be covered under this scheme by the end of the Twelfth Five Year Plan.

Sources: Economic Survey of Delhi, 2012-13, and Department of Urban Development, GoNCTD.

engaged in the construction of houses for the EWS (Economically Weaker Sections). However, here again, given the huge size of the target populace, the Government's initiative would be limited by the fact that the availability and allotment of land is under the jurisdiction of the DDA. In order to cater to a projected population of 23 million by 2021, the Delhi Master Plan Document (MPD-2021) is planning to add 20 lakh new dwelling units over the period 2001-2021, out of which 54 per cent of the units would be for the EWS and LIG (Low Income Group) categories.[18]

However, implementation issues in schemes aimed at supplementing housing facilities for the poor remain. The night shelters are often situated in 'difficult to reach' locations, and lack basic services. The regular functioning of these shelters also needs improvement.[19] The Government of the NCT of Delhi has submitted a detailed proposal to the Government of India under the Rajiv Awas Yojana, for undertaking slum surveys, mapping slums, and developing a slum information system. Some policy landmarks of the Delhi Government in the area of shelters and housing are listed in Box 5.2.

5.2.6 *Providing Legitimacy and Housing to the Rural Populace*[20]

Tenure security, legitimacy and identity are important for ensuring dignified living, apart from basic

18. An Approach to the Twelfth Five Year Plan (2012-17), Available at: www.delhi.gov.in accessed on 12th May 2013.

19. Ashray Adhikar Abhiyan representative's statement at the consultation organised by IHD.

20. Information source: Department of Urban Development, GoNCT.

services and housing. It is known that in Delhi, large areas of land meant for agricultural purposes get converted into unauthorised settlements, either just outside the *laldora* areas,[21] or even away from these areas. Provisions under the Delhi Land Reforms Act (1954) mandate authorities to serve notices to such settlements, which use these areas for non-agricultural purposes. While they are meant to counter unplanned development, these laws are often used to exploit the poor and other residents through rent-seeking and, in general, need to be revised by keeping in mind urbanisation and the growing demand for residential land within the city. To this end, the Government of the National Capital Territory of Delhi (GoNCTD) has taken some meaningful measures that have helped 'unauthorised settlements' to lose their tag of illegitimacy, allowed owners to sell and register the sale of property and also legitimise access to basic services for residents in this area. While this measure is directed mainly towards those living in unauthorised settlements, given the numbers of such settlements, both the regularisation and extension of *laldora* areas is estimated to benefit about 4 million persons.

The drive to legitimise a large section of Delhi's population was initiated in 2007, when all such settlements were invited to apply for regularisation. In 2007, 1639 residential welfare associations (RWAs) applied, and by 2012, 895 such settlements (of which 42 were *laldora* extensions) were regularised after the fixing of boundaries. Many settlements were unable to apply in 2007 and some could not be regularised due to land-related issues. In order to legitimise more such settlements, the GNCTD again invited such colonies to apply in July 2013. Apart from providing legitimacy, this move is likely to significantly bridge disparities by providing access to basic services and facilitate much-needed inclusion.

In summary, the highly urbanised city of Delhi is likely to face challenges in the housing sector due to the extremely high population density and lack of sufficient affordable housing facilities. Although the decline in housing shortage and improvement in housing conditions is a promising development, the number of people living in slums and slum-like conditions and the homeless is still large. While the ownership of houses is high in Delhi at 68 per cent, and even higher for the slums at 70 per cent, it is evident that houses in slums and those in affluent localities are not comparable. The one room/two room cramped living quarters usually found in the slums cannot be termed as decent housing. Many slum-owners also lack tenure security. Despite the congestion in housing, citizens living in rented houses in Delhi were found to be largely upbeat as regards the future outlook based on the findings from the Perceptions Survey, as 21 per cent were planning to buy a house within the next three years and 42 per cent of them were expected to be able to buy it. This share is higher for the affluent localities.

The various Government initiatives in housing are likely to have contributed to this positive outlook of the people. Central plans such as the JNNURM and the RAY (Rajiv Awas Yojana) have been launched with the aim of making Delhi a slum-free city, and the Delhi Government has been working in close coordination with the Centre for implementing these schemes, along with making houses for the EWS and building night-shelters.

5.3 Basic Services

One of the duties of the State is to provide all its citizens with adequate access to basic services such as water, sanitation, electricity and transport. Water, for instance, is an extremely precious natural resource, which must be used judiciously for there to be enough to go around, not just for the present generation, but also for those to come. However, as the 2006 Global HDR points out, access to this resource is also controlled by other factors such as poverty, inequality and government failures, due to which the poor and vulnerable segments of society can be 'locked out'.[22] Delhi too has a multi-tiered society with a huge gulf between the living standards of those at the bottom and those at the top. The aggregate level statistics need to be probed further to bring out the multiple situations faced by people from widely differing backgrounds and here an attempt has been made to analyse the basic services scenario

21. *Laldora* literally means 'red thread', which was in use in the past for demarcating the jurisdiction of a village. Presently, it denotes the boundary of the territory of a village within which the norms and controls of the municipality or urban development authority are not applicable. However, since these areas did not come under the purview of the Municipal Corporation of Delhi (MCD), haphazard development has taken place here. The land in these areas was supposed to be sold to a villager only so that outsiders would not increase the population density. *Source: http://articles.economictimes.indiatimes.com/2006-11-12/personal-finance/27467106_1_lal-dora-urban-villages-mcd-area*, Accessed on 14 May 2013.

22. Delhi Human Development Report, 2006, "Beyond Scarcity, Power, Poverty and the Global Water Crisis', Available at: *http://hdr.undp.org/en/reports/global/hdr2006/*, Accessed on 16 May 2013.

Table 5.1

Basic Facilities Available to Households in Delhi (Census, 2001 and 2011)

Sl. No.	Items	2001 (in '000)	Percentage of Total Households	2011 (in '000)	Percentage of Total Households
1.	Electricity	2372	92.86	3311	99.1
2.	Toilet facility	1991	77.96	2991	89.5
3.	Electricity and toilet facility	1874	73.77	2980	89.1
4.	Electricity available but no toilet facility	498	19.49	331	9.9
5.	Toilet available but no electricity	117	4.59	11	0.3
6.	No electricity and toilet facility	65	2.55	19	0.6
7.	Water supply				
	(i) Piped water supply	1924	75.33	2717	81.3
	(ii) Handpumps/tubewells	560	21.91	458	13.7
	(iii) Wells	1	0.04	3	0.1
	(iv) Other sources (river/canal/tanks)	69	2.72	163	4.8

Source: Socio-economic Profile of Delhi, 2011-12, Available at: *www.delhiplanning.nic.in,* Accessed on 14 May 2013.

with the help of disaggregated data in terms of the types of settlements, socio-religious groups, income groups and districts. Findings from the Perceptions Survey and Focus Group Discussions, 2013, constitute a useful source of information, helping one to gauge the pulse of the people in terms of how they view their access to various basic services as well as the quality of the latter.

An analysis of the provisioning of basic services over the last decade (Table 5.1) indicates that the Delhi Government has taken remarkable strides in this sphere. There is near-universal electrification, and 90 per cent of the households have access to sanitation facilities. The supply of drinking water by the Delhi Jal Board (DJB) now reaches 81 per cent of the households as opposed to 75 per cent ten years ago. Less than 1 per cent of the households are without both toilet facilities and electricity.

Drawing from the Perceptions Survey, data presented in Table 5.2 reveals people's perceptions about the improvements and/or deterioration in the provisioning of public services in Delhi over the last three years. Overall, electricity, bus services and street-lights are clear winners with a high proportion of the respondents claiming that these services had shown an improvement. A moderate share of the respondents reported an improvement in road conditions, water supply and garbage collection services. Sanitation, specifically the condition of public toilets, was rated the worst amongst all the public services. In the subsequent sections, the provisioning of basic services is discussed individually, and assessed not only at the aggregate level, but also from the point of view of the vulnerable segments which may still be underserved.

Table 5.2

Proportion of Respondents Reporting Perception of Change in Basic Services during the Last Three Years in Delhi

Public Services	Improved	Deteriorated
Power supply	56.6	3.0
Bus services	53.9	4.1
Street lights	42.0	6.0
Road conditions	29.3	15.3
Water supply	26.3	9.8
Garbage Collection	23.7	9.8
Public toilets	20.2	26.3

Source: Perceptions Survey, 2013.

5.3.1 Access to Water Supply

Urban development must give top priority to planning for water, toilets and sewerage as an integrated whole taking into account the likely expansion of the urban population (Draft Twelfth Five Year Plan)

As the global Human Development Report, 2006, puts it, "access to water for life is a basic human need and fundamental human right". Lack of safe drinking water can cause death, especially among children. Also, women and children invest considerable effort and time to collect and carry water.[23] Overall, it would not be an under-statement to say that poor access to water, drinking or otherwise, is not only be life-threatening, but also increases the vulnerability of people by restricting the options available to them towards fully utilising their potential for human development.

Among all the basic services, water and sanitation are areas wherein, as per the Perceptions Survey, 2013, the citizens of Delhi are facing considerable problems. While less than half (48 per cent) of the respondents reported water availability to be above average (that is, 'very good' or 'good'), a quarter (26 per cent) rated it as either 'very poor' or 'poor'. Around 10 per cent of the households did not have their own toilet facilities, and a recent Government Survey[24] has found that 56 per cent of the children living in slums and unauthorised colonies in Delhi defecated in the open, which compromised not only their health but also their security.

Water Availability

Water availability in Delhi improved considerably between 2001 and 2011. In 2011, approximately 81.3 per cent of Delhi's population received piped drinking water supplied by the DJB (Table 5.1), while the residual population accessed water from hand-pumps, tube-wells, wells, rivers, canals, etc. The situation reflects an improvement since 2001, when 75.3 per cent of Delhi's residents received DJB supply. The expansion in the coverage of drinking water supply took place despite a sharp increase in the number of households in Delhi over the period 2001-11 (from 2.55 million in 2001 to 3.34 million in 2011).[25] Disparity in access measured in terms of the distance to the source of drinking water shows a marginal improvement over the same period (Census, 2011). Thus, there is still considerable scope for correcting the disparity in access to drinking water within the household premises.

Delhi fares well as compared to other metros in supplying water to households within their premises (Figure 5.5), accounting for the highest share (86.5 per cent), higher than the metros of Mumbai, Kolkata, and Chennai. In terms of providing piped drinking water to households, Delhi is second only to Mumbai, among the four metros considered (Figure 5.6).

Figure 5.5

Water Supply in Metropolitan Cities (per cent)

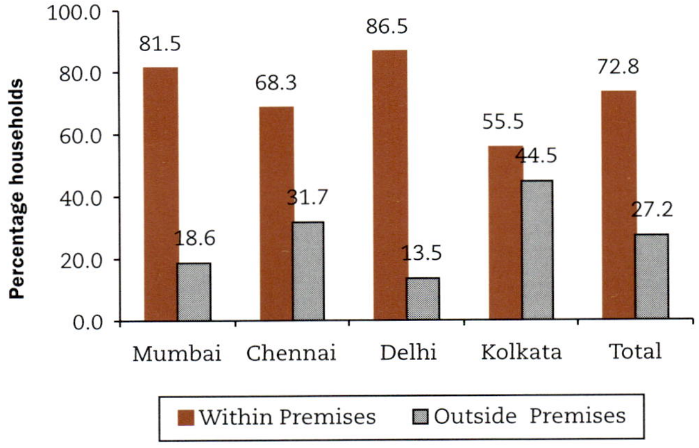

Source: NSS 65th Round (2008-09).

Figure 5.6

Source of Drinking Water in Metropolitan Cities (per cent)

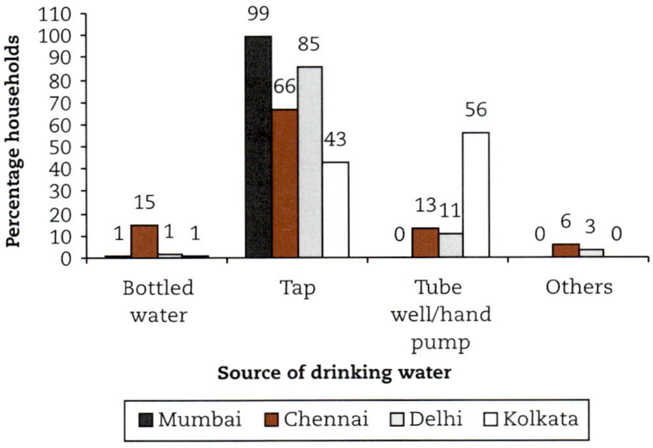

Source: NSS 65th Round (2008-09).

While the aggregate water situation has improved over the past decade, the distribution of water is not equitable across districts, with the peripheral areas receiving lower volumes per resident (Figure

23. Human Development Report, 2006, "Beyond Scarcity, Power, Poverty and the Global Water Crisis', Available at: *http://hdr.undp.org/en/reports/global/hdr2006/*, Accessed on 16 May 2013.
24. Report on 'Water, Sanitation and Hygiene—Report of the Baseline Survey 2012', from Mission Convergence, Available at: India Sanitation Portal, Accessed on 16 May 2013.
25. Census estimates, Available at: *http://delhi.gov.in/DoIT/DoIT_Planning/ES2012-13/EN/ES_Chapter percent202.pdf*, Accessed on 17 May 2013.

5.7) especially in the North, North-west, North-east and southern districts. The Perceptions Survey, 2013 also reveals a disparity among districts in terms of satisfaction with water availability (Figure 5.8). In the North-west and South-west districts, residents were found to be most dissatisfied with the availability of water, while in the east and New Delhi districts, residents rated water availability as high.

Figure 5.7

District-wise Availability of Drinking Water (percent) in Delhi

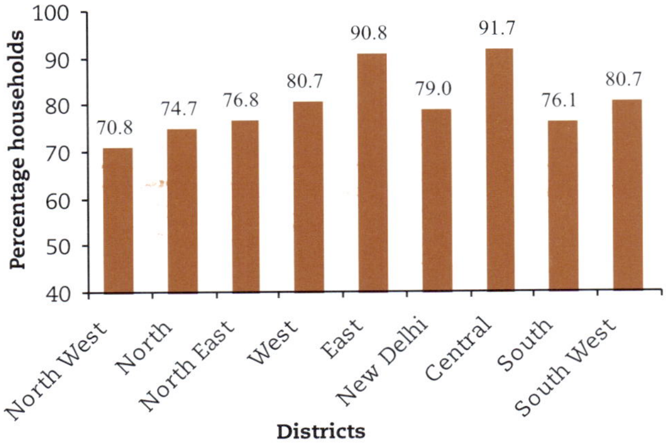

Source: Census, 2011.

The poor and under-privileged in Delhi receive subsidised water, but it comes at a price, in terms of time and cost. Hours of waiting in queues at water points and fights around water tankers are a common sight in the slums of Delhi. This is reflected in the high proportion of residents in unauthorised colonies and JJ clusters rating water availability as 'very poor/poor', while respondents from the settlements such as posh localities and approved colonies seemed more satisfied (Figure 5.9). Among the Delhi slums, which are solely dependent on government provisioning for water, just half the households have drinking water available within their premises and nearly 10 per cent have to go far away to fetch water.[26] The disparate access to drinking water is also brought out by the Perceptions Survey, which shows an increase in access to DJB piped water with increases in income.

Demand–Supply Scenario

The continued influx of people into Delhi creates an ever-rising demand for drinking water, which cannot be met by the existing production facilities (Figure 5.10). The total water supply from all sources in 2010 was around 845 MGD (million gallons water per day), including 745 MGD of surface water and 100 MGD of ground water. The total requirement in 2010 was 1080

Figure 5.8

Rating of Availability of Water Supply in Selected Districts (per cent respondents)

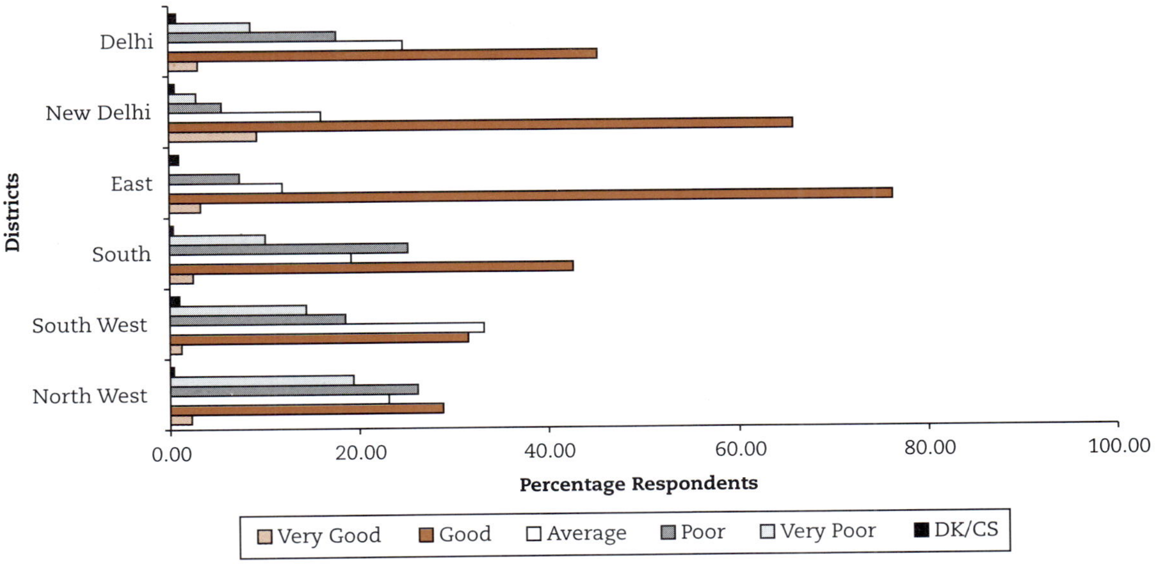

Source: Perceptions Survey, 2013.

26. For a detailed discussion on slums, see Section 5.4.

Figure 5.9

Rating of Water Availability (per cent respondents) in Different Settlement Types

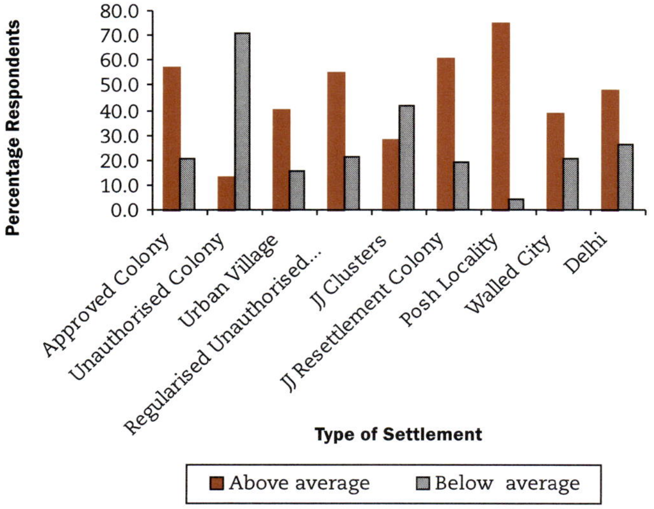

Source: Perceptions Survey, 2013.

Figure 5.10

Year-wise Production and Shortfall of Water

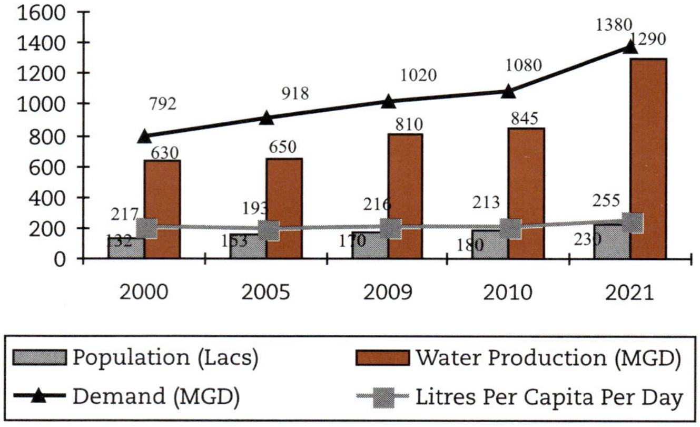

Source: Delhi Jal Board.

MGD, implying a shortfall of 235 million gallons per day. In 2011, the shortfall was less at around 165 MGD. On the basis of a projected population of 19 million and the DJB consumption norms of 60 GPCD, the water supply requirement is projected to be around 1140 MGD by the end of the Twelfth Five Year Plan.[27]

Deficits in the availability of raw water, the fast depleting groundwater and leakages from supply pipes are some of the main challenges faced by the DJB when tackling the increasing demand for water. The districts in South and South-west Delhi are worst affected by lowering ground water levels (below 20-30 meters from the ground level). DJB estimates a distribution loss of around 40 per cent of the total water supplied resulting from leakages alone.[28] Seven out of the nine revenue districts are reported to be precariously placed in terms of the availability of groundwater. The South and South-west districts have been declared as Notified Areas wherein there is to be no more extraction of groundwater. East, New Delhi, North-east, North-west and West Delhi districts have also been declared as 'over-exploited areas' by the Government.

27. Approach to the Twelfth Five Year Plan, Available at: *http://delhi.gov.in*, Accessed on 17 May 2013.

28. *http://delhi.gov.in/DoIT/DoIT_Planning/ES2012-13/EN/ES_Chapter13.pdf, Accessed on 17 May 2013.*

Water Quality

Poor quality of drinking water emerges as a major issue for Delhi-ites, as reflected in the Perceptions Survey, which reports that nearly half (47 per cent) of the respondents faced problems related to water quality in their daily lives. In terms of localities, a higher proportion of respondents from the Walled city (76 per cent), JJ clusters (59 per cent) and urban villages (56 per cent) reported issues with water quality. The FGDs corroborate these findings (Box 5.3).

The deteriorating quality of surface water and groundwater in Delhi has for long been an alarming development environmentally. The salinity of groundwater is increasing in South-west and North-west Delhi. In some areas of Shahdara and Kanjhawala, nitrate content has been found to be more than 1000 mg/litre, whereas the desirable limit of nitrate levels, according to Indian health standards, is a meagre 45 mg/litre.[29] The citizens of Delhi also incur high costs to procure water that is fit to drink by using systems like RO and Aquaguard, which the poorer segments of population cannot afford. The poor quality of surface water of the Yamuna, a river traversing a total distance of 48 km in Delhi, has for long troubled the city planners. The Yamuna accounts for 70 per cent of Delhi's water supply. However, the stretch of the river running through Delhi is extremely polluted as a result of the uncontrolled flow of untreated sewage and the discharge of industrial effluents. An additional reason is that no fresh water is available for dilution in Yamuna, as the entire fresh water from Wazirabad is used to meet

29. Indian benchmark data obtained from UNICEF, 2013.

Box 5.3

Water Availability and Quality: Findings from FGDs

In low-income localities such as the JJ clusters, JJ resettlement colonies and unauthorised colonies, there exist water supply as well as water quality issues.

- The Delhi Jal Board's piped water has not reached some JJ clusters covered in the FGD sample as well as many households in one regularised unauthorised colony. Some households depend on community standposts and some need to travel far to fetch water.
- Even in the areas where DJB water is available, there were issues cited regarding poor quality and severe shortages during the summer months. The seasonal water scarcity often led to fights colonies and sometimes people had to resort to buying water. Some of the better-off families augmented water supply from bore-wells where the cost had to be shared by the beneficiaries.
- Even many authorised colony residents cited issues about the quality of water including dirty water and foul-smelling water.
- Shortage during summer was a common complaint and some respondents reported that water bills were irregular and inflated.

Source: Focus Group Discussions conducted by IHD, 2013.

drinking water needs of the citizens of Delhi. It is alarming that the Yamuna has the lowest Dissolved Oxygen (DO) and highest count of total Coliform and faecal Coliform numbers among all rivers in the country. It also has one of the highest Biochemical Oxygen Demand (BOD).[30]

Water Tariff and Revenue

The issue of garnering resources to carry out the necessary investments in the water sector to deal with both the water deficit as well as its quality is problematic. Huge revenue losses have been incurred by the DJB due to unmetered connections, which constituted about 20 per cent of the total connections in 2011-12 (Economic Survey of Delhi, 2012-13). The tariff, while having a volumetric structure, that is, 'pay more as you use more', also provides a high subsidy for poor consumers consuming up to 20 kl per month, and free water for connections with monthly usage up to 6kl consumption. Till recently, the DJB did not have accurate estimates of the volume of raw water going for treatment and treated water available for distribution, and consequently could not estimate losses. Bulk meters have now been installed at water treatment plants to arrive at accurate estimates of the water supplied to consumers with consumption norms being applied for those without functional meters. Consumers are now also allowed to buy meters from the open market.

While the Perceptions Survey, 2013 showed that on an average, 80 per cent of the respondents across all the districts pay water bills, the incidence of non-payment was higher in the North-west (33 per cent) and South (26 per cent). Settlement-wise, the incidence of non-payment of bills was very high in the JJ clusters, wherein 69 per cent of the respondents reported not making any bill payments (Annexure 5.2). The non-payment would be partly due to the fact that two-fifths of the residents in these JJ clusters lack piped water supply.

Government Initiatives

Recognising the need for urgent reforms and capacity addition in the water sector, the Delhi Government has undertaken a number of initiatives during the Eleventh Five Year Plan period,[31] and these include:

30. Coliform is a form of bacteria. BOD is the amount of dissolved oxygen needed by aerobic biological organisms present in a body of water to break down organic material present in that water. The annual average of DO has ranged from 0.7mg/litre at Shahdara (downstream) to 7.6 mg/litre at Palla. The annual average of BOD has ranged from 2.07mg/litre at Palla to a high 54.5mg/litre at Khajuri Pantoonpul. These do not conform to the CPCB water quality standards for DO and BOD, which are 4mg/litre and 3mg/litre, respectively for class 'C' of river water.

31. *http://delhi.gov.in/wps/wcm/connect/DoIT_Planning/planning/important+links/an+approach+to+12th+five+year+plan+percent282012-17 percent29, Accessed on 18 May 2013.*

- One water treatment plant has been constructed and two more are being built.
- Three waste water recycling plants have been made operational and one is being built.
- The Sonia Vihar Water Treatment Plant with a capacity of 140 MGD has been made functional, resulting in improved supply in East and South Delhi.
- DJB has attended to the replacement of corroded and outlived pipes, reducing water supply leakage. Trunk mains near water treatment plants have been replaced by superior quality pipes and new meters have been installed.
- Rainwater harvesting is being promoted and subsidy is being provided by the Government for the installation of such systems. Since June 2001, the Ministry of Urban affairs and Poverty Alleviation has made rainwater harvesting mandatory in all new buildings with a roof area of more than 100 sq. m. and in all plots with an area of more than 1000 sq. m. that are being developed.[32]

In order to address water quality issues, Yamuna Action Plan-I (YAP-I), one of the largest river restoration projects, covering Delhi and some parts of Uttar Pradesh and Haryana, was initiated in 1993 as part of a joint effort by the Governments of India and Japan. However, cleaning the Yamuna remained an unfinished agenda under YAP-I and threw up the need for active people's participation. YAP-II focused on building new sewage treatment plants and expanding the capacity of old plants in order to address the most polluted stretch in Delhi. It also brought in NGOs to work at the community level on themes such as the socio-economic upgradation of the Community Toilet Complexes (CTCs) and the adjacent neighbourhoods, along with school health and hygiene programmes, etc. Now YAP-III has been approved for implementation of the selected projects by DJB, involving a total cost of about Rs.1657 crores.[33]

The Government's adoption of the *Bhagidari* or citizens' partnership approach for the provisioning of basic services has seen the involvement of Resident Welfare Associations (RWAs) in raising awareness about water conservation, water harvesting, and distribution of water through water tankers. Delhi's citizens have been enabled to pay water bills through the 'Jeevan' centres opened by the Government since 2009. These centres, which number more than 520, are open all day and are closed only during three national holidays.[34] The Delhi Government's efforts to improve the availability of water appears to have paid some dividends. Findings from the Perceptions Survey, 2013, reveal that on an average, 26 per cent of the respondents felt that the water availability situation had improved over the last three years. The share of respondents who felt that it had actually deteriorated was very low (10 per cent), and a majority (63 per cent) of the respondents felt that there had been no change in the water supply. The settlement-wise information, on the other hand, shows that a comparatively higher share of respondents from the unauthorised colonies (20 per cent) and JJ clusters (16 per cent) reported that the situation had worsened.

5.3.2 Sanitation

Water and sanitation facilities are complementary in nature and together are essential for a healthy population. The benefits of sanitation facilities go far beyond the obvious and are closely linked to human development. The benefits emanating from better access to sanitation facilities include better public health, improved work opportunities and enhanced dignity of the people.[35] In the context of an urban agglomerate like Delhi with a large number of slums, unauthorised colonies and homeless, the provisioning of reliable sanitation facilities is also closely entwined with improving the security of women and children who are ever so often forced to defecate in the open.[36]

Access to Latrine Facilities

At present nearly 90 per cent of the households in Delhi have access to latrines within their living premises (Census, 2011). However, 0.24 million

32. *http://www.rainwaterharvesting.org/policy/legislation.htm, Accessed on 18 May 2013.*
33. *http://delhi.gov.in/DoIT/DoIT_Planning/ES2012-13/EN/ES_chapter8.pdf*, Accessed on 20 May 2013.
34. *Source: http://www.governancenow.com/gov-next/egov/it-brings-delhi-govt-services-citizen-s-doorsteps, Accessed on 20 May 2013.*
35. *http://www.un.org/waterforlifedecade/sanitation.shtml Accessed on 20 May 2013.*
36. Even community toilets may be unsafe, as is discussed later in this section.

Box 5.4

More than half of the slum children in Delhi defecate in the open

This is the finding from a 2012 Baseline Survey on Water, Sanitation and Hygiene conducted by Mission Convergence across 19,683 households in Delhi. Mission Convergence or Samajik Suvidha Sangam (SSS) is a flagship project set up by the Delhi Government to converge various welfare entitlement schemes and services so that entitlements reach the poor and the vulnerable.

The Baseline Survey finds that 52 per cent of the children living in slums and unauthorised colonies defecate in the open. This share is as high as 79 per cent for children aged less than 3 years old. Amongst children above 3 years of age, 56 per cent of the girls and 48 per cent of the boys go outdoors for latrine purposes. The adverse impact on infants' health from such practices would be enormous and there are externalities in terms of impact on environment, especially on the immediate neighbourhood. The report finds the intensity of faecal deposition alarming with faeces flowing into storm drains, which, in turn, flows into the Yamuna untreated. Apart from issues of hygiene, the security risks that such practices pose for young children and women are not hard to imagine.

The Mission Convergence Report finds the highest shares of the practice of open defecation from the districts in the North-west, South and South-west. The main reason appears to be lack of community toilets and mobile toilets. The Survey Report highlights the need to build community awareness against such practices, alongside building more community toilets, increasing the number of seats in order to reduce waiting time, etc. The cleanliness and maintenance of public toilets is an issue that also needs urgent attention.

Source: *http://indiasanitationportal.org/category/content-type/media/statecity-news/delhi* and *www.hindustantimes.com*, Accessed on 5 June 2013.

households, comprising 7.2 per cent of the total, use public facilities and 0.11 million households (3.3 per cent) still use open spaces for defecation (see Box 5.4). This practice has serious implications not only for health and the environment, but also for the security of women and children, making them more vulnerable to exploitation.

The district-wise data for availability of latrine facilities shows that around 20 per cent of the households in New Delhi district used public facilities (Figure 5.11). The North-west district also shows the need for a lot of improvements in this regard.

Close to half the slum households did not have latrine facilities within their premises, according to Census data, which has important implications for the hygiene situation in and around slums, according to Census 2011 data. In quantitative terms, out of a total of 0.384 million households residing in the slums in Delhi, which comprise a little more than 10 per cent of Delhi's total population, nearly 0.192 million households did not have toilets within their premises. Among these, around 48,000 households were forced to defecate in the open, and the rest used community toilets.[37]

People's perceptions regarding public toilet facilities were found to be quite poor, according to the

Figure 5.11

District-wise Latrine Facilities in Delhi 2011

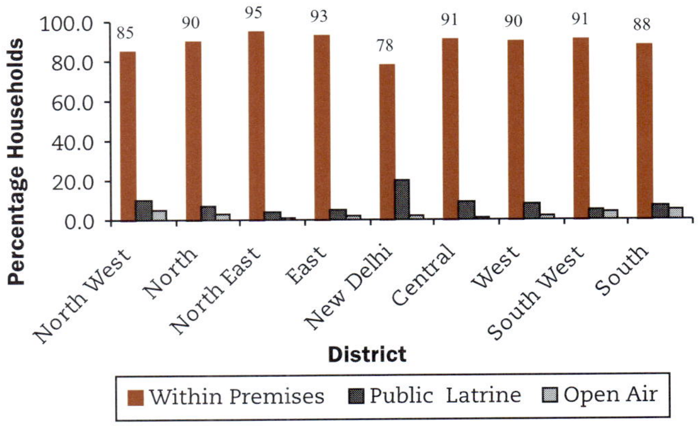

Source: Census, 2011.

37. A detailed discussion on sanitation facilities and other basic services in the slums follows in Section 5.4.

Perceptions Survey, 2013, with only 20 per cent of the respondents finding the facilities above average (i.e. very good/good) and more than half (54.5 percent) rating them as below average or very poor/poor (Figure 5.12). Only respondents from the South district were found to be relatively satisfied with the state of public toilets and a fewer proportion of respondents in New Delhi gave it a bad rating. This perception indicates that while some public provisioning has been made, the maintenance of such facilities in a regular and hygienic manner is lacking. These, in turn, impact the poorer segments of the population the most, since it is these very people who are the most dependent on public facilities. These findings are supported by the observations made during the FGDs, which reveal that a large proportion of respondents residing in the JJ clusters used the outdoors for defecation, having implications for hygiene and safety (Box 5.5). In one of the areas covered in the FGDs, women expressed fear in going alone to defecate near the railway lines.

Figure 5.12

Rating Cleanliness of Public Toilets (per cent respondents) in Different Settlement Types

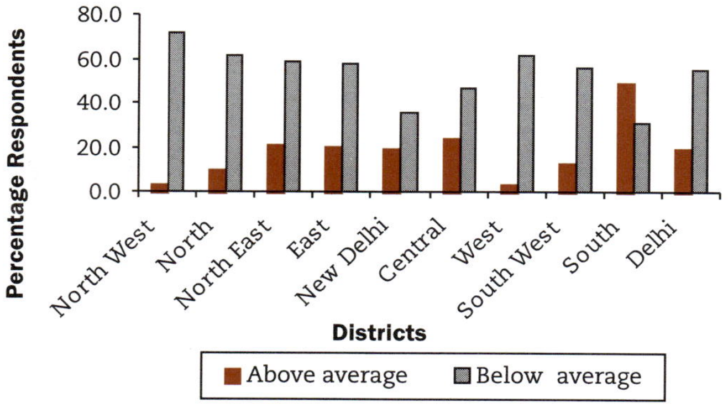

Source: Perceptions Survey, 2013.

Provision of Sanitation and Sewerage Facilities by the Government

The NDMC and the Delhi Cantonment Board are the two local bodies in charge of providing sewerage facilities in their respective areas. For the area under the jurisdiction of the MCD, the DJB is responsible for the same. Since the DJB is responsible for more than 95 per cent of the total area, the total sewage treatment is being taken care of by the DJB. At present, there are 19 treatment plants with a capacity of 514.75 MGD for sewage treatment. However, the capacity utilization is low at 62.5 per cent with around 321 MGD of sewage being treated (Economic Survey of Delhi, 2012-13). Around 1400 industrial units have installed Effluent Treatment Plants (ETPs) following Government directives and others are expected to be linked to common ETPs. The Government is also installing an Interceptor Sewerage System along the Najafgarh drain, the Shahdara drain and Supplementary Drain (ibid.).

Basic sanitation services to the low-income slum settlements are provided by the MCD. The current provisioning of sanitation services to slums follows standards set in the 1970s under the Environmental Improvement of Urban Slums scheme. The norms include provision of community toilets (1 seat for 50 users), and open and shallow street-side drains for household wastewater disposal that are linked to community standposts. Community toilets are usually linked to septic tanks and sometimes to underground sewerage wherever networks are available. The maintenance of community toilets is rendered more difficult due to vandalism. Underground sewerage networks for household toilets are available in some of the slum settlements. Sewers are also not provided to unauthorised colonies and rural villages. In most urban villages, the underground sewerage and drainage systems

Box 5.5

Open Defecations: Findings from the FGDs

Although households in many FGD localities reported having private toilets within their premises, some JJ clusters did not have such facilities. Some JJC residents go outdoors for defecation. Apart from hygiene-related issues of open defecation, there are safety issues in one particular area as women are scared to go alone near the railway lines. The absence of sewerage and garbage disposal services and uncovered drains are common problems in most areas, especially in some urban villages. Open garbage dumps constitute an environmental menace and the rainy season sees choked drains overflow, causing serious hygienic concerns and daily inconvenience.

Source: FGDs conducted by IHD in 2013.

are combined into a single network because of the existence of very narrow lanes. The outcome has been poor coverage of sanitation services, as a whole, and of underground sewerage, in particular.

Garbage Disposal and Drainage

Garbage collection and disposal, two other areas of State provisioning, are facilities which need improvement, and which, in many cases, have been privatized, accounting for the highest share, according to respondents of the Perceptions Survey (2013) (Figure 5.13). Around 20 per cent of the households reported dumping their garbage randomly in the open, or in the drains, in the absence of any systematic garbage collection service.

Figure 5.13

Where Household Garbage is Disposed of (per cent respondents in Delhi)

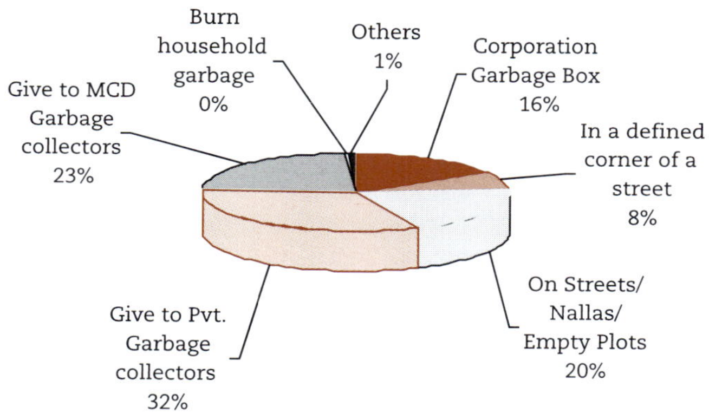

Source: Perceptions Survey, 2013.

Open dumping of garbage is the most prevalent in the South-west district (31 per cent), followed by the North-west district (27 per cent), as shown by the Perceptions Survey, 2013. The highest incidence of private collection of garbage occurs in the Central districts (72 per cent), followed by that in the East and North-east (43 per cent) districts. The system of garbage collection by the Government bodies varies in different districts. Corporation garbage boxes are used more in New Delhi and South Delhi while the incidence of garbage collection by MCD garbage collectors is higher in the North and North-west districts. A majority (65.5 per cent) of Delhi's residents feel that garbage collection and disposal facilities have remained the same over the last three years, but nearly 24 per cent also feel that they have improved (Annexure 5.3). The level of satisfaction with garbage collection services is higher in the Walled City, JJ resettlement colonies and approved colonies as compared to the JJ clusters and unauthorised colonies.

As discussed above, garbage dumped into open drains or overflowing into drain water during the monsoons poses a major health hazard for the residents. The drainage system in Delhi comprises internal drains that collect storm and wastewater from residential areas, and these flow into peripheral drains. The latter, in turn, join the main trunk drains and eventually this whole mass of water gets discharged into the Yamuna river. The length of the natural drain network in the city is 350 km, and this carries a discharge of 1,000 cubic meters, while the total length of man-made drains is 1,700 km over 12 municipal zones.[38] The industrial waste water generated in Delhi is about 40 MGD.

Area-wise, the drainage system in Delhi comprises the Najafgarh drain, the wildlife sanctuary area in Haryana territory, Shahdara area, the Bawana drainage basin, and Barapullah *nallah*, while the rest leads directly into the Yamuna River. A total of 22 drains fall into the Yamuna, out of which the Najafgarh drain alone contributes about 40.3 per cent of the total pollution to the Yamuna in Delhi followed by the Shahdara drain. The water quality monitoring results of the drains for the period April 2011 to March 2012 indicate that most drains are not meeting the standards with respect to Bio-chemical Oxygen Demand (BOD), Chemical Oxygen Demand (COD) and Total Suspended Solids (TSS) (Government of NCT of Delhi, Department of Environment, 2012).

While Delhi, as a whole, has around 59 per cent closed drainage, there is significant inter-district variation, with the New Delhi and Central districts faring far better than the other districts (Annexure 5.4). North-east Delhi stands out as the area with the poorest drainage with only 26 per cent coverage of the closed drainage. The poor state of drainage in some districts may be due to an outdated Master Plan for storm water drainage the period 1972-1976, which has not been revised till date. In order to rid the city of the perennial problem of waterlogging, the Delhi Government has decided to come out with a new Drainage Master Plan to streamline the entire sewerage network.

38. *http://jnnurm.nic.in/wp-content/uploads/2010/12/CDP_Delhi.pdf*, Accessed on 20 May 2013.

Solid Waste Management

The total solid waste generation in Delhi is around 8500 TPD (see also Annexure 5.5) (Government of NCT of Delhi, Department of Environment, 2012). The collection and disposal of municipal solid waste is carried out by the MCD, with the total number of *dhalaos* (landfills), metallic bins and open sites estimated at around 2500. The total sweeping staff available with the MCD and NDMC is in ratio of 1:216 persons and 1:326 persons, respectively, which is well above the prescribed norms of 1:500 (CPHEEO). The MCD incurs considerable expenditure in transporting the waste through long distances to the landfill sites.[39] Tackling the problem of availability of sufficient land for garbage disposal by augmenting the capacity of landfill sites also poses challenges.[40]

Government Strategies for Water and Sanitation

The DJB has been meeting its operating expenses since 2010-11 and has financially been in a position to invest in the water sector, as required.[41] Yet, equity in the distribution and access to water remains a challenge, with the peripheral areas of Delhi facing a disadvantage, and the persistence of quality-related problems, especially in the distribution network. Various interventions have been undertaken and many more are on the anvil to tackle these issues in the water sector, including demand management through tariff structures, and metering, reductions in leakages and containing of the demand for water by raising awareness about water conservation. There has been an increase in metering in the city and the Government expects 100 per cent metering of water connections during the next two years. Around 2-3 per cent of the pipes are replaced annually and flow meters are used to detect leakages. Pilot projects for using such meters in the distribution networks are on the anvil. Water conservation ratings can also help in assessing the efficiency of water use. A move from intermittent to continuous water supply is expected to improve ratings in Delhi. In this context, there is need for year-on-year performance measurements at the disaggregated levels such as the division/sub-division level.

A very important initiative in the sanitation sector has been that of the laying of an Interceptor Sewerage System along the Najafgarh drain, and Shahdara drain, and Supplementary drain across a 59 km stretch. The project is slated to ensure the protection of rivers and the major drains from any untreated effluents. It is expected that the sewage from over 1500 unauthorised colonies and other unsewered areas, including rural villages and JJ clusters would be trapped before it is permitted to reach the major drains. The project would ensure an improvement in the quality of water entering the river through three major drains that account for about three-fourths of the pollution.

A decentralised system of wastewater treatment might prove to be the right solution for unplanned settlements.[42] The DJB has also prepared a plan to provide sewerage facilities in the unauthorised colonies which have been regularized in 2012. In the unauthorised colonies, many public toilets have been constructed with JBIC (Japan Bank for International Cooperation) funds, in addition to public toilets constructed by the DUSIB. Decentralisation may also provide the solution for the garbage management system, if the capacity for management facility could be created at the ward level, since transport costs would then be reduced considerably. An increase in the capacity of waste processing, waste to energy conversion and waste recovery is also needed.

The Government has used the Bhagidari initiative, since 2002, to involve citizens in the campaign for a cleaner and healthier Delhi through the RWAs. The latter have been instrumental in improving the internal colony sewage systems, desilting sewers, overseeing work by the sanitary staff, and raising general public awareness regarding sanitation issues, among other things. The Delhi Government has adopted a ten-point strategy for comprehensive reforms in the water and sanitation sector in its approach to the Twelfth 12th Five Year Plan, (Box 5.6). With their emphasis on ensuring the universal supply of safe drinking water and more equitable water distribution, the proposed reforms would enhance the quality of life not only for the average citizen of Delhi, but also for the most disadvantaged and vulnerable strata of society.

39. Landfill sites are located on the Bhalswa GT Road, Gazipur and in Okhla. Two more landfill sites have been proposed.
40. According to a presentation made by Mr. M. Gupta, MCD, at the Stakeholders' Consultation organised by IHD on 8 July 2013 at New Delhi.
41. The discussion here draws from the presentation made by Ms. D. Mukherjee, CEO, Delhi Jal Board at the Stakeholders' Consultation organised by IHD on 8 July 2013 at New Delhi.
42. According to a presentation made by Mr. M. Gupta, MCD, at the Stakeholders' Consultation organised by IHD on 8 July 2013, at New Delhi.

Box 5.6

Mission Statement of the Delhi Government for the Twelfth Plan

- Potable & Safe drinking water to all residents of Delhi.
- 24x7 uninterrupted water supply in some pilot areas and more equitable distribution in the entire NCT.
- 100 per cent BIS Standard water quality to be made available to all consumers.
- Promotion of rainwater harvesting, groundwater recharge, regulated and controlled groundwater exploration.
- Complete measurement of water supply and distribution network at all levels with a 100 per cent metering system.
- Higher standards of treatment for wastewater.
- Use of treated waste water for all non-potable purposes.
- 95 per cent of total sewage generated to be collected, treated and disposed through interceptor sewers and normal sewage treatment network.
- Organisational restructuring of the DJB and promotion of a public–private partnership (PPP) approach to improve the management of the water and sewerage sector in Delhi.
- Non-revenue water level to be reduced to 30 per cent.

Source: An Approach to the Twelfth Five Year Plan (2012-2017), Available at: *www.delhi.gov.in*, Accessed on 21 May 2013.

In summary, it can be seen that despite improvement in access during 2001-11 access to water in Delhi is not equitable, with the unauthorised colonies and JJ clusters having much poorer access to water supply as compared to the other types of settlements. The residents in these and some other settlements also suffer due to the poor quality of water, which is sometimes muddy and foul-smelling. The Perceptions Survey, 2013, also found the residents of North-west and South-west districts most dissatisfied with the water supply.

The other main challenges that need to be addressed in the water sector include the deficit in raw water availability and the fast depletion of ground water. In particular, the lowering of the groundwater level has been adversely affecting districts in South and South-west Delhi. Leakage from the supply pipes also leads to considerable loss. Not just the deficient quantity, but the deteriorating quality of the surface water of the Yamuna also constitutes a major challenge for planners and policy-makers. The findings of the Perceptions Survey and FGDs also corroborate the issues pertaining to the water supply and quality, particularly in the low-income settlements. Supply problems are severe in summer and many residents complain of receiving foul-smelling water which is not fit for drinking. The better-off households resort to the use of bore wells, but these are costly and deplete groundwater.

There are some problems in raising revenue in the water sector including the prevalence of unmetered connections (20 per cent in 2011-12) leading to revenue loss. Till recently, the DJB was unable to estimate the volume of raw water going for treatment and the treated water available for distribution, and could not therefore estimate the losses accurately. Recently, the government has got bulk meters installed at various water treatment plants to be able to obtain accurate estimates of the water supplied to consumers and consumers are now also allowed to buy meters from the open market.

The sanitation sector is plagued by the fact that only 50 per cent of the slum-dwellers have access to private toilet facilities. Public toilets are also very poorly maintained, as perceived by the Delhi-ites. Many people, including small children, defecate in the open, leading to grave hygiene-related problems as well as security and environmental concerns. Open drains, lack of sewerage facilities in many settlements and inadequate garbage disposal facilities are among the other problems in this sector. In fact, the provision of sanitation facilities has been perceived by people to be one of the worst-performing areas of the government and immediate attention needs to be focused on this sector, especially in the slum areas.

5.3.3 *Electricity*

Electricity is a basic indispensable input in any modern day economy and is a key driver for development. It has become an essential service for providing decent living conditions in today's world and as such, provides a crucial underpinning for attaining human development goals. Electricity is an area wherein a majority of the Delhi-ites are satisfied with the efforts of the Government. According to the Perceptions Survey, almost 80 per cent of the households rated the availability of electricity as 'very good 'or 'good', that is, above average. Only a very small proportion (6 per cent) rated it as below average.

Demand–Supply Situation

Delhi has been electrified to a great extent and at present, electricity is the main source of lighting for more than 99 per cent of all the households in the NCT.[43] This is a significant improvement over 2001 when about 7 per cent of the households in the NCT did not have access to electricity. In per capita terms, the consumption of electricity stands at 1651.26 kwh, which is more than double the all-India average (778.71 kwh).[44] Electricity consumption has been growing steadily, increasing from about 13,000 million units in 2004-05 to 21,700 million units in 2011-12, signifying an increment of 64 per cent. Domestic users comprise a majority of the electricity consumers (81 per cent) in Delhi, followed by commercial (18 per cent) and industrial (1 per cent) users.

The average annual growth rate in power consumption during the Eleventh Plan period (2007-08 to 2011-12) was around 8.5 per cent (Economic Survey of Delhi, 2012-13). Power generation in the state, however, has been unable to keep pace with the enormous increases in demand and has shown considerable fluctuations during the last seven years. The gap between local generation and consumption of electricity has not been bridged for several years. In 2007-08, the gap was reduced to about 2,000 million units, but it has been widening since then to reach 13,700 million units in 2011-12 (Figure 5.14). The huge excess demand for power in the capital is met by the purchase of power from other states. Since 2004-05, more than half of the electricity available to the NCT is being purchased.

Figure 5.14

Electricity Generation, Consumption and Shortfall in Delhi

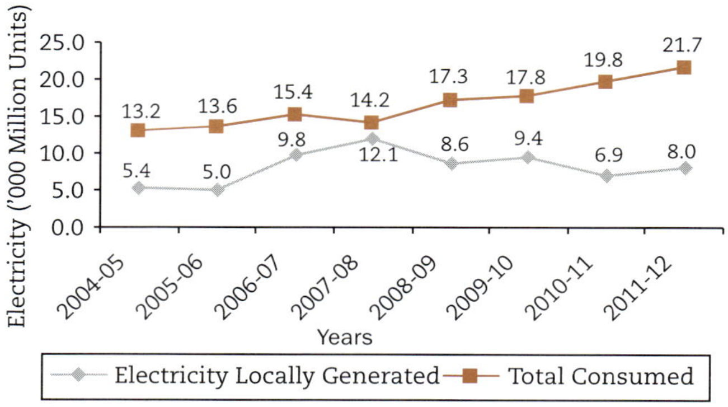

Source: Delhi Statistical Hand Book, 2012.

Power Sector Reforms

Up to 2002, when the Delhi Vidyut Board (DVB) was unbundled into six successor companies, the DVB was responsible for the generation and distribution of power to most parts of the Delhi NCT region. Around the beginning of the Tenth Plan, the DVB was restructured and unbundled as a part of the power sector reforms. Since then, with unbundling of the DVB, transmission and distribution (T&D) losses, which were largely responsible for negative returns in this sector, were reduced. Following privatisation, the Aggregate Technical and Commercial (AT&C) losses[45] also fell dramatically, from 52 per cent during the pre-reform era to 18.5 per cent in 2009-10 Economic Survey of Delhi, 2012-13). Some of the recent developments in the power scenario are delineated in Box 5.7.

Power Tariff and Power Cuts

Since the privatisation of the DVB, the spread of electricity has increased in the NCT and there have been significant reductions in transmission losses. However, the burden on the poor has intensified due to the frequent upward revision of power tariffs,

43. Census, 2011.The rate is marginally lower for the Scheduled Caste (SC) households.

44. The figures are for 2009-10, according to a reply to the Parliament question (PIB, Government of India, 14 March 2013).

45. AT&C is a better measure of efficiency as compared to transmission and distribution (T&D) losses since it also captures non-realisation of payments.

Box 5.7

Some Recent Developments in the Delhi Power Scenario

Generation: During 2011-12, installed capacity increased from 765 MW to 951 MW with the addition of GT-I of Pragati III Power Project, Bawana. In order to meet the steadily rising demand, two gas-based power projects, of 1500 MW and 750 MW, respectively, are being set up. A 1500 MW coal-based power project being set up in Haryana is expected to provide power to Delhi on an equal sharing basis.

Transmission: Delhi Transco, which is responsible for the planning, designing, construction and maintenance of 400 KV and 220 KV systems, has successfully met the challenges in this area. There is now a network of three 400 KV and twenty-nine 220 KV sub-stations associated with transmission lines. There has been considerable improvement in system availability, and reduction in transmission loss and in load-shedding.

Distribution: The distribution infrastructure is undergoing rapid improvement via the addition of power transformers, EHV cables, feeders and shunt capacitors.

Source: Economic Survey of Delhi, 2012-13.

especially during 2011-12.[46] In several instances, especially in the case of rented accommodation, electricity charges are fixed at a flat rate, which is much higher than the stipulated charge leading to financial pressure for these households. The rise in power tariff has not always been accompanied by assured power supply. The poor functioning of power plants is a widely cited reason for the shortage of power supply in the city. Illegal consumption of power is prevalent in slum settlements and illegal colonies, some of which have access to electronic appliances such as fans and televisions. There is thus a need for regularisation of the illegal residential colonies and slums, installation of meters and facilitation of payment for used electricity.[47]

While the Perceptions Survey, 2013, has shown a majority of Delhi's residents rating the availability of electricity as above average, disaggregated data reveal differing satisfaction levels across settlements. Specifically, as compared to the average figure of 80 per cent, only 57 per cent of the residents in JJ clusters and 67 per cent of the residents in the Walled city rated power availability as above average The district-wise rating reports South-west Delhi with the highest proportion (13 per cent) of residents who rated electricity supply to be 'very poor'.

Figure 5.15

Problems with Power Supply in Selected Settlements (per cent respondents)

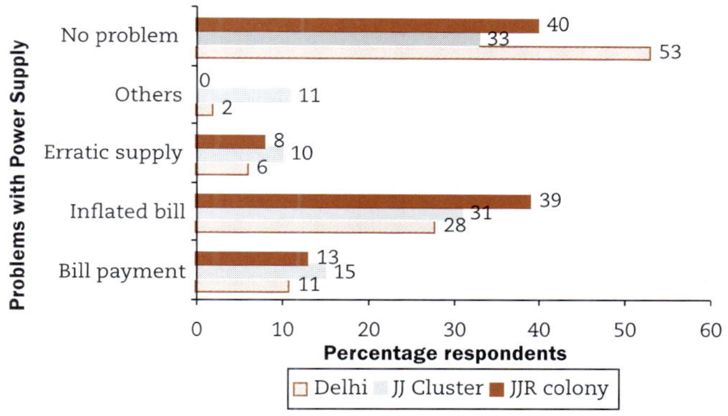

Source: Perceptions Survey, 2013.

The response of the people to the query as to whether they face any problem with power supply yielded an interesting response. As compared to 80 per cent of the respondents rating power availability as 'above average', the percentage share of respondents who said they had 'no problem' with power supply drops to 53 per cent (Figure 5.15).

Some of the main findings related to the power sector are as follows. *First*, a large proportion (28 per cent) of the respondents complained of inflated bills while others cited problems related to bill payment and erratic power supply as common issues. In terms of settlement types, respondents from the JJ resettlement colonies, JJ clusters, urban villages and

46. http://indiatoday.intoday.in/story/electricity-prices-hiked-in-delhi/1/202516.html and *http://www.ndtv.com/article/cities/delhiites-to-pay-more-for-power-from-friday-324953*, Accessed on 21 May 2013.

47. *http://news.nationalgeographic.co.in/news/energy/2011/09/110913-smart-meters-for-electricity-theft/*, Accessed on 21 May 2013.

Figure 5.16

Has Power Supply Improved in Last 3 Years? (per cent respondents)

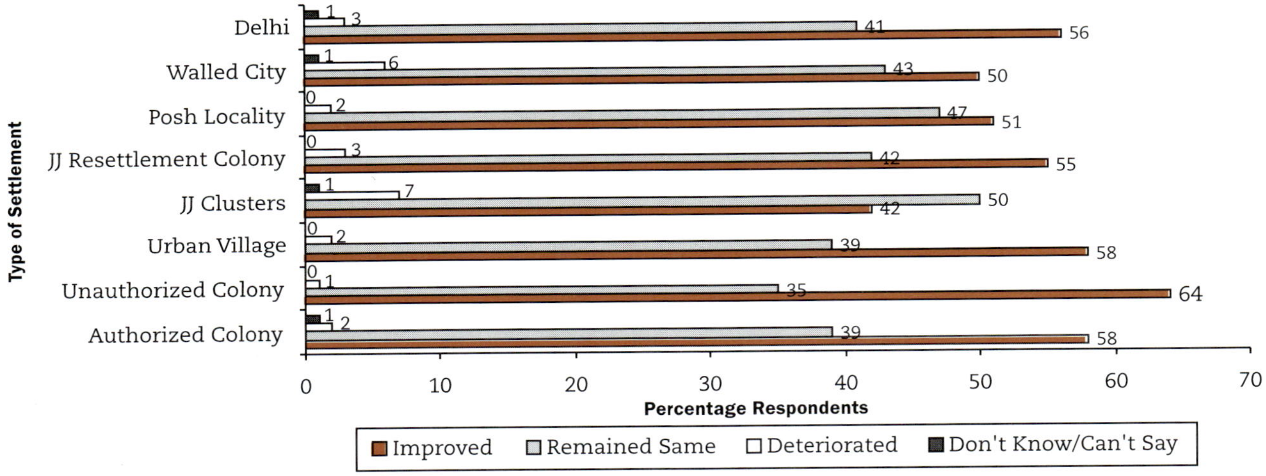

Source: Perceptions Survey, 2013.

Figure 5.17

Has Power Supply Improved Over the Last 3 Years? (per cent respondents)

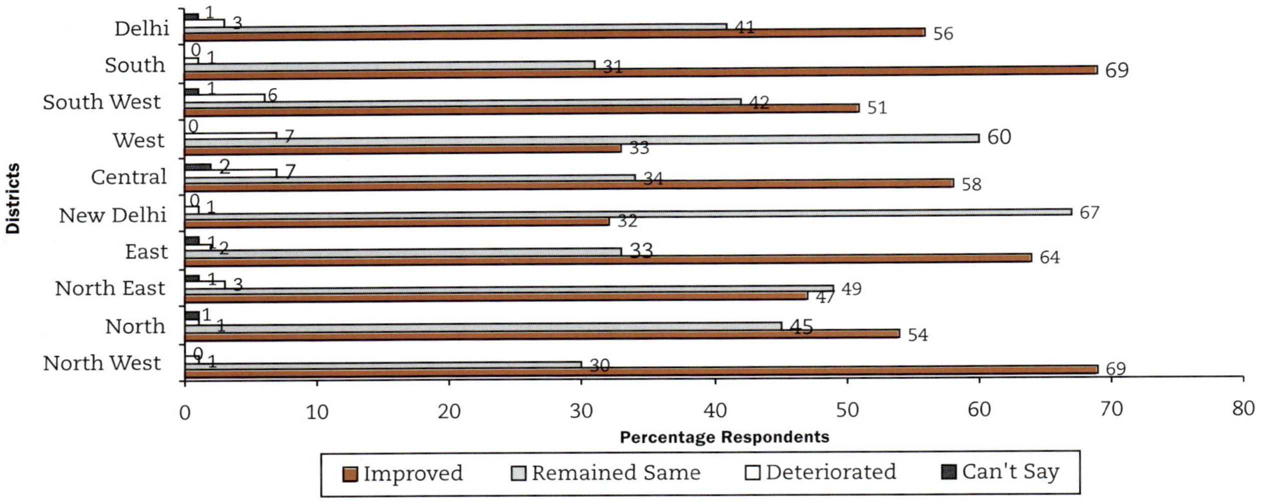

Source: Perceptions Survey, 2013.

the Walled City were among those citing inflated bills as a reason for dissatisfaction. These could also be attributable to either to the non-availability of electrical meters or forceful levying of fixed charges by landlords. About 17 per cent of the households in JJ clusters and urban villages reported that they did not pay for their electricity use according to meter readings but paid a fixed charge levied on them (a larger proportion of these respondents were residents of the South and South-west districts). Even in the posh localities and approved colonies, close to a quarter of the households reported this as a problem.

The district-wise data for those citing high electricity bills reveal a preponderance of such respondents in the South-west (46 per cent), Western (37 per cent) and Northern (29 per cent) districts. It is evident that there is a general feeling among the public that the cost of electricity has increased exorbitantly.

Second, as regards improvements in the electricity scenario over the last three years, more than half the respondents (56 per cent) felt that there had been an improvement in power supply in the city, while 41 per cent reported the feeling of a status

Box 5.8

Electricity Coverage in Poor Localities: Findings from the FGDs

The FGDs in 23 localities across Delhi found that mostly there is 100 per cent electrification with meters and payment through bills, except for one JJC in the South-west district, which gets power for four hours daily by using generators. Urban villages faced more problems with the supply of electricity especially in summer when there are a lot of power cuts. There was clear perception across the board that power has become very costly. There were reports of theft of electricity; people in authorised colonies and a regularised UC in the North-east complained of inflated bills. Residents of affluent areas, authorised colonies and even urban villages were satisfied with the functioning of street lights. In stark contrast, street lights were hardly functional in low-income settlements, including JJ clusters, JJ resettlement colonies, UACs and URCs, with obvious implications for safety of the residents.

Source: FGDs conducted by IHD.

quo, (Figure 5.16) and a small proportion (3 per cent) complained of it having deteriorated. The settlement type data finds the highest reporting of improvements by unauthorised colonies (64 per cent of the respondents), followed by the urban villages and authorised colonies at 58 per cent each. However, only 42 per cent of JJ cluster residents reported an improvement in power supply indicating an area for policy interventions in the power sector. The district-wise data show widely varying perceptions about a change in the power supply situation in the last three years (Figure 5.17).

Third, one of the benefits of the privatisation of electricity supply is improved efficiency in service delivery. A little over two-thirds of the respondent households (65 per cent) rated the power supply personnel as 'very good'/'good' and another 15 per cent rated them as average (Annexure 5.6). Respondents from unauthorised colonies gave the power personnel the best rating while the highest levels of dissatisfaction were expressed by the residents of JJ clusters, urban villages and the Walled City. Amongst the various districts, about 18 per cent of the households of the New Delhi, South-west and West districts gave a rating of 'poor' or 'worse'.[48] Such findings are also corroborated by a consumer survey conducted by DERC (2009),[49] which showed that consumers in Delhi were satisfied with stable voltage, regular visits by meter readers, regular receipt of bills and significant reductions in grievance redressal time.

Cooking Fuel

Liquid Petroleum Gas (LPG) or Piped Natural Gas (PNG) is used by 90 per cent of the urban and 75 per cent of the rural households in the NCT, (Census, 2011, Figure 5.18). Over the last decade, the more expensive and polluting fuels such as kerosene, wood and cowdung cakes have been increasingly replaced by LPG and PNG, more so in the urban areas. Yet, in the rural pockets, about 11 per cent of the population still depends on firewood. The use of LPG or PNG as cooking fuel is found to be relatively less in the SC households (80 per cent) (as per Census, 2011, estimates), compared to 91 per cent for Delhi as a whole. Almost 17 per cent of the SC households in the rural areas use firewood and 11 per cent use kerosene. Around one-fifth of the population still does not have a kitchen and 43 per cent of the households that cook in makeshift spaces outside the house still use firewood while 15 per cent use kerosene. Across the various districts of Delhi, the use of LPG and PNG is the lowest in North-west Delhi.

The Perceptions Survey reports variations across districts and settlements in the use of cooking gas stove. The districts of South-west Delhi (15 per cent) and West Delhi (16 per cent) were conspicuous in this regard, showing lower proportions of households using cooking gas stoves. The JJ clusters and JJ resettlement colonies also showed significantly lower levels of gas stove ownership. More than 90 per cent of the households in posh colonies, authorised colonies and urban villages owned gas stoves. One of the reasons for the low usage of cooking stoves in JJ colonies could be that LPG and PNG are only available against a proof of address, which many residents in JJ colonies do not possess and in the absence of which they are forced to buy cylinders from the open market on a premium. Another problem with LPG cylinders is the problem of pilferage. On several occasions, the weight of the cylinder delivered by authorised companies falls short of the stipulated weight. The grievance redressal mechanism is lengthy and ineffective. Access to PNG, which is the cleanest and safest cooking fuel, is more restricted than to LPG.

48. Data not presented here.

49. Available at: *http://www.derc.gov.in/consumer/Press percent20 Note/PressNote.htm*, Accessed on 21 May 2013.

Figure 5.18

Use of Cooking Fuel in Delhi (per cent households)

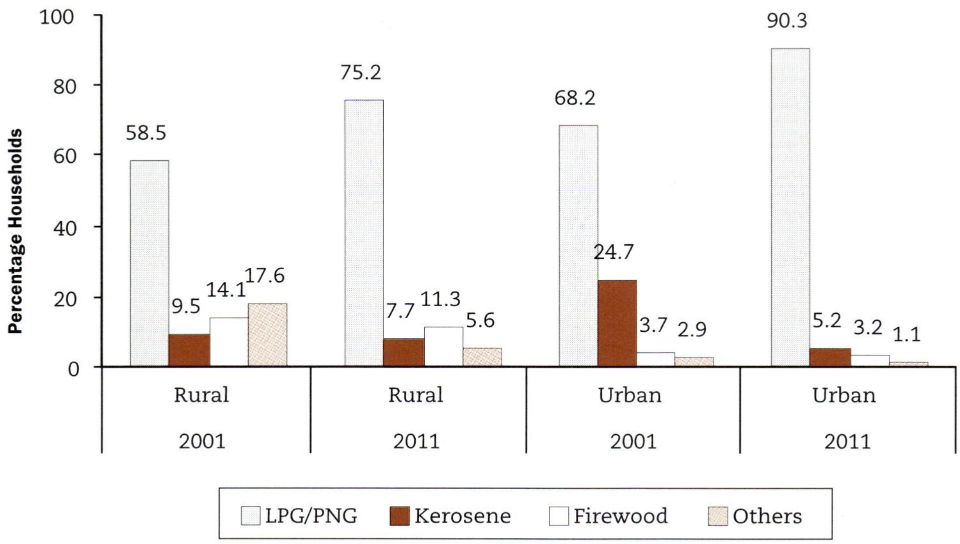

Sources: Census, 2001 and 2011 estimates.

The pipelines for this facility have not been laid out in several pockets of the city. It necessarily requires concrete walls to install the required equipment and leave out slum-dwellers and illegal constructions by design. The shift from LPG to PNG is highly desirable. It ensures uninterrupted supply to every household and has fewer chances of leakage and pilferage. It is also the cheapest option for domestic use.

The GNCTD has launched a new Plan scheme to provide free LPG connection with gas stove to all BPL households using kerosene. Under this scheme, more than 0.17 million households have already been covered and it is planned to make Delhi a kerosene free city by September 2013.

In summary, Delhi, with its high density of population, is likely to continue to be a power-deficit state. The supply in this city-state is augmented by the purchase of power from other states. The result has been nearly universal electrification. Findings from the Perceptions Survey, 2013, provide useful insights into the power situation in the state. The slum localities, particularly in the western side of the state, are reported as the most power-deficient. The residents of the poorer areas and slum settlements cite shortages in supply, and the high cost of electricity as problem areas. Issues of theft and unpaid usage of electricity, especially in slum settlements, persist. This situation partly converts to losses for the producers and is partially reflected in the frequent hikes in power tariffs and the absence of power.

It is, therefore, important to encourage the legitimate usage of power, accompanied with appropriate payments. The regularisation of illegal settlements and upgradation of slums is an important step in this direction. Privatisation has brought about positive changes in the grievance redressal mechanism and reduced transmission losses significantly. The Perceptions Survey, 2013, indicates that the districts of West and South-west Delhi require immediate attention in terms of power supply and efficiency of service providers. Installation of meters in the JJ clusters can be facilitated in order to generate accurate electricity bills.

5.3.4 Transport and Roads in Delhi

An efficient and people-friendly transportation system, along with roads that are in good condition, and adequate street-lighting constitute acceptable standards of living in a modern urban setting. In Delhi, rapid urbanisation, coupled with a rise in economic activities and personal income, have set in motion a massive upsurge in the demand for transport and an increase in the number of vehicles. Vehicular population in Delhi grew at the rate of 7 per cent over the periods 1999-2000 and 2011-12 (Economic Survey of Delhi, 2012-13). The number of registered vehicles is more than 7 million,[50] which is higher than the combined vehicular population of Chennai, Kolkata and Mumbai (Twelfth Five Year Plan, 2012-17, and Annual Plan, 2012-13, Delhi). A bulk of the demand for transport in Delhi has translated into the rising use of personalised vehicles, comprising more than 90 per cent of the total vehicular fleet. More vehicles on the streets are leading to congestion as well as to other health and environment-related problems. The Government of NCT has been actively promoting the use of public transport with the help of a number of measures to revamp the public transport system in view of the fact that a majority of the populace in the city uses public transport. The Bus Rapid Transport (BRT) system and the Delhi Metro are worth noting in this regard. A host of reform measures related to alternative modes of transport and improved road networks are also on the anvil. The Perceptions Survey, 2013, reports that buses and the metro are the most commonly used modes of transport in Delhi for commuting to work and educational purposes. According to the Perceptions Survey, 2013, one-tenth of the respondents belonged to the 'on foot' category, indicating that people also resort to walking to work or to educational institutions.

A study on transport demand forecasts[51] for Delhi predicts that the share of modal split for personalised vehicles like cars is expected to increase from 15.5 per cent in 2007 to 17.1 per cent in 2021 while the corresponding share for two-wheelers is expected to decrease from 25.5 per cent in 2007 to 20 per cent in 2021. The modal split in favour of public transport is expected to increase marginally for intra-city trips from 54.6 per cent to 59.7 per cent, and to decrease from 45 per cent to 40 per cent in the case of inter-city trips during the same time points.

The findings of this study as well as of the Perceptions Survey clearly indicate the predominance of the use of private transport. Thus, from both equity as well as efficiency perspectives, there is need for bringing about a fundamental change, which would contribute towards strengthening public transport. Walking and cycling to work and education centres could also be encouraged, as these promote a healthier lifestyle and do not cause pollution.

Transport Composition

The transport network in Delhi is still predominantly road-based though the Delhi Metro has definitely made its presence felt in recent years as a highly popular form of mass rapid transport. There has been an addition of 1.4 million vehicles over the three-year period of 2008-09 to 2012, reflecting a rapid expansion in Delhi's vehicular fleet.

Table 5.3 shows that together the share of two-wheelers (62 per cent) and cars (31.5 per cent) currently stands at more than 93 per cent of the vehicular population in Delhi, almost all of which are personalised vehicles. During the period 2008-09 to 2011-12, the overall compound annual growth rate (CAGR) for vehicles was 7.4 per cent, with taxis recording the highest growth rate (20 per cent), followed by goods vehicles (9 per cent), cars and jeeps (6 per cent) and two-wheelers (5.2 per cent). The per thousand population of vehicles has shown a phenomenal increase (70 per cent) over the period 2001 to 2011 (Figure 5.19 and Perceptions Survey, 2013), with personalised vehicles significantly contributing to this growth. However, the issues of vehicular congestion and the consequent pollution need policy attention.

Figure 5.19

Vehicles Per Thousand Population

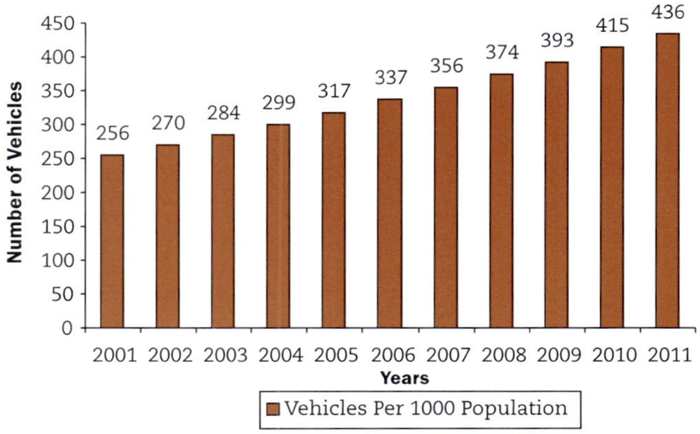

Source: Economic Survey of Delhi, 2012-13.

50. Delhi Statistical Hand Book, 2012. Some experts feel that this number is on the higher side since it may include vehicles that were registered some time ago but are no longer being used on the roads, according to Mr. D. Mohan, speaker at the Stakeholders' Consultation organised by IHD on 8 July 2013, at New Delhi.

51. Based on the study, 'Transport Demand Forecast Study and Development of an Integrated Road Cum Multi-Modal Public Transport Network', 2010, for the NCT of Delhi, commissioned by the Transport Department, GNCTD, carried out by RITES Ltd. in association with MVA Asia Ltd. and TERI.

Table 5.3

Registered Motor Vehicles in Delhi

Mode of Transport	2008-09	2009-10	2010-11	2011-12	CAGR (%)
Cars and Jeeps (Total)	18,59,370	20,13,680	21,73,323	23,43,113	8.0
Proportion of total share (%)	30.93	30.46	31.35	31.50	
2 W (Motorcycles and Scooters) Total	37,97,943	40,55,229	43,42,403	46,44,146	6.9
Proportion of total share (%)	63.18	61.34	62.64	62.44	
Auto Rickshaws Total	83,948	86,482	88,181	88,197	1.7
Proportion of total share (%)	1.40	1.31	1.27	1.19	
Taxis (Total)	40072	45240	57958	69780	20.3
Proportion of total share (%)	0.67	0.68	0.84	0.94	
Buses (Total)	55148	58047	61471	64033	5.1
Proportion of total share (%)	0.92	0.88	0.89	0.86	
Goods Vehicles etc (Total)	175250	193205	209370	228886	9.3
Proportion of total share (%)	2.92	2.92	3.02	3.08	
Total number of vehicles	6011731	6451883	6932706	7438155	7.4

Source: Delhi Statistical Hand Book, 2012.

Box 5.9

Curbing Vehicular Pollution in Delhi

The increase in the number of vehicles in the city has a strong adverse environmental impact. Also, studies have shown that vehicular pollution is a major contributor to respiratory and pulmonary diseases in cities like Delhi and elsewhere (Ingle, *et al.*, 2005; Rizwan, *et al.*, 2013; Central Pollution Control Board and Ministry of Environment and Forests, 2008).

Although much still remains to be done vis-à-vis emission from vehicles that use diesel as a fuel, it must be mentioned that significant improvements have been made to control vehicular emissions in Delhi, following which vehicular pollution has been curbed to a great extent. These include:

- Introduction of clean fuels like CNG for public transport and autos. Delhi has the largest fleet of CNG buses in the world.
- Introduction of Euro IV/Bharat Stage IV norms for tailpipe emissions of automobiles.
- Availability of diesel with 50 ppm sulphur content from April 2010.
- Phasing out of commercial vehicles that are over 15 years old.
- Introduction of battery-operated rickshaws for travelling short distances operating from nearby metro stations.
- Concessions of up to 30 per cent are being given on the price of the vehicles on the use of battery-operated vehicles having zero tailpipe emissions.
- VAT refund of 12.5 per cent is allowed for conversion of vehicles to clean fuels like CNG. (Economic Survey of Delhi, 2012-13.)

Pedestrian and Non-motorised Transport

"The pedestrians, bicyclists and non-motorised rickshaws are the most critical elements in mixed traffic" (Twelfth Five Year Plan, 2012-17 and Annual Plan, 2012-13, Delhi). Low-income groups are often the major users of non-motorised traffic and the growth of non-motorised vehicles has been more or less stagnant in recent years, with their CAGR being just around 1 per cent during the period 2008-09 to 2010-11 (Delhi Statistical Hand Book, 2012). The declining use of non-motorised transport reflects the conflicting nature of the transport-related demand from low-income groups vis-à-vis high-income groups and the former's relegation from road spaces.

Non-motorised forms of traffic are environment-friendly, but can only be used for short distance travel. Also in the existing conditions, an unplanned mix of fast- and slow-moving transport usually leads to more congestion, accidents and confusion. If people are at the heart of the road and transport infrastructure development policy, the current scenario in Delhi falls far short of the ideal, as it precludes the equitable distribution of road space and transport usage. There is an urgent need to modify infrastructure design to allow for mixed traffic. The construction of wide enough pavements for people to walk along and dedicated roads for cyclists would encourage people-friendly, non-polluting modes of transport. While the recent construction of the BRT corridor has dedicated lanes for non-motorised traffic and is a step forward in the right direction, a huge gap still needs to be bridged between conception and implementation to make a visible difference in the city.

Vehicle Ownership Patterns

The figures arrived at in the Perceptions Survey, 2013, indicate that 405 out of 1000 households own two-wheelers while the corresponding figure for cars is 159. Approximately 216 households own non-motorised vehicles including bicycles, rickshaws and *thela*s. When analysed by income and educational differences, the survey results reveal clear divergences in vehicle ownership patterns. The incidence of households owning two-wheelers and cars rises steadily as income increases. In the case of the lower middle or middle income brackets, the share of households owning two-wheelers is higher than those owning cars. In the case of higher income levels, two-wheeler ownership dips from 62.3 per cent (for the middle income category) to 55 per cent (for the highest income category) while car ownership spurts from 35.7 per cent to 59.2 per cent from the former to the latter. A similar pattern holds true for the educational categories. The Perceptions Survey, 2013, also reveals a positive outlook of the citizens of Delhi, as among the people who do not own two-wheelers or cars, 18.6 per cent plan to purchase two-wheelers while 8.6 per cent plan to purchase cars within the next two years.

The Public Transport System and People's Perceptions

Bus services in Delhi are currently provided by Private Stage Carriage operators (PSCs), the Delhi Transport Corporation (DTC), and the Delhi Metro Rail Corporation (DMRC), which provides connecting services to the metro rail system. These services are discussed in detail below.

- *PSCs in Delhi* comprised of cluster bus services, chartered buses and the Grameen Sewa vehicles for rural areas which constitute the measures that have been taken by the Government to meet the rising demand for bus services. On 15 March 2013, the Government also made the installation of GPS mandatory for chartered buses and Grameen Sewa buses to ensure the safety and security of passengers, which was to be effective from 30 April 2013.[52] In view of several allegations including many registered bus routes not being operational, lack of direct supervision, overcrowding, and buses being driven rashly leading to accidents, the Government issued a directive for taking all blue line buses off the roads in Delhi, which was implemented by June 2012. Of late, private chartered buses have also earned public ire following occurrences of various untoward incidents, which have fuelled safety and security concerns. The final blow was the recent infamous incident of gangrape in Delhi in December 2012, and in the wake of a public outcry and strict vigilant measures by the police, a large number of private chartered buses too went off the roads. The DTC plays a pivotal role in the multi-modal transit system of public transport in the NCR

52. Based on the article, "Now, GPS Mandatory for Chartered Buses", published in *The Times of India* on 19 March 2013, Available at: *http://articles.timesofindia.indiatimes.com/2013-03-19/delhi/37843233_1_gps-device-school-buses-gramin-sewa*. Accessed on 25 May 2013.

(Twelfth Five Year Plan, 2012-17, and Annual Plan, 2012-13,, Delhi.), transporting about 45 lakh passengers and covering a distance of 10 lakh kms. per day. Operating a fleet of 6029 buses, including 3775 low-floor and 1275 low-floor AC buses, the DTC is reported to have the world's largest eco-friendly CNG-based bus fleet (Twelfth Five Year Plan, 2012-17 and Annual Plan, 2012-13, Delhi). In order to make the DTC services more efficient, the issues that need to be addressed include the presently inadequate number of DTC buses and prolonged waiting time for commuters at many less frequent routes. Since buses are the most frequently used modes of public transport and perceived to be the most affordable, especially for low-income groups, it is recommended that the service and number of buses be fairly improved.

- An integral part of the Integrated Multi Modal Transport System, the Bus Rapid Transport System (BRT) will entail the construction of a total of seven BRT corridors built during the first phase in South Delhi (covering a distance of 14.5 kms, of which around 5.8 kms is already operational). With dedicated lines for motorised and non-motorised traffic, the BRT safeguards cyclists and pedestrians. People's feedback on the difficulties faced in reaching bus platforms situated in the middle of the road needs to be taken cognizance of and addressed. Motorised vehicles consisting of cars, two-wheelers and auto rickshaws, constitute more than 90 per cent of the vehicular traffic in the BRT corridor, and transport around 15-20 per cent of the commuters. On the other hand, while buses account only for 2.0-2.5 per cent of the total vehicles, they transport around 55-60 per cent of the total commuters.[53] The 'buses only' lane in the BRT leads to huge traffic jams and the loss of fuel due to prolonged queues at the traffic signals. A recent High Court order also favours the continuation of BRT and the Delhi Government has decided to extend the plan to other areas.[54] In a survey conducted by the Centre for Science and Environment (CSE) in 2008 amongst users of the BRT, 83 per cent of the commuters were reportedly happy with dedicated BRT lanes and wanted the BRT system to continue. A majority of the respondents felt that the BRT system should be expanded to other areas of Delhi and must be connected to the Delhi metro.[55]

- Metro Feeder Buses were introduced by the DMRC at selected metro stations for enabling commuters to interchange modes and connect to nearby places. However, metro feeder services have come in for repeated criticism due to the poor quality of buses and services, low frequency and overcrowding. Although there are 145 stations in the Delhi Metro network, covering nearly 190 kms, feeder buses cover a distance of 119 kms only. Recently, the DMRC has announced the introduction of 300 new feeder buses, within the year 2013.[56]

The findings from the Perceptions Survey, 2013, throw useful light on what the residents of Delhi have to say about the accessibility and quality of public transport in the capital city. The conclusions derived from their suggestions and comments are as follows:

- DTC buses (39.6 per cent), the metro (33.6 per cent) and chartered buses (12.2 per cent) were reported to be the three most frequently used modes of travel, based on a recollection of 30 days (excluding personalised modes of transport) (Perceptions Survey, 2013).

53. Available at: *http://www.dimts.in/pdf/Delhi_BRT_System_Lessons_Learnt.pdf*. Accessed on 21 May 2013.

54. Based on a report, "Government to Move SC if BRT Scrapped", published in *The Times of India* on 18 July 2012, Available at: *http://indiatoday.intoday.in/story/bus-rapid-transit-corridor-on-its-way-to-decongest-east-delhi/1/221933.html*, *http://indiatoday.intoday.in/story/sheila-dikshit-bus-rapid-transit-corridor-central-road-research-institute/1/208871.html* Accessed on 21 May 2013 "Delhi High Court Dismisses BRT Corridor Review Plea", posted in ndtv.com on 23 November 2012, Available at: *http://www.ndtv.com/article/cities/delhi-high-court-dismisses-brt-corridor-review-plea-296273*. Accessed on 21 May 2013.

55. Based on a survey "Delhi BRT System—Survey Report", conducted by CSE for DIMTS, Available at: *http://www.dimts.in/pdf/CSE-TrafficSurveyReport.pdf*. Accessed on 21 May 2013

56. Based on articles in *The Hindu*, "Metro Feeder Service: A Major Let-down", published on 23 December 2012, and TNN, "Metro Crowded, Few Feeder Buses", published on 13 February 2013. Available at: *http://www.thehindu.com/news/cities/Delhi/metro-feeder-service-a-major-let-down/article4231500.ece* and *http://articles.timesofindia.indiatimes.com/2013-02-13/delhi/37078811_1_feeder-buses-vaishali-corridor-lakh-commuters*. Accessed on 21 May 2013.

Table 5.4

Perceptions about the Bus Service in Delhi

Respondents	*Topmost 'Likes'*	*Second-most 'Likes'*	*Third-most 'Likes'*
Males	Affordability (31.7%)	Coverage (24.3%)	Safety (13.7%)
Females	Affordability (31.3%)	Coverage (23.8%)	Safety (13.9%)
	Topmost dislikes	Second-most dislikes	Third-most dislikes
Males	Overcrowding (31.3%)	No direct bus (18.01%)	Time consuming (11.4%)
Females	Overcrowding (31.8%)	No direct bus (17.04%)	Indecent behavior by bus conductors/ drivers/ co-passengers (10.4%)

Source: Perceptions Survey, 2013.

- A majority of the respondents felt that the services of DTC buses (54.2 per cent) and the metro (70.7 per cent) had improved over the last three years while close to half felt that the services provided by chartered buses had actually deteriorated (Perceptions Survey, 2013).
- Buses were still considered as the most accessible and usable mode of transport. Affordability, coverage and safety emerge as the three most important attributes that the people (of both sexes) like about the bus service in Delhi (Table 5.4) On the other hand, overcrowding and the absence of buses across all routes were cited as the downsides of the bus service in Delhi by both males and females.
- The male respondents disliked the relatively long time taken by buses to travel from one destination to another, while the female respondents cited the indecent behaviour of bus drivers, conductors and co-passengers as their reasons for disliking the same. Paradoxically, women found buses safe to travel in and did not see any link between the indecent behaviour of drivers/conductors and their safety considerations.

The Delhi Metro, an integral part of the Mass Rapid Transport System (MRTS), was introduced in Delhi in 2002 as an alternative means of providing safe, non-polluting and expeditious travel within the city. Presently spanning a length of 190 kms,[57] the Delhi Metro first started running between Shahdara and Tees Hazari stations on the Red line. Since then, it has expanded to other dedicated routes, viz., the Yellow, Blue, Green, Violet and Airport lines, which aim to cater to the travel needs of the entire NCR region. The phase-wise expansion of the Metro has ensured that the city does not come to a halt and consequently, inconvenience to commuters has been significantly mitigated. The work along Phases I and II of the Metro has been completed, and work on Phase III is currently underway. .

The Delhi Metro has made travel relatively much faster, easier and more comfortable for citizens, as they can avoid traffic snarls on the road and travel in air-conditioned comfort. The average number of daily passengers in the Metro has reportedly increased from 45,000 in 2003 to 2 million in 2013 (*Economic Times*, 17 March 2013), and on festive occasions and special days, the Metro ridership shoots up even more. An added advantage is that the Metro has not only made travel easier within Delhi but has also connected other adjoining areas in the NCR as well.

The satisfaction of commuters with this mode of travel is evident from the findings of the Perceptions Survey, 2013 (Table 5.5). The key factors favouring the Metro services were cleanliness and comfort. The male respondents also identified safety as a reason for preferring the Metro while the female respondents showed a preference for the presence of separate women's compartments, which could also be associated with safety. On the flip side, overcrowding, the non-availability of direct Metro facilities to various locations, the lack of toilets at all the metro stations and expensive fares were reasons whereby the Metro seemed to fall short of people's expectations.

57. delhimetrorail.com/project-updates, Accessed on 21 May 2013.

Table 5.5

Perceptions about the Metro Service in Delhi

Respondents	*Topmost 'Likes'*	*Second-most 'Likes'*	*Third-most 'Likes'*
Males	Clean (19.8%)	Comfortable (16.5%)	Safe (11.9%)
Females	Clean (18.8%)	Comfortable (16.6%)	Women's Compartment (16.2%)
	Topmost 'Dislikes'	Second-most 'Dislikes'	Third-most 'Dislikes'
Males	Overcrowded (32.4%)	No direct Metro (26.0%)	Toilets not available on all stations (16.0%)
Females	Overcrowded (31.7%)	No direct Metro (25.4%)	Toilets not available on all stations (15.5%)

Source: Perceptions Survey, 2013.

Responses from the Perceptions Survey about daily travel indicate that the percentage of people using the Metro is still the least among the lowest income groups and increases as one ascends the economic ladder, which is in contrast to DTC buses, for which the usage is seen to fall as one climbs up the economic ladder (Perceptions Survey, 2013). Such a finding rekindles the debate about whether the Metro, in its essence, is actually serving the masses, or is rather emerging as a premium transport mode. Similar concerns were expressed in a 2011 study on the work and livelihoods of the poor in the NCR region,[58] wherein the Metro was seldom found to be a mode of conveyance for poor workers. More thought and insight thus is required in this direction. However, in view of the fact that a major achievement of the Metro has been in terms of connecting satellite towns like Gurgaon in Haryana and Noida and Ghaziabad in Uttar Pradesh to Delhi, thereby benefiting commuters of these far-flung areas, it is expected that the proposed expansion of Metro services would soon touch the lives of the poorer strata. The Metro under Phases III and IV is envisaged to connect the satellite town of Faridabad in the extreme south of Delhi and the far-flung areas of Bawana in the extreme west, and would thus go a long way towards serving the working classes and poorer sections of the population.[59]

58. The study 'Livelihoods of the Poor and Vulnerable in NCR' was conducted by IHD in 2011 at the behest of Sir Dorabji Tata Trust (SDTT), Mumbai. Please refer to "Livelihoods of the Poor and Vulnerable in NCR—Final Synthesis Report 2012", p. 200, for details.

59. *Sources: www.delhimetrorail.com* and *http://www.dailypioneer.com/city/delhi-metro-phase-iii-a-landmark-for-city.html*. Accessed on 23 April 2013

Box 5.10

Recent initiatives by the Government in the Transport Sector

The Delhi government has been turning towards technology in a big way to solve the nitty-gritties of the problems plaguing the transport sector. The Global Positioning System (GPS) has been a useful tool in this respect. Some details of the recent efforts of the Delhi government in using GPS in the transport sector are presented below:

The Automatic Vehicle location system (AVL) through GPS was launched in 2010 to monitor crew behaviour, idling of buses etc. and help improve operational efficiencies and services to commuters.

Installation of GPS technology in buses would help the corporation keep a tab on the operation of buses from the time they leave the depot to the end of their journey. Reportedly in Dec 2012, 3,900 DTC low-floor buses and 379 cluster buses had GPS installed in them. The government has also installed GPS in 10,000 new autos. Installation of GPS would help keep a record of the route taken by drivers as well as address the safety aspect of commuters, especially female commuters.

The Delhi Govt. has issued a notice for making GPS compulsory in chartered buses and Grameen Sewa vehicles from April 30, 2013.

Source: Twelfth Five Year Plan, 2012-17, and Annual Plan, 2012-13, Available at: *http://www.delhi.gov.in/wps/wcm/connect/795c72804b89d45f9eaebf27c1af8e74/12TH-5YEAR-PLAN-2012-17-and-ANNUAL-PLAN-2012-13-one.pdf?MOD=AJPERES&lmod=-891377213&CACHEID=795c72804b89d45f9eaebf27c1af8e74*, Accessed on 21 April 2013.

Road Network and Street Lighting

From the Perceptions Survey we find that two fifths of respondents felt road conditions were below average in the city while a little over a third felt the same to be above average. District wise data show residents from New Delhi rating road conditions highly, while in the North East and North West districts road conditions were rated as poor. Above average ratings were given for roads in posh colonies and JJ resettlement colonies but respondents in JJ clusters and unauthorised colonies rated roads as poor. A large proportion of respondents (54.8 percent) felt that road conditions had remained the same in the last three years (Perceptions Survey, 2013).

The city road network in Delhi, reported to be about 33,198 lane kms long in 2012, has increased by 535 km since then. Multiple agencies are responsible for constructing roads in the city, such as the MCD, NDMC and the Public Works Department (PWD). Five national highways also run through Delhi as it is a wholesale trade centre for the whole of North India, leading to a lot of congestion on Delhi's roads. As a solution to the congestion problem, the Eastern Peripheral and Western Peripheral expressways are being constructed. (Twelfth Five Year Plan, 2012-17 and Annual Plan, 2012-13, Delhi.). The construction of flyovers, primarily over the busy traffic intersection points, has aimed at ensuring the smooth flow of traffic, and reducing fuel inefficiencies and time consumption.

Street lighting in Delhi was accorded a lot of attention prior to the Commonwealth Games in 2010 and superior quality lights were installed throughout the city, especially on the main roads. However, the arterial roads did not receive as much attention, and reports of poor illumination have surfaced in various parts of the city[60] in response to which policy interventions were put into place. The Perceptions Survey, 2013, reports that more than half the respondents rated the condition of street lighting as good, with the New Delhi district reporting the best street lighting and the Central and North-east districts reporting the poorest lighting. While 42 per cent of the respondents thought that street lighting had improved during the last three years, 49 per cent reported that it had remained the same. However, disparity in lighting across settlement types was highlighted in the FGDs wherein most of the poorer settlements such as the slums and unauthorised colonies reported inconvenience due to dysfunctional street lights, which was also reported as a great cause of concern for the safety of women and children.

To sum up, the Delhi Master Plan, 2021, aims at increasing the share of trips by public transport from the current 40 per cent to 80 per cent by 2020, which can only be achieved if the public transport system improves phenomenally along with other improvements in road space and infrastructure design, which would also accommodate non-motorised vehicles.[61] As mentioned at the inception of this chapter, one of the key policy objectives of the Government in recent years has been the strengthening of the public transport system and curtailing the usage of personalised vehicles. The Metro has been able to lure away people from using their private means of transport to a great extent. The Perceptions Survey, 2013, is also indicative of these behavioural changes, which indicate that a large proportion of the people from the reasonably well-off socio-economic categories have started taking to travelling by the Metro for both work and educational purposes, thus avoiding the use of personalised vehicles and reducing traffic congestion in the city. The Delhi Metro thus symbolises a major achievement for the Government in terms of providing a safe, convenient, expeditious and eco-friendly mode of travel, which has benefited the people of not only Delhi but of the entire NCR region as well. As part of the holistic urban planning system, the Government has also been promoting other alternative environment-friendly modes of travel, which can supplement the Delhi Metro and public buses. In fact, Delhi has the highest number of CNG buses in the world. Alternative modes of public transport like the Elevated Monorail, Light Railway Transit (LRT), and High Capacity Bus System (HCBS) are also on the anvil.

5.4 Slums and Some Other Deprived Settlements

Rapid increases in the slum population area signify a global phenomenon and are not confined to India

60. Based on the article, "How Inadequate Police Patrols and Street Lighting Make Parts of the Capital a Hotbed of Crime", Published in December 2012, Available at: *http://www.dailymail.co.uk/indiahome/indianews/article-2251297/How-inadequate-police-patrols-street-lighting-make-parts-Capital-hotbed-crime.html* and "Street Lighting in Delhi Should Match That of Developed Cities", Available at: *http://zeenews.india.com/news/delhi/street-lighting-in-delhi-should-match-that-of-developed-cities_789491.html*. Accessed on 15 June 2013

61. Sources: *http://www.cseindia.org/content/one-third-delhi-walks-work-are-our-roads-designed-safe-walking-and-cycling-latest-cse-survey* and *http://ncrpb.nic.in/latest_news/26Transport percent20Department, percent20Government percent20of percent20NCT percent20Delhi.pdf*. Accessed on 1 June 2013.

Figure 5.20

Slum Households by Average Occupancy

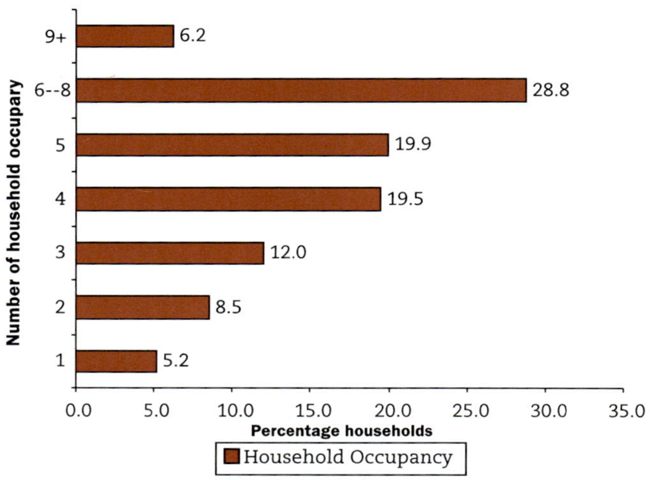

Source: Census, 2011.

Figure 5.21

Status of Basic Services

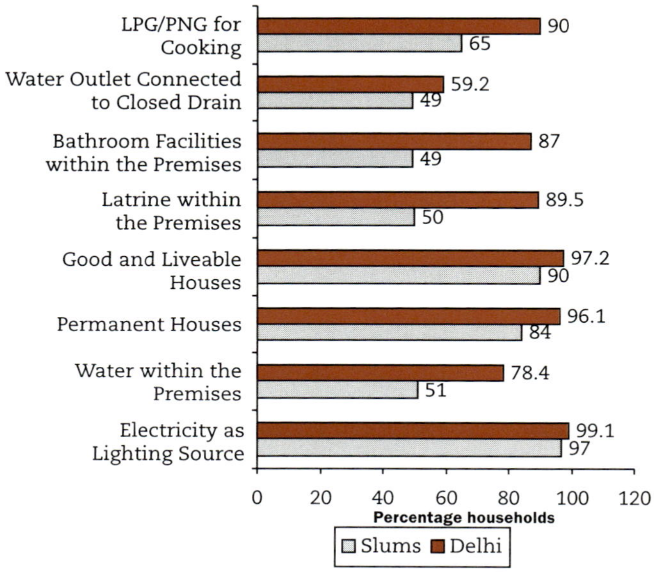

Source: Census, 2011.

alone. Recognising the substantial size of the slum population, their poor living conditions, as well as the challenges for including them in the mainstream population, the United Nations has set the target of achieving significant improvements in the lives of at least 100 million slum-dwellers by the year 2020, as part of the Millennium Development Goals (MDGs—target 11).

The number of slum households and slum population has increased substantially in Delhi over the decades, with the exception of the last decade. While in 2001, there were 0.42 million slum households (comprising a population of 2.15 million), in 2011, the numbers dropped to 0.384 million households (comprising a population of just over 1.9 million), thereby registering a decline. The Delhi Urban Shelter Improvement Board estimates for 2010 peg the number of JJ clusters as 643, with 0.4 million households and an estimated population of 2 million.

5.4.1 Housing

For Delhi, the Census 2011 data reveals that 84 per cent of the slum households stay in permanent houses and 9 per cent reside in semi-permanent houses. The average size of rooms in the slums is extremely small and the room density, that is, the number of people living per room is found to be very high. In 2011, 59 per cent of the slum households resided in single-room homes, 25 per cent shared two rooms, with household sizes of either 5 (20 per

Figure 5.22

Access to Three Basic Services (Water, Electricity and Sanitation) among Slum Households

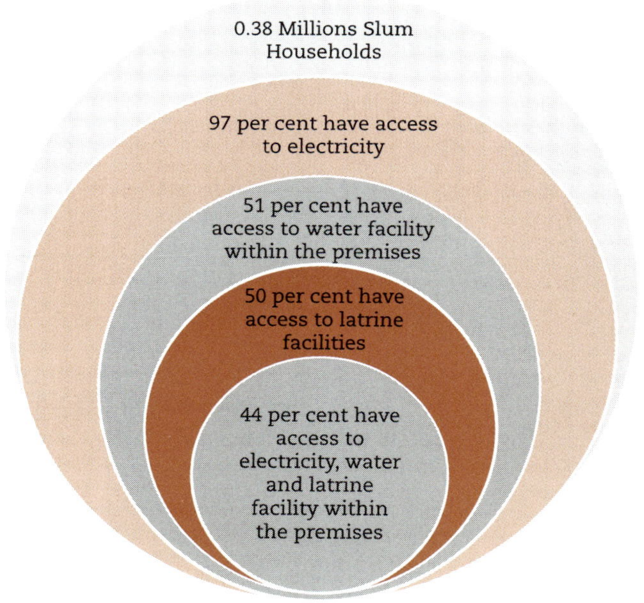

Source: Census, 2011.

cent households) or 6 people (nearly 35 per cent), thus clearly reflecting congestion and overcrowding (Figure 5.20).

Figure 5.23

Perceptions Regarding Performance of Basic Services for Selected Settlements

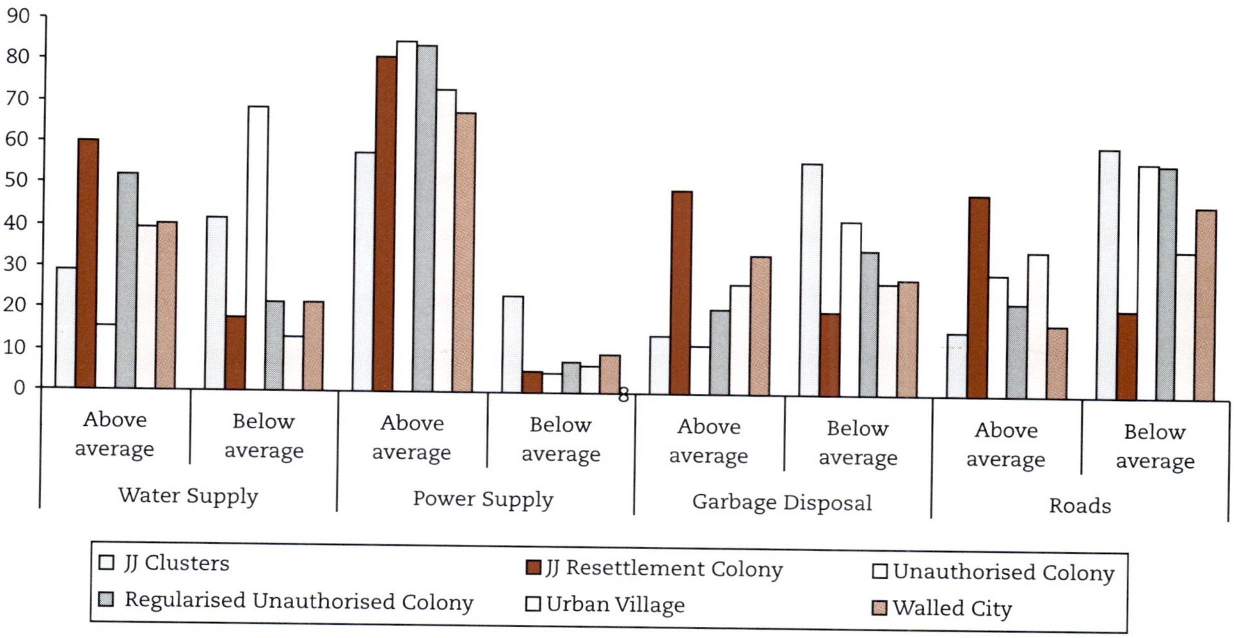

Source: Perceptions Survey, 2013.

5.4.2 Provisioning of Basic Services

When the Census, 2011, data on the provisioning of basic services to the slum and non-slum households is compared (Figure 5.21), it reveals that with the exception of electricity, slums lag behind the average level in terms of access to all the basic facilities, especially sanitation.

The gap between the figures for slums and the average figures for Delhi is the highest with regard to sanitation facilities. Combining the three important basic services of availability of water within the premises, electricity and latrine facilities, it is found that out of over 0.38 million slum households, only 44 per cent had access to all the three services (Figure 5.22), whereas, on an average for Delhi, approximately 76.5 per cent of the households had access to all these three basic services.

5.4.3 People's Perceptions about the Provisioning of Basic Services

Here we take a look at the findings from the Perceptions Survey by the type of settlements. The earlier discussion in this chapter indicated that JJ clusters[62] and unauthorised colonies were especially deprived in terms of access to basic services, and here we focus our attention on these very types of settlements.[63] The JJ resettlement colonies, urban villages and the Walled City are also discussed here since the residents of these areas also have issues in the area of provision of basic services, though not to the extent of the JJ clusters and unauthorised colonies (Figure 5.23). The vulnerability is the least in this sense in the approved colonies and posh localities, and these have therefore been kept out of the ambit of analysis in this section.

There is almost a unanimously positive perception about power supply in all the settlement types, except for the JJ clusters wherein more than 20 per cent of the respondents rated power supply as below average. The respondents from the JJ clusters,[64] urban areas and urban villages, regularised unauthorised colonies and the Walled City expressed garbage disposal and roads to be the problem areas as

62. Here the term *Jhuggi Jhopdi* clusters (JJCs) is used synonymously with slums.

63. The category of 'unauthorised colonies' includes both colonies that remain unauthorised and those that have been regularised. In this section, these are examined separately.

64. There is a possibility that the respondents' perceptions regarding roads and sanitation could be intermingled since in the FGDs, many respondents complained about flooded roads during rains, when open drains get clogged with garbage.

perceived by them. Water supply was a particular problem area for the residents of unauthorised colonies. On the other hand, respondents from the JJ resettlement colonies rated all these basic services quite highly.

5.4.4 Key Problems of Settlements

As part of the Perceptions Survey, respondents from the different types of settlements were also asked about the key problems faced by them in their respective localities. In keeping with the data depicted in Figure 5.23, sanitation figured as the most problematic area in four out of the six settlements considered (Table 5.6). In the unauthorised colonies, regularised and otherwise, water was reported to be the biggest issue for residents. The JJ clusters also clubbed power with sanitation as the key problem areas.

Table 5.6

Key Problems for the Settlements

Localities	*Most Problematic*	*Second Most Problematic*
Unauthorised Colony	Water	Roads
Urban Village	Sanitation	Roads
Regularised Unauthorised Colony	Water	Sanitation
JJ Clusters	Power and sanitation	Roads
JJ Resettlement Colonies	Sanitation	Roads
Walled City	Sanitation	Water

Source: Perceptions Survey, 2013.

5.4.5 Government Policy for Slums

The broad policy framework adopted in Delhi for slums is that no fresh encroachments shall be permitted on public land and that past encroachments, which have been in existence prior to 31 January 1990, will not be removed without providing alternatives. A three-pronged strategy has been adopted for dealing with the problems of JJs, as delineated below.

i) Relocation of the *jhuggi* households where the land-owning agencies are in a position to implement projects on the encroached land pockets as per requirements in the larger public interest. Submission of requests to the Slum and JJ Department for clearance of the *jhuggi* cluster for project implementation and with contributions of due share towards the resettlement cost.

ii) Institutionalisation of upgradation of JJ clusters and informal shelters in case of those encroached land pockets wherein the land-owning agencies issue No Objection Certificates (NOCs) to the Slum and JJ Department for the utilisation of land. However, the utilisation of land under this strategy is linked with the clearance of the project by the Technical Committee of the DDA.

iii) Extension of minimum basic civic amenities for community use under the scheme of Environmental Improvement in the JJ clusters and its component scheme of construction of 'Pay and Use Jansuvidha Complexes', containing toilets and baths, and also the introduction of mobile toilet vans in the clusters, irrespective of the status of the encroached land until their coverage is assured under one of the aforesaid two strategies.

5.5 Conclusions

Access to shelter for the citizens in Delhi is severely impacted by population pressures, accompanied by migration, and it has been compromised by the stark disparity in access to this basic facility. At the bottom of the pyramid, there are around 56,000 homeless people. Slum-dwellers constitute another vulnerable group living in congested housing, often without basic minimum services and lacking tenure security. The housing facility varies considerably depending on the type of settlement considered, from slums and unauthorised colonies at one end of the spectrum, to affluent colonies, at the other. The official figures of housing shortage show a declining trend and the present shortage is estimated at slightly over 1,50,000. This shortage paradoxically co-exists with a large number of vacant houses, indicating issues of affordability. In addition, given the large variation in housing facilities, as well as crowding due to the high incidence of large families living in one- or two-room premises, it appears that Delhi still has a long way to go before all its citizens are provided with decent housing. It is however, remarkable, that, according to the Perceptions Survey, 2013, around one-fifth of the people living in rented houses were largely positive about the future, with many of them reiterating the belief that they would be able to buy a house in the coming three years.

The provisioning of basic services has improved between 2001 and 2011 in all the four areas considered: water, sanitation, electricity and transport. The Delhi Government has succeeded in increasing the coverage of the services, particularly electricity connections, which are now nearly universal. The Government has spruced up the transport landscape of the city to a great extent, especially in the run-up to the Commonwealth Games held in 2010. Piped water connections are now available to 81 per cent of the households and sanitation facilities are available to nearly 90 per cent of the households.

In the Perceptions Survey, 2013, people perceived electricity, bus services and street lights to be the main services that had improved considerably over the last three years. The percentage share of people perceiving that that these services had deteriorated was very small. People, by and large, hailed the new additions to transport facilities such as the Metro and low-floor buses. A more moderate share of the respondents reported an improvement in road conditions (30 per cent), water supply (26 per cent), and garbage collection services (24 per cent). More than half the respondents felt that road conditions have maintained their status quo during the preceding three years, while 15 per cent felt that they had worsened. A large proportion (63 per cent) felt that water supply has remained the same while 10 per cent felt that it had deteriorated. Around two-thirds of the respondents felt that there was no change in garbage collection services during the last three years .Sanitation, specifically the condition of public toilets, was rated as the worst amongst all the public services.

5.5.1 Settlements

Moving from the aggregate frame, the settlement-wise analysis reveals a more nuanced picture. Although Delhi's natural population growth rate has been slowing down, every year nearly 2,50,000 people are added to the population of the city. Added to this is the pressure from the inflow of migrants into the city. While the new-comers provide invaluable services to Delhi's economy, the influx creates pressure on land, and also strains the available civic services and infrastructure. The various tiers of the Delhi society, with varying degrees of advantage and foothold, get reflected in the considerable differences in terms of the quality of services that they have access to. The disadvantaged masses are also handicapped by the fact that they can hardly afford private provisions and are the most dependent on government facilities.

The Perceptions Survey, 2013, indicates relatively poorer availability and functioning of all the basic services for the JJ clusters and unauthorised colonies. The poor quality of drinking water and water shortage in summers are particularly problematic issues for these people. Only half the slum-dwellers have access to private toilet facilities and the practice of open defecation poses great risks in terms of hygiene, security and environment. Open drains constitute an added woe for the residents of these settlements (and the residents of urban villages), as they turn the slums into stinking swamps during the monsoons when the drains are clogged with garbage dumped in the open. These poor and vulnerable segments of the population cannot afford access to private garbage collection systems like their counterparts who reside in the affluent settlements.

While slum-dwellers largely have access to electricity, they suffer from erratic supply and inflated bills. The residents of JJ resettlement colonies, urban villages and the Walled City, too, had issues with inflated bills. It is an interesting fact that unauthorised colonies reported the maximum improvement in power supply during the last three years. Dysfunctional street lights constituted an extremely important deficit area in the JJ clusters and unauthorised colonies, given the often precarious safety situation for the children and women residents there. Transport and roads were the other areas which need to be flagged for improvement. While the disadvantaged groups of people reap some external benefits from recent milestones such as the Metro and the introduction of low-floor buses, they face increasing costs and diminishing frequency of public bus services. Further, the inner roads in their own settlements are ill-lit and often not paved properly.

Social group-wise, the differences in perceptions were not very stark between the various groups, though the SCs were found to be marginally worse off than the other groups in terms of some of the basic services. The SC and Muslim households were found to face relatively more problems with regard to water availability while the Sikhs expressed most satisfaction regarding the same.

5.5.2 Variations across Districts

The North-west and South-west districts were found to be lagging behind the other districts in accessing many of the basic services. According to the Census information, water availability is poor in the North, North-west, North-east and South districts. The Perceptions Survey findings show residents citing poor availability of water in the North-west and South-west districts, as also salinity problems. The Samajik Suvidha Sangam (SSS) or Mission Convergence Report (2012) indicates that sanitation facilities are very poor in the North-west and South-west districts as well as in the South, since a higher percentage of the slum-dwellers in these districts are reported to defecate in the open. Yet cleanliness in the public toilets is given a thumbs-up by the respondents from the South district, which is an exception since all other districts have given poor rating to the same. In terms of drainage, the North-east district is the worst off as it has only 26 per cent closed drainage as opposed to an average of 59.2 per cent for Delhi.

Complaints about erratic power supply came mostly from the West and South-west districts, while a high share of inflated bill problems was reported by residents of the South-west, West and North districts. The New Delhi and West districts reported low proportions of respondents who felt that there had been improvements in the power supply over the last three years. Road conditions have largely remained the same during the last three years, according to more than half the respondents (55 per cent). The South district residents reported the maximum improvement (47 per cent), while 32 per cent of the residents of the Central district felt that road conditions had deteriorated. Overall, the South-west and North-west districts were found to be lagging behind in terms of the provisioning of basic services.

The discussion in this chapter points towards the need for a regular policy review for all the basic services in view of the fast-paced growth and changing conditions in Delhi. Simultaneously, the Government needs to play closer attention to the planning and implementation aspects of the same. In order to attain the eventual goals of a high level of human development for the citizens of Delhi, the Government initiatives also need to be focused further on the un-served and under-served groups/ pockets of people. The JJ clusters and unauthorised colonies have already been revealed as the most deprived in terms of shelter and basic services, and among the districts, the South-west and North-west districts also need a closer look.

5.6 The Way Forward: Some Policy Pointers

5.6.1 Housing

- The homeless need to be provided with adequate shelter, cheap food, and access to safe water and sanitation facilities, till such time that they can gain access to affordable housing.
- More focus and attention is needed for making the existing night shelters easily accessible and fully functional in terms of basic services. There is also need for separate shelters for women.
- There is a need to address the issue of crowding, especially in slums, where large families are forced to live in one or two rooms.
- A holistic approach to slum improvement and upgradation is already envisioned by the Government and needs to be carried forward by taking into account livelihood issues in the case of relocation.
- The availability of comprehensive data on slums and the homeless in Delhi would aid planning.
- More affordable houses are needed, as is evident from the fact that despite the housing shortage in the city, there are 11 per cent vacant houses in Delhi.
- Access to credit facilities at low rates of interest can be increased to bring houses within the financial reach of the people.

5.6.2 Water

- There is need for demand management by changing social attitudes towards the use and conservation of water.
- The Government's ongoing initiatives for rainwater harvesting should be continued and, in fact, accelerated, leakages from pipes reduced, regulation of groundwater use by deepening lakes, dams, reducing the number of tubewells undertaken, and more water treatment plants built. In this regard groundwater drawl charges and metering can be an option.

- Adoption of decentralized wastewater treatment may be made mandatory with reuse and recycle of treated wastewater in horticulture, cooling, flushing, etc. by individual units such as hotels, hospitals and shopping malls.

- In order to improve the quality of water, the target of the Twelfth Five Year Plan to supply 100 per cent BIS standard water quality to all, needs to be adhered to.

- For achieving equitable distribution of water, the DJB coverage must be fully extended to slums within their household premises.

- In order to raise revenue for resource generation, the Twelfth Five Year Plan proposes 100 per cent metering and reduction of non-revenue water level to 30 per cent.

5.6.3 Sanitation

- Public toilet facilities must be maintained in a clean and hygienic manner, and safety must be ensured.

- Public toilets for exclusive use of women are required.

- The eventual aim should be that all the vulnerable sections of the population have private toilets with water and sewerage connections, so that no one need suffer the indignity of open defecation.

- Settlements lacking sewerage networks must be provided with the requisite facilities and the drainage system needs replacement. Expansion of closed drainage is needed, especially in the North-east district.

- Decentralized waste management must be promoted at the local level, for which there is already an existing subsidy. In addition specific zonal level sites need to be allocated to set up environmental services for managing municipal solid wastes, biomedical waste and other types of waste.

- Garbage disposal systems must be improved with checks on the open dumping of garbage. People should be made aware about the problems resulting from the disposal of construction debris in the drains.

- Higher standards need to be adopted for the treatment for waste water, as recommended by the Twelfth Five Year Plan and the use of treated waste water for all non-potable purposes is recommended.

5.6.4 Electricity

- Tariffs must be rationalised to the extent possible in order to prevent their adverse impacts on the poor and the illegal use of power should be curbed to arrest revenue loss.

- Metering should be extended to all areas and complaints of inflated bills should be addressed regularly.

- Incentives should be used to promote renewable sources of energy and energy efficient measures, energy audits, etc. adopted.

5.6.5 Transport, Roads and Street Lights

- The bus network coverage and the number of buses need to be increased.

- Inter-state bus travel must be smooth and trouble-free within the NCR region to reduce pressures on Delhi.

- Services of public transport must be improved and surveillance measures like GPS immediately implemented to address the issue of safety and security.

- The multi-modal transport system network needs to be strengthened with the intermediate shifts of travel modes made smoother.

- Gender sensitizing of commuters and bus staff is needed and the helpline numbers should be widely circulated for ensuring safety.

- Functioning street lights are needed in all types of settlements, especially for the safety of women and children.

- Interior roads in the JJ clusters and unauthorised colonies need to be improved and maintained.

Annexure

Annex 5.1

Housing Shortage as per Census 1991-2011

Sl. No.	Items	1991	2001	2011
1.	No. of Households	1861576	2554149	3340538
2.	No. of Residential Houses	1802338	2452402	3313904
3.	No. of Shelter-less Households*	12200	24966	33506
4.	No. of Kutcha Houses (Non serviceable Temporary House for 2001)	182241	32976	93457
5.	Housing Shortage (c 1-2)+3+4)	253679	159689	153597
6.	Percent Housing Shortage (%)	13.62	6.25	4.59

Annex 5.2

Settlement-wise Residents Paying Water Bill (per cent)

Type of Locality	you pay a DJB water bill	
	Yes	No
Approved Colony	85.5	14.5
Unauthorised Colony	75.9	24.1
Urban Village	71.8	28.2
Regularised Unauthorised Colony	74.4	25.6
JJ Clusters	30.7	69.3
JJ Resettlement Colony	92.9	7.1
Posh Locality	96.7	3.3
Walled City	89.9	10.1
Delhi	79.7	20.3

Source: Perceptions Survey. 2013.

Annex 5.3

Perception in Change in Garbage Collection and Disposal Facilities over Last 3 Years (per cent respondents)

Type of locality	Improved	Remained Same	Deteriorated	Don't Know/ Can't Say	Total
Approved Colony	27.07	64.77	6.93	1.23	100.00
Unauthorised Colony	7.84	81.60	10.14	0.42	100.00
Urban Village	24.08	63.60	11.56	0.76	100.00
Regularised Unauthorised Colony	15.63	67.83	15.16	1.38	100.00
JJ Clusters	13.64	66.00	18.64	1.71	100.00
JJ Resettlement Colony	33.88	56.34	9.17	0.61	100.00
Posh Locality	21.88	73.38	4.74	0.00	100.00
Walled City	39.16	50.23	9.78	0.83	100.00
Delhi	23.70	65.51	9.77	1.02	100.00

Source: Perceptions Survey, 2013.

Annex 5.4

Drainage Facility for Waste Water Disposal

Area Name	Total Number of Households	Waste water outlet connected to		
		Closed Drainage	Open Drainage	No Drainage
NCT OF DELHI	3,340,538	59.2	36.6	4.2
North West	730,034	54.8	38.9	6.3
North	175,890	67.1	28.4	4.5
North East	395,060	25.9	72.5	1.5
East	354,385	60.8	37.9	1.3
New Delhi	30,385	84.5	11.8	3.7
Central	114,587	93.0	5.9	1.1
West	523,703	71.7	24.2	4.0
South West	462,772	65.2	29.5	5.3
South	553,722	60.0	35.2	4.8

Source: Census, 2011.

Annex 5.5

Solid Waste Management in Delhi, 2012

Sl. No.	*Particulars*	*Capacity/Quantity*
1.	Generation of Municipal Solid Waste (MSW)	8500 TPD
2.	MCDs Collection Dhalaos	168 Nos.
3.	Total Quantity of MSW through Sanitary Landfill Sites	5700 TPD
4.	Total Quantity of MSW treated	1000 TPD
5.	Proposed Quantity for treatment of MSW	8800 TPD

Source: DOE, Govt. of NCT Delhi, 2012.

Annex 5.6

Rating of Power Supply Personnel Across Settlements (per cent respondents)

	Authorized Colony	*Unauthorized Colony*	*Urban Village*	*JJ Clusters*	*JJ Resettlement Colony*	*Posh Locality*	*Walled City*	*Delhi Total*
Very Good/Good	68	80	65	50	55	68	46	65
Average	16	12	15	12	16	14	29	15
Poor/Very poor	5	4	11	15	7	6	10	7
DK/CS	2	0	5	4	5	6	7	3
Not Experienced	9	4	4	19	17	6	8	10
Total	100	100	100	100	100	100	100	100

Source: Perceptions Survey, 2013.

6

Public Safety

"Cities have the capability of providing something for everybody, only because, and only when, they are created by everybody."

—Jane Jacobs (1916–2006)

6.1. Introduction

The Human Development Report, 1994 cites *freedom from fear* as an essential component of human security (UNDP, 1994). The issue of safety and security and the meanings associated with these terms have traversed from physical safety to emotional well-being and human dignity. The protection of all, particularly vulnerable communities from hunger, illness, violence and discrimination has become increasingly important in the human development discourse. The World Development Report (World Bank, 2011) sheds light on the crucial relationship between security and development. It stresses that countries and areas characterised by insecurity, poverty, and social and political violence, are faring badly in terms of achievement of both the Millennium Development Goals (MDGs) as well as economic growth. To feel safe and to be safe are essential pre-requisites of a good quality of life for any individual. Safety is thus an important aspect of human development. A city that is completely free of crime, and provides a safe and secure environment for its residents, is perhaps a utopia. Crime is an everyday reality that affects urban centres across the world, and Delhi is no different.

This chapter first presents a background to crime and safety in an urban context, and the particular vulnerabilities faced by women and children, while concentrating on the unique case of Delhi. Using data from the National Crime Records Bureau (NCRB), the state of crimes in Delhi and their rate and composition are studied, in a comparative perspective with other major cities in the country. The results of the Perceptions Survey, 2013, are then presented and some interesting findings emerge. Current policy initiatives and strategies for the future are also discussed. An attempt has also been made to understand the implications of urban growth and planning on the safety of vulnerable populations like the poor, women and children. The subjective dimension of safety as experienced by different socio-economic groups as well as reported by the media, and the objective reality of safety as reflected by official data, are also presented and discussed. The policy and legal landscape following the brutal gang rape of a medical student in the city on 16 December 2012 has also been analysed along with the numerous efforts made by State and non-State institutions to address crucial issues regarding the safety of women in Delhi have also been highlighted.

6.2 Crime and Safety in an Urban Context

Urbanisation and urban growth are occurring at a rapid pace and according to the UNHABITAT (2012), more people in the developing regions would soon be living in urban areas as compared to rural areas. This global phenomenon creates enormous challenges in terms of the planning and distribution of resources for expanding urban populations, which could deepen existing disparities and differences based on economic, social and cultural grounds, thereby creating conflict and contestations (UNHABITAT, 2008). In the Indian context, urban centres are increasingly being associated with rising poverty and inequalities, which are attributed to many factors, one of which is exclusionary planning. Viswanath and Mehrotra (2007) and UNHABITAT (2008) point out that the 'Master Plan approach' to city planning has been criticised for being exclusionary. It is seen, that different socio-economic groups use and negotiate urban spaces and services differently such that all population groups do not have an 'equal right to the city'. For instance, private transport like cars and spaces such as malls, clubs and residential complexes are mostly used by the upper class. The poorer sections, on the other hand, use public transport and public spaces like buses, footpaths and roads, not just to commute, but also to earn their livelihoods (as in the case of hawkers, garbage collectors, fruit and vegetable vendors) (Viswanath and Mehrotra, 2007), owing to which they are more vulnerable to harassment, violence and abuse. Thus, the direction of urban planning, as it stands, is towards the creation not of equitable cities, but rather of divided ones, and Delhi is no exception.

Some of the glaring issues that need to be taken cognisance of and addressed are detailed below.

- The use of urban spaces is gendered, a fact that is often ignored in urban planning, resulting in the eclipsing of the specific needs of women and girls (UNHABITAT, 2013). According to Jagori (2011), the Delhi Master Plan, 2021, prepared by the Delhi Development Authority (DDA) does not use disaggregated data to understand the ways in which women make use of urban spaces and public services, which would allow for the inclusion of gender-sensitive features in planning. The City Development Plan (2006), too, does not seem to reflect any needs and concerns specific to women and girls (ibid). This is reflected in the lack of sufficient and well functioning public services such as street lights and safe public toilets in Delhi, which contributes to fear of violence in public spaces, and is likely to affect women and girls more severely. People, in general, and women and children, in particular, feel unsafe without street lighting and many either take alternate routes, or avoid dark areas altogether. According to a survey conducted by the Delhi Police in 2011, there were 650 unlit stretches in the city (Pandey and Haidar, 2013). In August 2012, a survey conducted by the Delhi Police revealed over 1500 areas in the city including areas near colleges, schools, residential areas and metro stations that were unlit and perceived as being unsafe (Anand, 2012).

- The lack of properly functioning, clean and safe public toilets poses serious health and safety concerns for women and girls who are vulnerable to urinary and reproductive tract infections, sexual harassment and even violence, as highlighted by a report by Sheikh (2008) on slums and resettlement colonies in Delhi. Again, while the better-off sections can easily access clean 'public' toilets in malls and restaurants, the poor are left with no options, as a result of which many reportedly resort to using open spaces, usually early in the morning or after dark to avoid being seen, all of which heighten their risks of being subjected to harassment and violence. The design of community toilet complexes, which have open roofs, allow men and boys to peep in and harass women and girls using the toilets, a concern brought out in the focus group discussions (FGDs) and Perceptions Survey, 2013. Incidents of men harassing women, and using the toilets meant for women, and the toilets being shut due to lack of water supply have also been reported (ibid.). Catarina de Albuquerque describes sanitation as more than a basic service, one which is deeply connected to the concept of human dignity, self-respect as well as safety from the threat of assault or harassment (UNHABITAT, 2013). A joint study conducted by Jagori, International Development Research Centre, and Women in Cities International in two *Jhuggi Jhopdi* (JJ) relocation colonies in North-west and North-east Delhi (2009-11), brings out the 'gender service gap', in terms of inequitable access to basic services like water and toilets for women. The findings also reveal how private interests had usurped the Municipal Corporation of Delhi (MCD) toilets and were charging residents for their use. Residents reported that they had to pay for these services or had to travel long distances to be able to access them. Incidents of violence and harassment have also been reported when women queue up to fill water or use toilets. The findings from the Perceptions Survey, 2013 and FGDs also reveal these concerns, particularly the fear of sexual harassment. Furthermore, the lack of sanitation could lead to conflict and possible violence. A study by Rodgers and Satija (2012) in selected slum settlements in Patna reveals that verbal and physical fights over makeshift toilets and water pumps are common.

- Another infrastructure-related issue in Delhi is the problem of boundary walls and setbacks around residential spaces, which have experienced a rise in anti-social activities like urinating in public spaces, and harassment. These contribute to a feeling of being unsafe, particularly by women (UTTIPEC, 2010). The high walls also block visibility and isolate pedestrians. Coupled with the lack of street lighting this results in people avoiding these 'public' spaces. The Perceptions Survey, 2013, brings out this issue quite strongly, with the women respondents revealing that they feel more unsafe as they move further away from their localities and into public spaces. This has resulted in women perceiving public spaces as negative, thus curtailing their mobility, which, in turn, impacts their participation in the life and the various employment and other opportunities that Delhi has to offer.

- A study by Jagori (2010a) finds that two out of three women report having faced incidents of sexual harassment more than once during the year under study. Spaces like the roadside and public transport were reported as unsafe. Over 80 per cent of the women respondents reported harassment in public transport or during transit and over 60 per cent reported facing verbal or physical harassment on the roadside. Findings from the Perceptions Survey reported in the earlier DHDR of 2006 also reveal public safety as a serious concern amongst the residents, with less than 20 per cent of the people feeling that the city was safe and half of them finding the city particularly unsafe for women.

- According to the research findings of another study by Jagori (2010b), the most vulnerable groups identified were young women below the age of 25 years, poor women (particularly homeless women), single women and Muslim women. Some of the factors giving rise to female insecurity included the lack of visible policing, the presence of men dealing with or consuming alcohol or drugs, crowded public transport and bus stops, poor lighting and societal attitudes. Less than 1 per cent of the women reported approaching the police in case of an incident of sexual harassment, which reflects the lack of trust for the police among the people (ibid.), a finding which also emerges in the Perceptions Survey, 2013.

- Children too emerged as vulnerable to crime and abuse. The Delhi Police reports[1] incidents of children running away from their homes, either of their own volition or to escape an uncomfortable situation at home as the two most significant reasons for children going missing. This is clearly indicative of a deep sense of dissatisfaction, even mistrust amongst children, owing to a lack of support and guidance on the part of their care-givers and the failure of the State to provide basic services for them. Vulnerability to violence and abuse of children is further compounded by poverty, and lack of shelter and basic services, thus rendering street children as the most vulnerable in cities. In fact, it has been noted that being victims of physical and sexual abuse and being denied basic rights could lead to a sense of social exclusion among children, which could potentially drive them towards anti-social behaviour and crime (UNICEF, 2012), also reflected in the findings of the IHD and Save the Children study (Box 6.1). In addition, the Delhi Master Plan, 2021, does not reflect the needs and concerns of children (Mobile Crèches, 2010).

Box 6.1

Street Children in Delhi: Findings from a Study by IHD and Save the Children

A survey undertaken in Delhi by the Institute for Human Development (IHD) and Save the Children in 2010 found close to 50,000 children below 18 years of age living on the streets (constituting 1 per cent of the child population).[2] Most of these children were located in the North and South-west districts. Out of these, a sample 1009 children were probed further and some of the main inferences that emerged from this exercise are as follows: *First*, over a quarter of the children surveyed constituted those who had run away, were living alone on the streets and were mostly involved in rag-picking and street vending, or working in dhabas. Half of them were illiterate and 20 per cent were girls. *Second*, a majority (over 70 per cent) reported living on the streets despite having a home due to reasons ranging from curiosity, escape from abuse at home, or having been victims of kidnapping, trafficking, losing their parents or losing contact with the latter, conflicts and natural disasters. *Third*, almost all children reported being subjected to verbal abuse (which they considered routine), while physical abuse was reported by 50 per cent of the boys and 33 per cent of the girls. Boys reported that they were beaten up mostly by the police and 50 per cent reported sleeping in public spaces. *Fourth*, over one-fifth of them reported using drugs, alcohol and other intoxicating substances, and nearly half of them reported being regular users of these substances. *Fifth*, the need to pay for toilet facilities and begging for water, or buying water from vendors due to fact that the community taps and handpumps were either absent or were malfunctioning was almost universal (90 per cent).

Source: 'Surviving the Streets', a study by IHD and Save the Children, 2011.

The issue that is part of an intense debate today is, "Safety for whom?" An inclusive city would go a long way towards closing the urban divide and making Delhi safer, thereby allowing all its citizens to exercise their social, economic, political and cultural rights freely without discrimination (UNHABITAT, 2008). The issue of crimes and violence against women and children has always been a concern but

1. *http://www.delhipolice.nic.in/parivartan/parivartan.htm*

2. According to the UNICEF definition cited in the study, there are three kinds of street children: children who run away from home, children who spend most of their time working on the streets, and children who live on the streets with their families.

it has now come into sharp focus, especially in the context of a series of brutal events that have occurred in the recent past, including the horrific gang rape of a 23-year old girl in December 2012, and that of a 5-year old girl in April 2013, to count a few. The incident of 16 December is being increasingly seen as a 'tipping point'[3] in the social, legal as well as policy landscape, as it invited massive social protests, thus making crimes against women '*everybody's business*'.[4] The major initiatives undertaken in the formulation of laws and policies are reflected in the recommendations of the Justice Verma Committee (constituted in December 2012), many of which have been also incorporated in the new the Criminal Law [Amendment] Act (2013). The media and civil society organisations were also instrumental in facilitating massive protests and meetings, spreading awareness in the process, and demanding fundamental changes within institutions such as the police and the judiciary. Although there is still a long way to go, the silence and apathy on the issue of crimes and violence against women has been broken. What is needed is a change not just in policing and laws, but also in societal attitudes, planning processes, and redressal mechanisms by promoting sensitisation and awareness among the public. These issues have been touched upon in the final section of this chapter.

6.3. State of Crime

6.3.1 The Total Crime Rate

Contrary to widespread perception, the crime rate in Delhi (based on a three-year average crime rate for 2004-2006 and 2010-2012) calculated using the official source of statistics, the National Crime Records Bureau (NCRB)[5] data declined over the period 2004-2006 to 2010-2012[6] (Figure 6.1). The NCRB data indicate that though the total cognisable[7] crime rate[8] (based on the Indian Penal Code [IPC])[9] for all major cities increased marginally from 293.8 to 310.6 per 100,000 population, the rate in Delhi (city) decreased from 397.9 to 314.3 per 100,000 during the same period (Figure 6.1). Bangalore reported the highest crime rate followed by Ahmedabad and Delhi, while Kolkata reported the least. Mumbai reported an increase in crime from 187.2 to 290.4 per 100,000 population (Annex Tables 6.1 and 6.2).

Figure 6.1

Total Cognisable Crime Rates in Major Cities (2004-06) and (2010-12)

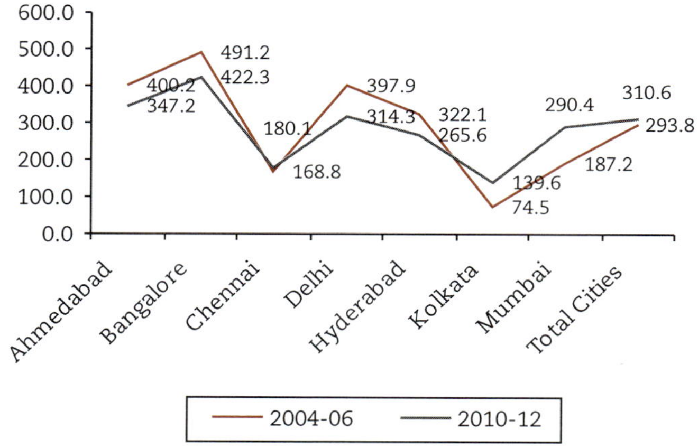

Source: Calculations using NCRB data, various years.

3. The term is used to describe a situation when a particular social phenomenon that was previously sporadic and disparate becomes generalised very rapidly (Malcolm Gladwell, 2000).
4. In conversation with Dev Nathan, Professor, Institute for Human Development (IHD), New Delhi at the stakeholder consultation on 'Safety in Delhi' held on 8 June, 2013 at the India International Centre, New Delhi.
5. The NCRB collects data on cognisable crimes from police stations in the states and Union Territories (UTs) and compiles them into detailed reports.
6. In 2004, the NCRB recorded crimes in 35 cities. Thereafter, crimes in 53 cities were recorded.
7. For the purpose of this report, only 'cognisable crimes' are being studied. The Indian Criminal Procedure Code (Cr.P.C.) classifies crime into: (a) Cognisable offence. and (b) Non-cognisable offence. In the case of the former, officers of the police are empowered to act without the permission of the magistrate, that is, without obtaining a court order; while in the case of the latter; the police must obtain a court order before arresting the person concerned.
8. Crimes per 100,000 population.
9. Cognisable crimes are further divided into crimes under the Indian Penal Code (IPC) and Special and Local Laws (SLL). IPC crimes include murders, attempt to commit murder, culpable homicide not amounting to murder, kidnappings, hurt, causing death by negligence, robbery, preparation and assembly for dacoity, robbery, burglary and theft, arson, riots, rapes, dowry deaths, kidnappings and abduction of women and girls, molestation, sexual harassment, importation of girls and cruelty perpetrated by husbands and relatives. Crimes included under the SLL include the Arms Act (1959), Narcotics Drugs and Psychotropic Substance Act (1985), Gambling Act (1867), Excise Act (1944), Protection of Civil Rights Act (1955), Terrorist and Disruptive Activities (Prevention) Act (1987), Prohibition of Child Marriage Act (2006), Indecent Representation of Women (Prohibition) Act (1986), Sati Prevention Act (1987), and SC/ST (Prevention of Atrocities) Act (1989).

The NCRB ranking, which is based on the total cognisable crime rate in the country, shows that Delhi ranks 31st among 53 cities in 2012. Thus, contrary to public perception and media reportage which projects Delhi as the most unsafe city in the India, it is pertinent to note that official data reveals a different story.

6.3.2 Types of Crimes

Delhi displays higher rates of violent crimes,[10] such as murder and kidnapping, as compared to other cities, which is an important cause for concern. However, an analysis of the percentage share of the types of crimes in Delhi between 2004-06 and 2010-12 makes it clear that the share of crimes against property were the highest during both time points, and have increased over time, while body crimes and crimes against women also recorded an increase from 6.8 to 9.9 per cent, and 6.7 to 9.5 per cent, respectively, over the same period (Figure 6.2).

Figure 6.2

Delhi: Composition of Crimes (per cent) (2004-06 and 2010-12)

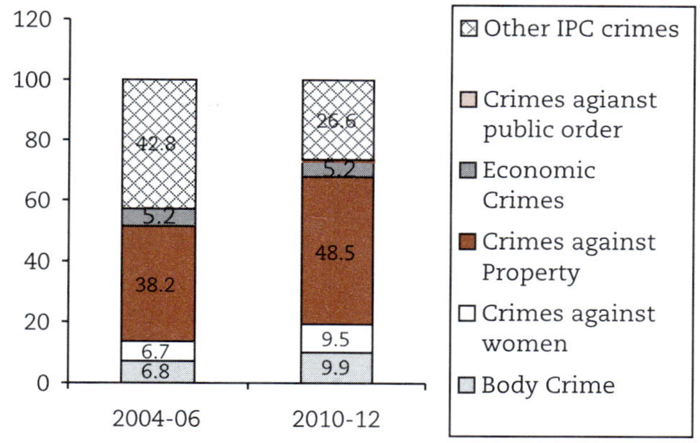

Source: Calculations using NCRB data, various years.

The percentage share of crimes against women in all the cities to the total IPC crimes have increased from 5.7 to 6.7 per cent over the period under consideration. Hyderabad recorded the highest percentage share for the same for both time points, followed by Delhi (Annex Tables 6.3 and 6.4).

6.3.3 Crimes against Women

Delhi does not feature amongst the top ten cities in terms of the rankings based on the total rate of cognisable crimes against women. It is ranked 16th amongst the 53 cities in 2012 (NCRB, 2012). The rank was 21st in the previous year. The overall rates of crimes against women[11] increased from 16.8 to 20.7 per 100,000 between 2004-06 and 2010-12, and there is considerable variability in these crime rates across cities (Figure 6.3). In the case of Delhi, the rate increased from 26.8 to 29.7 per 100,000 between the two time periods under study. In terms of the percentage share, Hyderabad recorded the highest share of crimes against women at both points of time (close to 10 per cent), followed by Delhi which showed an increase (from 6.7 per cent to 9.5 per cent) during the same period. (Annex Tables 6.3 and 6.4).

Figure 6.3

Crime Rates against Women in the Major Cities (2005-06 and 2010-12)

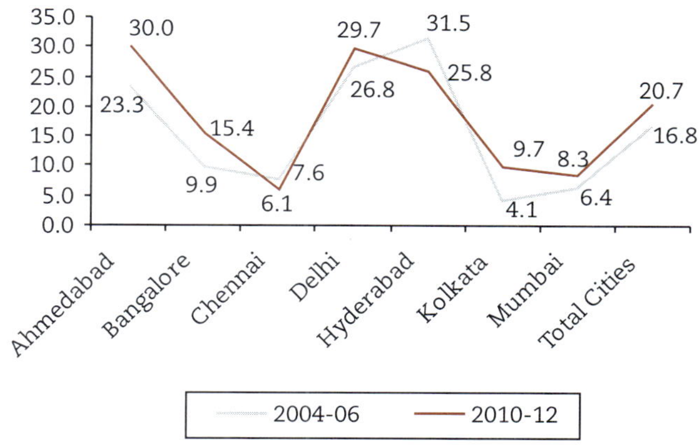

Source: Calculations using NCRB data, various years.

The most important point to be noted is that in terms of the rates of different kinds of crimes against

10. IPC crimes include violent crimes, viz., crimes against the body like murders, attempt to commit murder, culpable homicide not amounting to murder, kidnappings, hurt, causing death by negligence; crimes against property like robbery, preparation and assembly for dacoity, burglary and theft; crimes against public order like riots and arson; crimes against women include rapes, dowry deaths, kidnappings and abduction of women and girls, molestation, sexual harassment, importation of girls and perpetration of cruelty by husbands and relatives; crimes against children include rape, infanticide, kidnapping and abduction of children, foeticide, procurement of minor girls, buying and selling of girls for prostitution, abetment to suicide, exposure and abandonment; crimes against Scheduled Castes (SCs) and Scheduled Tribes (STs) like murder, rapes, robbery, burglary, arson, and, crimes under the Prevention of Atrocities against SCs/STs Act; economic crimes like criminal breach of trust, cheating, counterfeiting; and other IPC crimes.

11. (i) Rape (Section 376, IPC), (ii) Kidnapping and abduction for specified purposes (Sections 363–373, IPC), (iii) Homicide for dowry, Dowry deaths or their attempts (Section 302/304-B, IPC), (iv) Torture—Both mental and physical (Section 498-A, IPC), (v) Molestation (Section 354, IPC), (vi) Sexual harassment (Eve-teasing) (Section 509, IPC), (vii) Importation of girls (up to 21 years of age) (Section 366-B, IPC).

women, Delhi reported the highest rate of rapes (4.0 per 100,000 and 3.2 per 100,000, respectively, for the time points considered), despite showing a decline in the occurrence of the same. Delhi's position vis-à-vis other cities in terms of the rates of rapes is a cause for concern and highlights the need for intensive policy interventions. The rate of kidnappings and abductions was also the highest in Delhi and increased from 5.2 to 10.8 per 100,000. However, the perpetration of cruelty by husbands and relatives decreased slightly from 10.9 to 10.2 per 100,000 (Annex Tables 6.5 and 6.6).

If the rates of crimes against women are calculated as a proportion of the urban female population rather than of the total population, then the crime rate is found to decrease significantly from 58.2 to 49.8, between the years 2005-06 and 2008-09. However, between 2011 and 2012, the crime rate witnessed an increase to 63.6 per 100,000, thereby exceeding the 2005-06 level (Table 6.1).

Table 6.1

Crime Rates against Women in Delhi*[12]

Crime Category	2005-06	2008-09	2011-12
Rape	8.3	5.6	6.9
Kidnapping and Abduction	14.0	16.3	22.9
Dowry Deaths	1.6	1.5	1.4
Cruelty by Husband and Relatives	22.2	17.5	22.3
Molestation	9.7	7.3	7.9
Eve-teasing	2.5	1.7	2.2
Importation of girls	0.0	0.0	0.0
Total	58.2	49.8	63.6

Note: * Based on an average of the years 2005-06, 2008-09 and 2011-12.

Source: Calculated as a proportion of the urban female population on the basis of Census of India, 2001, from the NCRB, various years.

An assessment of the percentage share of the crimes to the total crimes against women in Delhi shows that the incidence of kidnappings and abduction increased from 19.3 per cent to 36.3 per cent during the period 2004-06 to 2010-12 (Figure 6.4). Kidnappings and abductions, and cruelty perpetrated by husbands and relatives together constituted more than 60 per cent of the crimes in 2004-06, and over 70 per cent of those in 2010-12. Rapes constituted 15.1 per cent of reported crimes against women in Delhi in 2004-06, and 10.8 per cent of those in 2010-12. Other crimes such as molestation and sexual harassment, and dowry deaths reported a slight decline over the period considered.

The share of rape in the crimes committed against women was 6.1 per cent in Bangalore in 2004-06, and increased to 7.2 per cent in 2010-12, while in Chennai, it increased from 7 to 14.6 per cent, and in the case of Mumbai, it fell from 17.6 per cent to 14.7 per cent. The percentage share of kidnappings and abductions to the total IPC crimes against women was the highest in Delhi during both the years under study (Annex Tables 6.7 and 6.8).

Figure 6.4

Delhi: Composition of Crimes against Women (per cent) (2004-06 and 2010-12)

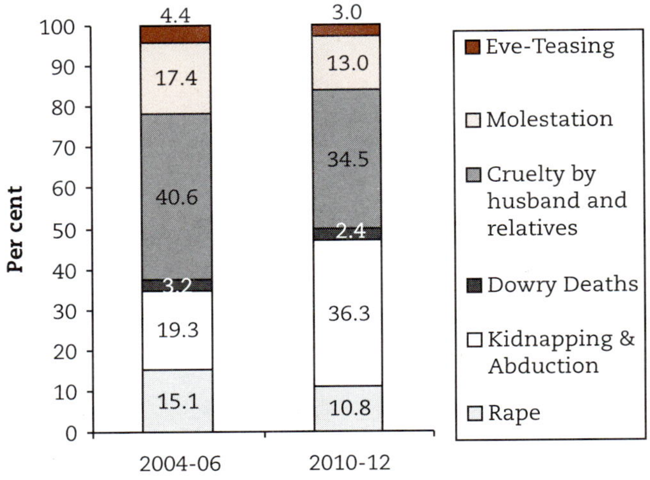

Source: Calculations using NCRB data, various years.

It is important to note the positive role of the media in highlighting crimes against women in the city as well in spreading awareness among people about the laws and policies that are in place to ensure their protection. However, indiscriminate reporting could also lead to the projection of Delhi as the centre for crimes against women, which, in turn, could lead to negative implications such as increased fear among people, and restricted mobility for women, among other adverse impacts. While the issue of women's vulnerability needs urgent attention in Delhi as well as in other parts of the country, there is also a need to place the city in a proper perspective. Moreover,

12. The rate of crimes against women in 2012 was calculated as a proportion of the urban female population, unlike during the preceding years wherein it was calculated as a proportion of the total population. Table 6.1 presents the rates of crimes against women based on an average for the years 2005-06, 2008-09 and 2011-12, and on the urban female population projections, using data from the Census of India, 2001.

as the preceding discussion has shown, two parallel situations emerge, that is, one, the subjective perception of feeling (un)safe, and two, the objective reality in terms of recorded crimes. However, it may also be noted that while the reporting of crime has increased over time, there is still considerable under-reporting of crimes due to various reasons such as reluctance by the police to register cases, and hesitation among the people to report certain crimes due to the social stigma attached to them, among other reasons.

6.3.4 Crimes against Children

Children constitute a vulnerable segment of Delhi's population in terms of safety and security. Delhi ranked second among 53 cities in 2011, according to rankings based on crimes against children. The NCRB data shows that the rate of overall crimes against children in all cities increased from 3.3 to 5.2 per 100,000 during the period 2004-06 to 2010-12. With a exceptions few, all the other 51 cities experienced an increase in the rates of crimes against children (Figure 6.5) during the period under study. Delhi recorded the maximum increase in the rates of crimes against children from 9 to 22.3 per 100,000 over the same period.

Figure 6.5

Crime Rates against Children in Major Cities (2004-06 and 2010-12)

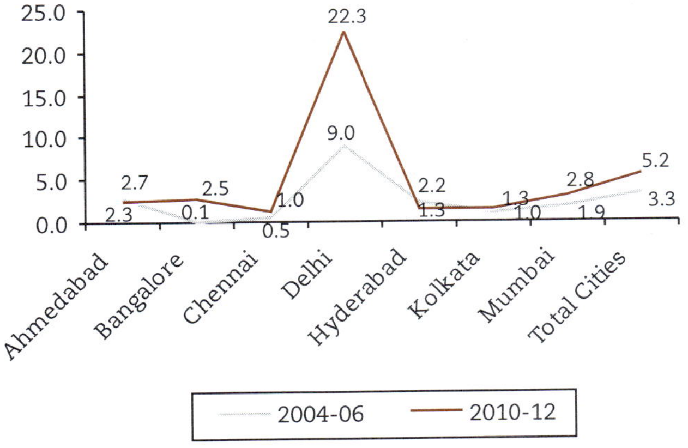

Source: Calculations using NCRB data, various years.

The rates of kidnapping and abduction of children in Delhi increased significantly from 4.5 per 100,000 in 2004-06 to 18.3 per 100,000 in 2010-12, and remained the predominant crime perpetuated against children (constituting over 80 per cent of the total crimes against children in 2010-12). This is notwithstanding the fact that some crimes against children like foeticide, infanticide, abetment of suicide, and procurement of minor girls, may be under-reported (Annex Tables 6.9 to 6.12). In addition, some crimes such as buying and selling of girls for prostitution may also go misreported as kidnappings and abduction.

Rape constituted a significant share of the total crimes reported against children, though its incidence declined from 22.2 per cent to 8.4 per cent over the period considered (Figure 6.6). Kidnappings and abductions constituted the largest share of total IPC crimes against children, and their incidence increased from 50 per cent to 82.1 per cent over the period under study. In other cities too, kidnappings constituted a large proportionate share and their incidence increased across cities, with Ahmedabad reporting the highest increase (from 23.6 to 81 per cent).

Figure 6.6

Delhi: Composition of Crime against Children (per cent) (2004-06 and 2010-12)

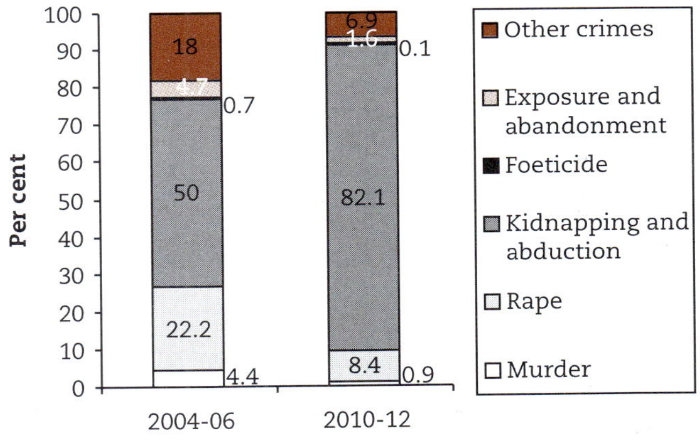

Source: Calculations using NCRB data, various years.

Children (considered as persons below 18 years of age) constituted a considerable proportion of those kidnapped in 2004-06, and this share increased dramatically in 2010-12, from 50 per cent to over 90 per cent, over the period under study (Table 6.2). It is pertinent to note that the sex composition of the kidnapped children varies substantially with age. The proportion of male children is higher than that of female children in the below 15-years age group, while the older age groups (15-18 years) comprised a larger proportion of females (Table 6.2).

The media reports cases of many missing children daily and out of more than 0.175 million children

Table 6.2

Age- and Sex-wise Composition of Victims of Kidnappings and Abductions (%)

Year	Delhi/ All-India	Total Number of Cases Reported	Up to 10 Years (%)		10-15 Years (%)		15-18 Years (%)		Above 18 Years (%)		Total (%)	
			Male	Female	Male	Female	Male	Female	Male	Female	Total Male	Total Female
2004-06	Delhi	1414	8.0	5.9	6.1	11.5	3.5	18.0	15.5	31.4	30.7	66.9
	All-India	23,383	1.2	0.9	1.2	3.8	1.3	10.2	27.3	54.1	31.0	69.0
2010-12	Delhi	3648	9.9	4.8	23.2	18.0	11.3	26.0	2.9	4.0	47.2	52.8
	All-India	43,565	1.6	1.1	2.9	6.5	2.1	21.7	15.2	48.9	21.8	78.2

Source: Calculations using NCRB data, various years.

reported missing in India between 2009 and 2011, a majority were reported to be missing from Maharashtra, Delhi and Madhya Pradesh (*Hindustan Times*, 2013). In Delhi, on an average, 14 children are reported missing daily, according to the Crime in Delhi Report (Delhi Police, 2012). Given the gravity of the situation, a recent directive of the Supreme Court ordered that the cases of missing children be taken more seriously and recorded as criminal cases, which require immediate investigation. According to a study by Navsrishti (2011), the maximum cases of missing children were reported in the North-east, East and South-east districts in Delhi. Three-fourths of those registered as missing were found by the police and others, while the rest remained missing. There were glaring gaps in the standard operating procedures (SOPs) and the police were known to ignore cases of those missing children who belonged to the socio-economically weaker sections (ibid.).

Thus, it is clear from official data that the crime rates against children in Delhi are among the highest, with rape and kidnappings constituting the main crimes, which is an issue of crucial concern for both the government and the police. The protection of children in the city needs to be accorded top priority and critical attention needs to be paid in terms of improving the formulation as well as implementation of laws and social policy. While the media has been quite active in raising awareness and spreading information about the issue, urgent steps still need to be taken for ensuring better policing and implementation of laws, and most importantly, for spreading awareness to guarantee the safety of children. More studies are needed to understand the ways in which crimes against children are reported, in order to attain a better understanding of the crime profile, as well as for instituting more effective policies to facilitate the improved protection of children.

6.3.5 Charge-sheets and Convictions

In terms of police investigations, the pendency rate increased from 43.7 per cent to 51.9 per cent from 2005 to 2007, and then decreased to 45 per cent in 2011, while the charge-sheeting rate has remained more or less the same, though it decreased a little in 2007 (Table 6.3). In 2011, the pendency rate was reported to be 45 per cent and the charge-sheet rate was 55 per cent. In 2012, the charge-sheet rate increased significantly to 70.4 per cent, which was a positive development, while the pendency rate decreased slightly to 42.1 per cent. At the level of the courts, the conviction rate has been decreasing since 2005, while the pendency rate remains high (and was

Table 6.3

Delhi: Status of Police and Court Cases Dealing with General IPC Crimes (2005 to 2012) (per cent)

Years	Police Cases (%)		Court Cases (%)		
	Charge-sheet	Pendency	Conviction	Acquittal	Pendency
2005	56.3	43.7	8.9	5.5	85.6
2006	53.7	46.3	9.6	5.1	85.3
2007	48.1	51.9	9.7	5.3	85.0
2008	55.2	44.8	5.8	3.1	91.1
2009	52.6	47.4	5.4	3.9	90.7
2010	50.0	50.0	4.6	4.3	91.1
2011	55.0	45.0	5.3	5.7	88.9
2012	70.4	42.1	7.1	6.2	86.7

Source: Calculations using NCRB data.

almost 90 per cent in 2011). Between 2011 and 2012, the conviction rate increased from 5.3 per cent to 7.1 per cent, the rate of acquittal increased slightly from 5.7 to 6.2 per cent, while the pendency rates declined from 88.9 per cent to 86.7 per cent.

Table 6.4

Delhi: Status of Police and Court Cases Dealing with Rape from 2005 to 2012 in Delhi (per cent)

Years	*Police Cases (%)*		*Court Cases (%)*		
	Charge-sheet	*Pendency*	*Conviction*	*Acquittal*	*Pendency*
2005	68.7	31.3	7.2	38.3	54.5
2006	91.8	8.2	8.2	24.5	67.3
2007	84.2	15.8	9.1	23.8	67.1
2008	87.6	12.4	6.8	15.5	77.6
2009	87.7	12.3	10.2	11.4	78.4
2010	86.0	14.0	7.8	14.6	77.6
2011	77.2	22.8	9.9	13.9	76.3
2012	69.8	30.2	14.8	15.2	70.0

Source: Calculations using NCRB data.

As regards the cases of rape, at the level of the police, the pendency rate has been seen to be increasing since 2006. The rate of cases charge-sheeted has also seen to be increasing, however, with a slight decrease in 2011 and a significant decrease in 2012 (Table 6.4). One can see that in 2012, the rate of charge-sheeting by the police fell to 69.8 per cent, while the pendency rate increased to 30.2 per cent from the previous year. At the level of the court, the conviction rate has increased since 2005, and remains higher than that of general crimes. The pendency rate of court cases has also been seen to be increasing, while the acquittal rate has been decreasing (which can be attributed to the larger number of pending cases). The rate of acquittal in rape cases is still much higher than that of general IPC crimes. However, at the level of the court, the conviction rate has increased significantly from 9.9 to 14.8 per cent from 2011 to 2012, while the acquittal rate has increased to 15.2 per cent and the pendency rate has fallen from 76.3 to 70 per cent in the same period. Overall, the picture of the police and court cases dealing with rape is slightly better than that of the total IPC crimes shown in Table 6.3.

6.4. Findings from the Perceptions Survey, 2013

The Perceptions Survey, 2013, collected information relating to various aspects of crime and safety of the population, in general, and women, in particular. The broad areas of inquiry included: (i) rating Delhi in terms of personal safety, (ii) how safe/secure people felt living in their localities, (iii) rating the security of women and girls in the city in three spaces apart from their homes, viz. the localities in which they resided, public transport and at the workplace, (iv) whether crime has increased, decreased, or stayed the same during the last three years, (v) whether the respondents have experienced crime, and the nature of these crimes, (vi) level of satisfaction with the police, in terms of their prompt response to a problem and their being easily approachable and easy to talk to, and (vii) the steps that can be taken to improve people's safety/ security in Delhi.[13]

In addition to the Survey, Focus Group Discussions (FGDs) were carried out in six localities. In particular, the FGDs were conducted only with women in various locations across the city to understand the issues that specifically concern women's safety. In addition, interviews were also conducted with the police personnel in police stations at various locations in the city to better understand their perspective. In the FGDs, the key points of discussions included identification of the areas considered most unsafe; the people who were the most unsafe; threats and incidents of crime, perceptions about the police; coping mechanisms; gender-based violence; perceptions about the increase or decline in crime; the response of the State on the issue of crime; and, recommendations on how to make Delhi safe(r).[14] Some of the main findings based on the responses to the Survey questionnaire are delineated below.

6.4.1 How Do People Rate Delhi in Terms of Personal Safety?

Delhi was rated as 'below average' in terms of personal safety by nearly 38 per cent of the respondents, (a combination of poor: 30.7 per cent or very poor: 7.2 per cent ratings; see Figure 6.7). However, nearly 30 per cent of the respondents reported that the levels of personal safety in the city were 'above average'.

13. It needs to be noted that the Perception Survey, 2013, mainly addressed public safety issues. In relation to women, the Survey was confined to probing about women's safety in public spaces. Women's security within their homes was beyond the scope of this survey.

14. It may be noted that the Perceptions Survey, 2013, was carried out soon after the incident of 16 December 2012, which is likely to have influenced the responses.

Interestingly, variations in the perception of safety by the district and type of locality were reported. A majority of the respondents in New Delhi surprisingly rated personal safety in the city-state as poor and very poor (56.3 per cent). This was followed by the districts of South Delhi (49.7 per cent), North-west Delhi (41.2 per cent), Central Delhi (39.4 per cent), and West Delhi (38.6 per cent), where the respondents rated levels of personal safety as lower than the all-Delhi average (Figure 6.8).

Figure 6.7

People's Rating of Personal Safety in Delhi (%)

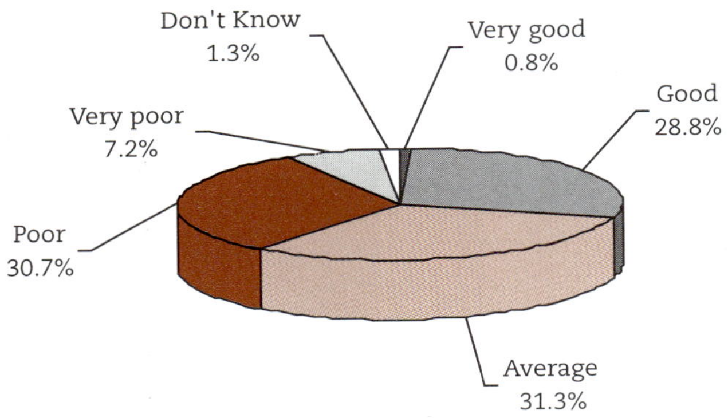

Source: Perceptions Survey, 2013.

Figure 6.8

District-wise Rating of Personal Safety (%)

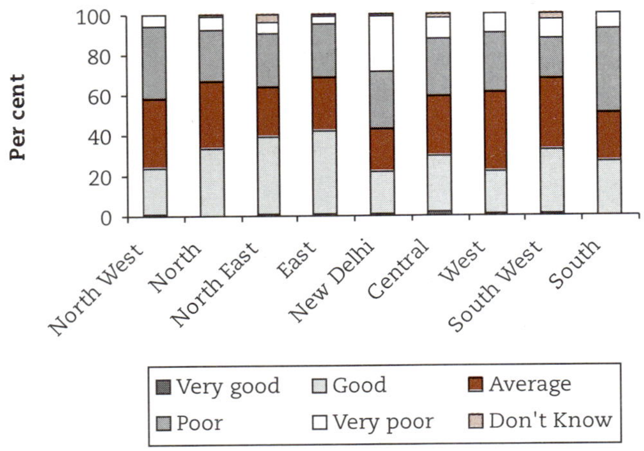

Source: Perceptions Survey, 2013.

When the data is disaggregated by the type of locality, it is interesting to note that again the residents of posh localities rated personal safety in Delhi as most unfavourable (with 46.2 per cent of the respondents rating it as poor or very poor). This was followed by respondents in the Walled City (41.9 per cent), *Jhuggi Jhopdi* (JJ) clusters (40 per cent), authorised colonies (39.9 per cent), JJ resettlement colonies (36.9 per cent), urban villages (34.9 per cent) and unauthorised colonies (31.0 per cent).

There were also substantial differences between the perceptions of men and those of women. As compared to men (31.8 per cent), far fewer women (26.8 per cent) thought that the level of personal safety was good or very good in the metropolis, showing a gender difference in perceptions of approximately 5 percentage points.

When the data is disaggregated by caste, there was not much difference between the general, Scheduled Castes (SCs) and Other Backward Castes (OBCs) (the percentages that reported personal safety as good or very good were 30.1, 29.7 and 29.6 per cent, respectively). However, Scheduled Tribes (STs) reported higher insecurity, although their population in rather insignificant in the city. It is also interesting to note that migrants across all caste groups rated Delhi much higher on the parameter of personal safety than the non-migrants.

6.4.2 How Safe Do People Feel in Their Localities?

In response to the question as to how safe they felt while living in their localities, a majority of the respondents (51.4 per cent) reported feeling secure or very secure (3.6%) (Figure 6.9). Another 26.5 per cent felt secure sometimes, and overall, less that 20 per cent of the population felt insecure, or very insecure.

Figure 6.9

How Safe Do People Feel in Their Localities? (%)

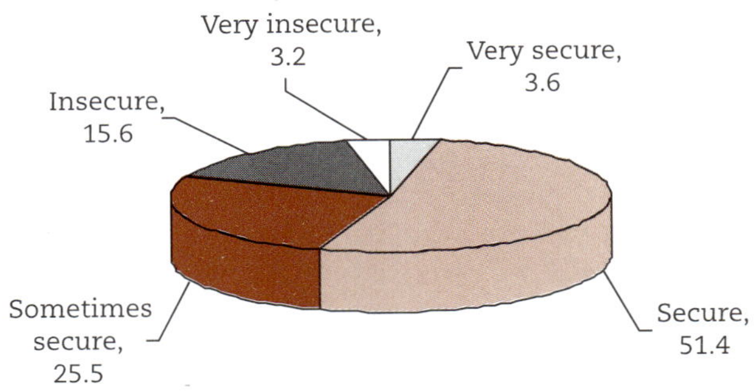

Source: Perceptions Survey, 2013.

Across the districts, New Delhi emerged as the safest locality with 71.6 per cent of respondents from this district saying that they felt secure or very secure. This is quite paradoxical, and needs to be read in tandem with the results of the earlier question, wherein residents of New Delhi (disproportionately) felt that Delhi, on the whole, was more unsafe, while at the same time, they felt the safest in their own localities. As regards the other districts, the corresponding figures were Central Delhi, 61.8 per cent, North-east Delhi, 70.0 per cent, and North Delhi, 62.7 per cent, respectively.

When disaggregated by colony type, the responses on safety showed the respondents from unauthorised colonies feeling the most secure in their localities (with 63.9 per cent reporting that they felt secure and 2.5 per cent reporting that they felt very secure). A possible explanation for this could be the sense of familiarity and comfort that the poor and vulnerable populations who live in these settlements feel within their immediate neighbourhoods. This was followed by respondents from the Walled City (62.4 per cent), authorised colonies (57.2 per cent), urban villages (52.5 per cent), posh localities (49.5 per cent), JJ resettlement colonies (49.4 per cent) and JJ clusters (40.8 per cent), in that order. In general, it can be seen that people felt safe in their own localities, and there was not much difference by gender for this perception (56.1 per cent for men and 53.5 per cent for women). When disaggregated in terms of age, there was little variation in the data on feeling secure in one's locality until the 60-plus age group. Senior citizens reported feeling relatively less secure (52 per cent) in comparison to the aggregate (55.2 per cent).

6.4.3 *How Do People Rate Women's Safety—At Their Workplace, in Public Transport and in Their Own Localities?*

Perceptions of safety for women threw interesting light on the subject of their safety and security. The general opinion was that women were most safe in spaces closer to their homes, that is, in their own localities, followed by their workplaces, and were the least secure while using public transport (Figure 6.10).

6.4.4 *Women's Safety at the Workplace*

The workplace was not perceived as a very safe place for women, as only less than one-fourth of the respondents felt that the workplace was secure/very secure for them. When the data is disaggregated by sex, it is interesting to note that men marginally felt that the workplace was safer for women than the women themselves. Given the extremely low workforce participation rate for women in Delhi, gender stereotypes prevail, and these are likely to play a role in the perceptions of both men and women in terms of women's work and their workplaces. When the data was disaggregated by age, it revealed that the elderly, in general, felt that the workplace was more unsafe for women. Similarly, by work status, retirees and pensioners thought the workplace to be (most) unsafe for women.

Figure 6.10

People's Ratings of Women's Safety at Their Workplace, in Public Transport and in Their Own Localities (per cent)

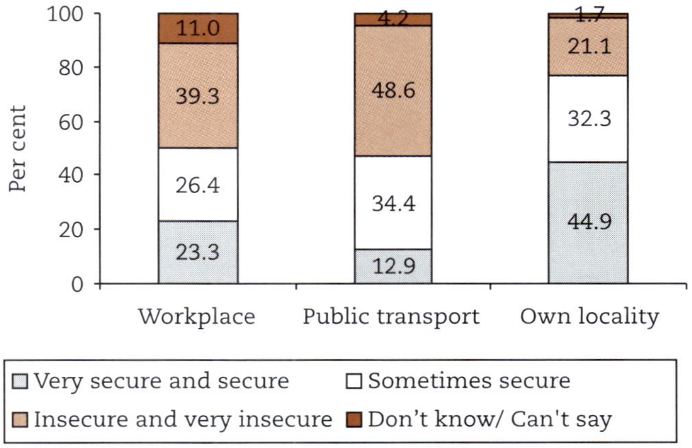

Source: Perceptions Survey, 2013.

6.4.5 *Women's Safety While Using Public Transport*

Perceptions about the security of women while travelling by public transport were not positive. Only a small proportion of the respondents thought that public transport was very secure (0.4 per cent) or secure (12.5 per cent) for women. This perception came out quite clearly in the FGDs too. Women felt that buses were the worst type of public transport in terms of safety, since they were harassed by both the young and old, illiterate and educated men. Also, perceptions about the safety of public transport for women decreased with increasing education levels. The illiterate and the less educated respondents perceived public transport to be more safe than those who were educated up to the graduate level and above.

6.4.6 *Women's Safety in Their Own Locality*

At the aggregate level, the dominant perception about women's safety that emerged from the Survey was that women were the most secure within their own communities and localities, as opposed to when they were at their workplaces or while using public transport. However, when this data was disaggregated by the locality of residence, the respondents from posh colonies, JJ resettlement colonies and JJ clusters felt women to be least secure within their own localities. In other words, the 'rich' and the 'poor' localities were considered to be the most unsafe for women. On the other hand, urban villages, unauthorised colonies and the Walled City were rated as most secure by their residents.

The FGDs provided useful indications about spaces within the localities which were considered to be unsafe by women. Public toilets, in particular, were considered very unsafe, and women expressed reluctance to visit them alone. Unlit roads and parks were also considered to be unsafe (Box 6.3). Incidents of chain snatching and sexual harassment were reportedly common near alcohol shops and parks. As a group of women from Satyawati Colony, Ashok Vihar, stated, "Parks in the vicinity are unsafe as groups of men can be seen gambling. Stray incidents of chain snatching, especially by boys on motor bikes are common." The respondents from Sultanpuri said, "The railway *fatak* (barrier) area is very dangerous. That is where the boys hang out. Girls have to cross that area to reach their school and these boys harass them. A teenaged girl reported facing sexual harassment by local boys even when they were walking on the road. Another girl said, "When we go to the toilets, they harass us by teasing us and throwing stones at us." Lack of street lighting and dark areas were perceived as unsafe. The need for more police presence and patrolling at night was highlighted.

6.4.7 People's Perceptions about the Incidence of Crime over Time

The results of the Perceptions Survey indicate that Delhi's residents share a near universal perception that crime has increased over time. There is a general perception that all kinds of crime have increased during the last three years with almost 95 per cent of the respondents reporting that both big and small crimes had increased. This emerged very clearly in the FGDs too. Groups of both men and women articulated that over time, Delhi has become an unsafe city and that crime has increased. The FGD respondents felt that small crimes (such as sexual harassment and stealing) had increased. The incidence of '*chhura maarna*' (knifing) was reported widely during the discussions.

However, marked variations in perceptions about the incidence of crime were evident when the data was disaggregated by districts. While 81.4 per cent of the respondents in New Delhi felt that big crimes had increased, and 15.0 per cent felt that crime had actually declined, the corresponding figures for North-west Delhi were 97.7 per cent and 0.7 per cent, respectively. In the case of small crimes, the trend was similar, but the variation between districts was less. The relatively positive outlook on the overall crime scenario in the former case may be attributed to better policing and other infrastructure in the 'most important' district of Delhi—the heart of the city, which is home to most of its political class and bureaucracy. Interestingly, as has been seen earlier, it is pertinent to note that while residents of New Delhi felt most safe in their localities, at the same time, they also felt most strongly that Delhi on the whole was unsafe!

6.4.8 Experiencing Crime

The Perceptions Survey, 2013, reveals that close to one-tenth (9.3 per cent) of the respondents or their family members had been victims of some crime during the last three years. There was considerable district-wise variation in these perceptions, ranging from 2.8 per cent in South-west Delhi to 17.3 per cent and 17.5 per cent in the Central and West Delhi districts, respectively (Figure 6.11).

Figure 6.11

District-wise Percentage of Respondents and Their Families Reporting an Experience of Crime (during the Preceding 3 years) (per cent)

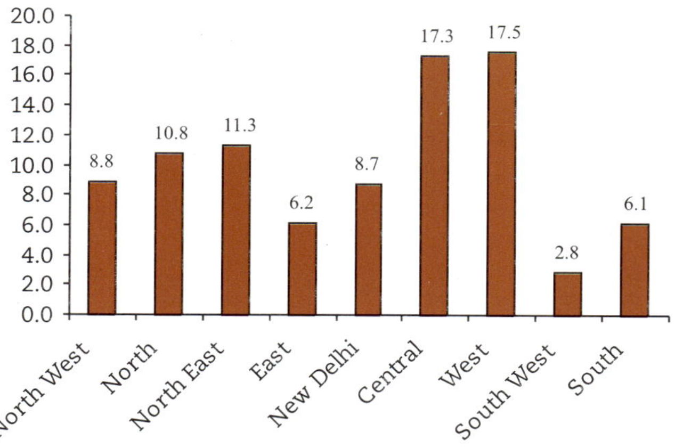

Source: Perceptions Survey, 2013.

When the data was disaggregated by locality type, it was found that the residents from posh localities reported having experienced some form of crime at a rate which was almost double that of the average figure for Delhi as a whole (18.5 per cent of the residents in posh localities reported having experienced crime as against the all-Delhi average of 9.3 per cent). On the other hand, the residents of authorised colonies, JJ clusters and the Walled city reported experiencing crime rates less than the average for Delhi.

6.4.9 Nature of Crime

The Perceptions Survey also tried to assess the kinds of crime that were experienced by the respondents. The most common crimes reported by the respondents or their families were thefts (69.2 per cent); robberies (16.7 per cent); crimes against women, which included sexual harassment (6.0 per cent), family violence (2.4 per cent), and sexual assault (0.7 per cent); and other crimes (fraud 2.9 per cent, vandalism, 1.6 per cent, and others, 0.6 per cent). With regard to the composition of criminal offences by income categories, it was found that thefts had more likely been experienced by those belonging to the lower income groups, robberies by those in the higher income groups, and, not surprisingly, the reporting of sexual harassment was also higher amongst the higher income groups.

6.4.10 Satisfaction with the Police—Promptness, Approachability and What Needs to be Done

The residents of Delhi, in general, did not report satisfaction with the performance of the police force. In terms of the promptness of response, about one-fourth (23.8 per cent) of the respondents reported being satisfied with this important keeper of law and order, including 0.8 per cent who were 'very satisfied' and 22. 6 per cent who were 'satisfied' (Figure 6.12).

The little faith that people reposed in the police was expressed in the FGDs, wherein people said that the police did not respond in time, and that they were left to fend for themselves. In one of the FGDs, women lamented, "*Yahan hamein apni suraksha khud karni padti hai*" (here we have to protect ourselves). Harassment by the police was also commonly cited in various FGDs by residents of the poor settlements across the city. Several instances of policemen slapping and misbehaving with residents in the poor settlements were also reported. When the responses were disaggregated by income classes, it was seen that the respondents belonging to the high income category reported being the 'most dissatisfied' with the police response in terms of promptness (39.1 per cent reported being 'dissatisfied', and another 11.2 per cent reported being 'very dissatisfied').

When the respondents were asked about the approachability of the police, it was found that in the aggregate, a little over one-fifth (22.3 per cent) of the respondents were satisfied with their interactions while 18.9 per cent chose not to reply (Figure 6.13). In the FGDs, the respondents voiced the need for a larger police force, especially female police personnel and wanted the police to treat citizens amicably, or in a friendlier manner.

In response to the question as to the two most important measures that were needed to enhance safety and security in the city, the respondents to the Perceptions Survey offered some useful suggestions, such as increases in police patrolling coupled with immediate action against any crime, implementation of stricter laws for 'safety for all', and improvements in police behaviour.

Figure 6.12

People's Rating of Promptness Displayed by the Police (%)

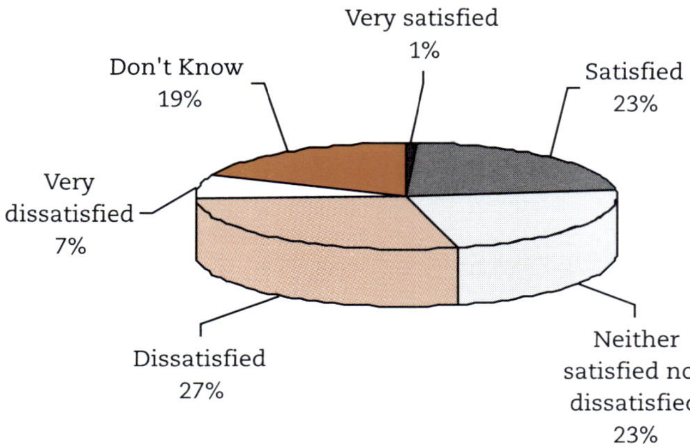

Source: Perceptions Survey, 2013.

Figure 6.13

People's Ratings about the Approachability of the Police (%)

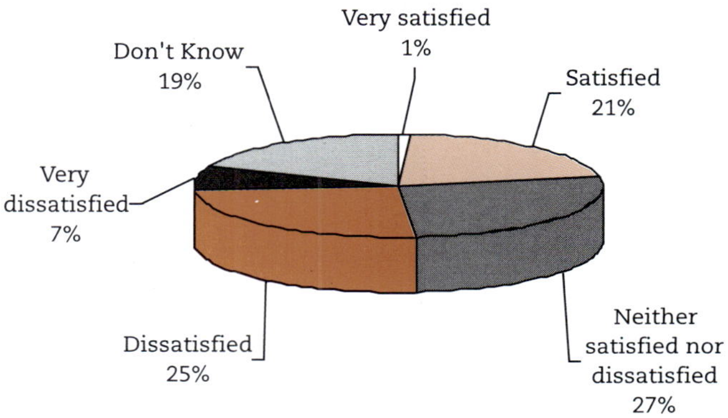

Source: Perceptions Survey, 2013.

Box 6.2

Interviews with the Police

In order to get a more balanced view of people's perceptions, it was felt necessary to also engage with the police. Interviews held with police officers during the course of the Perceptions Survey, 2013, brought forth some useful inferences. The police felt that the public and the media did not understand the difficulties and challenges faced by them in their everyday functioning, and cited many concerns related to their workplace. Following are some excerpts from the interviews of the police personnel.

- "The condition of women officers is much better now than a few years back. However, I face trouble in coming from my house to this police station everyday, as there are drug addicts who stare at me and give me dirty looks."—A female police officer.
- "People treat us like dirt; they do not give us any authority. I sometimes feel fear when I go out, especially in my civilian clothes. I want to leave my job as I do not get any holiday to go back to my village." —A male police officer.
- "After the December 2012 gangrape case, women officers (have to) report for duty at night. Sometimes when we don't answer the phone the first time, people complain. It is not easy."— A female police officer.
- "There is no basic infrastructure here in the police stations, there is no regular water and the toilets are not cleaned. We can't go home. People expect us to do so much, but look at the way we function. Police personnel should be posted near their homes. Also our working hours are so long, there should be shifts."— A male police officer.

Box 6.3

Unsafe Areas, Most Vulnerable and Threats to Safety in Delhi—Findings from the FGDs

What are the most unsafe areas in the city?

The areas around alcohol shops and gambling dens were perceived to be very unsafe. Dark spaces such as parks were also considered unsafe and susceptible to crimes, especially crimes against women.

Who is the most vulnerable in the city?

Apart from women, children were perceived to be most vulnerable in the city. There is a sense of fear and this was articulated in the FGDs. Parents discussed their fears about the safety of their children, especially if they were unaccompanied while travelling or while at play. In particular, mothers said that they did not send young girls out of the house alone.

Who is a threat to safety?

The FGDs with both men and women revealed that it was mostly men who commit crimes. It was also perceived that unemployed youth were more likely to be the perpetrators of crimes such as theft and robbery. Women reported that it was generally men who harassed women, especially in public transport.

The FGDs held with only men revealed that there was a general sense that if a woman is harassed while she is out of her home, it is usually her fault. Western influences, especially the incidence of women wearing Western clothing, was seen to be responsible for the rising crimes against women.

To sum up, the Perceptions Survey, 2013, reveals some interesting findings and paradoxes. While a majority of Delhi's population felt safe in the areas wherein they resided—their localities and their neighbourhoods, they felt that crime had increased over time and did not rate Delhi favourably in terms of personal safety. Women rated personal safety more poorly than men, and the STs rated it more poorly that the others. At the same time, migrants across all caste groups found Delhi to be safer than their non-migrant counterparts.

Children and senior citizens emerged as vulnerable groups. Senior citizens felt far more unsafe in their own localities, and also had less positive perceptions about women's safety, in general. In the FGDs, almost all the female respondents expressed fear for their children's safety and cited fearsome events that had occurred within their localities.

People's perceptions about the lack of women's safety in the city were significant. The survey revealed that most women did not feel safe in public spaces, with the workplaces and public transport emerging as spaces perceived to be the least safe for women.

People's perceptions about the police were not very positive. There was a general sense of fear as well as dissatisfaction in dealing with the police, which points towards the need for more police, including policewomen, and a more responsive police.

6.5 Recent Initiatives and Strategies for the Future

In this broad landscape of crime and safety in Delhi, most of 2012 and the first quarter of 2013 saw an increase in the reporting of both overall crime, and crime against women. While there is a tendency for such statistics, especially if fuelled by media reports, to cause alarm, it may be argued that an increase in the reporting of crime is a positive development in the case of Delhi, where the incidence of reported crime is much lower than in other parts of the world.

The brutal gang rape that occurred on 16 December 2012 brought to light the inadequacies in planning and policing, as also the appalling civic apathy on the part of the people, many of whom just neglected the victims as they lay helpless on the road. All this could be attributed not just to the failure of the State, but also to the failure of the people. Thus, besides the need for systemic changes within the policing and planning processes, what is also required is a change in societal attitudes and a positive consciousness amongst the citizens. Some of this change was observed in the massive social protests wherein the participants included both men and women, and civil society organisations, who were fighting for immediate action and justice for the victim. The change was that crimes against women were now perceived as 'everyone's problem' rather than as women's problems alone, also indicated by the responses to the questions posed to the police, the State, and the public. The responses also revealed that crime against women is a structural problem, and in need of strong long-term solutions at the levels of the law, policy and society. They also highlighted the role of the social media in not just raising awareness, but also mobilising people for collective action, thereby bringing forth its potential as a tool that could be constructively utilised for crime prevention and reduction.

What also emerged is the need to gain a perspective on the socio-economic and psychological factors that lead to crime and violence in the society. These factors need to be analysed against a society that is marked by sharp inequalities (also indicated in the other chapters in this DHDR). These inequalities need to be examined in an urban landscape characterised by inequitable access to resources and opportunities as well as discrimination in various areas. It is also a common perception, for instance, that the police often ill-treat the poor and the homeless, and do not consider them at par with the affluent sections. In the Perceptions Survey, 2013, as well as in the FGDs, people across the income groups highlighted the lack of appropriate response from the police. There is a general mistrust and lack of faith in the police, particularly amongst the socio-economically weaker sections, whose members also cite facing police harassment. There is thus a critical need to make some changes within the police force through sensitisation, training and even collaborative exercises with the people in order to create an atmosphere of trust and cooperation by making the police more accessible and responsive to their needs.

6.5.1 An Overview of Existing Schemes and Initiatives

6.5.1.1 Schemes and Initiatives for Women and Girls

There have been some positive policy developments aimed at ensuring the protection of women and girls in the private and public spheres. The Report of the Working Group on Women's Agency and Empowerment under the Twelfth Five Year Plan proposes two such programmes, viz., *Ujjawala*, a scheme meant for the prevention of trafficking for commercial sexual exploitation of girls/women through the rescue, rehabilitation and re-integration of victims of trafficking; and the setting up of 'One Stop Crisis Centres' for cities with a population of more than 2.5 million with the aim of provisioning shelters, police desks, legal, medical and counselling services, and 24*7 helplines, amongst other measures.

In addition, laws that seek to address the safety of women include: the Supreme Court Vishakha Judgement (1997), a landmark in the protection of women from sexual harassment (including even verbal harassment) at the workplace resulting in the formation of the Committee on the Sexual Harassment of Women at the Workplace (Prevention,

Prohibition and Redressal) Act, 2013. Under this Act, the case has to be registered under Section 509 of the Indian Penal Code (word, gesture or act intended to insult the modesty of a woman). In terms of violent crimes against women, the Justice Verma Committee, which was constituted on 23 December 2012, proved to be a landmark in the policy and legal landscape, and made some crucial suggestions on the definitions and laws related to rape, sexual assault, child sexual abuse, medical examination of victims, legal procedures to deal with such crimes as well as reforms pertaining to education and electoral procedures (PRS Legislative Research, 2013). The Committee stressed the need to review the existing laws on violence such as acid attacks, offences against women in the conflict areas, and the trafficking of women and children. A major achievement of the Justice Verma Committee has been its move to make a case for offences such as stalking and 'eve teasing', which are often considered 'minor', to be considered serious offences instead. Another major element in the new law is that it penalises police officers for not registering an FIR in cases under certain IPC sections.

Amongst the various government initiatives, the *Stree Shakti*, a collaborative capacity building project, was initiated by the Government in 2002, with the aim of focusing on issues pertaining to the health, well-being and empowerment of the socio-economically weaker women. As part of this initiative, Gender Resource Centres have been established to offer training in life skills, literacy, health, education and the awareness of legal rights so as to empower women and girls. Other government initiatives include the publication of an information booklet by the National Commission for Women (NCW) for college students and young women, providing details on women's rights and emergency helpline numbers. The Delhi Government has also started a helpline for women under the number 181.

In terms of planning, the enhancement of street lighting, and establishment of 'Multi-Utility Zones' (MUZs) are being carried out, and as part of these initiatives, the Delhi Development Authority (DDA) established a Unified Traffic and Transportation Infrastructure Planning and Engineering Centre (UTTIPEC), in 2008, whereby it seeks to develop guidelines on pedestrian safety, designing of infrastructure like roads, and street lights, to support women, informal workers and others (Jagori, 2011) .

The Delhi Police too have taken numerous steps in order to ensure the safety of women and to make the process of lodging complaints easier (Delhi Police, 2012). One of these measures is the establishment of the Crime against Women Cell (now renamed as the 'Special Police Unit for Women and Girls') in all the districts of Delhi. Complaints regarding stalking and obscene calls can be made on the helpline number 1096 of the Anti-Stalking Cell and Anti-Obscene Calls Cell. Help desks for women and the helpline number 1091 have also been established. As part of the *Parivartan* scheme launched in 2005 in North-west Delhi, women beat officers have been stationed in different areas in the city to interact with women and to understand their problems and concerns as part of a general awareness programme to prevent violence against women in both the public and private spheres as well as to prevent child sexual abuse. The programme is a collaborative effort of the police, civil society organisations, and professionals, in order to strengthen the capacity of the police as well as the community to protect women and children from violence. In addition, women police in civilian clothes have been deployed at various places. Crisis intervention centres to support victims of sexual assault have also been established.

Although the launch of these initiatives is a positive move, it is equally essential to ensure that that they are implemented in their true spirit and are subjected to regular monitoring and review. However, the challenges that continue to prevail include the persistence of the patriarchal norm and mindsets in society, which can only be changed through education and awareness. Norms of respect and gender equity need to be mainstreamed into school and college curricula and sensitisation programmes need to be launched in schools and colleges and incorporated into everyday conversations to promote long-term and sustained change in society.

6.5.1.2 Schemes and Initiatives for Children

A number of laws meant to protect children are in place, but the implementation process is marked by serious flaws. For instance, the Juvenile Justice Act 2000 (JJ Act) was enacted to strengthen laws to protect children in conflict with the law and children in need of care and protection through measures that were sensitive to the child's development needs and facilitated his/her rehabilitation through institutions covered under this Act. However, with the duration of stay of children in these institutions limited to three years, there is a lack of continuity in interventions, which could, in turn, hamper the child's future.[15]

The issue of child sexual abuse and the need to implement the Protection of Children from Sexual Offences Act, 2012 (POCSO), is another area that needs attention. A new initiative of the Delhi Commission for the Protection of the Child (DCPDR) proposes measures to ensure the protection of children in schools through interventions such as banning the hiring of people with a criminal record of sexual or physical violence, the appointment of one female guard in school buses, locking of the school buses and vans in school when they are not deployed on duty, amongst others (Rahman, 2013). However, the actual implementation of these policies needs concerted efforts and attention.

Given that a large number of children are reported missing every year, the Delhi Police has taken many steps towards the protection of children, particularly for improving reporting and coordination of missing children (Delhi Police, 2012). These include: the use of the Zonal Integrated Police Net (ZIPNET) for recording information about missing children; the registration of all cases of missing children as kidnappings; and launch of a scheme called *Pehchaan* in 2011 to maintain photographic records in order to protect children from the socio-economically weaker sections and residing in slums and resettlement colonies. Initiated in the areas which have reported the maximum number of missing children, more than 64,000 children have been given photographs under this scheme. Units such as the District Missing Persons Unit (DMPU) at the district level and the Missing Persons Squad at the city level, the Anti-Human Trafficking Unit (AHTU) in each district, and a special investigative unit which takes on unresolved cases of missing children, have also been established. Delhi Police is also teaming up with NGOs to carry out rescue operations. With Delhi being regarded as the hub for child trafficking, the Delhi Government has announced a high level committee headed by the DCPCR with the aim of curbing the trafficking of children.

In the sphere of improving life skills, a special community policing programme called *Yuva* was launched in order to offer life skills, literacy and vocational skills to young underprivileged adults. An initiative called *Bacchon ki Phulwari*, aimed at providing a healthy and safe environment for children of working mothers, was also undertaken. However, despite all these policy efforts and existing laws such as POCSO, Child Labour (Prohibition and Regulation) Act, 1986, JJ Act, 2000, and Commission for the Protection of Child Rights Act, 2005, amongst others, numerous children still go missing daily in Delhi, are forced to work in hazardous jobs, land up on the streets and are exposed to violence, abuse and exploitation, and experience the denial of their basic rights to health, safety and education. These incidences expose the serious policy gaps that exist with devastating impacts on the future lives of the affected children. The State is responsible not just for each child's current well-being, but also for his/her future 'well becoming' (Roelen and Sabates-Wheeler, 2011), and a strong political will is required to ensure the implementation of policies.

6.5.2 *Emerging Policies and Strategies*

It is clear that crime in Delhi is a cause for concern, with women and children often emerging as the particularly vulnerable groups. What is also evident is the positive role of the public and the media in bringing about change and bringing people closer to policy formulations. The process of policy formation needs to be more participatory than ever before. Institutions need to be more responsive, approachable and accountable, and trust needs to be fostered between the public and the police. While designing policy, categories matter. Within the policy space, women and children are often clubbed together, especially in relation to crime and safety. It is imperative to understand and engage separately with crimes against children *per se* and to develop child-specific policies to protect them. In the post-16 December 2012 landscape, efforts are being made to bring in reforms in the criminal justice system by facilitating the speedy trials of cases of crime against women. Similar efforts should also be made for cases dealing with crime against children. Apart from this, the profile of the perpetrators also needs closer analysis. Official data shows that the profile of the perpetrators of crime in Delhi has seen a change with criminal activities disproportionately concentrated among the youth vis-à-vis other sections of the population, which needs crucial policy attention. It must also be understood that safety is not merely an issue of policing; in fact, it needs to be placed within the wider socio-economic and political framework of the planning and provisioning of basic

15. As pointed out by Mr. Shubhra Sanyal, Professor, National Institute of Criminology and Forensic Science (NICFS), New Delhi at the stakeholder consultation on 'Safety in Delhi' held on 8 June 2013 at the India International Centre, New Delhi.

Box 6.4

Key Policy Suggestions

- Reforms in the criminal justice system like the police, judiciary, and rehabilitation and intervention mechanisms, which include capacity building and better coordination among various departments to ensure efficiency and accountability and facilitate the building of trust among citizens.
- Inclusive urban planning and services to ensure safety and equitable access for all citizens.
- The use of Information and Communication Technologies (ICTs) in crime reduction and prevention.
- The innovative and constructive use of media, including new media, as a tool to bring about social and attitudinal changes, building on citizens' spirits, dealing with civic apathy as well as sensitisation and spreading of awareness about important issues.
- Encouraging more research in the sensitive areas of crime, safety and social protection, so as to better inform the formulation and implementation of social policy.

services. Inclusive planning must aim at maintaining continuity in different kinds of urban spaces used by different people and allow for the development of more public and shared spaces so that people from varying socio-economic groups are able to interact with each other and avail of the advantage of living in an urban set-up on an equal footing. The Draft Strategic Framework for Women's Safety in Delhi, 2010 outlines seven areas of intervention to make Delhi safe, viz., urban planning and design of public spaces; provision and management of public infrastructure and services; public transport; policing; legislation, justice and support to victims; education; and civic awareness and participation. In addition, serious changes need to be promoted in societal attitudes towards the vulnerable groups, along with sensitisation, civic sense and respect for the law, beginning with homes and schools, without which policies would not have the desired impact (Jagori, 2011).

Some policy suggestions have thus been made to this end and focus on five main areas that need to be addressed (Box 6.4).

6.5.2.1 Reforms in the Criminal Justice System

Strengthening the Law Enforcement Machinery

- Law enforcement services should be brought under the Delhi Government in order to make police functions efficient and accountable.
- The police force should be freed of duties that do not require law enforcement such as security provision, orderly and summon duties, and should be allowed to focus on law enforcement and the protection of citizens.[16]
- There is a need to strengthen the transport, excise and other enforcement departments of the Delhi Government in order to lessen the burden on the police. Similarly, municipal bodies like the MCD, NDMC, and Delhi Cantonment Board should have their own enforcement force to lessen the burden on the police. [17]
- The number of female police staff[18] should be increased and their needs and concerns including with regard to safety should be met.

16. There is a severe shortage of police staff in India for the safety of its citizens, with one police officer per 761 common citizens, in contrast with the large number of police staff deployed for VIP security (three police officers for one person). Delhi has 448 police officers per 1,00,000 persons. The highest police–citizens ratio was reported in the Andaman and Nicobar Islands (1064) while Bihar recorded the worst (65), according to Mohan (2012). There were reportedly 180 police stations in Delhi in 2011 as compared to 129 in 2005, and the total police strength in 2011 was 48,959 as compared to 30,314 in 2005, according to the Statistical Abstract of Delhi, Government of NCT of Delhi (2012).
17. Suggested by Mr. Kamlendra Prasad, Director of the National Institute for Criminology and Forensic Sciences, New Delhi, at the Consultation on the "Second Delhi Human Development Report—2013" on 8 July 2013 at the India International Centre, New Delhi.
18. Delhi Police has announced that it would increase the strength of female police officers (over 2500 police officers) at all police stations in the capital, (Mohan, 2013).

- Financial and other incentives like better ranks should be offered to the police to instil pride in them and to boost their morale.[19]
- There is also a need for proper reporting[20] of all crimes,[21] even 'small crimes'[22], especially against women and children.
- A board elaborating cases concerned with crimes against women and children should be displayed at all police stations.
- The police personnel should be sensitised, particularly in dealing with crimes against women,[23,24] children,[25] and the socio-economically weaker sections.[26]
- Resources should be dedicated to the implementation of social programmes such as *Yuva* and *Parivartan*, organised by the police, and regular monitoring and evaluation should be conducted on the basis of detailed feedback from the residents in order to measure progress of these programmes on the ground.
- The possibility of extension of the *Bhagidari* system to policing could be explored, and the institutionalisation of community policing and neighbourhood watch schemes (on the lines of Police *Mitras*) should be encouraged, thus giving citizens a stake[27] in their safety and well-being, as well as building trust between the people and the police. [28]

---

19. The present system of performance evaluation of police officers focuses on crime reduction and control, with often negative implications such as under-reporting of crimes and preventive action, which, in turn, leads to many arrests and encounters. This highlights the need to design a more holistic evaluation system. This is as per the Prakash Singh judgement in 2006 on police reforms. Although some of the mechanisms to initiate this have been set up in Delhi, they are yet to be operationalised (Kotwal, 2013).
20. Police offiials are known for refusing to register FIRs both small and big crimes despite being legally obliged to do so, in accordance with the provisions of Section 154, Cr. PC (National Legal Research Desk, 'Delhi Police : Standard Operating Procedure (SoP) for Investigation of Rape Cases') and under the 166 Cr. PC wherein a public servant disobeys the law, with intent to cause injury to any person. There is increasing under-reporting and criminals are not being brought to book. This is despite every FIR register bearing the label, 'Burking or writing an incorrect report is an offence punishable under section 218 IPC (Bureau of Police Research and Development, 2013).
21. The increase in the incidence of crimes may be reflective, to an extent, of better reporting and should be encouraged so as to facilitate easy approachability and trust.
22. Among crime prevention measures, the 'broken windows theory' has emerged to be quite influential, according to which tackling petty crimes like littering, vandalism and broken windows could lead to the prevention of more serious and violent crimes (Herbert, 2013). If applied to crimes against women, it would suggest taking crimes considered to be minor such as sexual harassment very seriously and having a zero tolerance policy towards minor crimes, which, in turn, could lead to reductions in serious violent crimes against women. The new law based on the Justice Verma Committee does take a positive step in this direction.
23. Protocols need to be adhered to while registering FIRs and questioning the victims of rape. Rape cases are referred to as 'Special Report Cases', which need to be monitored by the District Commissioner of Police of the district. The case has to be investigated by a female investigating officer and the victim has to be examined by a female doctor only upon obtaining the victims consent if she is above the age of 12 and that of her guardian in case she is younger. Every effort has to be made to ensure that the woman's identity remains secret. Evidence has to be collected carefully and handled with care. These are among the many other protocols that need to be adhered to National Legal Research Desk (n.d.).
24 Mr. Uday Sahay, Chairman and Managing Director of SAUV Communications Private Limited and former Indian Police Service (IPS) Officer, New Delhi, also suggested that government hospitals should be equipped to deal with rape victims and the police should come to the hospital to take the victim's statement and register the case.
25. As per POCSO (2013), while dealing with child victims, a female police officer not lower than the rank of sub-inspector has to come to the residence of the child to record his or her statement, no child is to be detained in the police station at night, police officers visiting the child have to be in plain clothes, the medical examination of a female child is to be conducted by a female doctor in the presence of the child's parent or guardian, among other stipulations.
26. The police is generally known to have a pro- rich bias as pointed out by Buncombe, (A (2013).
27. In conversation with Dr. T.N. Mishra, former Director, National Police Academy and former Director, CBI, who feels that this could potentially help people's self esteem and confidence and give them a stake in the process
28. In the words of Prime Minister, Dr. Manmohan Singh at the Conference of Directors General of Police in 2005, cited in the Ministry of Home Affairs document on Community Policing (p. 3), "The basis of police authority cannot be mere law; it has to be trust of the community as well." Refer to Draft Project Proposal/Business Case on Police–Community Partnership (PCP), Prepared by Micro Mission 2 (Community Policing) of the Prime Minister's National Police Mission, 2008-11.

- The need for change within the police force as per public demands also needs to be analysed and understood. The police should not be viewed as merely a coercive instrument of the executive, but also as a facilitator, a provider of services to the public. In this context, the setting up of a Public Relations Committee for the police that would comprise people from all fields and facilitate public interaction may be considered, thus creating a positive image of the police vis-à-vis the public.[29]

Reforms within the Judiciary

- Special fast-track courts should be institutionalised to address the perpetration of violent crimes against women and children in order to expedite these cases and ensure conviction.
- Proper implementation of POCSO and reviewing of the IPC Acts regarding rape and sexual abuse should be ensured.[30]
- The State should assure monetary compensation, counselling and all possible medical treatment to rape victims.[31]
- Stronger punishments are needed for crimes considered to be 'minor', such as sexual harassment, stalking, etc. in order to prevent more serious crimes in the long run.
- Special protection and encouragement should be given to witnesses of violent crimes.

Rehabilitation and Intervention Mechanisms

- Reforms must be initiated in the juvenile justice laws to bring them in line with UNICEF recommendations, that is, moving away from judicial proceedings and custodial sentencing to social and community solutions, counselling, probation, community service and other alternatives.[32]
- Continuity of child care interventions must be ensured from rehabilitation to re-integration (including the provision of education, vocational training, skill development, recreation and employment) for children in need of care and protection as well as children in conflict with the law, by involving experts as well as relevant stakeholders.
- Ensure proper and sensitised training of Personnel dealing with children (both those in care of need and protection as well as in conflict with the law), whether at shelter homes, or during the investigation processes.
- There is need for linkages between various legislations and departments dealing with children to ensure that the main principles of international law focusing on the protection of child rights are upheld.

6.5.2.2 Urban Planning and Services

Participatory and Inclusive Urban Planning

- Involvement of women and children, elderly as well as minority groups, in planning processes through scientific safety audits and regular feedback.
- Inclusive city-wide planning by building community centres.
- Installing of sufficient street lighting within and outside localities.
- Widening of pavements and pedestrian amenities, and reduction of setbacks in order to create visibility of the streets and mixed space use in these areas.
- Creation of more stops and slowdowns in highways.
- Reviewing of the Master Plan, 2021, to ensure that children's needs and concerns such as

29. In conversation with Dr. T.N. Mishra.
30. Since these do not appropriately apply to the special case of child sexual abuse (which should be recorded as a separate offence) and do not offer protection to children who have been subjected to sexual abuse, specialised counselling mechanisms need to be put into place to deal with these children, according to excerpts from Dr. Asha Bajpai's chapter on "Child Sexual Abuse and Law", (Bajpai, n.d.)
31. As per the recommendations made by the National Commission for Women, cited in the Legal India website.
32. Based on UNICEF, 2010; Dasgupta, 2010.

safety, well-being, and 'well-becoming' are met.[33]

Transport

- Installation of Geographical Information Systems (GIS) in public transport as well as autos and taxis.
- Prominent display of helpline numbers and driver and cab/bus/auto information inside these modes of transport.[34]
- Regulation of all forms of transport and conducting of regular checks.
- Avoiding overloading of buses and provisioning of more frequent buses.
- Checking of all forms of transport, especially during the night.
- Implementation of prohibition of tinted windows in all forms of transport with resultant penalties for violations.
- Presence of police in buses and metros, especially at night.

Municipal Services

- Building more community toilets in slums and resettlement colonies as well as free public toilets in public spaces for women, while maintaining enough distance between the men's and women's toilets; ensuring regular monitoring and upkeep of these facilities (including security provisioning) to prevent misuse and to ensure the safety of users.
- Building of well-maintained roads for access to schools, clean and usable toilets (separate for girls and boys), and better security around schools to be provided by school authorities.
- Ensuring that social welfare schemes cater to all and are available in all areas without discrimination.

Security Provision by Service Providers

- The onus of providing security should be with the concerned service providers. Thus, apart from providing services like public toilets, monuments, parks, buses, schools, etc., the owners of these services should also be responsible for providing safety to the users of these services.[35] A successful example of this is the Delhi Metro, which provides security at all the stations and is perceived to be relatively safe as per the findings of the Perceptions Survey, 2013, and this could be extended to the above-mentioned public services.[36]
- This would make the service providers accountable for the safety of their users as well as ensure that no anti-social or criminal activities take place in these public spaces.

6.5.2.3 Use of Technology to Track and Curb Criminal Activity and Map Unsafe Locations

The Delhi Police has been working towards the installation of technical systems to enhance the reporting and tracking of criminals and victims via web-based integration of information systems, information exchange programmes, ZIPNET, enhanced databases, and digital crime mapping in collaboration with other departments and NGOs. However, there is still a level of mistrust where the police are concerned, which could be tackled through the implementation of a range of positive measures and more interactions with the public such as the *Jan Sampark* initiative.

The following are some suggestions whereby technology could be used to address crimes as well as spread awareness:

- Electronic registration of FIRs and other complaints across local police stations, which could then automatically enter the central database.

33. Mobile Crèches Citizen Report (2002-2007) reiterates that street children, beggars, children of sex workers, child sex workers, children of migrant sex workers and children with disabilities are the most vulnerable, and shelter, sanitation infrastructure, education infrastructure, crèches and day centres and other amenities need to be ensured for them, which are currently either absent or in a deplorable condition (Mobile Crèches, 2011).
34. Suggested by Dr. Kalpana Viswanath, Senior Advisor, 'Safe Delhi Initiative', Jagori, Consultant, UN Women, Project Director, Gender-inclusive Cities Project, Women in Cities International/Femmes et Villes International, during an internal consultation at IHD, New Delhi.
35. Suggested by Mr. Kamlendra Prasad, Director of the National Institute for Criminology and Forensic Sciences, New Delhi, during a personal interview on 30 June 2013.
36. Suggested by Mr. Uday Sahay.

- A web portal should be maintained for the city wherein the citizens' experiences regarding crime and safety could be shared. This portal could also be used to share new policies, laws and events on the issues of crime and safety. A provision to receive important alerts on the phone or sending SOS messages could be explored (for example, 'VithU', an emergency application available for smart phones).[37, 38]

- Mapping of these different kinds of crimes could be done on the basis of the above information.

6.5.2.4 Innovative and Constructive Role of the Social Media and Other Media Like TV, Films, Plays

- Building and promoting norms, which inculcate a respect for the law, starting at the school level, by integrating them into the curricula.

- Building and promoting norms of mutual respect and responsibility amongst the citizens (particularly towards women and girls), which could also be integrated into the school curricula.

- Tackling public apathy through awareness and sensitisation regarding the safety and well-being of women, children, youth and the elderly within localities and public spaces; affording encouragement to citizens to help victims of accidents as well as assaults, and assuring them protection from police harassment.

- Spreading awareness about the rights of the people, laws and government schemes, amongst the vulnerable sections, particularly children and youth.

- Facilitating the formation of neighbourhood and community watch groups, both in posh colonies and slum settlements.

- Spreading awareness about crimes against children and laws therein, in schools as well as residential areas for creating awareness not only amongst parents, guardians and teachers, but also amongst the children themselves.

- Need for social media to screen their own content and ensure that images and messages which condone violence against anyone in any way are immediately reported and removed.[39]

6.5.2.5 Promotion of Research in the Area of Crime, Violence and Safety

- Conduct in-depth longitudinal research studies to understand how urbanisation in the country is panning out and how it impacts planning, governance and safety and security.

- Collection of disaggregated data on how different groups use and experience public spaces (over a period of time).

- Carrying out in-depth research to understand how men, women, girls and boys, the differently-abled, the elderly, transgendered persons, and the poor, experience violence and crimes in order to inform more specific policies for their empowerment and protection. Conduct more evaluation studies on the existing programmes to understand how they are operating on the ground.

---

37. A research study conducted across six countries (Canada, Germany, the Netherlands, Spain, the United Kingdom, and the United States) reported that over 80 per cent of the respondents felt that there was a communication gap between the police and the citizens, reflected in the lack of knowledge on the part of the citizens about local police activities. They felt that the police needed to communicate with the people through digital channels of communication. Almost 50 per cent felt that social media could be used to prevent crime. Many suggested that a citizens' portal should be maintained so that information about crime and safety could be shared on an anonymous basis (Accenture, 2012). Such information could be used to map local crimes, as has been done in Brazil, Venezuela, Panama, Argentina and Chile via Wiki Crimes (*Al Jazeera*, 2011).

38. VithU, is an emergency App, that, at the click of the power button of a smart phone, twice consecutively begins sending out alert messages every two minutes to contacts that are fed into the App by the user, as the designated receivers or guardians. The message says, "I am in danger. I need help. Please follow my location."
The receiver will receive a link to the person's location every two minutes and get the person's updated location. Also, the user will get updates on the 'Crime Scene in India' and a 'Tips Feed' option, exclusively giving her safety tips in an emergency situation.

39. Recently, Facebook came under serious criticism from various women's groups for not dealing with the images and messages promoting gender-based violence, as a result of which the company has committed to review its guidelines and crack down on such offensive content (Bruns, 2013). This was also pointed out by Ms. Nandita Bhatla, Senior Technical Specialist at the International Centre for Research on Women (ICRW), New Delhi.

- Review state budgets to understand the extent to which the needs and concerns of women and children are being captured.[40]
- Improve understanding of the NCRB data, how data on crime are collected, how IPC crimes are categorised, and what challenges come in the way of the recording of crimes.[41]
- Undertaking of detailed research to understand how different socio-economic groups view crime and what they expect from the police; tools such as safety audits and accessibility audits can be used to include vulnerable sections in the planning processes.[42]

All the above measures will certainly go a long way in improving public safety in Delhi. However, as we have seen in the beginning of the chapter, crime and violence are manifestations of multiple factors. Crime needs to be located in the wider context of societal attitudes and norms, which also influence the functioning of diverse state institutions such as the planning authorities and the criminal justice system. As such, legal reform and (mere) policing, although important, will not have the desired impact on crime. Civic norms and mindsets appropriate for a progressive city are yet to develop fully, not just in Delhi, but the country as a whole. This is evident from the occurrence of heinous crimes against women in spite of the recent enactment of harsher laws. Given that the issue of public safety has come to the centre of public discourse, it is now an opportune time for building trust and mutual respect among the citizens, as well as the citizens and the state, and for concerted and relentless efforts by all stakeholders towards a safe(r) Delhi.

Annexure

Annex Table 6.1

Three Year Average of Category-wise IPC Crime Rates in Major Cities during 2004-06

Types of Crimes	*Ahmedabad*	*Bangalore*	*Chennai*	*Delhi*	*Hyderabad*	*Kolkata*	*Mumbai*	*Total Cities*
Body Crimes	41.9	69.1	35.9	27.2	97.6	13.1	30.1	43.1
Crimes against Women	23.3	10.2	5.2	26.8	31.5	4.2	6.4	16.8
Crimes Related to Property	145.3	191.5	38.7	151.9	115.7	24.5	92.9	103.1
Economic Crimes	13.3	31.6	4.8	20.8	37.1	8.9	13.7	17.8
Crimes against Public Order	3.4	8.3	0.6	0.7	2.8	1.4	1.6	4.6
Other IPC Crimes	172.9	180.5	98.6	170.45	37.4	22.4	42.5	108.5
Total IPC Crimes	400.2	491.2	168.8	397.9	322.1	74.5	187.2	293.9

Source: Calculations using NCRB data.

40. According to the latest report by HAQ and CRY (2013), the Delhi State Budget (2013-2014) allocation for children is 18 per cent, signifying a negligible increase of 0.07 per cent over the previous year, with many programmes pertaining to health and social protection experiencing a decline in allocations (HAQ and CRY, 2013).
41. In discussion with Ms. Vrinda Grover, Senior Advocate and Ex-Executive Director, MARG, Human Rights Lawyer and Advocate for Women's Rights, at the Consultation on the "Second Delhi Human Development Report, 2013, on 8 July 2013, at the India International Centre, New Delhi.
42. Based on Politzer, 2012.

Annex Table 6.2

Three-Year Average of Category-wise IPC Crime Rates in Major Cities during 2010-12

Types of Crimes	*Ahmedabad*	*Bangalore*	*Chennai*	*Delhi*	*Hyderabad*	*Kolkata*	*Mumbai*	*Total Cities*
Body Crimes	29.3	58.2	28.9	31.2	68.0	23.5	48.1	43.3
Crimes against Women	27.9	15.4	5.2	29.7	28.2	9.7	12.3	20.7
Crimes Related to Property	92.5	174.5	29.6	153.0	84.6	28.9	142.6	99.3
Economic Crimes	9.1	45.3	8.3	16.2	33.9	15.0	23.5	20.8
Crimes against Public Order	2.8	5.8	1.2	0.7	7.0	2.4	3.7	5.2
Other IPC Crimes	185.5	123.2	107.0	83.6	44.0	59.9	60.1	121.3
Total IPC Crimes	347.2	422.3	180.1	314.3	265.6	139.6	290.4	310.6

Source: Calculations using NCRB data.

Annex Table 6.3

Composition of IPC Crimes within Major Cities Based on a Three-year Average during 2004-06 (per cent)

Types of Crimes	*Ahmedabad*	*Bangalore*	*Chennai*	*Delhi*	*Hyderabad*	*Kolkata*	*Mumbai*	*Total Cities*
Body Crimes	10.5	14.1	14.2	6.8	30.3	17.6	16.1	14.7
Crimes against Women	5.8	2.1	3.0	6.7	9.8	5.6	3.4	5.7
Crimes Related to Property	36.3	39.0	21.5	38.2	35.9	32.9	49.6	35.1
Economic Crimes	3.3	6.4	3.1	5.2	11.5	11.9	7.3	6.0
Crimes against Public Order	0.8	1.7	0.5	0.2	0.9	2.0	0.9	1.6
Other IPC Crimes	43.2	36.8	57.8	42.8	11.6	30.0	22.7	36.9
Total IPC Crimes	100.0	100.0	100.0	100.0	100.0	100.0	100.0	100.0

Source: Calculations using NCRB data.

Annex Table 6.4

Composition of IPC Crimes within Major Cities Based on a Three-year Average during 2010-12 (per cent)

Types of Crimes	*Ahmedabad*	*Bangalore*	*Chennai*	*Delhi*	*Hyderabad*	*Kolkata*	*Mumbai*	*Total Cities*
Body Crimes	8.5	13.8	16.0	9.9	25.8	16.9	16.5	13.9
Crimes against Women	8.1	3.8	2.9	9.5	10.7	7.0	4.5	6.7
Crimes Related to Property	26.5	41.5	16.6	48.5	31.4	20.7	49.0	31.7
Economic Crimes	2.6	10.8	4.7	5.2	12.9	10.8	8.0	6.7
Crimes against Public Order	0.8	1.4	0.6	0.2	2.5	1.7	1.3	1.7
Other IPC Crimes	53.5	28.7	59.2	26.6	16.6	42.9	20.6	39.2
Total IPC Crimes	100.0	100.0	100.0	100.0	100.0	100.0	100.0	100.0

Source: Calculations using NCRB data.

Annex Table 6.5

Three-year Average of Category-wise IPC Crime Rates against Women in Major Cities during 2004-06

Crime Category	*Ahmedabad*	*Bangalore*	*Chennai*	*Delhi*	*Hyderabad*	*Kolkata*	*Mumbai*	*Total Cities*
Rape	0.9	0.6	0.5	4.0	1.3	0.2	1.1	1.5
Kidnapping and Abduction	2.2	0.7	0.4	5.2	1.2	0.5	0.6	1.8
Dowry Deaths	0.1	0.8	0.4	0.8	0.5	0.1	0.1	0.5
Cruelty by Husband and Relatives	18.2	4.7	3.1	10.9	21.8	1.9	1.9	8.2
Molestation	1.4	2.7	1.2	4.7	2.7	1.2	2.2	2.7
Eve-teasing	0.5	0.4	2.0	1.2	4.0	0.3	0.6	2.0
Importation of Girls	0.0	0.0	0.0	0.0	0.0	0.0	0.0	0.0
Total	23.3	9.9	7.6	26.8	31.5	4.1	6.4	16.8

Source: Calculations using NCRB data.

Annex Table 6.6

Three-year Average of Category-wise IPC Crime Rates against Women in Major Cities during 2010-12

Crime Category	*Ahmedabad*	*Bangalore*	*Chennai*	*Delhi*	*Hyderabad*	*Kolkata*	*Mumbai*	*Total Cities*
Rape	1.0	1.1	0.9	3.2	0.8	0.3	1.2	1.7
Kidnapping and Abduction	3.2	2.7	0.6	10.8	0.5	1.0	0.9	3.4
Dowry Deaths	0.2	0.7	0.2	0.7	0.5	0.1	0.1	0.5
Cruelty by Husband and Relatives	24.0	6.2	2.4	10.2	20.1	4.4	2.0	10.3
Molestation	1.4	4.0	0.9	3.9	2.3	2.3	3.1	3.4
Eve-teasing	0.2	0.6	1.1	0.9	1.4	1.6	1.0	1.4
Importation of Girls	0.0	0.0	0.0	0.0	0.0	0.0	0.0	0.0
Total	30.0	15.4	6.1	29.7	25.8	9.7	8.3	20.7

Source: Calculations using NCRB data.

Annex Table 6.7

Composition of IPC Crime against Women within Major Cities Based on a Three-year Average during 2004-06 (per cent)

Crime Category	*Ahmedabad*	*Bangalore*	*Chennai*	*Delhi*	*Hyderabad*	*Kolkata*	*Mumbai*	*Total Cities*
Rape	3.8	6.1	7.0	15.1	4.1	4.7	17.6	8.8
Kidnapping and Abduction	9.3	6.8	4.7	19.3	3.8	10.9	9.4	13.3
Dowry Deaths	0.5	7.9	5.8	3.2	1.6	1.2	1.2	3.0
Cruelty by Husband and Relatives	78.2	47.5	41.2	40.6	69.1	46.5	29.0	47.6
Molestation	6.0	27.2	15.3	17.4	8.6	30.1	33.8	15.6
Eve-teasing	2.2	4.5	25.9	4.4	12.7	6.4	8.9	11.7
Importation of Girls	0.0	0.0	0.0	0.0	0.0	0.1	0.0	0.0
Total	100.0	100.0	100.0	100.0	100.0	100.0	100.0	100

Source: Calculations using NCRB data.

Annex Table 6.8

Composition of IPC Crime against Women within Major Cities Based on a Three-year Average during 2010-12 (per cent)

Crime Category	Ahmedabad	Bangalore	Chennai	Delhi	Kolkata	Hyderabad	Mumbai	Total Cities
Rape	3.4	7.2	14.6	10.8	3.6	3.4	14.7	8.3
Kidnapping and Abduction	10.7	19.2	9.2	36.3	10.3	2.1	10.3	16.5
Dowry Deaths	0.8	4.5	3.2	2.4	1.0	2.0	1.0	2.6
Cruelty by Husband and Relatives	79.9	39.7	39.8	34.5	44.9	78.0	24.8	49.5
Molestation	4.6	25.3	14.0	13.0	23.8	9.0	37.2	16.5
Eve-Teasing	0.6	4.1	19.2	3.0	16.1	5.6	12.1	6.6
Importation of Girls	0.0	0.0	0.0	0.0	0.3	0.0	0.0	0.0
Total	100	100	100	100.0	100	100	100	100

Source: Calculations using NCRB data.

Annex Table 6.9

Three-year Average of Category-wise IPC Crime Rates against Children in Major Cities during 2004-06

Crime Category	Ahmedabad	Bangalore	Chennai	Delhi	Hyderabad	Kolkata	Mumbai	Total Cities
Murder	0.1	0.0	0.1	0.3	0.1	0.0	0.1	0.1
Infanticide	0.0	0.0	0.0	0.0	0.0	0.0	0.0	0.0
Other Murder	0.0	0.0	0.0	0.0	0.0	0.0	0.0	0.0
Rape	0.2	0.1	0.2	1.9	0.5	0.1	0.5	0.6
Kidnapping and Abduction	0.3	0.1	0.1	4.5	0.5	0.3	0.2	1.1
Foeticide	0.0	0.0	0.0	0.0	0.0	0.0	0.0	0.0
Abetment of Suicide	0.0	0.0	0.0	0.0	0.0	0.0	0.0	0.0
Exposure and Abandonment	0.5	0.0	0.0	0.3	0.9	0.0	0.0	0.2
Procurement of minor girls	0.0	0.0	0.0	0.0	0.1	0.1	0.0	0.0
Buying of girls for prostitution	0.0	0.0	0.0	0.0	0.0	0.0	0.0	0.0
Selling of girls for prostitution	0.0	0.0	0.0	0.0	0.0	0.0	0.0	0.0
Other crimes	1.6	0.0	0.0	1.9	0.0	0.4	1.0	1.2
Total	2.7	0.1	0.5	9.0	2.2	1.0	1.9	3.3

Source: Calculations using NCRB data.

Annex Table 6.10

Three-year Average of Category-wise IPC Crime Rates against Children in Major Cities during 2010-12

Crime Category	Ahmedabad	Bangalore	Chennai	Delhi	Hyderabad	Kolkata	Mumbai	Total Cities
Murder	0.0	0.1	0.1	0.2	0.0	0.0	0.1	0.1
Infanticide	0.0	0.0	0.0	0.0	0.0	0.0	0.0	0.0
Other Murders	0.0	0.0	0.0	0.0	0.0	0.0	0.0	0.0
Rape	0.1	0.2	0.5	1.9	0.3	0.2	0.8	0.5
Kidnapping and Abduction	1.9	1.6	0.5	18.3	0.4	0.6	0.7	3.1
Foeticide	0.0	0.0	0.0	0.0	0.0	0.0	0.0	0.0
Abetment of Suicide	0.0	0.0	0.0	0.0	0.0	0.0	0.0	0.0
Exposure and Abandonment	0.3	0.1	0.0	0.4	0.1	0.0	0.1	0.1
Procurement of Minor Girls	0.0	0.2	0.0	0.0	0.0	0.1	0.0	0.0
Buying of Girls for Prostitution	0.0	0.0	0.0	0.0	0.0	0.0	0.0	0.0
Selling of Girls for Prostitution	0.0	0.0	0.0	0.0	0.0	0.1	0.0	0.0
Other Crimes	0.0	0.3	0.0	1.5	0.4	0.3	1.1	1.3
Total	2.3	2.5	1.0	22.3	1.3	1.3	2.8	5.2

Source: Calculations using NCRB data.

Annex Table 6.11

Composition of IPC Crime against Children within Major Cities Based on a Three-year Average during 2004-06 (per cent)

Crime Category	*Ahmedabad*	*Bangalore*	*Chennai*	*Delhi*	*Hyderabad*	*Kolkata*	*Mumbai*	*Total Cities*
Murder	4.8	6.1	2.9	4.4	11.1	2.9	11.1	4.3
Infanticide	0.0	0.0	0.0	0.0	0.0	0.0	0.0	0.1
Other Murders	0.0	0.0	0.0	0.0	0.0	0.0	0.0	0.0
Rape	4.8	28.3	13.7	22.2	26.8	19.7	26.8	19.3
Kidnapping and Abduction	23.6	30.3	22.7	50.0	37.9	46.4	37.9	29.3
Foeticide	0.0	0.0	1.4	0.7	0.0	0.3	0.0	0.6
Abetment of Suicide	0.0	0.5	0.2	0.0	0.0	0.1	0.0	0.2
Exposure and Abandonment	51.5	0.0	3.5	4.7	18.3	1.3	18.3	7.3
Procurement of Minor Girls	5.5	5.6	2.2	0.0	3.3	0.5	3.3	0.7
Buying of Girls for Prostitution	0.0	1.5	0.2	0.0	0.0	0.4	0.0	0.6
Selling of Girls for Prostitution	1.2	3.0	0.4	0.0	0.0	0.1	0.0	0.2
Other Crimes	29.1	24.7	52.8	18.0	2.6	28.2	2.6	37.5
Total	100.0	100.0	100.0	100.0	100.0	100.0	100.0	100.0

Source: Calculations using NCRB data.

Annex Table 6.12

Composition of IPC Crime against Children within Major Cities Based on a Three-year Average during 2010-12 (per cent)

Crime Category	*Ahmedabad*	*Bangalore*	*Chennai*	*Delhi*	*Hyderabad*	*Kolkata*	*Mumbai*	*Total Cities*
Murder	0.0	3.6	8.2	0.9	3.1	0.6	2.9	2.4
Infanticide	0.0	0.0	0.0	0.0	0.8	0.0	0.2	0.2
Other Murders	0.0	0.0	0.0	0.0	0.0	0.0	0.0	0.0
Rape	6.3	8.3	46.3	8.4	22.1	12.1	27.0	9.2
Kidnapping and Abduction	81.1	66.9	44.7	82.1	27.5	48.6	26.3	59.4
Foeticide	0.0	0.3	0.0	0.1	1.9	0.0	0.3	0.4
Abetment of Suicide	0.0	0.0	0.0	0.0	1.6	0.4	0.3	0.2
Exposure and Abandonment	12.1	2.8	0.0	1.6	8.1	0.0	4.3	2.8
Procurement of Minor Girls	0.2	7.8	0.0	0.1	0.0	9.0	0.1	0.9
Buying of Girls for Prostitution	0.0	0.0	0.0	0.0	0.0	0.6	0.1	0.2
Selling of Girls for Prostitution	0.0	0.0	0.0	0.1	0.4	4.8	0.0	0.2
Other Crimes	0.2	10.4	0.8	6.7	34.5	24.0	38.7	24.1
Total	100.0	100.0	100.0	100.0	100.0	100.0	100.0	100.0

Source: Calculations using NCRB data.

7

People's Perceptions

7.1 Introduction

Having moved progressively from the traditional sense of the term that looked at income, education and health, 'human development' has today come to encompass various meanings including the opportunities available to people, their capabilities, empowerment, and equity, among other things. Different aspects such as leisure, contentment, a feeling of safety and security, and aspirations have increasingly found space in the measurement and understanding of people's well-being and quality of life. Therefore, the aim of this chapter is to focus on certain aspects of well-being, as reported by the people of Delhi, in order to attain a holistic understanding of the state of human development in the capital state.

As has been discussed in detail in Chapter 2, Delhi has a very diverse populace. With a population of more than 16.7 millions, it has been growing by about 0.3 million persons per year since 2007 (Economic Survey of Delhi, 2013). It is also a city of migrants, most of whom come here in search of employment, better wages, educational opportunities and, as such, a better quality of life.

Inevitably, rapid urbanisation and economic growth, coupled with the demands of a growing population, have resulted in a significant advancement of infrastructural facilities in the city, particularly in the road and transport sector, along with considerable improvements in the provisioning of several basic amenities. On the other hand, issues such as the poor quality of services and growing disparities between various sections of the population continue to be a matter of concern. While the other chapters of the report focus on the actual progress made by the Government in terms of the provisioning of facilities and access to better livelihoods, education, healthcare, basic services and safety, the focus in this chapter is on peoples' ratings of their own lives, an assessment of their surroundings, their suggestions for facilitating better livelihoods, a review of what they like and dislike about the city, the type of assets they own in their households, and their aspirations regarding the products they wish to purchase in the coming years. This exercise is thus relevant as it is increasingly being argued that "policy-makers should take the subjective well-being of the population as their goal and think of all other goods like education, health and income as means to that end" (Layard, 2012). Therefore, by examining people's perceptions about their lives, their localities, their neighbourhoods and the city that they live in, policy-makers can acquire a better understanding of the challenges that need to be addressed for bringing about improvements in the well-being of the residents of Delhi.

This chapter aims to bring out the voice of Delhi's citizens. It is primarily based on the Perceptions Survey, 2013, the findings of which are supplemented with Focus Group Discussions (FGDs), which were conducted in different localities in Delhi, with a particular focus on the poorer localities (for the survey design and other details, see Annexure to Chapter 1).

The questionnaire that was administered to the respondents for the Perceptions Survey, along with the FGDs, covers the following issues, which are presented and discussed in this chapter:

- People's satisfaction levels with respect to the quality of their lives, health, neighbourhoods, work, education and other aspects of well-being.
- Leisure activities, eating out, etc.
- The availability of economic opportunities as perceived by various socio-economic groups.
- Evaluation of basic services, schools and other schemes that are offered for the benefit of the city's residents.
- Household and locality level dynamics and people's assessments of the best and worst services available in the city.
- The nature and extent of assets owned by the households, their assessment of what is lacking, and their plans for the future in terms of asset ownership.
- Feeling of financial stability amongst the respondents
- Ratings of people's interactions with different government personnel, the functioning of social protection schemes, and the process of acquiring ownership of identification documents in the city.
- People's listings of the things they like/dislike about Delhi and the main problems they face here in their daily lives.

Box 7.1

Studying Perceptions

Both subjective and objective realities are important for studying human development. For example, apart from objective measures such as whether a person has access to drinking water, it is important to know what people feel about this service. Are they satisfied? Do they think that it has improved or deteriorated? However, both subjective and objective evaluations cannot always be mapped on to each other. It is possible that those having water supply of inferior quality may be more satisfied than those having quality water supply in their homes if the water supply for the former group was comparatively more regular. Thus, subjective evaluations such as satisfaction levels or perceptions of change can lead to results that are different from more objective measures. To illustrate further, it has been repeatedly seen that satisfaction levels among recent migrants are higher than those among older migrants and also non-migrants. Why is this so? A possible explanation is that a large proportion of the migrants come to Delhi in a quest for work, that is, to escape poverty and unemployment in their place of origin. Thus, while these migrants more often than not have worse living standards than those of the non-migrants, it has been observed that they still rate their satisfaction levels higher than the latter. This could be because they are comparing their present conditions with those prevalent in their places of origin, which they may consider to be comparatively inferior (spatial reference points). Figure 7.1 depicts how people's socio-economic backgrounds, expectations, secondary data, and spatial and temporal reference points coalesce to influence their perceptions.

Figure 7.1

Factors Influencing People's Perceptions

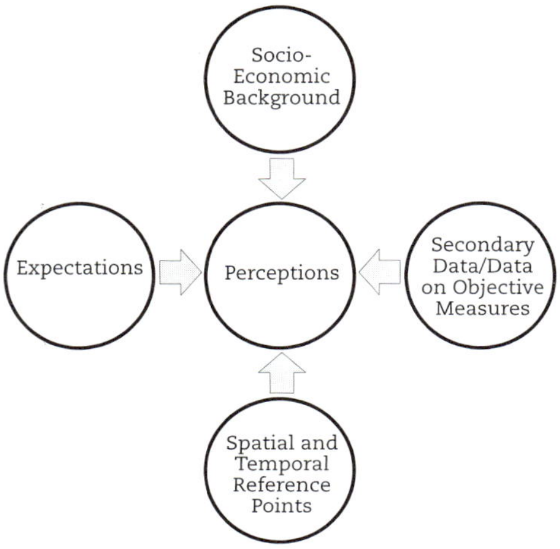

The issues highlighted above are addressed in this chapter through an analysis of people's perceptions rather than objective indicators, though the latter do exert a major influence in terms of forming people's perceptions. It is equally important to point out at the outset that perceptions are also determined culturally. For example, if we were to look at the happy planet index, we would find that Bangladesh is ranked quite highly with the people there reporting higher levels of well-being than their counterparts in many of the richer nations.[1] This could partly be explained by the fact that the people in Bangladesh have a larger positive perception of well-being on account of their experiences of traditional institutions of family and religion, which inform various dimensions of their lives. Box 7.1 illustrates some of the factors that are likely to contribute towards shaping people's perceptions and opinions.

7.2 Satisfaction Levels among the Residents of Delhi

In order to understand and measure the subjective life satisfaction/sense of well-being of the people of Delhi, the respondents in the survey were asked how satisfied they were with various aspects of their lives, including the parameters of healthcare, neighbourhood characteristics, immediate family, overall achievements in life, work/education, and the general quality of life. These attributes of life in Delhi were explored on the basis of the assumption that they contribute to a person's assessment of his/her overall well-being. The responses were recorded on a scale of one to five, beginning with 'very satisfied', and moving on to 'satisfied', 'neither satisfied nor dissatisfied', 'dissatisfied' and 'very dissatisfied'.[2]

This section of the chapter first studies the overall life satisfaction index (see Box 7.2), before examining in some detail two of its components which outline a significant difference in people's perceptions.

7.2.1 Overall Satisfaction with Life

To start with, different questions measuring the various aspects of well-being outlined above were combined[3] to form a composite index of 'satisfaction

1. Sourced at :*http://www.happyplanetindex.org/* (Accessed June 6, 2013).
2. For most analyses in this chapter, the responses 'very satisfied' and 'satisfied' have been combined into one measure of satisfaction. Similarly, the responses 'dissatisfied' and 'very dissatisfied' have been combined into one measure of dissatisfaction.
3. The correlation between various variables for the index was studied before identifying its components.

with life'.[4] The index thus generated was then scaled by using two cut-off points so that the population could be distributed into three sets of respondents, *vis-à-vis.*, those exhibiting low, average and high levels of overall satisfaction[5]

Box 7.2

A Note on Indices

A series of indices have been constructed on the basis of the Perceptions Survey, 2013, and have been presented under various sections in the chapter. These indices assess people's overall satisfaction with life, their evaluation of the basic amenities available to them in terms of both access and quality, their ratings of safety and security, and their assessment of employment opportunities available in Delhi as also the quality of schools in the city.

In general, the construction of an index to examine the broad issues of well being, life satisfaction, human development, and economic environment, among other indicators, can be justified on the grounds that a composite measure makes it easier to summarise and present issues that may otherwise be difficult to comprehend, especially for policy-makers. This is particularly true in the case of issues that are multi-dimensional in nature and require the holistic measurement of more than a single variable, such as 'satisfaction with life'. Using just one indicator in such cases may lead to under-identification of the groups of individuals that should be targeted through policy. For example, a study by the Oxford Poverty and Human Development Initiative (OPHI) research team that used a new measure of global poverty found that eight Indian states accounted for more poor people than those in 26 poorest African countries combined,[6] and this had important implications for policy-making. Similarly, in this chapter, we are interested in arriving at overall evaluations, for example, access to and the quality of different basic services taken together, for the purpose of identifying localities or socio-economic groups that perceive a general deficiency in provisions of the same.

Largely, the composite index reflects that the majority of those who live in Delhi were highly satisfied with their lives although this could, to a large extent, be a cultural artifact (see Box. 7.1). However, as expected, perceptions differed between socio-economic groups (such as gender, age, education levels) and by income levels, activity status and locality,[7] with the difference in satisfaction levels being the most stark when disaggregated by these latter three groups (see Figures 7.2, 7.3 and 7.4)

Figure 7.2

Distribution of Population Based on the Level of Satisfaction with Life (Index), by Income Group

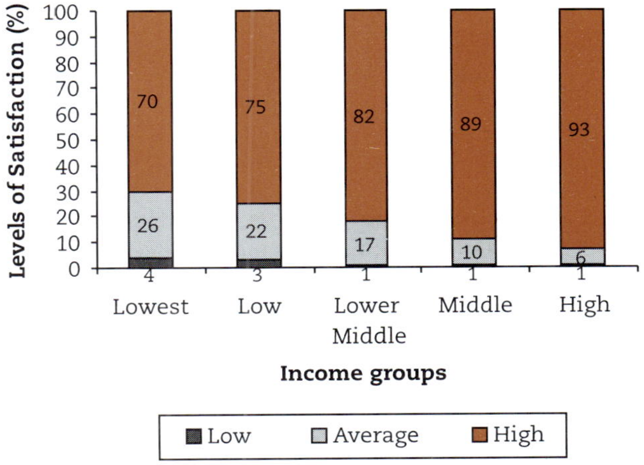

Source: Perceptions Survey, 2013.

Figure 7.2 clearly shows that a larger proportion of people with higher incomes were more satisfied with life than those with lower incomes, which is not surprising, given that material well-being is generally seen as an important criterion for life satisfaction.[8]

When the socio-economic factors are explored further, the resultant analysis of the life-satisfaction index by activity status (depicted in Figure 7.3) shows that among the different occupational groups, casual wage labourers account for the lowest proportion of people reporting a high degree of life-satisfaction and

4. Confirmatory Factor Analysis showed a high degree of internal consistency between these variables, which meant that they could be combined into a composite index.
5. This could also be read as 'dissatisfied', 'neither satisfied'/'dissatisfied' and 'satisfied'. This is the methodology that has been followed in constructing all the indices in this chapter. The meaning associated with the cut-off points changes in accordance with the question asked.
6. *http://www.bbc.co.uk/news/10609407*. See also the OPHI website: *http://www.ophi.org.uk* (Accessed May 15, 2013).
7. The analysis is based on a general classification of monthly household incomes. These are: Lowest, Low, Lower Middle, Middle, and High. For details of income categories see Annexure 1.1
8. A similar finding was reported for the Quality of Life study conducted by the Economist Intelligence Unit (EIU) in 2005. Under this study, the EIU had developed a 'quality of life' index that linked subjective life-satisfaction surveys with the objective determinants of the quality of life such as income. The index was calculated to obtain a ranking of 111 countries.

Figure 7.3

Distribution of Population Based on the Level of Satisfaction with Life (Index), by Activity Status

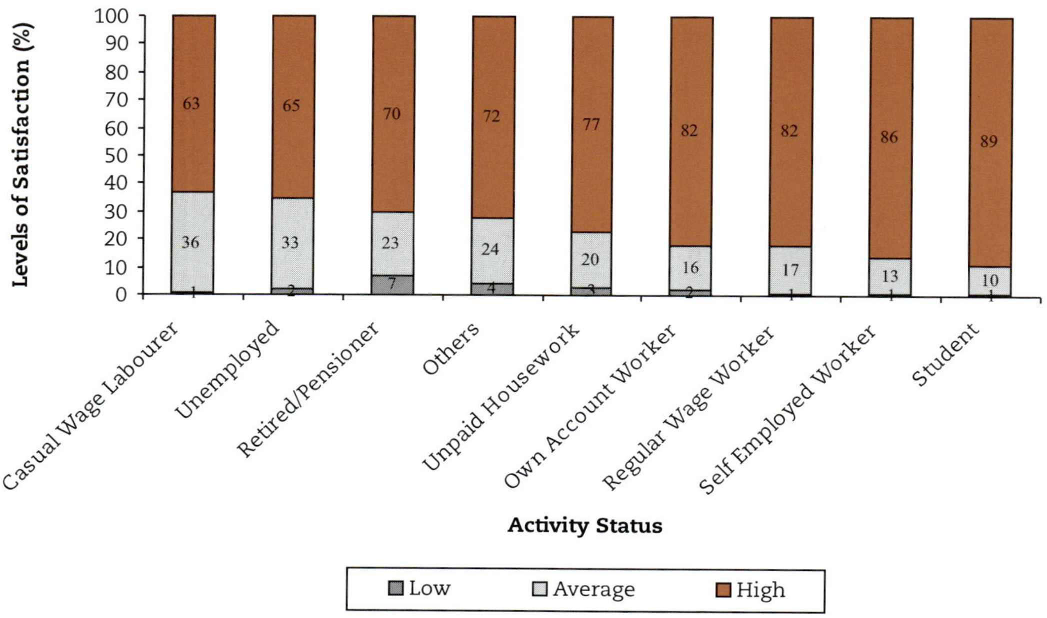

Source: Perceptions Survey, 2013.

are closely followed by the unemployed. On the other hand, 89 per cent of the students report being highly satisfied with their lives.

Figure 7.4

Distribution of Population Based on the Level of Satisfaction with Life (Index), by Locality

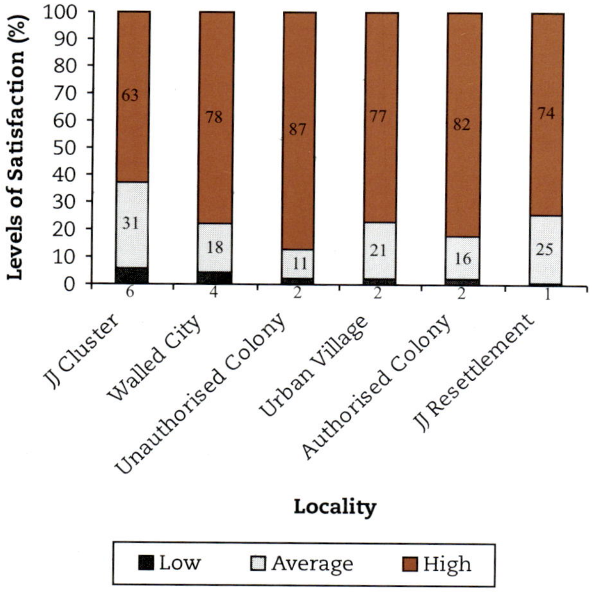

Source: Perceptions Survey, 2013.

Figure 7.4 studies the life-satisfaction index by locality type. It is evident that a large proportion of the people living in *Jhuggi Jhopdi* (JJ) clusters are not very satisfied with their lives, and this has interesting implications when compared with the proportion of those who are 'highly satisfied' in the JJ resettlement colonies. This finding suggests that some basic steps undertaken by the State Government in terms of the development of the JJ clusters in Delhi under their resettlement scheme could have contributed to the positive impact on people's assessment of their life-satisfaction levels.[9]

7.2.2 "How Satisfied Are You with the Quality of Your Life?"

Following the methodology of the 'Quality of Life Index' study (see Footnote 8), which used only one question to measure subjective life-satisfaction, this section explores the responses to the comparable question asked in the Perceptions Survey which was: *"How satisfied are you with the quality of your life?"*

9. Hence, even though the residents of JJ resettlement colonies are often disadvantaged due to relocation, their higher satisfaction levels as compared to their counterparts living in the JJ clusters could be a result of tenure security, legitimacy, improved amenities and as such, a result of the spatial factors discussed in Box. 7.1.

On the whole, a significant proportion of the respondents (75 per cent) reported that they were 'satisfied' or 'very satisfied' with the quality of their life. About 17 per cent of the respondents said that they were 'neither satisfied nor dissatisfied' while about 8 per cent reported that they were 'dissatisfied'. However, the perception of satisfaction was not consistent among Delhi's population when disaggregated by their backgrounds (Table 7.1).

Table 7.1

Proportion of Respondents Satisfied with the Quality of Their Life (in %)

Monthly Household Income	*Respondents Satisfied*	*Age*	*Respondents Satisfied*
Lowest	64	15-19 years	79
Low	72	20-29 years	75
Lower Middle	80	30-45 years	75
Middle	82	45-60 years	75
High	85	60 years and above	72
Activity Status		*Type of Settlement*	
Student	82	Posh Locality	91
Regular Wage Workers	78	Unauthorised Colony	81
Own Account Worker	78	Authorised Colony	77
Self-employed Employer	76	JJ Resettlement Colony	75
Unpaid Housework	73	Urban Village	74
Retired/Pensioner	69	The Walled City	72
Unemployed	66	JJ Clusters	56
Casual Wage Worker	51		
Level of Education of Respondent		*Caste Groups*	
Illiterate	66	SCs	70
Primary Educated	66	STs	70
Middle School	74	OBCs	75
Matric	77	General	77
Higher Secondary	79		
Graduate and Higher Education	85		
Gender			
Male	76		
Female	74		

Note: All figures have been rounded off. *Proportion of respondents answering the question "How satisfied are you with your quality of life?"

Source: Perceptions Survey, 2013.

Following is a summary of the findings presented in Table 7.1:

- *First*, the elderly, women, the Scheduled Castes (SCs), Scheduled Tribes (STs), those having lower education levels, casual wage earners and those living in JJ clusters accounted for a higher proportion of people who were less satisfied than their counterparts.

- *Second*, conforming to the findings for the overall index, a higher proportion of people in the higher income groups reported satisfaction with the quality of their life when compared to those belonging to the lower income groups.

- *Third*, disaggregated by activity status and locality indicated that casual wage labourers and respondents from the JJ clusters constituted the largest proportion of those dissatisfied with the quality of their life (similar to the overall life-satisfaction index). Only 51 per cent of the respondents among the casual labourers and 56 per cent of the residents of JJ clusters rated the quality of their life as satisfactory, which is much lower than the average figure for the capital city at 75 per cent.

Box 7.3

Dissatisfied Casual Wage Labourers: Who Are They?

The lowest incidence of satisfaction was observed amongst the casual wage labourers, who accounted for 9 per cent of all respondents. Also, those who were dissatisfied had lower education levels and belonged to households with lower income levels. About 71 per cent of the dissatisfied casual wage labourers were illiterate or educated only up to the primary level.

Dissatisfied Women: Was Are They?

While at the aggregate, a larger proportion of women were found to be less satisfied than men with the quality of their life in Delhi, among the younger age groups, surprisingly, a larger proportion of the women were actually found to be more satisfied (than men). Dissatisfaction with the quality of their life was found to afflict a larger proportion of women over the age of 29 years, and could be possibly associated with the competing demands of work, home, marriage and childbirth, which affect a majority of women in Delhi.

7.2.3 How Satisfied Are You with Your Own Health Status?

The Perceptions Survey found a higher proportion of the respondents to be satisfied with their health status (80 per cent) in comparison to those satisfied with the quality of their life (75 per cent). Also, as regards the overall satisfaction of life index, the difference amongst the sexes was relatively small, with the male and female respondents reporting more or less similar levels of satisfaction.[10] However, it was found that the differences in satisfaction by gender varied across age groups when it came to the question of health. The satisfaction levels among both men and women declined with age, but the decline in women's perceptions about their health was much more pronounced. Possible explanations for this could be the added burden of childbirth, household responsibilities and 'double burden of work' that women have to engage with as they get older.

The dissatisfaction levels for males and females, disaggregated by various age groups, revealed that in the youngest age group (15-19 years), a smaller proportion of the women were dissatisfied than men (see Figure 7.5). However, this gets reversed remarkably in the older age groups, with a larger proportion of the women reporting dissatisfaction with health as compared to men. While about 3 per cent of the males in the age bracket of 20-29 years are dissatisfied, about 6 per cent of the females belonging to this bracket reported to be dissatisfied. In the next age bracket (30-45 years), about 5 per cent of the males and 10 per cent of the females are dissatisfied. The proportion of the dissatisfied among both men and women increases with age but the percentage of dissatisfied women is around 28 per cent among those aged 60 years and above, while the corresponding figure among men is about 19 per cent.

The differences in perceptions among men and women relating to health are fairly alarming. It is possible that the 'double burden of work', coupled with ageing, are responsible for the greater proportion of dissatisfied respondents amongst women. An additional analysis of dissatisfaction across income groups by gender indicates that while respondents belonging to the lower income groups were, in general, more dissatisfied with their health status, the difference in the proportion of the 'dissatisfied' between males and females was also greater among the lower income groups, with a larger proportion of the women being more dissatisfied (see Figure 7.5). In the light of such perceptions reported by women regarding their health and the quest for universalisation of healthcare (discussed in Chapter 4), it would be pertinent for policy-makers to explore further reasons behind such dissatisfaction and to identify the need for special healthcare provisions for women, especially poor women.

Figure 7.5

Proportion Dissatisfied With Their Own Health by Age (in%)

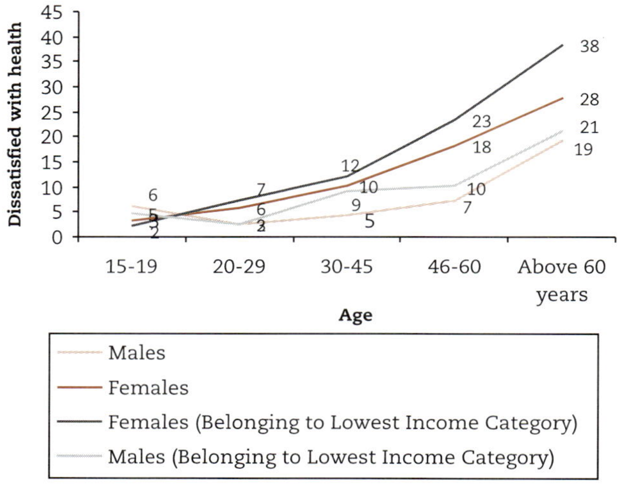

Source: Perceptions Survey, 2013.

7.3 Evaluation of the Economic Environment by the Residents

This section first looks at the index of economic environment in Delhi by gender and income groups, followed by analyses of the individual components that are used in the index.

7.3.1 Overall Evaluation of the Economic Environment

To start with, the rating of overall employment opportunities in Delhi has been examined. This has been done by calculating an index to arrive at a composite rating of the employment opportunities (or the economic environment index) by combining the responses to questions on the rating of employment opportunities for men, those for women, and the change in employment opportunities during the last three years.

10. The proportion of men who reported a high level of satisfaction on the 'satisfaction with life' index was 80 per cent as compared to 77 per cent of women.

The methodology used to generate the above index is the same as the one described in the previous section for the life-satisfaction index. After the responses to the above questions were combined, the cut-offs were used to divide the population into various categories including those who gave a lower rating to the overall economic environment in Delhi, those who thought that it was average, and those who perceived it to be good.[11]

The overall distribution for the economic environment index showed that 23 per cent of the respondents gave a low rating to employment opportunities in Delhi whilst 46 per cent evaluated it positively. Furthermore, the difference between the proportion of men and women in terms of their evaluation of the overall economic environment for Delhi was found to be quite small (Figure 7.6).

Figure 7.6

Distribution of Population Based on the Rating of the Overall Economic Environment (Index), by Gender

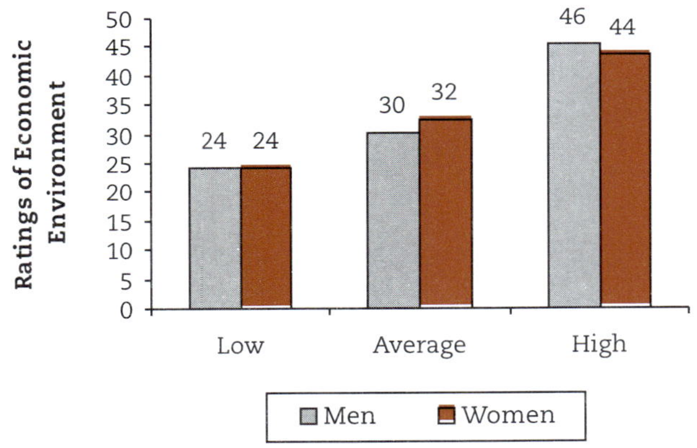

Source: Perceptions Survey, 2013.

There was a marginal difference between men and women when it came to the proportion of people within each group who gave a positive or average evaluation of the economic environment in Delhi (Figure 7.6). This is interesting because studies have shown that women plan their careers less as compared to men, and this difference in aspirations should be reflected in their evaluation of the economic environment (Department of Education, Oxford Learning Institute; De Vries, *et al.*, 2006). On the other hand, the results here could signify a reflection of the way in which the respondents in Delhi perceive the economic environment with no prior expectation of men and women having different opinions.

When people's rating of the overall economic environment is cross-tabulated with the income levels of their households, it is found that a greater proportion of those belonging to the higher income categories rate it higher as compared to those belonging to the lower income groups (Fig. 7.7).

Figure 7.7

Distribution of Population Based on a Rating of the Overall Economic Environment (Index), by Income Group

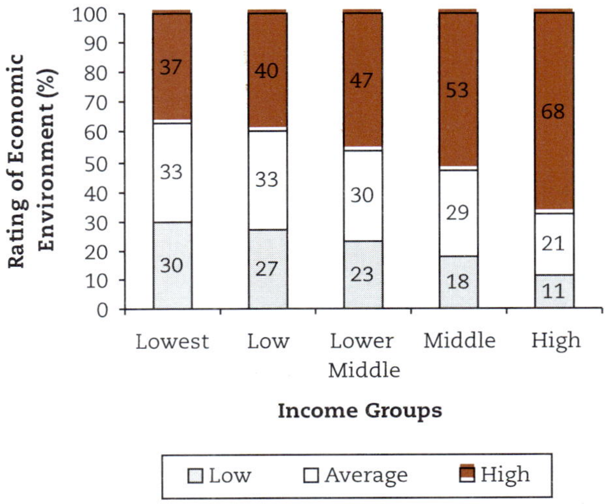

Source: Perceptions Survey, 2013.

7.3.2 Rating of Availability of Employment Opportunities

Disaggregation of the economic environment index into the three individual questions that were used to construct the index brings forth some interesting findings. These should be seen in conjunction with the findings of the FGDs (Box 7.4), as it facilitates a better understanding of people's perceptions towards the economic environment in Delhi.

- How do you rate the availability of employment opportunities for men?
- How do you rate the availability of employment opportunities for women?

The results derived from the responses to the above questions show that perceptions about the availability of work were, as such, optimistic. Almost half of the respondents reported that employment

11. This can also be interpreted as low rating=negative evaluation and high rating=positive evaluation, or low rating=dissatisfaction with the economic environment and high rating=satisfaction with the economic environment.

Figure7.8

Proportion Who Feel That Employment Opportunities are Good For Men and Women (in%)

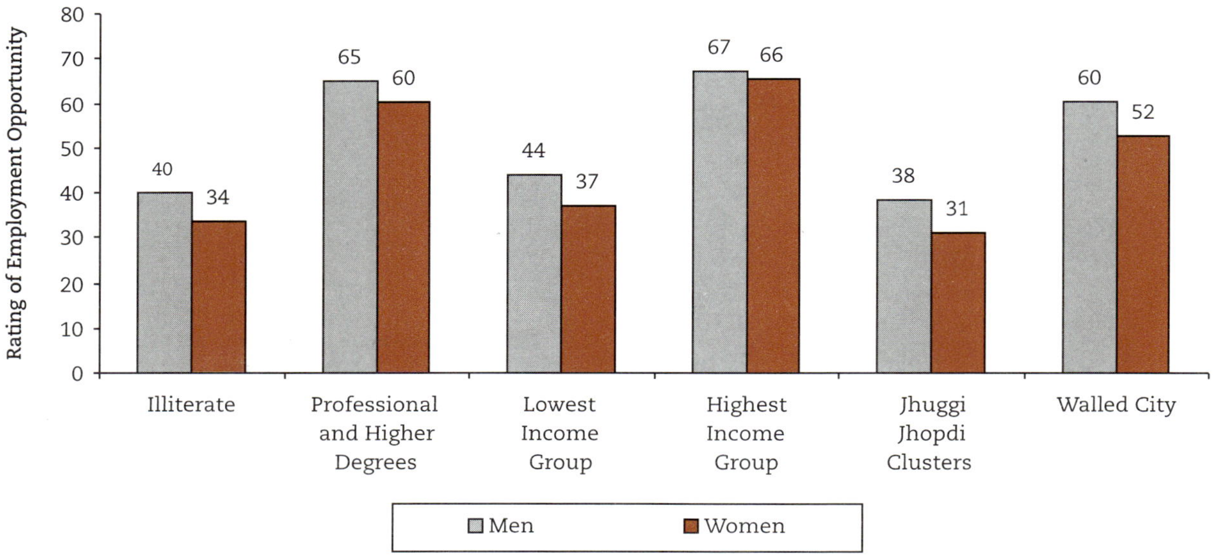

Source: Perceptions Survey, 2013.

opportunities for men were good in the city, while for women, about 45 per cent said that the opportunities were good. Almost 30 per cent of the respondents rated employment availability to be average for both men and women. Even though the difference in the perceptions regarding job opportunities for men and women is not very large, the results do reflect the more difficult labour markets that exist for women.

7.3.3 Have the Employment Opportunities Increased, Decreased or Remained the Same during the Last Three Years?

With respect to the change over time, more than half of the respondents (52 per cent) felt that the employment opportunities had remained the same during the last three years, but it is encouraging to find that despite the slow growth in employment and the recent economic crisis, more than one-third of the respondents felt that employment opportunities in Delhi had improved.

A related question then is: Who are the people who think employment opportunities are good (high rating)? Which groups feel that opportunities are poor (low rating)?

From the data collected during the Perceptions Survey, 2013, it emerges that employment opportunities are perceived to be fewer by a larger proportion of those belonging to the lower income groups. About 21 per cent respondents felt that employment opportunities for men were poor, for women it was 27 per cent. When studied by income groups, on the other hand, only 10 per cent of those belonging to the highest income category rated employment opportunities as poor for both men and women. The Work Participation Rates (WPRs)[12] by women across settlement types also re-affirm this finding (Table 7.2). The WPR for women is found to

Table 7.2

Work Participation Rates (15-59 Years) among Women, by Settlement Type

Posh Localities	15
Authorised Colonies	9
The Walled City	7
JJ Resettlement Colonies	7
JJ Clusters	6
Unauthorised Colonies	3
Urban Villages	3

Source: Perceptions Survey, 2013.

12. The Work Participation Rate (WPR) has been calculated for the population within the age group of 15-59 years.

Box 7.4

Work Opportunities: Findings from the FGDs

- *Women's Views on Their Work*

  The FGDs with communities in various low-income settlements revealed that social issues continue to constrain women's work and to some degree, reflect the reasons behind the low WPR of women in Delhi. Despite having the inclination as well as the ambition to engage in work, women report that owing to the prevalence of cultural taboos, the men in their families were reluctant to allow them to work. In some households, home-based work is permissible but the women feel that such kinds of work are exploitative. Lack of education was also cited as a reason for not getting work, and this relates to the findings of the Perceptions Survey as well as to the perception that work opportunities improve with educational status. Also, many women reported the need for dual incomes because poverty compelled them to engage in work.

- *What Aspirations Do You Have for Your Young?*

  The following responses were obtained to the above question:

  - "We want our children to receive good quality education.": Discussions with the respondents revealed that low-income households considered education to be the only tool for upward social mobility.
  - "We want government jobs for our children.": A common aspiration among communities was the desire for government jobs for their children, as this ensured stability, status and a decent income. As regards the boys, the respondents aspired for them to become police personnel while for the girls, they aspired for them to become teachers.

- *What Measures by the Government and Civil Society Can Help in Improving Your Livelihoods?*

  The responses to the above question were:

  - Improving the quality of education;
  - Ensuring better terms of work with social security and improved wages;
  - Providing high quality and meaningful vocational training for both men and women;
  - Providing swift transfer of identity cards in case of migrants, especially BPL cards; and
  - Reducing corruption.

Source: Perceptions Survey, 2013, and FGDs.

be higher among the higher-income localities (posh localities, authorised colonies, The Walled City areas), followed by the low-income settlements (JJ clusters and JJ resettlement colonies), and then the middle-income areas such as unauthorised colonies and urban villages.

The different settlement types also showed wide variations in perceptions regarding employment opportunities for both men and women. Figure 7.8 shows how perceptions regarding the employment opportunites for men and women differ by place of residence, household income and literacy levels. A larger proportion of the respondents in the JJ clusters and JJ resettlement colonies were much more pessimistic about the same, while a larger proportion of the respondents in the Walled City and authorised colony residents were the most optimistic.

7.3.4 Perceptions Related to the Main wage Earner

A question related to the economic environment that was asked in the survey pertained to the level of satisfaction with work felt by the main wage earner in the household. The question asked was, "*How satisfied are you with your work?*", which was measured on a five-point scale, similar to the other questions pertaining to satisfaction. Satisfaction levels with work among the main wage earners of the households were found to be highly related with the skill level of the occupation (as also income and education levels). While close to 94 per cent of the professionals reported work satisfaction, less than two-thirds (60 per cent) of the unskilled low-paid workers reported the same.

The results of the Perceptions Survey showed that people's confidence with regard to the stability of their household incomes was also linked to the skill level of the job being held by the main wage earner (MWE). This aspect was investigated by posing the question, "*How confident are you about the stability of your household's main income?*" This question was measured on a four-point scale.[13] Overall, about 63 per cent of the households reported that they were confident about the stability of their respective household incomes. However, there were large variations in the people's responses based on the skill level of the occupation of MWEs, their income and education levels. In households where the MWE fell in the category of an unskilled low-wage earner, about half of the respondents reported that they were not confident at all. As regards the skilled low-paid workers, the respondents were found to be a little more optimistic (56 per cent), and said that they were confident; this proportion increased amongst service workers (64 per cent), even more so among semi-professional households (77 per cent), and was the highest among the respondents in the professional category (87 per cent). It can be said that the poor and the less educated are less confident about the stability of their household's main income.

7.4. School Admissions, Quality of Education, and Professional and Technical Courses

Education is a key variable in understanding human development and is instrumental in augmenting human capabilities. The poor also perceive education as the only tool for upward mobility (see Box 7.4). Chapter 3 of this Report presents and discusses the aspects and issues pertinent to education in Delhi. Here people's perceptions on some aspects of the education processes are presented, including their perceptions on the process of school admissions, satisfaction with the quality of education from the lens of both parents and students, and an evaluation of the opportunities for higher education available in Delhi.

The Perceptions Survey, 2013, reveals that about 62 per cent of the student population was studying in government schools, and the rest in private and other schools. According to the Economic Survey of Delhi, 2012-2013, 38 per cent of Delhi's students study in private schools, which suggests that the Perceptions Survey, 2013, is representative of the school-going population in Delhi.

7.4.1 Evaluation of the Overall Quality of Schooling

An index for measuring people's perceptions of the overall quality of schooling in Delhi was calculated by combining the following questions:

- How do you rate the facilities/infrastructure (like buildings) in your child's school?
- How do you rate the overall discipline in your child's school?
- How safe do you feel your child is while he/she is at school?
- How easy or difficult was the process of admissions in the case of your child?

The composite measure of the quality of school based on the above questions was used to divide the population into those who evaluated the quality of the school as 'good', 'average' or 'bad'. Similar to the evaluation of the overall economic environment, this can also be read as those who are 'satisfied' with the quality of school, are 'neither satisfied nor dissatisfied' and those who are 'dissatisfied'.

Based on the index of quality of schooling, it has been found that approximately 80 per cent of the respondents found the overall quality of the school where their children were studying to be good while the rest thought it to be average (18 per cent) or bad (2 per cent). The overall school quality received a good rating (Figure 7.9) from a larger proportion of respondents whose children were in private school.

Figure 7.9

Distribution of Population Based on the Overall Rating of Quality of Their Child's School (Index), by School Type

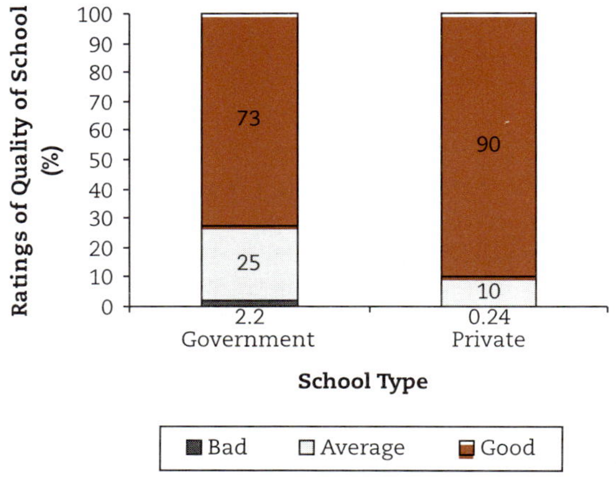

Source: Perceptions Survey, 2013.

13. Scale readings were 'Most Confident', 'Confident', 'Less Confident' and 'Not Confident At All'

When probed by income levels, a higher proportion of the people belonging to the lower-income groups reported the school quality to be bad or average (Figure 7.10). This could imply that those belonging to the higher-income groups had access to better schools in Delhi and also perhaps differential access within schools.

Figure 7.10

Distribution of Population Based on the Overall Rating of Quality of Their Child's School (Index), by Income

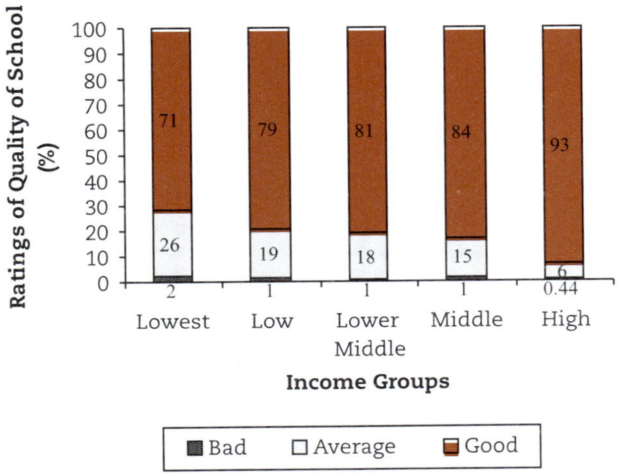

Source: Perceptions Survey, 2013.

To understand better the perceptions about educational opportunities in Delhi, (school and technical educational opportunities) some relevant questions from the survey were examined and the findings are reported below.

7.4.2 "How Difficult or Easy Was It to Get Your Child Admitted to School?"

Issues relating to children's admissions have been widely debated in the context of Delhi. Schools have been directed to follow a point system, which is intended to minimise the biased selection of students. Despite the introduction and implementation of this system, admission-related difficulties are known to be commonplace.

Contrary to common opinion, the results of the Perceptions Survey, 2013 tell us that a majority of the people (62 per cent) felt that the process of school admissions in Delhi was easy and about 11 per cent found it to be very easy. A small percentage felt that the processes of admission in schools were difficult (4 per cent) or very difficult (2 per cent). The income group-wise data for school admissions reveals that a larger proportion of those belonging to the lowest income category found the processes of admission to be more difficult. Greater ease of access to school admissions was reported by a large proportion of the people in the income categories of low and lower middle. A majority of the children belonging to these income categories were also found to attend government schools, which are bound by law to admit students and could explain the greater ease in attaining admissions for most of them. In the case of those belonging to the income ranges of lower middle and highest, the perceived difficulty in securing school admissions again showed an increase. Among those belonging to the highest income category, the proportion of respondents indicating the processes of admissions to be difficult or very difficult was the highest at about 12 per cent. It is possible that *first*, with increases in incomes, the demand for private school admissions increases (which are often discriminatory in their process of admissions), and *second*, households with higher incomes may have ambitions to send their children to particular private schools, thereby making the processes of admission even more competitive for themselves.

7.4.3 How Satisfied Are You with Your Child's Education in School?

While government school results have improved significantly in the recent past, it is important to know how people rate the quality of education that their children are receiving in the same. Dissatisfaction with schooling was found to be higher amongst those whose children were studying in government schools (Figure 7.11). While overall,

Figure 7.11

Proportion of Parents Satisfied/Dissatisfied with the Quality of Their Child's Present School Education, by Type of School

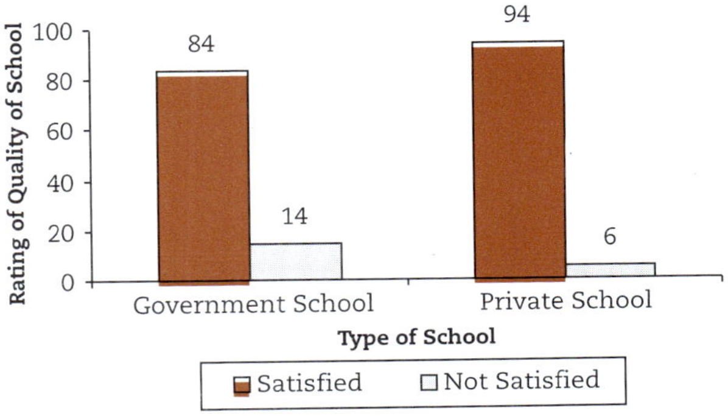

Source: Perceptions Survey, 2013.

about 90 per cent of the respondents were satisfied with their child's education, such a high level of satisfaction was not uniform across socio-economic groups and localities. A larger proportion of those belonging to the lowest income category and those living in localities such as JJ clusters and JJ resettlement colonies were more dissatisfied with their children's education. In the case of those belonging to the lowest two income categories considered, close to 12 per cent reported being dissatisfied with their child's education, with the figure dropping to 10 per cent, 9 per cent and 2.5 per cent, respectively, in the subsequent income brackets.

The results of the FGDs in the low-income localities showed that the respondents were highly dissatisfied with the quality of education in government schools. They reported dissatisfaction with the teaching quality, discipline, school amenities, infrastructure, and mid-day meals. These FGD findings corroborate the trends in the rating of satisfaction with education across settlement types from the Perceptions Survey, 2013, wherein more than 18 per cent of the respondents from the JJ clusters and about 15 per cent from the JJ resettlement colonies reported dissatisfaction with the quality of education that the children in their households were receiving. The residents of urban villages also reported dissatisfaction levels that were higher than the average (12 per cent). These three settlement types, along with the unauthorised colonies, also accounted for almost 70 per cent of the illiterates (as detailed in Chapter 3 on Education). Those who expressed slightly lower dissatisfaction were the residents of authorised colonies, unauthorised colonies, and the Walled City areas. Residents of posh localities reported the lowest level of dissatisfaction (3 per cent).

7.4.4. How Do You Rate Your Satisfaction Level with Your Present Education?

The Perceptions Survey also administered questions to students with regard to satisfaction levels with their education. Of the 7 per cent of the respondents who were students, 17 per cent (including both male and female) said that they were 'very satisfied' with their current level of education. However, there was a difference of almost 10 per cent between the proportion of male and female students, who reported being 'satisfied', with the female students reporting a higher level of satisfaction than their male counterparts.

The data collected also indicated a clear divide in ratings of satisfaction by the respondents with regard to education in government schools vis-à-vis private schools. The proportion of students studying in private schools and reporting being 'very satisfied' with their education was much higher than their government school counterparts (27 per cent vis-à-vis 14 per cent). The proportion of those 'dissatisfied' was also higher among those enrolled in government schools as compared to private schools (9 per cent and 2 per cent, respectively). Thus, it is evident from the satisfaction levels with education reported by both parents as well as students that government schools are lacking in many aspects, and are not able to sustain high satisfaction rates among the populace, and this holds true more so for the lower income groups and poorer localities. These are also supported by the findings from the FGDs.

7.4.5. How Do You Rate the Availability of Technical and Professional Courses in Delhi?

Apart from being the political centre of the country and a major centre of work and employment, Delhi is also a hub for higher education and attracts students from across the country as well as internationally.

When asked to evaluate the educational opportunities in Delhi, more than 80 per cent of the respondents reported that that they felt that educational opportunities for technical/professional courses were 'good' or 'very good', while 16 per cent of the respondents perceived them to be 'average' and 3 per cent felt that they were 'poor'. The results of the Perceptions Survey, 2013, point towards a positive association between the education of the respondent and his/her perception of the availability of educational opportunities in Delhi. Amongst those who are illiterate, less than 5 per cent felt that education opportunities in the city state were 'very good', while 14 per cent of those with professional degrees gave a 'very good' rating to the same. Again, amongst the illiterates, 5 per cent felt that the availability of educational opportunities was 'poor' but this figure was much lower, at 0.5 per cent, for those holding professional degrees. The reason for this could be that the well-educated can be expected to be more aware of the available educational opportunities in the city and may be able to find jobs commensurate with their skill and aspirations.

It has been reported in the chapter on Education that a significant proportion of the students/migrants come to Delhi for education-related purposes. In order to get a better understanding of this trend, data was collected on the perceptions on education on the basis of the number of years that the migrants have spent in Delhi. The findings reveal that the more recent was the migrant, the greater was the likelihood of his being optimistic about the education opportunities in Delhi. Almost all the people who had migrated to Delhi during the preceding year rated educational opportunities to be 'good'; for those coming in over the preceding 2-5 years, this figure was 90 per cent, while it was less than 80 per cent for those who had migrated within the last 11-20 years. Overall, it emerges that perceptions regarding education in terms of schooling as well as the availability of technical/professional courses was influenced by the economic and educational backgrounds of the respondents.

7.5 Households in Delhi: What They Lack, What Assets They Own and What They Plan to Purchase

Interpersonal relationships, leisure activities, a feeling of economic stability, all these have an impact on the feeling of well-being among individuals and the general sense of contentment amongst people. In addition, the ownership of assets makes daily chores and life at home more comfortable for people, while some assets like housing also act as a major source of economic security. In order to get a feel of the people's perceptions of their daily lives, including their household amenities, assets and aspirations regarding the same for themselves, the following set of questions was posed to the respondents:

- What does your household lack?
- Which of the following assets do you have in your household?
- Which of the following assets are you planning to buy in the next two years?

Various categories of answers were reported for the open-ended question on what was lacking in the respondents' households (Table 7.3). While many reported lacking household assets (17 per cent), a significant proportion also reported attributes like income (7 per cent), employment (8 per cent), better education (2 per cent), and family members (2 per cent). About 8 per cent reported that they did not lack anything and that 'all was well' in their households. 'Household durables' was the most common response to what was lacking in homes (17 per cent) (Table 7.3).

The household deficiencies mentioned in Table 7.3 above were further disaggregated by income groups and occupations. This revealed that the demand for more income, employment and household durables, on the whole, was much higher amongst the lower-income categories. Expectedly, the lack of employment was most felt amongst the unemployed (15 per cent), and was followed by casual wage labourers (11 per cent), and was much lower (at 6-7 per cent) among other worker categories such as regular workers and own account workers.

Table 7.3

The Top Twelve Things That Are Lacking in Households (in %)

Household Durable Consumer Appliances	17
Car	16
House	13
Computer/Laptop/Internet	9
Motorcycles	9
All Is Well/ Do Not Lack Anything	7
Job/Employment	8
More Income	7
Cooking Assets like LPG Cylinder and Stove	3
Better Education	2
Identity Card (BPL, APL, Aadhaar, PAN, Passport)	2
Water Facilities	1

Note: All figures have been rounded off.

Source: Perceptions Survey, 2013.

In response to the query: "*Which of the following assets do you have in your household?*" and "*Which of the following assets are you planning to buy in the next two years?*" (Table 7.4), it was found that electric fans, cooking gas stoves and televisions had near-universal ownership in the households surveyed. Aspirations were high for the purchase of assets such as laptops and desktops (with and without the Internet facility), followed by motorcycles, cars and air conditioners.

An analysis of the data obtained from the Perceptions Survey, 2013, on the demand for assets based on household income groups found that among the lowest income groups (Lowest), refrigerators had the highest demand; about 16 per cent of the households reported that they were planning to buy it within the next two years; this was followed by durables such as coolers (15 per cent) and motorcycles (14 per cent).

About 4 per cent of the respondents belonging to this income group reported owning a car, about 12 per cent said that they felt that a car was lacking in their households, and about 7 per cent reported that they were planning to buy a car in the next two years. This demand for cars among the poorest is indicative of the growing needs and aspirations of the residents of Delhi.

Table 7.4

Asset Ownership and Proportion of People Planning to Purchase Assets in the Next Two Years (in %)

	Have the Asset	*Planning on Buying Asset for the First Time*
Motorcycle scooter/moped	44	9
Cycle/cycle-rickshaw/thela	25	2
Car	15	7
Electric fan	96	Negligible
Cooler	70	6
TV	91	2
Cable	80	4
Air-conditioner	17	7
Refrigerator	68	6
Cooking gas stove	92	3
Laptop/desktop without Internet Facility	12	9
Laptop/desktop with Internet Facility	14	11

Note: All figures have been rounded off.
Source: Perceptions Survey, 2013.

Amongst the highest-income groups, the aspirations for durables indicated a different set of preferences. More than one-fifth of households (22 per cent) reported that they were planning to buy a car, followed by laptops/desktops with Internet connections (16 per cent).

Aspirations to buy a house were highest amongst respondents from the lowest-income category as 16 per cent of them reported that they were planning to buy a house within the next three years. For the low and lower-middle income brackets, this proportion was 12 per cent, while it had the smallest incidence among those in the high-income category (5 per cent).

At the aggregate level, approximately 7 per cent of the respondents reported that they did not lack anything in their house (Table 7.3). When disaggregated by income, large disparities were found in the perceptions of the same. While almost one-fourth of the respondents from the highest household income bracket reported that their households did not lack anything, such households constituted 1 per cent among the lowest-income bracket.

When studied by occupations and activity status, it was found that retired persons showed a reasonably high level of contentment in this regard. More than one-fifth of the respondents (22 per cent) reported not lacking anything in their households, though what they reported as lacking constituted *enough income* (13 per cent) and *family members* (8 per cent), amongst other things. While issues of security, pensions, and economic support were found to be important requirements of the elderly, which could be bolstered through various government interventions, the need and responsibility of family members to care for the elderly emerges.

7.6 Assessments of Neighbourhoods/Localities in Terms of Basic Services and Safety and Security

7.6.1 How Satisfied are You with Your Neighbourhood?

A large majority of the respondents (78 per cent) reported being satisfied with their neighbourhoods. Although at the aggregate level, the people's satisfaction levels with their locality/neighbourhood were, in general, very high, they did differ across localities/neighbourhoods, thus depicting a picture of two opposing realities in Delhi (see Figure 7.12). A higher proportion of those living in more 'tenure-secure' settlements were satisfied with their locality. In other words, JJ clusters and unauthorised colonies had a lower proportion of the people expressing satisfaction with their neighbourhoods vis-à-vis other settlements and compared to Delhi as a whole.

Figure 7.12

Proportion of People Satisfied with Their Neighborhoods, by Locality

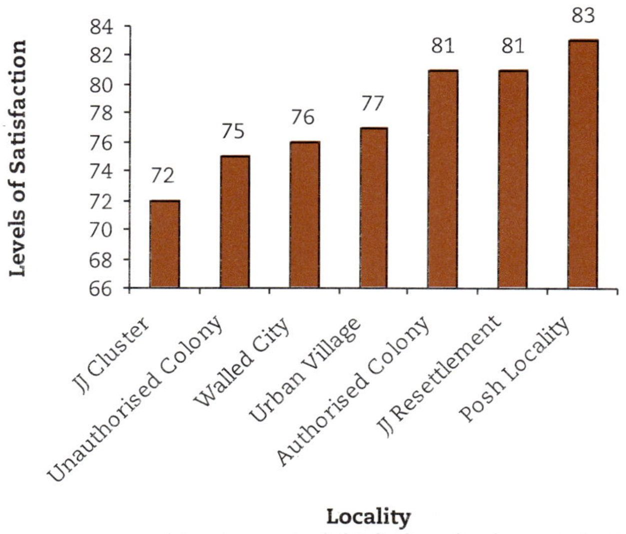

Source: Perceptions Survey, 2013.

Box 7.5

What Are Your Three Most Preferred Leisure Time Activities?

What do Delhi-ites enjoy doing during their leisure time? What is people's preferable idea of leisure? How do the choices of women differ from those of men; of young people from those of the elderly? The Perceptions Survey, 2013, tried to investigate the same and asked people to report *three of their most preferable leisure time activities*. The following results were found:

- A combined analysis of all the leisure activities mentioned by the respondents revealed that watching television was the most popular leisure time activity (almost 63 per cent of the respondents), followed by outings/meetings with family and friends (53 per cent).
- A disaggregated analysis by sex revealed that both men and women were more or less equally fond of watching television. While a higher proportion of males reported being fond of sports (12 per cent), reading (18 per cent), watching movies (15 per cent), and surfing the Internet (7 per cent), women reported being fonder of going for outings (56 per cent), and shopping (11 per cent).
- The age-specific analysis shows an interesting distribution of leisure activities. A higher percentage of those in the youngest age groups (15-19 years) were interested in engaging in sports (24 per cent), listening to music (34 per cent), and surfing the Internet (9 per cent). Watching movies was the most common activity in the subsequent age group of 20-29 years. Reading was most popular among the youngest two age groups of 15-19 years and 20-29 years (37 per cent and 20 per cent, respectively) and was the lowest among 30-45 year-olds (11 per cent) and 46-60 year-olds (13 per cent); however, amongst those who were 60 years and above, reading had regained some of its popularity (20 per cent).
- For the respondents in the 30-45 year age group, reading as a leisure activity was reportedly affected by household and work responsibilities that the men and women engaged in and was possibly replaced by watching television, which was most popular for this age group (65 per cent). Interest in watching television was also found to increase with increases in income, but this is likely to be associated with higher rates of TV ownership in the higher income groups.
- Preference for sports as a leisure activity was reported by around 7 per cent of the respondents for all income brackets though it was much more popular amongst the highest-income group (13 per cent). While it is commonplace to see children and youth playing in all corners of the city and all available spaces, the youth, especially those belonging to lower-income groups mentioned the lack of open spaces as one of the four most important issues/problems in their lives. It is likely that a lower preference for sports amongst the lower-income groups is associated with the lack of availability of spaces for children/youth to play in.
- Outings/meetings with family and friends were found to decline significantly with increases in income. Following from this, it was the also the most popular activity among the lesser educated, as about 65 per cent of them preferred spending time with family and friends. However, amongst those holding professional degrees, it was the third most preferred activity, at 35 per cent. Preference of meeting with friends/family was reported by 40 per cent among the youngest but by 60 per cent in the highest age bracket.
- Activities such as reading, surfing the Internet and shopping show an expected increase with increases in income (as they are associated with education levels and surplus income). These also seemed to be the avenues which replaced activities such as outings/meetings with friends and family.

Note: Percentages not adding to hundred due to multiple-type response.

7.6.2 Evaluation of Different Basic Services Taken Together[14]

In order to assess whether people's perceptions about the availability and quality of basic services varied across locality, an index for the evaluation of basic amenities was calculated. It combined questions on both the rating and evaluation of basic services[15] like power, water, sanitation, garbage disposal, roads, and street lighting,[16] and the cut-off points distributed the population into those who rated basic amenities as 'low', 'average' and 'high'.[17]

From the findings presented in Chapter 5 on shelter and basic services presented earlier, it is evident that there exist wide disparities in the provisioning of basic services in terms of both their quantity and quality, and that these disparities also emerge clearly from people's overall rating as depicted by the index on perceptions relating to basic services.

Respondents reporting lower ratings of basic services in higher proportions are largely from the JJ clusters, the Walled City, and unauthorised colonies (Figure 7.13). It needs to be noted that as compared to respondents in the JJ clusters and unauthorised colonies, the respondents from the Walled City also reported a higher proportion of those who gave a high rating to basic amenities. What ails the provisioning of basic services in the Walled City emerged quite clearly from the FGDs where the respondents cited congestion and overcrowding in their localities as the factors that made the integration of modern service delivery systems such as water, drainage, and sewerage into their localities difficult. Thus, despite being authorised tenements, they are unable to receive services at par with other areas of the city, leading 29 per cent of them to rate satisfaction with basic services as 'low'.

Figure 7.13

Distribution of Population Based on Rating of Various Basic Amenities (Index), by Locality

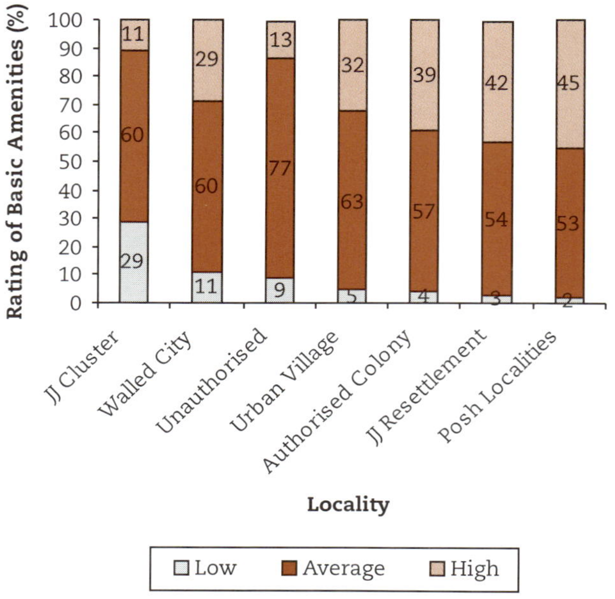

Source: Perceptions Survey, 2013.

7.6.3 Evaluation of Overall Safety and Security

In order to get a composite picture of people's perceptions of safety and security, and to assess whether it varied by locality, an index was generated, which combined the question on perceptions of safety and security in the localities along with questions on perceptions of the safety and security of women at their workplaces, in public transport, and in community areas. The index of safety and security was further broadened to include the perceptions of changing crime levels in Delhi, with respect to both big crimes and smaller crimes. After combining the responses to the various questions, cut-off points were used, which distributed the population into those who rated overall safety and security as 'bad', 'average' and 'good'.

The results show that the highest proportion of respondents who rated overall safety and security as bad belonged to JJ clusters (Figure 7.14). There was

14. The evaluation of different basic services taken separately is presented in Chapter 5 of this report.
15. Typical question for rating: "How do you rate the <insert name of basic service> in your locality—'very good', 'good', 'average', 'poor', 'very poor'?" Typical question for evaluation: "Has <insert name of basic service> improved, deteriorated or remained the same over the last three years?"
16. Although it could be the case that people's evaluation of street lighting went beyond their neighbourhood, Cronbach's alpha and factor analysis showed a high degree of internal consistency between street lighting and other components, and therefore, it was included in the construction of the basic services index. Cronbach's alpha is a measure of internal consistency, that is, how closely related a set of items is as a group. A 'high' value of alpha is often used (along with substantive arguments and possibly other statistical measures) as evidence that the items measure an underlying (or latent) construct. (Source: UCLA: Statistical Consulting Group, Available at: *http://www.ats.ucla.edu/stat/spss/faq/alpha.html* (Accessed May 25, 201)
17. This can again be understood as 'low rating'='dissatisfaction', 'average rating'='neither satisfaction nor dissatisfaction', 'high rating'='satisfaction'.

no significant difference in the rating of safety and security by gender.

Figure 7.14

Distribution of Population Based on Their Rating of Overall Safety and Security, by Locality

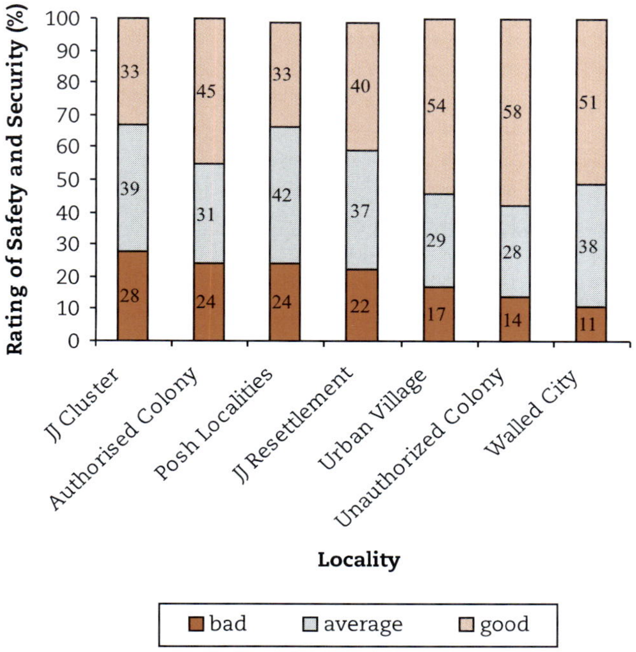

Source: Perceptions Survey, 2013.

7.6.4 Deficiencies and Problems in Locality

In view of the differences in satisfaction levels across localities in terms of basic services and safety, it was felt necessary to probe further as to what was lacking in these localities and which service delivery issues were the most pressing.[18] In terms of the respondents' answers to what was lacking in their locality, the issue of safety and security was cited by the largest proportion (22 per cent) followed by the issue of sanitation (19 per cent). Responses to questions on the most problematic basic service-related issue also revealed that sanitation was the most critical and pressing issue across all income groups of respondents. While the issues of sanitation were universally raised across settlement types and income groups, they were more of concern in the lower-income settlements. This has also emerged from the findings delineated in Chapter 5 on Shelter and Basic Services.

18. These were analysed on the basis of two questions: 'What does your locality lack' and 'What is the most problematic and the least problematic service/issue in your locality'.

When the results were disaggregated further, the issue of safety and security was more pronounced in the highest-income bracket (30 per cent) and the two lowest-income brackets (23 per cent each), while in the middle-income brackets, a much smaller proportion reported it (18 per cent) as an issue. This corroborates the findings delineated in Chapter 6 on Safety and Security, which indicates that the rich feel the most insecure in the city.

With respect to the most problematic service/issue, sanitation was again reported by about one-third of the respondents across almost all income categories. Water supply as a service was rated the worst by a higher proportion of respondents in the three lowest-income groups (20-23 per cent), thereby highlighting the problems faced by these people with regard to the availability of water in their localities.

Table 7.5

The Most Problematic and Least Problematic Issues Faced by Residents Belonging to Different Income Groups

Income Groups	*Most Problematic Issue*			*Least Problematic Issue*
	Most Dislikes	*Second Most Dislikes*	*Third Most Dislikes*	*Most Likes*
Lowest	Sanitation	Water	Power	Power
Low	Sanitation	Water	Roads	Power
Lower Middle	Sanitation	Water	Roads	Power
Middle	Sanitation	Roads	Safety	Power
Highest	Sanitation	Safety	Pollution and Roads	Power
Total	Sanitation (30%)	Water (20%)	Safety (12%)	Power (33%)

Source: Perceptions Survey, 2013.

7.7. Exploring Delhi: What People Like and Dislike about the City

With the main aim of gauging what people liked and disliked about the city as a whole, the Perceptions Survey elicited responses to the following two open-ended questions: "*Please mention the two most important things that you like about Delhi.*" and "*Please mention the two most important things that you dislike about Delhi.*"

Approximately one-fifth (21 per cent) of the respondents reported liking the historical monuments and museums in Delhi; the second most

Box 7.6

Open Spaces, Playgrounds and Gardens

Parks, gardens and playgrounds were reported to be lacking as basic services by almost 10-14 per cent of the respondents across different income groups. The results of the FGDs indicated that a large proportion of the people from the low-income communities such as slums, and resettlement colonies raised the issue of unsafe and unhygienic open spaces. They reported that empty spaces inevitably became garbage dumps, and at the same time, they were not well-lit, and did not have any security provisions. In one of the JJ clusters in West Delhi, a mother said, *"Pehle to khelne ke liye jagah hoti thi. Ab wahaan metro aa gayi hai."* (Earlier there was an open space to play. Now that space has been appropriated by the Delhi Metro). In the face of growing infrastructure needs and development, the demands on open spaces seem to be increasing. Open spaces do not make it to the top of the list of what is lacking in the locality, but they seem to be of relevance to all income classes and social groups in Delhi.

The need for such spaces is voiced more strongly by some groups. For instance, during the FGDs, children mentioned the lack of open spaces to be the most important problem for them, while among the youth, it was the third most important problem (see Table 7.8).

likes were received by the transport facilities (19 per cent), followed by religious places (17 per cent), good employment opportunities (9 per cent), and the general way of life in Delhi (7 per cent) (Table 7.6). In terms of what people disliked, one-third of the respondents (31 per cent) reported lack of safety and security, followed by crowding and congestion (12 per cent), heavy traffic (12 per cent), poor sanitation (10 per cent), high inflation (10 per cent), and high pollution levels (7 per cent). As such, these attributes that people disliked about Delhi were uniform across, age, gender, and type of locality, among other factors.

In order to get a more nuanced understanding of what people liked and disliked about the city, the FGDs in the low-income settlements probed the questions delineated in Table 7.6 further (see Tables 7.7 and 7.8). The findings from the FGDs presented some paradoxes and were quite contrary to *a priori* expectations. These findings are detailed below.

- *Employment*: Both male and female respondents appreciated the availability of 'some work' (which possibly is even more limited in the case of poor migrants coming from various parts of the country). At the same time, with regard to the question, *"What is the most pressing issue that you face in daily life?"*, the lack of jobs and job security were the most pertinent for both the sexes. What emerges is that while employment opportunities are, as such, felt to be lacking by those residing in the low-income settlements, the possibilities of finding 'some work' were appreciated by these respondents.

- *Transport Systems*: While men, in general, were appreciative of the transport system in Delhi as a whole, women specifically appreciated the Metro service. It is important to note that women, on the whole, reported

Table 7.6

The Two Most Important Things That Respondents Like and Dislike about Delhi (in %)

Top Five Likes		*Top Five Dislikes*	
Historical Monuments and Museums	21	Law and Order, Lack of Safety and Security of the People and Prevalence of Crime	31
Better Transport Facilities	19	Crowd and Congestion	12
Plenty of Religious Places	16	Heavy Traffic	12
Better Employment Opportunities	9	Poor Sanitation, Garbage Strewn in Public Spaces and Inefficient Sewerage System	10
All Is Well in Delhi	7	Very High Rate of Inflation/Price Rise	10

Note: All figures have been rounded off.

Source: Perceptions Survey, 2013.

disliking the transport system in Delhi, which could possibly be due to issues of safety and overcrowding, among other reasons (see Chapter 5 on Basic Services for more details).

- *Safety*: Those living in the poor localities pointed to lack of safety as a major issue. For women it was the topmost concern, while men rated it at the third place amongst their other concerns. A linked problem was that of alcoholism. The FGDs revealed that the easy availability of alcohol in these localities led to greater violence at home as well as harassment on the streets.

- *Availability of Electricity and Health Facilities*: While the residents of Delhi, in general, view access to electricity and the availability of healthcare facilities as basic to metropolitan living, amongst the poor, especially the migrants, these facilities were cited as major contributors to an improved quality of life. It is not surprising, therefore, that among women, both these services were rated as the third most liked aspect of their life in Delhi.

- In order to facilitate an understanding of the particular problems of children, the youth and the elderly, they were separately asked to rank the most pressing issues they faced (see Table 7.8). While some issues were common across the general findings for all of Delhi, some specific concerns were raised by the following groups:

- *Youth*: The youth residing in low-income localities were particularly concerned about employment opportunities, especially opportunities which are commensurate with their education/expectations. One young daily wage worker said, *"Kitne din baap ka kha sakte hain, jo milta hai le leta hoon."*, (For how long can I live off my father, I take whatever employment I get).

Table 7.7

Most Liked and Disliked Aspects of Delhi as per Men and Women Living in Poor Localities

	Liked Aspects	
	Men	*Women*
1	Availability of Some Work	
2	Transport Systems and Road Network	The Metro
3	Way of Life in Delhi	Electricity and Health Facilities
	Disliked Aspects	
1	Sanitation, Open sewers and Drains	Safety
2	Water Supply issues	Alcoholism
3	Safety	Transport Systems

Source: Focus Group Discussions (FGDs) (Ranking of Issues in Poor Localities across Delhi).

The youth also reported the lack of open spaces for playing and the lack of affordable housing as issues of concern for them. With exorbitant land prices and bleak economic prospects, the youth find no avenues to escape living in already overcrowded tenements.

Table 7.8

Common Problems Faced by Different Groups of People

	Women	*Men*	*Youth*	*Children*	*Elderly*
Most Common Problem	Lack of employment and, Safety and Security	Job security and Job opportunity	Unemployment and inappropriate employment	Open spaces for playing	Lack of pension/ income security
Second Most Common Problem	Sanitation issues and lack of toilets	Water and Sanitation	Quality of education	Quality of education and schools	Lack of easy work
Third Most Common Problem	Water	Price rise	Open spaces for playing	Lack of electricity	Lack of support systems
Fourth Most Common Problem	Alcoholism amongst men	Safety, especially 'Women's Safety'	Affordable housing	Lack of other recreational activities	Water-logging

Source: Focus Group Discussions (Ranking of issues in poor localities across Delhi).

- *Children*: Both parents and children reported the need for open spaces, better quality education, electricity (to aid studies) and also opportunities for recreational activities such as music, dance and art, among others, which were by and large, reported to be missing in government schools.

- *The Elderly*: The elderly reported the lack of support systems and income as issues of importance to them. Many also wanted to be engaged in low intensity work. Waterlogging in their localities was also a common inconvenience.

7.8 Rating of Dealings with Government Officials, Social Protection Schemes and Identity Cards

Amongst other things, social protection and government subsidies are beneficial in augmenting human capabilities, especially amongst the poor and vulnerable groups. While government services and their provisioning are important, it is public personnel and their everyday interactions with the people, which is of essence to be assessed.

7.8.1 Rating of Government Officials

Delhi is governed by various departments, but there are some that come into frequent contact with citizens in their day-to-day life. In the course of the Perceptions Survey, 2013, the respondents were asked to rate their interactions with personnel from different government departments as 'good', 'average' and 'poor'.[19] What emerged was a clear hierarchy amongst the different service providers (Table 7.9). The Delhi Metro Rail Corporation (DMRC) personnel had the highest proportion of respondents, with about 79 per cent of the respondents rating their interactions as 'good', followed by the electricity departments (Bombay Suburban Electric Supply [BSES] and North Delhi Power Ltd. [NDPL], 65.5 per cent), the Delhi Transport Corporation (DTC)/bus services (43 per cent), the Delhi Jal Board (DJB) (35 per cent) and the Delhi Traffic Police[20] (14 per cent). The Municipal Corporation of Delhi (MCD) and the Delhi Police were at the bottom of the rating ladder with 12 per cent and 10 per cent of the respondents, respectively, rating their interactions with their personnel as 'good'.

Table 7.9

Rating of (any) Interactions Had With Personnel Belonging to Different Government Departments (in %)

Name of Department	*Good*	*Poor*
Delhi Metro Rail Corporation (DMRC)	79	3
BSES and NDPL	66	9
Delhi Transport Corporation (DTC) and Bus Services	43	13
Delhi Jal Board (DJB)	35	22
Delhi Traffic Police	14	30
Municipal Corporation of Delhi (MCD)	11	40
Delhi Police	10	46

Note: All figures have been rounded off.
Source: Perceptions Survey, 2013.

7.8.2 Which of the Following Identity Cards Are Owned by Any Member of Your Household?

Identification cards and other proofs are important documents for the purpose of accessing social provisioning, security and formalisation of the workforce. During the FGDs in the low-income settlements, a large number of the respondents reported the lack of identification documents, which came in the way of their availing of the facilities and benefits meant for them. In order to better understand this issue, information on the households' ownership of select documents which served as identity proofs was sought (including driving licence, voter ID card, UID, bank account, PAN card, passport). The Perceptions Survey, 2013, data revealed that the most widely owned document of identification was the voter ID card, owned by at least one member in 88 per cent of the households, followed by bank accounts (81 per cent) and UID cards (71 per cent).

For residents of JJ clusters, the reported ownership of UID and voter ID cards was the highest (90 per cent, and 93 per cent, respectively). The ownership of bank accounts was lower at 65 per cent and that of PAN cards much lower, that is, owned by approximately a quarter of the respondents (26 per cent). Voter ID cards were found to be owned by large proportions of the respondents across all socio-economic groups. Amongst the migrants, 51 per cent of those settled in Delhi over the last year already had voter ID cards,

19. Many reported that they had not interacted with some department personnel.

20. This is understandable as many in the city only commute by public transport and as such do not have reason to interact with the traffic police.

Box 7.7

Functioning of Some Key Social Protection Schemes

During the FGDs conducted in different low-income settlements, the functioning of key schemes such as the Public Distribution System (PDS), the mid-day meal schemes in schools, pension schemes, and subsidies and scholarships for school books and uniforms were explored.

The PDS was reported to be functioning well in some settlements but not in others, with no clear picture emerging as to what factors made it work and what did not. The common problems associated with the PDS were reported as irregularity of supply, untimely distribution, non-disbursal of the promised amounts, and non-disbursal of certain commodities (in many localities, only rice and wheat are reported as being disbursed).

A few settlements reported that their children were receiving mid-day meals on a regular basis, but issues concerned with the poor quality of food offered, inadequate amounts of food and hygiene-related issues were pointed out by the respondents. Some parents alleged that teachers siphoned off school rations and also carried home cooked food on a regular basis. Parents reported, "*Kabhi kabhi khaana accha hota hai, par us din khaana kum padta hai.*" (Sometimes the quality of food is good, but those days the food falls short). They further said, "*Khaana accha bhi ho to hum school par bharosa nahin kar sakte—humein bachchon ke saath khaana bhejna hi padta hai.*" (Even if the food is good, we cannot rely on it—we have to send food with our children, just in case the food served at school is insufficient or inedible).

Near universal distribution of money for books and uniforms in schools was reported by children living in the low-income settlements. A majority of the settlements reported problems such as partiality of the teachers towards children from certain communities and withholding of part of the disbursal amount by teachers.

In the case of pension schemes (widow, old-age, and disability), more or less all the beneficiaries reported that they were regularly receiving their pensions, however, they raised the issue of inadequacy of the pension amount. Amongst all the schemes the disbursement of pension amounts was found to be the most efficient.

Sources: FGDs and Perceptions Survey, 2013.

while over three-fourths of those who had migrated to Delhi during the last 10-20 years had the same. The migrant population suggested the need to allow the transfer of identity proof documents, especially the Below the Poverty Line (BPL) card. This suggests that migrants and those who live in less 'tenure-secure' areas feel a greater need for legitimacy and recognition by the Government.

7.9 Conclusions

Perceptions are subjective assessments and, therefore, formulating clear conclusions and policy prescriptions based on them alone is not advisable. However, perceptions are important indicators of well-being and as mentioned in the introduction to this chapter, the subjective well-being of the population also needs to be taken into consideration by policy-makers.

- In this light what emerges is that a larger proportion of the vulnerable groups such as women, the SCs, the elderly, and lower-income households do feel less satisfied with their lives, as compared to their counterparts. The maximum differences in perceptions with respect to satisfaction with life emerge across income groups, and there seems to be a positive association between satisfaction and levels of income. This suggests that life satisfaction in Delhi is closely linked to material well-being and can, therefore, be directly targeted by policy-makers.

- The two most important issues that emerge, in general, are sanitation and safety in the city. Both these issues cut across income, gender, age, settlement types and socio-economic categories. However, they are seen to be more critical to some groups (for instance, safety in the case of the women of Delhi, and sanitation for low-income settlements). This suggests the urgent need for policy-makers to focus on the condition of safety and security in the city, which is also apparent from the findings of Chapter on Public Safety. The results also give some indication as to the localities that can be prioritised for the provisioning of better sanitation facilities.

- In these averages, it is important to note issues specific to certain focus areas like education and employment as well as specific to certain groups such as children, women, youth, the elderly, the poor, etc. A universal concern amongst the respondents from low-income settlements was the quality of education being imparted in government schools. With the respondents pointing towards education as the only tool for their upward social mobility, the need for not only textbook learning but also meaningful and quality vocational training and placements came up as useful policy pointers. The lack of recreational activities like art, dance and music in government schools come up as priority areas for children from low-income settlements. The fact that a large proportion of the respondents expressed the desire to have government jobs for their children owing to the stability in tenure and pay that these jobs ensured, what emerges is the need to formalize work opportunities and enforce better terms of work. These would contribute towards a feeling of greater financial stability amongst the less skilled and poorer households.

- It is also important to note that income levels, education, the skill level of occupations and place of residence are all linked and, therefore, similar patterns are observed across these variables. In this context, it becomes even more important to break this cycle of deprivation to ensure social mobility in the city. This can be done through focused and better implementation of affirmative action policies, the Right to Education (RTE) Act and other similar schemes that are primarily targeted at the traditionally disadvantaged populations.

- Another important focus of the poor during the FGDs were identification documents—as seen above, the poor have more voter identity cards but lack other identification proofs which may allow them to avail of other facilities. This is particularly true for migrants. The FGDs indicate a need to transfer identification and beneficiary identification, especially in the case of BPL cards. As is being advocated, the Aadhar–UID card may constitute a significant step in this direction (as almost 71 per cent of Delhi's population reported that they had received it). This would also go a long way towards providing legitimacy to particularly those sections of the population that are at the risk of being marginalised in the a\rapidly growing city like Delhi.

- Some particular issues stood out with respect to women, such as their health and labour markets. The fact that a larger proportion of women are significantly more dissatisfied than men with respect to their health (especially after the age group of 20-29 years) could indicate the pressure of competing demands post matrimony and childbirth and also possibly being denied rest, time and priority with respect to health expenditures. It is imperative to explore further the factors that lead to such negative perceptions with respect to health among women. This is also suggestive of a need for welfare schemes that target women, especially mothers and working women.

- As reported in the FGDs, with respect to labour markets, it was found that often women face barriers both at the household level and at a broader level. At the same time, some women complained that they were forced to work out of compulsions such as poverty. Women's access to labour markets needs to be broadened by addressing their competing needs of managing home and work. Apart from sensitising members of the household, other external factors like safety, flexibility that comes from part-time and home based work, better transport connectivity, etc., need to be factored into the planning process and also promoted as an inherent part of human resource practices in both the public and the private sectors.

- Similarly, with respect to the youth living in poor localities, issues of employment, affordable housing and open spaces become critical; for the elderly in these localities, issues of safety and sanitation are not reported to be as critical as are issues of both social and economic support. For the youth, better employment-generating schemes and spreading awareness of these schemes through local employment centres might take care of a lot of issues reported by them. For the elderly, it appears that an otherwise well-functioning pension scheme can be made meaningful by revising pension amounts.

- The assessment of government department personnel by people has revealed the higher ratings of the very modernised Metro system and the recently privatised electricity suppliers. The third most highly rated was the DTC, which has also made massive efforts to modernise its fleet. This indicates the possibility that these modernisation efforts and the resultant change in institutional values greatly impact people's assessment of these departments and their personnel. There is a need to modernise government departments, make them more efficient and reliable, improve service delivery and train employees in better service delivery. Apart from modernisation, departments such as the police need to instil faith among people, especially the poor, by being more accessible, prompt and gender- sensitive.

On the whole, the analyses in this chapter show that in Delhi, there is a stark mapping of subjective life satisfaction to objective determinants of well-being for groups and localities. Stated differently, the poor, the weak, the uneducated, the women, in general, are also less satisfied with their lives. This is compounded by the contextual effect of localities where it is equally evident that the poorer localities are the ones that are more deprived. The latter is true even when one considers provisions (basic services, safety and security) that are perceived as being the responsibility of the Government and favouring the poor. This suggests that the results of the Perceptions Survey, to a large extent, corroborate the hard data. Looking at the satisfaction with life Index, for example, policy-makers can clearly identify that it is the vulnerable groups who are dissatisfied in Delhi, and this can be rectified by targeted policy towards increasing incomes. Similarly, it is also evident that improving the provision of basic amenities and safety and security in the poorer localities would also go a long way in improving the life satisfaction of those living in these localities. On the whole, people in Delhi are fairly optimistic about their well-being, which puts an added burden on the Government to identify and support those who are not. Using perception-based indicators to bring about policy changes can ensure a more holistic development of the people of Delhi.

8

Looking Ahead: A Perspective for an Inclusive City

8.1 The Context

The city of Delhi today has evolved into a huge progressive metropolis, aspiring to attain global standards in terms of infrastructural facilities, social services (healthcare, education, sanitation, etc.) among other things. It is home to about 17 million people. Most of these people, along with the thousands who migrate to the city, dream of building their future in this vibrant urban agglomerate. The city is, in effect a microcosm of India, wherein people from different parts of country and even outside have sufficient space to preserve their cultures and languages, and to contribute and participate in the city's development while enjoying its vibrancy. A city of hope for its citizens, it is expected to meet their aspirations, fulfil their dreams, and protect them from varied shocks and stresses.

Being the capital of the country, Delhi is the seat of power for both the Union Government as well as the Delhi State Government. Delhi today finds a place amongst the top 40 cities of the world in terms of the ranking of wealth and is also one of the most prosperous states in the country in terms of per capita income. The citizens of Delhi, regardless of which type of settlement they live in, enjoy many facilities, such as access to good roads, bridges, flyovers, transportation services like the recently introduced low-floor buses, Metro, flyovers, and public parks, among other things.

Another conspicuous feature of Delhi is the huge in-migration that it faces from the neighbouring as well as other states, including even far-off states. Around 75,000 people migrate every year to the city largely in search of livelihoods and better educational opportunities, bringing optimism and hope for the future. The National Capital Region (NCR) was planned to ease some of this pressure (both of migration and natural growth) off the National Capital Territory (NCT) of Delhi. There are indications that these plans have yielded some results, as the rate of migration has been stabilising in Delhi, with the migrants settling in the other areas of NCR. Apart from the regular migrants, Delhi also encounters daily commuters and a sizeable 'floating' population that travels to the city for work, access to medical care, education and other purposes for a short period of time during the day. Thus, the multiple facilities in the city cater not only to the city's resident population, but also to the additional variable population. Any assessment of progress in Delhi from the perspective of human development thus needs to take all these ground realities into consideration.

The Delhi Government's policies have been increasingly attuned to meeting the people's needs. The Government has initiated a spate of measures and programmes to improve service delivery at every level, including the *Bhagidari* initiative, Mission Convergence, creation of Citizens' Service Bureaus, and *Jeevan* centres, all of which underscore the Government's continuous commitment to provide basic services and amenities to the people with a sense of accountability. The specific aim of Mission Convergence, launched by the Delhi Government in 2008, was to make Delhi "a more inclusive city by integrating the existing social security schemes and delivering them through a unified structure in a decentralised manner with a particular focus on empowering women through interventions in the areas of livelihood, health, non-formal education and legal literacy". The enactment of the Delhi (Right of Citizens to Time-bound Delivery of Services) Act, 2011, has been accompanied by an electronic service level agreement (e-SLA), signed by the Municipal Corporation of Delhi (MCD) for at least six services, including the issuance of birth/death certificates and certain licences. In fact, the Government has decided to increase its reliance on e-governance to foster and enforce accountability.

What has been the journey like since 2006, when stock-taking was done with the publication of the first Delhi Human Development Report? This Report, in its previous chapters, has made an assessment of various aspects of human development such as employment and livelihood opportunities, basic services, education, healthcare as well as public safety. The entire assessment, based on various sources of statistics and documents, has been made primarily through the lens of the disadvantaged and the marginalised population, and is balanced by a large and representative survey of the perceptions of around 8,000 people of Delhi. This is because no amount of physical investment or government initiatives can be said to be completely successful until they receive the stamp of people's approval. Based on the discussions in the preceding chapters of this Report, this concluding chapter attempts to identify the positive gains made by Delhi and the major concerns and challenges inherent in a growing city of such diversity.

8.2 Some Major Achievements

As has been brought out in detail in various chapters of this Report, Delhi has taken large strides in several areas of human development. Some of them are briefly highlighted below.

8.2.1 Enhanced Incomes

Delhi has experienced tremendous growth in the per capita income of its residents, which was about 7 per cent per annum during the seven-year period of 2005-06 to 2012-13. This has enabled Delhi to become the richest state in the country, with a current per capita income of about Rs. (2 lakhs) per year which is about three times higher than the national average. This significant growth in the per capita income, along with several social welfare policies, led to a reduction in poverty to a single-digit figure (9.9 per cent) in 2011-12, from the level of about 13 per cent during 2004-05. Although, as has been widely pointed out, this official poverty estimate may be an under-estimation, particularly in a burgeoning metropolis like Delhi where the cost of living is very high, there is still no doubt that at least the level of absolute poverty has been steadily declining in the state.

8.2.2 Expansion in Employment Opportunities

An important factor behind the reduction in absolute poverty is the tightening of the labour market. There has been an increase of 1.3 million workers during the 12-year period from 1999-2000 to 2011-12, when it reached a figure of 5.56 million. Although the female workforce participation rate (WPR) is quite low at approximately 11 per cent, this rate too has been increasing from the below 1 per cent level during the period 1999-2000 to 2011-12. This has been accompanied by a reduction in the female unemployment rate. A noteworthy feature of Delhi's workforce is the high share of regular workers at two-thirds of the total and a very small share of casual workers (3.5 per cent), which is quite in contrast to the overall urban India scenario, with the corresponding percentages being around 43 and 15, respectively. Moreover, there has been a significant increase (of about 10 per cent) in the proportion of regular workers in Delhi at the cost of casual and self-employed workers during the period 1999-2000 to 2011-12, with females registering a much more impressive rise of 19 per cent, thereby reaching the current level of 77 per cent. The earnings of workers have also increased significantly.

The earnings of regular workers witnessed an increase of 5 per cent per annum during the seven-year period from 2004-05, and the increase for females was higher vis-à-vis the males. The increase in the earnings of casual workers was even larger, registering a double-digit rate, which was nearly double of the corresponding all-India figures. These positive trends in the labour market became more important in the wake of the entry of a regular stream of migrants to the city for livelihoods, who have been successfully absorbed by the city. The migrants have benefited from the increasing prosperity of the city while also contributing enormously to its development.

The positive features in the labour market are also reflected in the survey of people's perceptions, which reveals that about one-third of the respondents perceived that work opportunities in Delhi have improved over time, with a similar proportion reporting that the work opportunities continue to be average. What is more important is that two-thirds of the households consider their household incomes to be stable.

8.2.3 Improved Access to Basic Services

Notwithstanding the large influx of migrants, the city witnessed an overall improvement in housing during the ten-year period between 2001 and 2011, with the housing shortage declining from about 0.25 million to 0.15 million during this period. There has been an improvement in the quality of houses, and the ownership rate of homes is high. Despite the housing congestion, citizens living in rented houses were found to be largely upbeat about the future outlook, as found by the Perceptions Survey, 2013, as 21 per cent of the people felt that they could buy a house within the next three years, while 42 per cent of these people expected that they would be able to do so. The Government's initiatives in the housing sector are likely to have contributed to the positive outlook of the people. Aiming to make Delhi a slum-free city, Plan programmes such as the Jawaharlal Nehru National Urban Renewal Mission (JNNURM) and the Rajiv Awaas Yojana have been launched, along with the schemes for constructing houses for the economically weaker sections (EWS) and building night shelters for the homeless. The city has also performed well vis-à-vis other metros in providing water to its citizens, with over 80 per cent of the households receiving water within their premises.

The provisioning of electricity and transport services has also seen significant improvements. The electricity has near-universal coverage. The supply of power has greatly improved post-2002, following wide-ranging reforms in the power sector, and presently, 99 per cent electrification of households has been achieved in Delhi. Nearly 80 per cent of the respondents of the Perceptions Survey rate power supply in the city as 'above average'. Also, the services of the power supply personnel in addressing complaints was given a positive rating, with more than two-thirds of the respondent households rating it as 'above average'. In the transport sector, the citizens have significantly benefited from the advent of the Metro, low-floor buses, construction of several flyovers, and erection of streetlights. The Perceptions Survey, 2013, reveals that the Metro service is widely hailed as a welcome addition to the Delhi transport landscape. People expressed their satisfaction with the cleanliness and comfort levels in the Metro along with the safety it afforded to people, especially for women. The Perceptions Survey reports affordability, coverage, and safety as the most liked attributes of the bus service in Delhi by both males and females.

8.2.4 Expansion in Educational Opportunities

During the last few years, there has been a significant growth in educational opportunities in Delhi. With respect to most educational indicators, Delhi is ahead of the rest of India. Delhi recorded a literacy rate of 86 per cent in 2011, signifying an improvement of more than 4 percentage points since 2001. Although there is a gender gap in literacy, it has been declining over time. The Gross Enrolment Ratios (GERs) in Delhi in 2010-11 at the primary and upper primary levels are 127 and 108, respectively, which are higher than the corresponding figures of 116 and 85, respectively, at the all-India level.

The city also provides myriad opportunities for higher education, as evidenced by the inflow of many out-of-state students. In terms of overall literacy, Delhi, at 86 per cent, is far ahead of the all-India level. On an average, the number of years of schooling in Delhi is 7.5, as compared to about 5 years for all-India in 2010. The share of people with higher educational qualifications such as graduation and post-graduation is 17 per cent, vis-à-vis the corresponding share of 7 per cent at the all-India level. Not surprisingly, the Perceptions Survey, 2013, reveals a huge proportion (around 90 per cent) of the respondents to be satisfied with their children's education, with the levels of satisfaction increasing with rising levels of income. Educational opportunities for the technical/professional Census were also rated highly, with four-fifths of the respondents rating these as 'above average'.

8.3 Emerging Priorities and Strategies

The considerable progress in Delhi on several fronts from the human development perspective must be balanced against setbacks and slow progress in other areas, such as the persistent disparities, low work participation of women and high level of informalisation in employment despite economic growth. Ensuring a safe environment for the citizens is also a very important concern. Overall, some of the issues that emerge as priority areas in the various chapters discussed in the *Report* are discussed next and the strategic responses for addressing the same indicated alongside.

8.3.1 Reduce Inequalities and Promote Universalisation of Basic Services, Health and Education

Although Delhi is doing well, on an average, in terms of income, employment creation, infrastructural facilities and basic services, as compared to most parts of India, it faces an increasing challenge of disparities and the exclusion of large sections of the residents across localities, social and occupational groups. These disparities persist in terms of income, type of employment, human capital (education and healthcare), and access to basic services, particularly sanitation. Huge gaps exist between the vulnerable and most marginalised groups vis-à-vis the well-off residents.

Income and Type of Employment

Despite a high average per capita income of around Rs. 2,00,000 (two lakhs) per year, the number of people living Below the Poverty Line (BPL) in Delhi was 1.7 million in 2011-12, reflecting the inequality present in Delhi. As is widely acknowledged, the present poverty line is an under-estimation of the vulnerability of people and settling the poverty line higher in a metropolis like Delhi would add to the number of poor. The inequality is also partly a reflection of the types of employment accessed by different segments of the population. As many as about 85 per cent of all workers in Delhi are engaged in informal employment, taking into account those working in both the formal and informal sectors, which reflects the high degree of informalisation of employment in the city. Although this percentage is lower than the corresponding overall Indian average, this is hardly comforting for Delhi with its high growth of prosperity. This usually implies lower average earnings as well as inferior working conditions vis-à-vis the organised sector. Nearly four-fifths of all workers and 97 per cent of the informal sector workers have no access to social protection. Even with regard to the regular workers, the fact that a high proportion of them have no written contracts and no social security, poses a major challenge. Some occupations are very vulnerable, such as sales (particularly retail) and service workers, domestic servants, transport workers, vendors and hawkers, security guards and construction workers. The manufacturing sector workers, whose number, contrary to expectations, has shown an increase, are, as a whole, quite vulnerable, as is evident from their declining labour productivity. A large number of them are engaged in subsistence activities in a poor work environment. The Perceptions Survey, 2013, also finds that for those wherein the main wage earner is engaged in unskilled low-paying jobs, the proportion of households considering their income to be stable is low.

Access to Services

Along with improvements in basic services during the last ten years, gaps and disparities in terms of access to these services remain. An estimated 56,000 people are homeless in Delhi. Although housing shortage has declined over the years, as per official figures, persistent inequity continues to exist in terms of access to decent housing. Further, overcrowding exists alongside the fact that more than 10 per cent of the houses are lying vacant. More than half of the lowest income households live in one-room dwellings, whereas 40 per cent of the households in the top income groups live in houses with three or more rooms. Around 40 to 45 per cent of the people from the two lowest income category are paying monthly rents in the range of 20 per cent to 40 per cent of their household incomes.

The existence of a large homeless population that has to take shelter at railway stations, under flyovers, on the pavements, and any other public space they can find, is a challenge that Delhi needs to address urgently. The night shelters provided by the Government are inadequate in number and suffer from various drawbacks in their present form, including the lack of basic facilities such as water and sanitation.

Although access to water and sanitation facilities has improved over time, considerable disparities still remain, with slums and settlements such as unauthorised colonies faring rather poorly, especially in the sanitation sector. Water continues to be riddled with major supply and quality issues, and coupled with the significant deficit in sanitation facilities, leading to both uneven human development as well as environmental concerns.

Delhi compares well *vis-à-vis* other metros in terms of water availability as well as access to drinking water within household premises. The poor do receive water on concessional rates, but the supply is plagued by shortages, especially in the summer months, and it also suffers from poor quality in some localities thereby endangering the health and hygiene of the users. The Perceptions Survey, 2013, reports that close to three-fourths of the respondents from the unauthorised colonies and around 40 per cent of those residing in *Jhuggi Jhopdi* (JJ) clusters rated water availability as below average. The residents of poorer settlements reported that though water pipelines had been laid, arrangements for the provisioning of clean water were inadequate.

While nearly 90 per cent of the households in Delhi have access to sanitation facilities within their premises, the remaining use public facilities or open spaces. In terms of the people's perceptions, it has been found that the availability of sanitation facilities is the most common problem area followed by the availability of water and roads. The Focus Group Discussions (FGDs) conducted revealed that though community toilets have been built, their lack of cleanliness and maintenance pushes many slum residents to defecate in the open, which also has security implications, especially for the women. Overall, lack of sanitation is one of the major challenge areas wherein vast gaps remain, especially in terms of the achievement of equitable access.

The state of basic services available to the households living in slums is particularly poor. They lag behind the average levels for Delhi in terms of access to all basic amenities, except for electricity. Amongst the households living in slums, just around two-fifths have access to bathroom and latrine facilities within their premises, which is far lower than the corresponding shares for Delhi as a whole. More than half of the children in the slums defecate in the open with grim consequences for hygiene, security and the environment. There is a huge gap even with regard to the availability of water within the household premises. It is only in the area of power supply that the slums are at par with the rest of Delhi, with 97 per cent of them having been electrified, though affordability of this service is an issue. The contrasting situation of slum-dwellers vis-à-vis Delhi as a whole becomes apparent when we see that as compared to an average of more than 75 per cent of the households in Delhi accessing the three services of water within their premises, electricity and sanitation facilities combined, the corresponding share for slum households is less than 45 per cent.

Access to Healthcare and Education

Healthcare

The health scenario in Delhi shows a mixed performance, with commendable achievements, but burdened by some pressing concerns and challenges. Life expectancy has improved over the last three decades, along with the state of public health facilities. The life expectancy at birth of 72 years for Delhi is higher than the national average of 68 years, with near-similar levels across gender. Public spending on health in absolute terms has also shown a significant increase during the period 2006-07 to 2012-13, with Delhi probably being the first state in the country to spend almost 10 per cent of its total budget on health. Primary healthcare facilities in Delhi have expanded tremendously, which has found an echo in the Perceptions Survey, 2013, according to which 75 per cent of the state's population indicated its 'habitual preference' for public health facilities. In low-income groups, this indicated preference was almost universal. Also, the lower costs of services or affordability, effectiveness and technical competence are the domains wherein public health services are rated highly by the populace.

Concerns, however, persist on quite a few fronts. Firstly, despite a steady reduction in recent years, the incidence of early childhood mortality continues to be high in Delhi. A significant proportion of the burden of deaths during infancy occurs during the neo-natal period, partly resulting from poor hygiene and care practices, as well as less than universal coverage of institutional childbirths. In the case of both maternal and child health risks, the available evidence also suggests the existence of socio-economic inequalities in terms of access to and use of healthcare services. Secondly, Delhi faces the twin challenges of both infectious as well as chronic diseases. While periodic health risks from common infections such as dengue, viral fevers and diarrhoea persist, recent trends indicate a growing predominance of chronic diseases such as cardiovascular ailments, diabetes, cancers and respiratory diseases. With the growing prevalence of chronic diseases, it is the poor who face a higher risk of both exposures to the risk factor and occurrence of the disease. Thirdly, the health service system continues to face a few challenges with regard to the delivery of equitable, quality health services. A shortfall in the numbers of the required health workforce, in the face of a growing demand for services often leads to overcrowding and poor service quality. Health facilities are less than optimally distributed in spite of a steady expansion in absolute numbers. Lastly, notwithstanding a number of government-sponsored schemes and programmes, financial protection against health shocks remains inadequate. Poor awareness of the schemes often leaves low-income, vulnerable families inequitably exposed to the risks of financial catastrophe and illness-induced impoverishment.

Education

Access to educational opportunities, even for basic education, remains disparate for different segments of the population in Delhi, thus impacting their capabilities. The Scheduled Castes (SCs) and the Muslims have very low representation in the sphere of higher education. For the SCs, even at the elementary level, the Gross Enrolment Ratio (GER) levels are very low and decline gradually from the primary to the successively higher levels. This demonstrates the difficulty in making the transition from one level of schooling to another for SC children. The findings of the Perceptions Survey, 2013, help in identifying the challenge areas in education. It reports that more than two-thirds of the illiterate population in the sample are residents of four types of settlements, viz. the JJ clusters, unauthorised colonies, JJ resettlement colonies, and urban villages. A little over half the primary or middle school level graduates were also found to reside in such settlements, pointing towards the need for strategic interventions aimed at improving the education and skill sets of these persons. The survey also finds a majority of service workers to be either illiterate or having acquired differing levels of school education. This unskilled populace with low levels of education comprises 20 per cent of the respondent sample and also needs to be treated as a target area for policy interventions.

Gender

There is a considerable gender gap in literacy in Delhi which needs to be addressed. Although the male–female gap in literacy has been narrowing over time, literacy rates in Delhi are a long way behind other comparable metropolises. Workforce participation is an area wherein women lag behind men by a huge margin. Despite the rise in the number of women workers and the work participation rate during the last one decade or so, the female labour force participation in Delhi remains at a low level of around 11 per cent, which is much lower than the corresponding average figure for urban India. While traditional surveys fail to fully capture the contribution of women in economic activities, the levels of women's participation in economic activities in Delhi are certainly less than desirable when compared with other major cities of South-east Asia and East Asia, especially China. Of course, the income effect and higher proportions of adolescents and young adults being enrolled in educational institutions have also contributed to the lower participation of women. However, at the same time, there are supply side and institutional bottlenecks such as the lack of appropriate work opportunities, supportive institutions, and lack of public safety, which discourage women from taking up work. This is also evident from the fact that around three-fourths of the women above the age of 15 years are engaged in unpaid housework, and the proportion is even higher among illiterates and those with lower levels of education.

8.3.2 Towards Some Strategies

Focus on Informal Sector Enterprises and Workers

Given the rising proportion of informal sector workers without social protection, there is a need for drafting an integrated strategy/plan for informal sector enterprises, which would entail support for clean ancillary manufacturing activities and IT-enabled services, and ensure proper conditions of work, a workforce environment and conditions of employment including social security. The manufacturing sector in Delhi, which is overwhelmingly unorganised and accounts for around 27 per cent of the workforce, has much lower productivity than the service sector. The provision of cheap credit, enhanced technology and improved skills to this sector should be an important part of the plan. It is also imperative to promote the growth of a healthier and cleaner manufacturing sector, besides providing a fair deal to the informal sector workers.

The plan should be integrated with the provisions for effecting improvements in living conditions. Since it is largely the informal sector workers who live in JJ clusters and other areas with poor public access to basic amenities, the plan for promoting a healthy informal sector should also include the provision of housing, healthcare, education, sanitation and accessibility (such as the construction of better feeder and tertiary roads) for the informal sector households. The needs of the migrant workers should also be given special attention.

It should be an aim to provide social protection to all informal workers within the next decade. Education and health services should be made more accessible to the informal sector workers by locating the public service delivery units, including health centres and schools, in the localities where they mostly live. This *Report* demonstrates the reliance of the informal workers on the public sector for the delivery of services, and despite the increasing role of the private sector, the role of the public sector remains paramount.

Formalisation and Universalisation of a Minimum Level of Social Security

The registration of informal sector workers should constitute an important part of the focus on informal sector workers. The facility of the Aadhaar card has already reached three-fourths of the population of Delhi, and the rest need to be covered at the earliest. This would greatly facilitate reaching out social benefits to the targeted groups. However, it is only one hurdle, though an important one. The provision of some important benefits such as old age pension, health insurance, subsidised foodgrains and shelter should be upscaled in terms of coverage as well as improvements in quality and efficiency. The recent initiative by the Government of Delhi in this regard would facilitate the provision of food security to a large section of Delhi's residents. Easily identifiable exclusion criteria may be adopted for certain categories of people such as government employees, income tax payers, and those owning large houses, to name a few.

The direct cash transfer method has also been adopted in some cases in Delhi, the results of which have shown promise. However, before scaling up, all its implications should be studied carefully. The migrants, who are often missed out, should be accorded special care and in their case, portability of social security benefits is very important. Hence, the Aadhaar Card has an important role to play in this regard. The upscaling and innovative methods, already initiated in some cases, could go a long way towards universalising the provision of social security to the population of Delhi. A large number of dormitories may be constructed for the temporary migrant workers as has been done in China. This would considerably reduce their vulnerabilities. The aim should be to provide the four critical social provisions—food, health insurance, old age pension and shelter—to all the citizens of Delhi within the next seven to eight years.

The above measures would not only reduce the vulnerability of the poor, but would also lead to a further tightening of the labour market. The increase in social wages and benefits would also help them enhance their bargaining power. This would further lead to a rise in wages, thereby bridging the gap between the earnings of formal and informal sector workers. This would also lead to a process of the gradual formalisation of the informal workforce. The Delhi Government has already taken several steps in this direction and now needs to upscale them in mission mode. This has already been achieved, to a large extent, in several countries such as Brazil and should be attainable in Delhi too. The apprehension that it would contribute to the further influx of migrants to the city is largely exaggerated as evident from the fact that the rate of migration in Delhi is now stabilising and more migrants are settling in other towns of the NCR, and in fact, even in the smaller and medium towns of the country.

Universalisation of Elementary Education

All 6-14 year old children should be in school, including those from the disadvantaged groups and children with special needs. There should be 100 per cent retention and completion of eight years of schooling by 2020. There should be an aim to increase unity in the girls' to boys' ratio in enrolment. Child labour should be eradicated by identification and mainstreaming of child workers in schools, and by providing them special training for becoming a part of the mainstream. Other out-of-school children should be mainstreamed in a similar manner.

Universalisation of Health Coverage

The avowed goals of the health system in Delhi should be to envision universal coverage with equity and quality. Reducing infant mortality, particularly neonatal deaths, necessitates ensuring universal institutional delivery in a time-bound manner and coverage of all the vulnerable communities/low-income settlements with an appropriate package of home-based neonatal and post-delivery care. In order to aid the process of regular monitoring, the Mother and Child Tracking System (MCTS) needs to be well-integrated as a part of the Health Information System and to serve as a key instrument of monitoring and evaluation of programme interventions. The next priority should be to strengthen primary healthcare by setting up an equitable, efficient and responsive network of clinics with adequate infrastructure, including both physical as well as human resources. The spatial inequalities in coverage can be minimised through the introduction of ICT-based, need-oriented norms for planning new clinics and health facilities.

As a model for universal health coverage (UHC) for the other states, the Delhi Government could consider developing the Primary Urban Health Centres (PUHCs)/dispensaries into 'Wellness Centres' with a dedicated cadre of Public Health Technical Officers 'owning up' each Wellness Centre. The latter would be responsible for introducing lifestyle modification interventions in the neighbourhood, and for acting as the first point-of-care to offer clinic-based services, consultations, and surgical/hospitalisation procedures in accordance with the prevalent diseases, case compositions in health facilities, and services that are in high demand.

Lastly, there is need to universalise adequate financial protection for covering all incidences of ill-health or disease, hospitalisation and accident/trauma incidents, with minimal exclusion norms. The requisite strategy would be to ensure the availability of cashless medical services—both clinic- and hospital-based—for the poor and vulnerable population, and ultimately offer a 'Common Standard Health Entitlement Package' (CSHEP) for free medical services to all through a 'Universal Health Entitlement Card' (UHEC). This scheme could, in fact, be the flagship financial protection entitlement that would integrate all the present financial protection mechanisms under multiple agencies the Rashtriya Swasthya Bima Yojana [RSBY], Delhi Government Employees Health Scheme (DGEHS), Delhi Arogya Kosh/Nidhi, and free beds for members of the EWS into a single, prepaid smart-card with the provision of differential credit/cash allowances according to the type of beneficiary. The UHEC could be valid for all the services enlisted under the CSHEP, with the option for 'recharging' UHEC credits in a manner similar to the purchase of prepaid mobile phone credits by cellphone users. Pilots could also be initiated to identify and test the appropriate services for inclusion under the CSHEP, their standard schedule of charges and other modalities, and robust, randomised experiments could be undertaken to assess the potential utility/sustainability and logistic issues for phased migration to a UHEC-based system.

Enhancement of the Economic Empowerment of Women

As pointed out earlier, discounting the income effect and the higher enrolment of young adults in educational institutions, the participation of women in economic activities is quite low. The participation of women needs to be enhanced through various measures, on both the demand and supply side. Women's access to the labour market can be broadened by taking into consideration their competing needs for managing both home and work. Apart from sensitising the members of the household, other external factors like ensuring safety, flexibility (as in part-time and home-based work), better transport connectivity and the imparting of appropriate skills for the emerging jobs need to be factored into the measures for intervention in this area. An important key to making Delhi an inclusive city is to expand gainful employment opportunities for women at a fast rate.

Improving the Access to and the Quality of Service Provisions

Public Health: There is a need to build an equitable, efficient, responsive network of clinics with adequate infrastructure including both physical as well as human resources and consolidating the already impressive network of primary level health facilities. The Perceptions Survey, 2013, reports that public facilities are clearly preferred by people over private facilities for hospitalisation and even for the non-hospitalised services, people are increasingly turning to public healthcare. The publicly-provided health services in Delhi appear to be on the right track in facilitating equitable access and usage of health facilities and scaling up the infrastructural aspects of service delivery to levels that are commensurate with the growing demand. However, what still remains a crucial aspect of healthcare provision is ensuring a health service delivery system that remains responsive to people's needs and expectations while balancing both interpersonal and technical aspects of service quality.

Education and Skills: It is also imperative for Delhi to aim towards becoming a fully literate and universal primary educated state with 10 years of average schooling among its residents. For achieving this, an action plan needs to be prepared and integrated with the ongoing programmes, with greater funding and support from the Delhi Government. Secondly, the strategic planning should also cover upgradation of skills among people living in the unauthorised colonies, particularly the weaker sections such as SCs and Muslims. Thirdly, the Government should ensure that there is 100 per cent transition of students till the secondary level of education and students must have attained an adequate level of learning. This necessitates a strategy for effectively monitoring and supervising the transition, identifying the causes of drop-outs from school, and periodically assessing the achievements of the programme. The Delhi Government also needs to expand schools at the secondary level and strengthen the infrastructure in schools and colleges. More importantly, accommodation and transport facilities should be efficiently planned for students. An important strategy relates to the filling up of all vacancies for teachers in schools and colleges. Towards this end, the Delhi Government should take initiatives to hold discussions with responsible agencies.

An important challenge pertains to the learning achievements in schools, which needs to be addressed through implementation of multiple strategies entailing the hiring of qualified teaching staff, employing optimum infrastructure, and regular assessments of students, teachers and the establishments themselves. Lastly, the State Government may consider establishing a set-up to promote innovation in education for the creation of an efficient and dynamic institutional culture in the state.

Provision of Access to Shelter, Basic Amenities and Services for the Poor: Notwithstanding the impressive improvements that have taken place in the provision of basic services and amenities in Delhi, huge gaps continue to exist between the poor and non-poor localities in most of the cases. One of the important thrusts of the human development effort for the next 5-7 years in the capital could be to bridge these gaps. The challenge lies more in the delivery of basic services and various amenities discussed earlier in this *Report*. Like many other big cities in the country, Delhi too is becoming an increasingly divided city, with the divisions becoming more glaring in view of the rising prosperity of some sections of its society. The provision of access to high quality basic services including clean potable water, clean toilets, transport facilities, particularly feeder buses, and a minimum level of decent housing, should be categorised as an important goal for the next 5-7 years. The lack of sanitation in most parts of the city, particularly in the areas inhabited by the poorer populations, has also emerged as an important challenge that needs to be addressed urgently. The cleaning of the Yamuna too is closely linked with sanitation, apart from addressing environmental concerns. Although the availability of transport has considerably improved in the capital in recent years, considerations of speed and efficiency have sidelined the average pedestrian and daily commuters, making road usage lopsided in favour of the more affluent sections of society which own and drive motorised vehicles on Delhi's increasingly crowded roads. These concerns and issues necessitate a periodic review of the policies in each sector and regular feedback from citizens for the purpose of drawing up appropriate policies or modifying existing ones in accordance with the rapid development of Delhi as a millennium city.

In this context, some salient measures should aim to provide equitable access to clean water and sanitation facilities to all, to upgrade drainage and sewerage systems, provide functional street lights to low-income areas, and provide shelter and housing for all through housing credit, in-situ up-gradation, etc.

8.3.3 Enhancing Physical Safety and Environmental Security

Physical Safety

The issue of public safety has assumed increasing significance among the residents of Delhi, particularly the women, after the brutal gang-rape of a woman in a city bus on 16 December 2012. However, an analysis of the official crime statistics reveal that the crime rate against women has declined from 2004-06 to 2010-12, though the rates of rape and kidnapping remain the highest during both time periods among all metropolitan cities. In addition, what is even more of a challenge is the safety of children, with crimes against them recording the maximum increase in the rates of all crimes between 2004-06 and 2010-12. More gender-sensitive urban planning, ensuring well-lit streets and safe public toilets could provide a sense of security, particularly among women and children. The Perceptions Survey, 2013, has been very useful in identifying the challenge areas in people's safety and security. Approximately only one-third of the respondents rated personal safety in Delhi as 'good' or 'very good'. The feeling that crime had gone up over the years was near-universal. Most women did not feel safe in public spaces with the workplace and public transport emerging as spaces perceived to be the least safe for them. The Perceptions Survey recorded a high degree of dissatisfaction among the respondents vis-à-vis the police due to the lack of promptness on the part of the police in responding to a situation, as well as the lack of approachability, which are stumbling blocks in the effort to deal with the incidence of rising crime.

The right to live in a safe and secure environment is the basic right of all citizens of a progressive society and is, in fact, an integral part of human development, to enable people to realise their capabilities fully. The Delhi Government is conscious of this and has taken several effective steps in the wake of the tragedy that occurred on Delhi's streets in December 2012. Albeit, this is a complex issue, requiring several dimensions of interventions, in both the short and medium terms. Some of the critical thrust areas in this direction are as follows: initiating reforms within the criminal justice system and strengthening law enforcement agencies like the police, through capacity building and sensitisation; encouraging greater engagement with the public; reforming the judiciary and expediting cases dealing with violent crimes; and introducing rehabilitation and intervention mechanisms to ensure protection of the children and youth. In addition, the use of technology and surveillance in crime reduction and prevention is crucial.

Safety could itself be made a basic service by encouraging and executing participatory and inclusive urban planning and services, a safe and more efficient public transport system, clean and well-functioning public toilets, and well-lit roads, which would transfer the responsibility of ensuring safety to the providers of these basic services. An inclusive city would go a long way towards bridging the urban divide and making Delhi a safer city to live in, wherein all its citizens can exercise their social, economic, political and cultural rights freely, without fear or discrimination.

Crimes in society, and specifically those against women, can be located in structural inequities and a deep-rooted patriarchal system that sanctions such crimes. In this context, the biggest challenge that needs to be addressed is the persistence of patriarchal norms and chauvinistic mindsets, which can only be changed by spreading education and awareness. The norms of inculcating respect and gender equity need to be incorporated into school and college curricula, while simultaneously sensitisation programmes need to be launched and their implementation monitored regularly to ensure healthier social and gender-based interactions in society. Only such measures can bring about long-term and sustained change. The media too can be used in an innovative and constructive manner, especially as a tool to facilitate social and attitudinal change, build zeal among the citizens, and deal with civic apathy more pro-actively, while simultaneously creating awareness among the public about important social issues.

Environmental Security

Human development is sustainable only to the extent that the environment is not harmed beyond repair and a healthy legacy is left behind for the coming generations. However, in Delhi, many environmental concerns arise due to the lack of private toilets, open drains in some areas, especially in the slums, open garbage disposal and the resultant contamination of the surface water in the Yamuna river. The Yamuna, Delhi's lifeline for water availability, is, in fact, severely affected by the uncontrolled flow of untreated waste from human settlements, as well as from industrial effluents. Open defecation leads to the flow of faecal matter into the river via open drains, as well as the contamination of the immediate environment in the neighbourhood. In many parts of Delhi, the groundwater suffers from high salinity and nitrate content. The Government has set into motion initiatives for addressing the pollution in Yamuna, through the execution of the Yamuna Action Plan in two phases, while the third phase is on the anvil.

However, there is also a need to raise public awareness further against contamination of the river water, which still remains a major challenge. The rapid depletion of groundwater due to its excessive use is another issue of serious concern. Some of the ways of ensuring conservation of water would be through demand management by changing social attitudes towards the use and conservation of water. The Government's ongoing initiatives for rainwater harvesting should be continued and accelerated, leakages from pipes reduced, groundwater use regulated by deepening lakes and dams, the number of tubewells reduced, and more water treatment plants built.

In Conclusion: The above strategies, as mentioned earlier, are in addition to several other aspects of human development discussed in this as well as the preceding chapters of this *Report*. These issues, strategies and goals need to be monitored closely and regularly, and accompanied by strong commitment and appropriate institutional arrangements through the participation of the citizens. The Government of Delhi has already taken several measures and innovative steps in this direction. These need to be expanded, accelerated and strengthened. The governance efforts of Delhi operate in a constrained space because of the multiplicity of authorities in several areas, giving rise to the problems of accountability. It is thus imperative to find ways to effectively tackle this issue to ensure the success of the above strategies and efforts for enhancing human development. Delhi cannot become a world-class city unless it is an inclusive one, wherein all its citizens share the benefits of its rising prosperity and there are no deprivations and vulnerabilities.

References

Accenture (2012), "Are Police Forces Maximizing Technology to Fight Crime and Engage Citizens?", The Accenture Citizen Pulse Survey on Policing, Available at http://www.accenture.com/SiteCollectionDocuments/PDF/Accenture-Are-Police-Forces-Maximizing-Technology-to-Fight-Crime-and-Engage-Citizens.pdf#zoom=50WHO (2002), Accessed on 20 June 2013.

Agewell Foundation (2012), "Comprehensive Study on the Status of Older Persons—Delhi and NCR", New Delhi, Available at: http://www.agewellfoundation.org/pdf/Agewell%20Study%20Oct-2012-website%20(1).pdf, Accessed on 13 April 2013.

Agrawal, Y.P. and S. Chugh (2003), "Learning Achievement of Slum Children in Delhi", *Occasional Paper NIEPA*, Available at: http://www.nuepa.org/Download/Publications/Occasional%20Paper-34schugh.pdf, Accessed on 18 May 2013.

Al Jazeera (2011), "Citizens Figure Crime Using Social Media", 21 August, Available at: http://www.aljazeera.com/indepth/features/2011/08/201182173025315608.html, Accessed on 21 June 2013.

Anand, J. (2012), "Delhi's Underbelly: 1500 Dark Spots", *Hindustan Times*, 30 August, Available at: http://www.hindustantimes.com/India-news/NewDelhi/Delhi-s-underbelly-1-500-dark-spots/Article1-922085.aspx, Accessed on 30 May 2013.

Bajpai, Asha, Chapter on "Child Sexual Abuse and Law", cited in the Childline website, Available at: http://www.childlineindia.org.in/Child-Sexual-Abuse-and-Law.htm, Accessed on 15 June 2013.

Bhardwaj, Alok (2010), "BRT System in Delhi—Present and Future Scenario", *DIMTS Ltd.*, Available at: http://www.dimts.in/pdf/Symposium-on-Publi-Transportation/BRT-System-in-Delhi-Presen-and-Future-Scenario.pdf, Accessed on 16 May 2013.

Bruns, M.K. (2013), "Facebook's Turning Point on Sexual Violence", CNN International, Available at: http://edition.cnn.com/2013/05/29/opinion/kinsey-bruns-facebook-rape, Accessed on 3 June 2013.

Buncombe, A. (2013), "One Rule for the Rich and Another for the Poor: Outcry as India's Richest Man Mukesh Ambani Gets 'VIP' Police Protection", *The Independent*, 22 April, Available at: http://www.independent.co.uk/news/world/asia/one-rule-for-the-rich-and-another-for-the-poor-outcry-as-indias-richest-man-mukesh-ambani-gets-vip-police-protection-8583507.html, Accessed on 1 July 2013.

Bureau of Police Research and Development (BPRD), "Maintenance of Police Records", Delhi Police, Available at: http://bprd.nic.in/writereaddata/linkimages/2102736297-Maintenance%20of%20Station%20records.pdf., Accessed on 3 April 2013.

Cameron, A., M. Ewen, M. Auton and D. Abegunde (2011), *The World Medicines Situation*, (Third edition), World Health Organisation, Geneva

Census (2011), Primary Census Abstracts, Registrar General of India, Ministry of Home Affairs, Government of India, Available at: http://www.censusindia.gov.in/2011census/PCA/pca_highlights/pe_data.html, Accessed on 14 July 2013.

———. Provision Population Totals, Paper 2, Registrar General of India, Ministry of Home Affairs, Government of India, Available at: http://www.censusindia.gov.in/2011-prov-results/paper2/census2011_paper2.html, Accessed on 12 April 2013.

———. SRS Bulleting (2012), Sample Registration System, Vol. 47, No. 2, Registrar General of India, Ministry of Home Affairs, Government of India, October.

———. (2011), "Provisional Population Totals: NCT of Delhi Profile", Available at: http://censusindia.gov.in/2011census/censusinfodashboard/stock/profiles/en/IND007_NCT%20of%20Delhi.pdf, Accessed on 16 July 2013.

Central Pollution Control Board and Ministry of Environment and Forests (2008), "Environmental Health Series. Epidemiological Study on Effect of Air Pollution on Human Health (Adults) in Delhi", New Delhi.

Chaudhury, R.R., R. Parameswar, U. Gupta, S. Sharma, U. Tekur and J.S. Bapna (2005), "Quality Medicines for the Poor: Experience of the Delhi Programme on Rational Use of Drugs", *Health Policy and Planning*, Vol. 20, No. 2, pp.124-36.

Chugh, S. (2011), "Dropout in Secondary Education: A Study of Children Living in Slums of Delhi", *NUEPA Occasional Papers*, Available at: http://www.nuepa.org/Download/Publications/Occasional%20Paper%20No.%2037.pdf,Accessed on 18 May 2013.

Das, J. and J. Hammer (2004), "Strained Mercy: The Quality of Medical Care in Delhi", *World Bank Policy Research Working Paper 3228*, The World Bank, Washington DC, March.

———. (2005), "Money for Nothing: The Dire Straits of Medical Practice in Delhi, India", *World Bank Policy Research Working Paper 3669*, The World Bank, Washington DC, July.

———. (2007), "Location, Location, Location: Residence, Wealth, and the Quality of Medical Care in Delhi, India", *Health Affairs*, Vol. 26, No. 3, pp. w338-51.

Dasgupta, M. (2010), "Rehabilitation through Education for Juveniles in Conflict with Law", *Working Paper No 238*, Summer Research Internship 2010, Centre for Civil Society, Available at: http://www.ccs.in/ccsindia/interns2010/meghna-dasgupta_rehabilitation-through-education-for-juveniles.pdf, Accessed on 12 July 2013.

De Vries, J., C. Webb and J. Eveline (2006), "Mentoring for Gender Equality and Organizational Change", *Employee Relations*, Vol. 28, No. 6, pp. 553-72.

Delhi Police (2012), "Crime in Delhi", Available at: http://www.delhipolice.nic.in/, Accessed on 3 March 2013.

DHDR (2006), *Delhi Human Development Report 2006 – Partnerships for Progress*, Government NCT of Delhi, Oxford University Press, New Delhi.

DIMTS Ltd. (2008) "Delhi BRT System—Survey Report", Survey conducted by the Centre for Science and Environment, New Delhi, Available at: http://www.dimts.in/pdf/CSE-TrafficSurveyReport.pdf, Accessed on 20 May 2013.

———. "Delhi BRT System—Lessons Learnt". Available at: http://www.dimts.in/pdf/Delhi_BRT_System_Lessons_Learnt.pdf, Accessed on 13 May 2013.

Directorate General of Employment and Training (DGET) (Various Years), *The Employment Review*, Ministry of Labour and Employment, Government of India, New Delhi.

Directorate of Economics and Statistics (DES) and Office of Chief Registrar (Births and Deaths), GNCTD (2012a), Annual Report on Registration of Births and Deaths in Delhi—2011, New Delhi.

———. (2012b), Report on Medical Certification of Cause of Deaths in Delhi—2011, New Delhi.

———. (2013), Annual Report on Registration of Births and Deaths in Delhi—2012, New Delhi.

Directorate of Economics and Statistics, Government of Delhi (2006), *Household Consumer Expenditure in Delhi (Based on NSS 60th Round—State Sample)*. (Mimeo).

Directorate of Health Services (DHS) (Various Years), Department of Health and Family Welfare, GNCTD, Annual Reports, 2011, 2012, 2013, New Delhi.,

Economic Survey of Delhi (2012-2013), Planning Department, Government of NCT of Delhi, New Delhi.

Garg, C.C. and A.K. Karan (2009), "Reducing Out-of-pocket Expenditures to Reduce Poverty: A Disaggregated Analysis at Rural–Urban and State Level in India", *Health Policy and Planning*, Vol. 24, No. 2, pp. 116-28.

Giedion, U., E.A. Alfonso and Y. Diaz (2013), "The Impact of Universal Coverage Schemes in the Developing World: A Review of the Existing Evidence", *UNICO Studies Series 25*, The World Bank, Washington DC.

Gladwell, M. (2000), The Tipping Point: How Little Things Can Make a Big Difference, Little Brown, Boston.

Goli, S., R. Doshi and A. Perianayagam (2013), "Pathways of Economic Inequalities in Maternal and Child Health in Urban India: A Decomposition Analysis", *PLoS ONE 8(3): e58573. doi:10.1371/journal.pone.0058573.*

Government of National Capital Territory of Delhi (GNCTD) (2012a), Approach to the Twelfth Five Year Plan, Available at: http://www.delhi.gov.in/wps/wcm/connect/DoIT_Planning/planning/important+links/an+approach+to+12th+five+year+plan+%282012-17%29, Accessed on 26 April 2013.

———. (2006), Delhi Human Development Report, Government of Delhi, New Delhi.

———. (2012b), Statistical Abstract of Delhi, Available at: http://delhi.gov.in/DoIT/DES/Publication/abstract/SA2012.pdf, Accessed on 2 July 2013.

———. (2013) Directorate of Health Services, Department of Health and Family Welfare, Available at: http://www.delhi.gov.in/wps/wcm/connect/doit_health/Health/Home/Directorate+of+ Health+Services/Publication, Accessed on 6 May 2013.

———. Government of National Capital Territory of Delhi and UNDP Homeless Survey (2010), New Delhi.

———. *An Approach to the Twelfth Five Year Plan (2012)*, Available at: http://delhi.gov.in/wps/wcm/connect/doit_planning/Planning/Important+Links/An+Approach+to+12th+Five+Year+Plan+percent282012-17percent29, Accessed on 10 April 2013.

———. (2012), *Delhi Statistical Hand Book 2012, New Delhi.*

Government of NCT of Delhi and Transport Department (2010), "Transport Demand Forecast Study and Development of an Integrated Road-cum-Multi-Modal Public Transport Network for NCT of Delhi", Available at: http://www.delhi.gov.in/wps/wcm/connect/d8707180436ea1acbf5affeaf072cdcf/Final_TDFS_DIMTS_RITES+Study.pdf?MOD=AJPERES&CACHEID=d8707180436ea1acbf5affeaf072cdcf, Accessed on 16 May 2013.

Government of India (GoI) (2006), "National Urban Transport Policy", Ministry of Urban Development, Available at: http://urbanindia.nic.in/policies/TransportPolicy.pdf, Accessed on 28 May 2013.

———. (2013), *Economic Survey 2012-13*, Ministry of Finance, Government of India, Oxford University Press, New Delhi.

HAQ and CRY (2013), 'Delhi State Budget 2013—2014 Disappoints Children Once Again', Available at: phttp://www.wghr.org/dnloads/Budget_for_Children_2013-2014_Delhi_Final.pdf, Accessed on 8 April 2013.

Herbert, W. (2013), "What a Mess: Chaos and Creativity", *Huffington Post*, 20 February, Available at: http://www.huffingtonpost.com/wray-herbert/what-a-mess-chaos-and-cre_b_2726060.html, Accessed on 26 May 2013.

High Level Expert Group (HLEG),(2011), Planning Commission (HLEG), Government of India, New Delhi.

High Level Expert Group Report on Universal Health Coverage for India, Available at: http://uhcforward.org/sites/uhcforward.org/files/India_report.pdf, Accessed on 16 July 2013.

Hindustan Times (2013), "Missing Children Cases to be Treated as Kidnapping", Available at: http://www.hindustantimes.com/India-news/Mumbai/Missing-children-cases-to-be-treated-as-kidnapping/Article1-1058573.aspx, Accessed on 2 June 2013.

IAMR (2011), "Towards Social Inclusion", India Human Development Report, Planning Commission, Government of India, New Delhi.

IHD–IRMA (2010), *Informal Employment and Poverty in Urban India,* Various Papers (Mimeo), Institute for Human Development, New Delhi, and Institute of Rural Management Anand, Anand.

IHD—Save the Children (2011), "Surviving the Streets", Institute for Human Development and Save the Children, New Delhi.

Ingle, et al. (2005), "Exposure to Vehicular Pollution and Respiratory Impairment of Traffic Policemen in Jalgaon City, India", *Industrial Health*, Vol. 43, No. 4, pp. 656-62.

Institute for Human Development (IHD) (2007), "Shelterless Persons in Delhi: Challenging Inclusive Growth Policies", Department of Social Welfare, NCT of Delhi.

———. (2012), "Livelihoods of the Poor and Vulnerable in the NCR: Final Synthesis Report", IHD-SDTT Study, New Delhi (Mimeo).

International Institute of Population Sciences and Macro International (2010), District Level Household Survey 3, 2007-08, India, IIPS, Mumbai.

Jagori (2010a), "Understanding Women's Safety towards a Gender-inclusive City: Research Findings (2009–10)", Available at: http://www.endvawnow.org/uploads/browser/files/understanding_womens_safety.pdf, Accessed on 16 April 2013.

———. (2010b), "Safe Cities Free of Violence against Women and Girls", Report of the Baseline Survey Delhi, New Delhi, Available at: http://jagori.org/wp-content/uploads/2011/03/Baseline-Survey_layout_for-Print_12_03_2011.pdf, Accessed on 12 March 2011.

———. (2011), "Safe Cities Free of Violence against Women and Girls Initiative: A Draft Strategic Framework for Women's Safety in Delhi 2010", New Delhi, Available at: http://jagori.org/wp-content/uploads/2006/01/Strategic_Framework.pdf, Accessed on 31 March 2013. Jagori and Women in Cities International (2011), "Excerpts from the Final Report on the Action Research Project on Women's Rights and Access to Water and Sanitation in Asian Cities", .

Jeemon, P. and K.S. Reddy (2010), "Social Determinants of Cardiovascular Disease Outcomes in India", *Indian Journal of Medical Research*, Vol. 132, No. 5, pp. 617-22.

Kar, S.S., J.S. Thakur, N.K. Virdi, S. Jain and R. Kumar (2010), "Risk Factors for Cardiovascular Diseases: Is the Social Gradient Reversing in Northern India?", *Natl Med J India*, Vol. 23, No. 4, pp. 206-09.

Kotwal, N. (2013), "Why the Delhi Police Chief Will Not Step Down", *The Hindu*, 4 May, Available at: http://www.thehindu.com/opinion/op-ed/why-the-delhi-police-chief-will-not-step-down/article4683364.ece, Accessed on 2 July 2013.

Layard, Richard (2012), "Why Measure Subjective Well-being?", *OECD Observer No. 290-291*, ISSN 0029-7054, pp. 22-23.

Marmot, M. (On Behalf of the Commission on Social Determinants of Health) (2007), "Achieving Health Equity: From Root Causes to Fair Outcomes", *The Lancet*, Vol. 370, No. 9593, pp. 1153-63.

Marmot, M., T. Atkinson, and J. Bell (2010), "Fair Society, Healthy Lives: The Marmot Review, Strategic Review of Health Inequalities in England Post-2010", Executive Summary, Available at: http://www.instituteofhealthequity.org/projects/fair-society-healthy-lives-the-marmot-review, Accessed on 16 July 2013.

Mazumdar, S. and P.G. Mazumdar (2013), "Health and Healthcare in Delhi: Towards Universalisation with Equity and Quality", *Background Paper on Health for the Second Delhi Human Development Report*, Institute for Human Development, New Delhi (Processed).

Ministry of Health and Family Welfare (MOHFW) (2005), *Report of the National Commission on Macroeconomics and Health*, Government of India (GoI), New Delhi, August.

———. (2009), *National Health Accounts—India 2004-05*, Government of India (GoI), New Delhi.

Ministry of Housing and Urban Poverty Alleviation (MoHUPA) (2007a), "National Urban Housing and Habitat Policy", Available at: http://mhupa.gov.in/policies/duepa/HousingPolicy2007.pdf, Accessed on 5 May 2013.

———. (2007b) Report of the Technical Group [Eleventh Five Year Plan: 2007-12] On Estimation of Urban Housing Shortage, Available at: http://mhupa.gov.in/ministry/housing/HOUSINGSHORTAGE-REPT.pdf, Accessed on 5 May 2013.

———. (2012), Report of the Technical Group on Urban Housing Shortage (Tg-12) (2012-17), Available at: http://mhupa.gov.in/W_new/urban-housing-shortage.pdf, Accessed on 12 May 2013.

Misra, A., R.M. Pandey, J.R. Devi, R. Sharma, N.K. Vikram and N. Khanna (2001), "High Prevalence of Diabetes, Obesity and Dyslipidaemia in the Urban Slum Population in Northern India", *Int J Obes Relat Metab Disord*, Vol. 25, No. 11, pp. 1722-29.

Mobile Crèches (2010), "Situational Analysis of Chilren under Six in Delhi 2002-2007-A Citizens' Report", Mobile Creches Publications, New Delhi.

Mohan, R.V. (2012), "Over One-fifth of the Country's Police Force Just on Paper", *The Times of India*, 24 December, Available at: http://articles.timesofindia.indiatimes.com/2012-12-24/india/35990966_1_vip-security-police-vacancy-police-force, Accessed on 22 May 2013.

———. (2013), "Delhi Police to Hire 2508 Policewomen'", *The Times of India*, 5 January, Available at: http://articles.timesofindia.indiatimes.com/2013-01-05/delhi/36160777_1_women-police-police-stations-women-cops, Accessed on 10 July 2013.

MOSPI (2012), "Children in India—2012: A Statistical Appraisal", Report by the Ministry of Statistics and Programme Implementation, Government of India.

National Advisor on Homeless to the Commissioners of the Supreme Court (2012), Report on Urban Homeless, Available at: http://www.righttofoodindia.org/data/homelessness_data/July_2011_report_urban_homeless_national_advisor_on_homeless_to_the_comiissioners_of_supreme_court.pdf, Accessed on 18 June 2013.

National Sample Survey Organisation (NSSO) (2006), "Morbidity, Health Care and the Condition of the Aged", *Report No. 507 (60/25.0/1)*, NSSO 60th Round (January-June 2004), Ministry of Statistics and Programme Implementation, Government of India, March.

———. (2007-08), "Education in India—Participation and Expenditure", *Report No. 532*, NSS 64th Round, Ministry of Statistics and Programme Implementation, Government of India, New Delhi.

———. (2012), "Un-incorporated Non-agricultural Enterprise Survey (excluding construction)", 67th Round (2010-11), Government of India, New Delhi.

———. (2013), "Key Indicators of Employment and Unemployment in India, 2011-12", NSS 68th Round, Ministry of Statistics and Programme Implementation, Government of India, New Delhi.

———. (Various Years), *Quinquennial Surveys of Employment and Unemployment*, 55th Round (1999-2000), 61st Round (2004-05), 66th Round (2009-10) and 68th Round (2011-12), Government of India, New Delhi.

National Commission for Enterprises in the Unorganised Sector (NCEUS) (2008), "Report on Conditions of Work and Promotion of Livelihoods in the Unorganised Sector", Academic Foundation, New Delhi.

Navsrishti (2011), "Missing Children! A Big Challenge in MCT of Delhi", Available at: http://navsrishti.org/n/reports/MissingChildren.pdf, Accessed on 5 May 2013.

National Crime Records Bureau (NCRB) (2011), "Crimes against Children", Chapter 6, Available at: http://ncrb.nic.in/CD-CII2011/cii-2011/Chapter%206.pdf, Accessed on 4 April 2013.

NCRB (National Crime Records Bureau), Ministry of Home Affairs, New Delhi, Available at: http://ncrb.gov.in/, Accessed in January -July 2013.

National Legal Research Desk (n.d.), "Delhi Police : Standard Operating Procedure (SoP) for Investigation of Rape Cases", Available at: http://nlrd.org/resources-womens-rights/rape-laws/government-notifications-advisories-rape-laws/delhi-police-standard-operating-procedure-sop-for-investigation-of-rape-cases, Accessed on 2 June 2013.

NIMS, ICMR and UNICEF (2012), "Infant and Child Mortality in India: Levels, Trends and Determinants", National Institute of Medical Statistics (NIMS), Indian Council of Medical Research (ICMR) and UNICEF India Country Office, New Delhi, India.

Palacios, R., J. Das and C. Sun (2011), "India's Health Insurance Scheme for the Poor: Evidence from the Early Experience of the Rashtriya Swasthya Bima Yojana (RSBY)", Centre for Policy Research, New Delhi.

Pandey, N. and F. Haidar (2013), "Invitation to Crime: City Has 650 Unlit Stretches", *Hindustan Times*, 26 July, Available at: http://www.hindustantimes.com/India-news/NewDelhi/Invitation-to-crime-City-has-650-unlit-stretches/Article1-725606.aspx, Accessed on 5 August 2013.

Planning Commission (2011a), "Faster, Sustainable and More Inclusive Growth, An Approach to the Twelfth Five Year Plan", Available at: http://planningcommission.nic.in/plans/planrel/12appdrft/appraoch_12plan.pdf, Accessed on 10 June 2013.

———. (2011b), "Report of the High Level Expert Group on Universal Health Coverage for India", Government of India, New Delhi.

———. (2013), *Twelfth Five Year Plan (2012-17)— Social Sectors, Volume III*, SAGE Publications, New Delhi.

Politzer, M. (2012), "Challenges for the Differently-abled", *Live Mint* and *The Wall Street Journal*, 16 September, Available at: http://www.livemint.com/Politics/NpeQcpIH9JsqfrV7YcBPIK/Challenges-for-the-differently-abled.html, Accessed on 31 May 2013.

PRS Legislative Research (2013), Summary of Justice Verma Committee Report, Available at: http://www.prsindia.org/parliamenttrack/report-summaries/justice-verma-committee-report-summary-2628/, Accessed on 21 May 2013.

Rahman, Naziya Alvi (2013), "Soon, More Child Safeguards", *The Times of India*, Gurgaon edition, 23 April, p. 4, Available at http://articles.timesofindia.indiatimes.com/2013-04-23/delhi/38762613_1_draft-policy-child-rights-school-transport, Accessed on 23 April 2013.

Rastogi, T, K.S. Reddy, M. Vaz, D. Spiegelman, D. Prabhakaran, W.C. Willett, M.J. Stampfer and A. Ascherio (2004), "Diet and Risk of Ischemic Heart Disease in India", *Am J Clin Nutr*, Vol. 79, No. 4, pp. 582-92.

Reddy, K.S., D. Prabhakaran, P. Jeemon, K.R. Thankappan, P. Joshi, V. Chaturvedi, L. Ramakrishnan and F. Ahmed (2007), "Educational Status and Cardiovascular Risk Profile in Indians", *Proc Natl Acad Sci*, USA, Vol. 104, No. 41, pp. 16263-68.

Registrar General of India (RGI) (2011), "Statistical Report of 2009", Report No. 1 o 2011, Sample Registration System, Government of India, New Delhi.

———. (2012), "SRS Bulletin", Vol. 47, No. 2, Sample Registration System, Government of India, New Delhi, October.

Rizwan, S.A., Baridalyne Nongkynrih and Sanjeev Kumar Gupta (2013), "Air Pollution in Delhi: Its Magnitude and Effects on Health", *Indian Journal of Community Medicine*, Vol. 38, No. 1, Indian Association of Preventive and Social Medicine.

Rodgers, D. and S. Satija (2012), "Understanding the Tipping Point of Urban Conflict: The Case of Patna, India", *Working Paper No. 5*, Available at: http://www.urbantippingpoint.org/output/projectpublications/, Accessed on 16 March 2013. Roelin, K. and R. Sebates-Wheeler (2011), "A Child-sensitive Approach to Social Protection: Serving Practical and Strategic Needs", International Conference: on 'Social Protection for Social Justice', Institute for Development Studies, UK.

Sahai, N. Sanjiv and Simon Bishop (2009), "Bus System Reform in Delhi", *DIMTS Ltd.*, Available at: http://www.dimts.in/pdf/Bus_System_Reform_in_Delhi.pdf, Accessed on 13 May 2013.

Sarkar, P.K., Saikat Bose and Pritha Ghosh (2007), "A Critical Appraisal of Traffic and Transportation Sector in Delhi and Possible Solutions", *Department of Transport Planning, School of Planning and Architecture*, New Delhi.

Selvaraj, S. and A.K. Karan (2009), "Deepening Health Insecurity in India: Evidence from National Sample Surveys since 1980s", *Economic and Political Weekly*, Vol. XLIV, No. 40, 3 October, pp 55-60.

Sen, Amartya (1999), *Development as Freedom*, Oxford University Press, Oxford.Sheikh, S. (2008), "Public Toilets in Delhi: An Emphasis on the Facilities for Women in Slum/Resettlement Areas", CCS *Working Paper No. 192,* Summer Research Internship Programme 2008, Centre for Civil Society, Available at:http://www.ccs.in/ccsindia/downloads/intern-papers-08/Public-toilets-in-Delh-192, Accessed on 17 April 2013.

Shiva Kumar, A.K., L.C. Chen, M. Choudhury, S. Ganju, V. Mahajan, A. Sinha and A. Sen (2011), "Financing Healthcare for All: Challenges and Opportunities", *The Lancet*, Vol. 377, No. 9766, pp. 668-79.

Singh, A., P.K. Pathak, R.K. Chauhan and W. Pan (2011), "Infant and Child Mortality in India in the Last Two Decades: A Geospatial Analysis", *PLoS ONE 6(11): e26856. doi:10.1371/journal.pone.0026856.*

Social Statistics Division (2012), "Children in India 2012—A Statistical Appraisal", Ministry of Statistics and Programme Implementation, Government of India, New Delhi, Available at: http://mospi.nic.in/mospi_new/upload/Children_in_India_2012.pdf, Accessed on 12 February 2013.

Tanahashi, T. (1978), "Health Service Coverage and Its Evaluation", *Bulletin of the World Health Organisation*, Vol. 56, No. 2, pp. 295-303.

The Economist Intelligence Unit (2005), *"Quality of Life Index", The Economist*, Available at: http://www.economist.com/media/pdf/QUALITY_OF_LIFE.pdf, Accessed on 25 May 2013.

The Gazette of India (2000), Ministry of Law, Justice and Company Affairs (Legislative Department), The Juvenile Justice (Care and Protection of Children) Act, Available at: http://wcd.nic.in/childprot/jjact2000.pdf, Accessed on 1 June 2013.

———. (2005), The Protection of Women in Domestic Violence Act, 2005, Available at: http://wcd.nic.in/wdvact.pdf, Accessed on 5 June 2013.

The Times of India (2013a), "Cases of Missing Children under 14 to be Treated as Kidnapping",16 April, Available at: http://www.indianexpress.com/news/cases-of-missing-children-under-14-to-be-treated-as-kidnapping/1103131/, Accessed on 2 June 2013.

———. (2013b), "Analysing the POCSO Act 2012", 25 April, Available at: http://kushmanda.com/index.php/the-protection-of-children-from-sexual-offences-pocso-act-2012/ and http://dpjju.com/index.php?option=com_content&view=article&id=561&Itemid=257, Accessed

Twelfth Five Year Plan (2012-17) and Annual Plan (2012-13), "Write-up on 'Road Transport' under the Transport Sector", Available at: www.delhi.gov.in, Accessed on 10 May 2013.

UNDP (1990), *Human Development Report 1990: Concept and Measurement of Human Development*, Oxford University Press, New York.

UNHABITAT (2008) State of the World Cities 2010/2011: Bridging the Urban Divide, London & Sterling, VA: Earthscan.

———. (2012), "State of the World Cities 2012-13: Prosperity of Cities", Bounford.com, Cambridge, UK and Progress Press Ltd., Malta.

———. (2013), "State of Women in Cities 2012-13: Gender and Prosperity of Cities", Bounford.com, Cambridge, UK and Progress Press Ltd, Malta

UNHCR (2010), "Quick Facts, Shelter and Human Rights", Canada, Available at: http://www.humanitarianforum.org/data/files/resources/802/en/shelter_human_rights.pdf, Accessed on 4 April 2013.

UNICEF (2010), "Good Practices and Promising Initiatives in Juvenile Justice in the Cee/Cis Region", Imprimerie Courand et Associés—ICA, Geneva.

———. (2012), "State of the World's Children 2012: Children in an Urban World", New York, USA

———. (2013), "Water in India: Situation and Prospects", UNICEF, FAO and SaciWATERs, India.

UTTIPEC (2010), "Removal of Boundary Walls and Reclaiming of Setbacks into Public Realm", Available at: http://uttipec.nic.in/writereaddata/linkimages/9614247194.pdf, Accessed on 31 May 2013.

United Nations Development Programme (UNDP) (1994), *Human Development Report 1994*, Oxford University Press, New York.

Viswanath, K. and S.T. Mehrotra (2007), "Shall We Go Out?", Women's Safety in Public Spaces in Delhi", *Economic and Political Weekly*, Vol. 42, No. 17, pp 1542-48.

Xu, K., D.B. Evans, K. Kawabata, R. Zeramdini, J. Klavus and C.J.L. Murray (2003), "Household Catastrophic Health Expenditure: A Multi-country Analysis", *The Lancet*, Vol. 362, No. 9378, pp. 111-17.

Yuko, Tsujita (2009), "Deprivation of Education: A Study of Slum Children in Delhi, India", UNESCO, *2010/ED/EFA/MRT/PI/12*, New Delhi.

World Bank (2011), *World Development Report 2011: Conflict, Security and Development*, World Bank, Washington DC.

Glossary

Words in common usage not explained in the text

Ahaar	Food
Arogya	Illness
Awas	Shelter/Housing
Bacchon	Children
Bhagidari	Partnership
Bharat	India
Dhabas	Local eating joints
Dhaloas	Place for garbage disposal/ management
Dwar	Door
Gaon	Village
Jal	Water
Janani	Mother
Jansuvidha	People's convenience
Jeevan	Life
Jhuggi/Jhopdi	Shanty
Karyakram	Programme
Kosh	Fund
Mamta	Care
Mela	Fair
Mitra	Friend
Nidhi	Fund
Nirman	Development
Parivartan	Change
Pehchaan	Identification
Phulwari	Garden
Rashtriya	National
Sakshar	Literate
Sampark	Contact
Sarkar	Government
Shishu	Child
Stree Shakti	Women's Empowerment
Suraksha	Security/Protection
Swasthya	Health
Thela	Hand cart
Ujjawala	Brightness
Vidyut	Electricity
Yojana	Scheme
Yuva	Youth

Notes:

Aadhaar: Aadhaar is a 12-digit individual identification number issued by the Unique Identification Authority of India on behalf of the Government of India to satisfy a certain verification process. This number will serve as a proof of identity and address anywhere in India and will be of help in accessing services like banking, mobile phone connections and other government and non-government services in due course.

Cognisable crime: In the case of such crimes, officers of the police are empowered to act without the permission of the magistrate, that is, without obtaining a court order.

Crime rate: Crimes per 100,000 population.

Crude death rate: Number of deaths occurring during the year per 1,000 population estimated at midyear.

Drop-out: Students who fail to attend classes for a fairly long period. Drop-out at the primary level may be calculated with respect to the cohort who enter class I and fail to pass schooling in class V.

Formal (Organised) Sector: Incorporated private enterprises employing 10 or more workers and all public sector enterprises belong to the formal sector.

Formal Employment: Persons who are not in informal employment and have access to social security benefits and security of tenure are considered to be in formal employment.

Gross Enrolment Ratio: The proportion of students enrolled in a particular level of education to the eligible age group of child population.

Infant Mortality Rate: Number of deaths under one year of age occurring during a given year, per 1,000 live births occurring among the population of the given geographical area during the same year.

Informal (Un-organised) Sector: It comprises all unorganised enterprises, defined as all unincorporated private enterprises (owned by individuals or households) that employ less than ten workers.

Informal Employment: It includes all those employed persons, whether employed in unorganised enterprises or in the organised sector, who have no access to social security benefits and security of tenure.

Labour Force Participation Rate: Percentage of persons in the labour force to total population.

Labour Force: All employed and unemployed persons constitute the labour force.

Life expectancy at birth: Average number of years that a newborn could expect to live if he/she were to pass through life subject to the age-specific mortality rates of the present period. It reflects the overall mortality level of a population and summarises the mortality pattern that prevails across all age groups – children and adolescents, adults and the elderly in a population.

Maternal Mortality rate: Proportion of the maternal deaths during a given time period per 100,000 live births during the same time-period.

Pratibha Vikas Vidyalaya: Literally means a school where talent is developed. This is a category of school supported by the government to search for and develop talent of poor and meritorious students.

Rashtriya Madhyamik Shiksha Abhiyan: A scheme of Government of India with the objective of universalising secondary education.

Sakshar Bharat: Literacy programme in India which literally means "all are literate in India".

Sarva Shiksha Abhiyan: Flagship scheme of Government of India with the objective of universalising elementary education.

Sex ratio: The ratio of females per thousand males in a population.

Total Fertility Rate: Number of children that would be born to a woman if she were to live to the end of her child-bearing years and bear children in accordance with current age-specific fertility rates.

Unemployed: Persons who are not engaged in any economic activity but are willing to work.

Unemployment Rate: Percentage of unemployed persons to the total labour force.

Usual Principal and Subsidiary Status (UPSS) of Employment: The NSSO collects data on employment and unemployment using three broad measures or approaches namely (I) Usual status (II) Current Weekly Status and (III) Current Daily Status. The usual status is further categorized at two levels: Usual Principal Status (UPS) and Usual Principal and Subsidiary Status (UPSS). Usual status relates to the activity status of a person during the reference period of last 365 days preceding the date of survey. Current weekly status of a person is the activity status obtained for a person during a reference period of 7 days preceding the date of the survey. Current Daily Status of a person is determined on the basis of his/her activity status on each day of the reference week.

Work Participation Rate: Percentage of persons in the workforce to total population.

Workforce: All employed persons constitute the workforce.

Yuva Nirman: Literally means 'youth development'. The Government of NCT of Delhi has framed 'Yuva Nirman Scheme` under "The Delhi Higher Education Aid Trust" under which scholarships are provided on a merit-cum-means basis to the socially and economically backward students of the State Universities and affiliated institutes.